SOUTHERN EUROPE SINCE 1945

SOUTHERN EUROPE SINCE 1945

Tradition and modernity in Portugal, Spain, Italy, Greece and Turkey

Giulio Sapelli

Translated by Ann Fuller

Longman
London and New York

Longman Group Limited,
Longman House, Burnt Mill,
Harlow, Essex CM20 2JE, England
and Associated Companies throughout the world.

Published in the United States of America
by Longman Publishing, New York

First published 1995

ISBN 0 582 070643 CSD
ISBN 0 582 070651 PPR

British Library Cataloguing-in-Publication Data

A catalogue record for this book is
available from the British Library

Library of Congress Cataloging-in-Publication Data

A catalogue record for this book is
available from the Library of Congress

Set by 8 in 10/12 Times
Produced by Longman Singapore Publishers (Pte) Ltd.
Printed in Singapore

CONTENTS

LIST OF FIGURES AND TABLES

Figures

Tables

ACKNOWLEDGEMENTS

This book is the result of many years of study and research during which time I have been able to count on the friendship of many scholars and the help of various institutions.

In particular, I would like to mention Maurice Aymard and our frequent discussions at the start of this project when I was Director of Studies at the Maison des Sciences de l'Homme and Ecole des Hautes Etudes en Sciences Sociales. I would also like to thank Antonio Elorza and Paco Comin for the help they gave me during my studies in Madrid, and Paco Bonamusa and Pere Gabriel who enabled me to teach and study at the Autonomous University of Barcelona.

My most sincere and affectionate thanks go to Kemal Karpat, that most excellent and affable teacher. Not only did he encourage me to start my studies on modern Turkey, but he also offered valuable advice and help with the final manuscript.

This book covers a great deal of geographical territory and my studies led me to many places. The expenses involved were considerable and I could not have managed without the financial help given to me by the Milan Chamber of Commerce, Industry, Artisans and Agriculture through the good offices of its president, Piero Bassetti, and by FORMEZ thanks to the interest expressed in the project by its president, Sergio Zoppi. Other organizations, ISVEIMER, FIME and SME, also gave financial help. I thank them all.

Special thanks go to my friends at the Foundation Giulio Pastore for their help and affection, and to the Calouste Gulbenkian Foundation whose contribution facilitated my stay in Portugal.

I remember, with gratitude, the Bibliothèque Internationale d'Histoire Contemporaine of Nanterre, the Maison des Sciences de l'Homme of Paris, the London School of Economics, the Banco de España and the Casa de Velásquez in Madrid, the City of Barcelona library, the library of the Calouste Gulbenkian Foundation, and the National Library of Lisbon. These libraries were much more than mere reading rooms, thanks to the help given to me by the personnel.

I wrote the first version of this book during a three-month stay at the Fondation des Treilles in Provence. This oasis is the perfect place for scholars. Here they can concentrate in an atmosphere where culture, civilization and good taste create peace for the spirit. Here Anne Gruner Schlumberger, with her exquisite courtesy and *simpatia*, offered hospitality, help and understanding. My debt to her is great, as is my grief at her death.

I would like to thank Ann Fuller not only for her translation of this book but also for her help in editing it. My thanks are also due to Francesca Carnevali for her constructive criticism.

Acknowledgements

Very special thanks go to Marisa de Gioia for her help over the many years we have worked together at the Giangiacomo Feltrinelli Foundation in Milan and for her ability to curb my natural intellectual disorder and spur me on.

This book is dedicated to my wife Francesca, for her support and encouragement.

Giulio Sapelli
Milan, 23 April 1994

INTRODUCTION

My aim in writing this book is to contribute towards a greater understanding of the European experience. It is a comparative study of the historical, political and socio-economic aspects of Southern Europe, as I am certain that this is the best methodology for finding solutions to the problems under discussion.

The short-term approach to this work, requested by the editor, has its drawbacks. However, the editor's wishes were not the only justification for choosing to cover the period after the Second World War to illustrate the specific characteristics of Southern Europe and the countries (Portugal, Spain, Italy, Greece, Turkey) which form it. The reason for choosing the short-term approach was influenced by other, more weighty, considerations.

I am convinced that the accelerated process of economic, social, political and cultural change which has taken place over the last 50 years has been decisive for both the growth of Southern Europe and the differentiation between the southern countries and the continental ones. In fact, understanding the nature of the change and the specific characteristics of the area comes from a clear understanding of the inter-twining of economic growth and social and political dynamics. In this sense, the disadvantages of the short-term approach are nullified by the methodology of comparison and by the possibility of a close examination of the historical social processes.

Part One of this book synthesizes, in Chapter 1, the specific characteristics of Southern Europe and gives an overview of the theses presented for consideration. The second chapter deals with foreign politics and the international collocation of the countries under study, as these two factors have had great historical influence.

In Part Two the central theme is the social implications of economic growth. Chapter 3 covers emigration and return migration. This is possibly the most significant social aspect of the central theme. Chapter 4 is devoted to the enormous changes in the rural societies of Southern Europe. The central theme of Chapter 5 is an investigation of the various roads to industrialization which covers economic growth and the advent of capitalist markets. Chapter 6 is an analysis of the effects of capitalist markets, and the relation between economy and society, defined as induced capitalism, which developed in the countries of Southern Europe. The specific socio-economic formation of the area is derived from the inter-twining of tradition and modernity with capitalist forms of production and forms of pre-modern social reproduction.

Part Three deals with an analysis of the political society expressed by the specific socio-economic aspects of the area. Chapter 7 presents the neo-caciquist model as the key to understanding the links between strong clientship, low political institutionalization and weak parties which exist in these countries. Chapter 8 presents an analysis of the various Southern European dictatorships. The persistence of these dictatorships is one of the most specific characteristics of Southern Europe. The analysis covers the differences in their growth, their development and the various reasons for their collapse, and reaches the conclusion that the consolidation of democracy was atypical. Chapter 9 discusses the rapidity with which ideological polarization was overcome and democracy was learnt in these countries until the end of the 1980s.

The fourth, and concluding, part of the book examines the unsolved problems which reveal the process of modernization without development which is common to the whole area. This process is seen in the lack of relationship between economic growth and political institutionalization.

The incapacity to elaborate strong rules of civil conduct is typical of Southern European countries. This is clearly shown by the conflicts between state and nation, by the epidemics of violent action and the de-legitimization of the elites, by the decline of the relationships between faith and politics and the rise of integralist religious movements, and by the start of the breakdown of such stability in the party system as had previously been so rapidly established.

My Southern European adventure is not over. Working on this book has convinced me that I must write another on the anthropology of the enormous changes which, here, have had an economic, historical and sociological interpretation.

There are two technical points I would like to comment on here. The first concerns the names of the many political parties mentioned. The first time a party is named I have given the English translation, followed by the initials by which the party is commonly known and the original name in brackets. Generally speaking only the initials are used subsequently. The complete list, in alphabetical order of the initials, can be found in Appendix II.

Figures of international fame are mentioned only by surname. National politicians are nominated by name and surname except where there is no danger of confusion.

Part One

SOUTHERN EUROPE

Chapter 1
MANY EUROPES

I Southern Europe?

Is it legitimate to define the countries which border the northern shores of the Mediterranean as 'Southern Europe' and to distinguish the area thus formed from the rest of Europe? This is not an idle question. Today the individual characteristics of each of the countries which make up Europe are known to everyone. When the Maastricht Treaty was signed in 1992, it seemed that the unification of Europe could be carried out easily. The treaty spelt out the time-frame for arriving at the single European market. However, since then not only has economic integration proved to be very difficult but the political differences between the various European countries have become more marked. Conflicts of interest and opinion have become stronger. Because of this, it is important to understand why and how these conflicts arose and to find a solution that can reconcile the emergence of strong nationalist feelings with the sought-after harmony of a united Europe. The understanding of each country's specific identity can be useful for the creation of common institutional, social and economic policies.

Even if we can no longer think of ourselves as just Europeans, we can try to understand the reasons for these feelings and we can work more efficiently if we have a greater knowledge of our differences, contrasts and even similarities. Perhaps the moment has arrived to accept that, between the overpowering rise of national identities and a European identity, it is possible to feel oneself subject of only a part of the culture and history of Europe. Once we used to think that we could be citizens of the world, but we are not yet citizens of Europe, and we are no longer just citizens of our own country. This indicates that one single Europe does not exist: many Europes do.

It is not easy to understand the reasons for the different experiences of each sub-area of the European continent. The differences and similarities between areas formed by specific groups of nations are based on various factors. I plan to discuss these distinguishing factors one at a time. The following pages will analyze in more detail the points presented in this introduction.

II An introduction to the socio-economic formation of Southern Europe

There is little doubt concerning the vital importance of the choices made in international politics after the Second World War. After the fall of Soviet power in 1989, these were debated once again. But until that moment Portugal, Spain, Italy, Greece and Turkey had shared, in different measures, the common fate of forming the group of countries confronting the countries of the Warsaw Pact on the Southern European and Middle Eastern flank of Nato. The consequences of this position have been both politically and economically important. However, international politics could not exert enough influence on Southern Europe in such a way as to shape its experience. Southern Europe has specific characteristics that are rooted in a socio-economic structure different to that of Continental Europe (including the British Isles), Central Europe and Eastern Europe. The long- and short-term historical differences of the last two areas *vis-à-vis* the Southern European area are immediately evident, while they become less so when looking at Continental Europe and Great Britain. A fairly simple way of analyzing the question is to look at OECD[1] statistical data gathered over the last thirty years.

However, one thing must be made quite clear: not all the countries of Southern Europe are on the Mediterranean nor are all the Mediterranean countries part of Southern Europe. Those countries which, until a short time ago, formed Yugoslavia are not part if it. These have a completely different history from Italy, Portugal, Spain, Greece and Turkey. Slovenia, Croatia, Serbia and Bosnia Hercegovina share their history with Central and Eastern Europe not only because of ancient roots but also because they are among those countries which followed the Soviet example after the Second World War, thereby rejecting the possibility of a capitalistic economy and a democratic parliamentary system. From this point of view, the conflict which started in 1948 between the then Yugoslavia and the USSR is not important as it does not alter the problem. On the other hand, France is a typically Continental European country with its own clear and specific identity, and is not part of Southern Europe. Braudel was very explicit on this subject when he wrote:

> Since the time of Caesar, and well before, up until the great barbarian invasions in the Fifth century, the history of France was a fragment of Mediterranean history. The events which occurred around the middle sea, even if they happened a long way from the shores of France, determined the country's life. But, after the invasions (leaving aside the exceptions like the belated wars for the domination of Italy), France identified with, above all, Central and Eastern Europe.[2]

The most important difference between the countries of Southern Europe and those of Continental Europe and the British Isles is the early industrialization of the latter.

The following figures and tables regarding social structure show a whole series of consequences following the late industrialization of Southern European countries. These figures and tables relate to four separate periods covering the years from 1960 to 1989, and they allow comparisons between the group of Continental European countries formed by Germany, France and Great Britain, and the countries of Southern Europe.

Data for the years immediately following the Second World War is not included here as too many different methods of data collection were used. Methods became standardized in 1960.

The data on which the figures are based can be found in Appendix I together with other statistical data.

Figure 1.1 shows that Germany, France and Great Britain had more labour force as a percentage of total population than all of the Southern European countries –

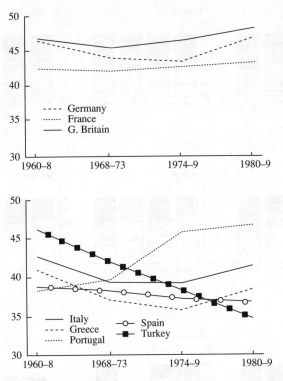

Fig. 1.1 Total labour force as percentage of total population (average for period)

with the exception of Portugal where, in the second half of the 1970s, the labour force was larger than in the other southern countries.

The most significant figures are those relating to the percentage of workers in agriculture, in industry and in the service sector (Fig. 1.2).

Southern Europe not only had a slower rate of decline in the number of agricultural workers but, excluding Italy, very high percentages were reached for the service sector workers without prior peaks of employment in industry, which is an experience typical of Germany, France and Great Britain.[3] This peculiarity of the southern experience starts to lose its relevance, except in the case of Greece and Turkey, over the last period (1980–9).

Until the 1980s, total unemployment (male and female) was higher in the Southern European countries (Fig. 1.3)

The reason for the jump from agriculture straight to services lies in the non-growth mechanism in force since 1968–73 (excluding Turkey) and, at the same time, in the fall of GDP per capita also in Germany, France and Great Britain. This non-growth mechanism is clearly shown by the trend in the yearly percentage changes of GDP per capita (Table 1.1) and of value added in agriculture, industry and services (Table 1.2) for the four periods.

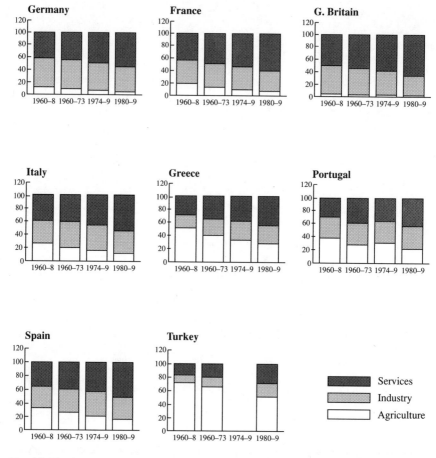

Fig. 1.2 Employment by sector as percentage of total employment (average for period)

The data shows that the country with the strongest growth indicators is Turkey. The reason for this is the low level of the starting point and the impressive economic structure of a social system still solidly based on agriculture.

Most Europeans do not consider Turkey as part of Europe. But Turkey can lay claim to being European not only because of international and military alliances but also because it has achieved a system of parliamentary democracy (of European origins) which has no equivalent in the Middle East.

The common element which emerges in the countries identified as South European is the rapid growth and the rapid change from a mostly agrarian society to one strongly oriented towards the service sector. The peculiarity of this development emphasizes a very important aspect of the socio-economic structure of these countries. The following pages will show that these societies have not been able to reach a high and stable systemic integration which could mirror the slow and constant changes in their social structures. They have been shaken up by convulsive contradictions over a very short period. In spite of the contemporary displays of

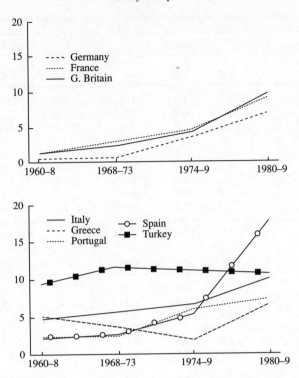

Fig. 1.3 Unemployment as percentage of total labour force (average for period)

Table 1.1 GDP per capita – yearly percentage changes (average for period)

	1960–8	*1968–73*	*1974–9*	*1980–9*
Germany	3.1	4	2.5	1.7
France	4.2	4.5	2.3	1.6
G. Britain	2.4	3	1.5	2.1
Italy	5	3.9	3.2	2.3
Greece	6.7	7.8	2.6	1.1
Portugal	5.7	8.9	1.3	2.1
Spain	6.4	5.7	1.1	2.1
Turkey	3.2	3.4	2.9	1.9

Source: OECD – see Ch. 1, n. 1.

Table 1.2 Value added – yearly percentage changes by sector (average for period)

	1960–8			1968–73		
	Agr.	Ind.	Ser.	Agr.	Ind.	Ser.
Germany	1.7	4.3	4	0.6	5.1	4.8
France	1.7	6.9	5	1.4	7	5.7
G. Britain	2.2	2.7	3.4	3.3	1.9	4.6
Italy	2.6	7.1	5.4	−0.4	5.2	4.8
Greece	3.9	8.8	7.8	4.8	11.8	7.4
Portugal	2.3	8.8	7.2	−0.6	9.5	8.6
Spain	1.9	10.8	6.8	3	9.3	5.6
Turkey	2.1	9.4	6.6	1.1	7.8	7.7

	1974–9			1980–9		
	Agr.	Ind.	Ser.	Agr.	Ind.	Ser.
Germany	0.3	1.4	3.1	1.8	0.6	2.7
France	1.1	2.4	3.5	1.8	0.8	2.9
G. Britain	0.4	−0.2	2.7			
Italy	1.4	3.5	4	1.1	2.1	2.9
Greece	0.8	3.3	4.6	2	0.5	2.1
Portugal						
Spain	1.5	1.5	3.4			
Turkey	5.5	5.4	5.3	1.9	5.4	4.6

Source: OECD – see Ch. 1, n. 1.

intense, violent and armed political and social conflict,[4] all the countries examined here have developed, however, a remarkable capacity for social integration. Following Lockwood's theory,[5] they have been able to establish non-conflictual relations between social groups.

Considering the intense process of change that these countries have gone through, social mobility in Southern Europe has not been as intense and constant as could have been imagined. The aim of this book is to show that the actions of individuals are marked by individualistic and vertical relationships rather than collective and horizontal ones. Southern Europe is a land of clientship and patronage and is characterized by the presence of status systems not by contractual ones. Late industrialization, insufficient penetration of market mechanisms and the overwhelming presence of the state in social and economic life are all factors which have been decisive in forming the economic and social life of these countries.

III Agrarian society and the persistence of traditions

Italy was the first of the Southern European countries to be integrated into an institutional system of international free trade which was one of the characteristics of its post-war economic, social and political history. Italy was a moving force with its very strong level of integration both with Continental Europe and with international trade. The increase in the latter is one of the main causes of the economic development in the second post-war period. Another factor which sets Italy apart from the other Southern European countries and societies is the lateness with which the others joined the EEC. As we all know, this process is still unfinished mainly because of the monetary policies which have been pursued.

However, this process has thrown light on the profound differences within Europe. We will see that these were largely determined by a general process which is not primarily economic but institutional and social, or rather, political. The late creation of market economies has been a distinctive element in Southern Europe's history since the end of the Second World War. But market forces have been implemented from above: from the institutional system rather than from the foundation of society. First in Italy, then in Spain, Greece, Portugal and finally Turkey, the protectionist, restrictive, administrative trappings which burdened, and which in some ways still burden, the economies of these countries were dismantled by decisions made by their political elites. This was not due only to the external shocks imposed by the international economic situation, nor was it a functional adjustment of the social sub-systems to the invisible hand of a self-regulated market. Instead, it was a specific, differentiating and suffered process in which both the role of the modernizing elites and the legacy of the past acted to define the framework in which to operate. The culture of the management groups and the personal creed of the protagonists of the large collective mobilization movements were essential in shaping this process.

The agrarian vicissitudes of the Southern European countries bear witness to this. In the first place, the importance of the landowning structure was one of the characteristics which shaped the history of three of these countries: Italy, Spain and Portugal. But the way in which the advance of capitalism in the rural areas influenced economic growth and social change was different in each of these three countries.

In the south of Italy the absentee landlords had, for centuries, influenced the relations between agrarian structure and economic growth. After the Second World War the collective movement of farmers from below and political reforms from above, transformed the large estates into small- and medium-sized holdings and into capitalistic leaseholdings, freeing a part of the labour force for the increasing industrialization of the country and for internal and external emigration. In Italy there was agrarian reform without a social revolution.

In Spain dormant estates transformed themselves into engines of capitalism thanks to the flight of the workers from the rural areas and to the virtuous circle created by increases in labour costs and mechanization, aided by the progressive dismantling of the administrative trappings.

In Portugal inertia was an age-old fact in a millennial balance, both in the estate-owning south as in the small-holding north. The military revolution gave rise to the rebellion of the seasonal labourers and the political mobilization which destroyed the dominance of the estate-owners. When the collective enthusiasms had died down and the soldiers had retreated to their barracks, the agrarian counter-revolution and democratic political reform laid the basis for the creation of a system of large, medium and small capitalistic holdings in the south of the country.

But the most characteristic thing about Southern Europe's agrarian vicissitudes is the polarization of its land property structures. While the north of Portugal was made up of small-holders, who played a decisive role in repelling the military and communist revolution of 1974, the south was made up of large estates. The same can be said of Galicia, Euskady (the Basque provinces) and Catalonia which were in contrast to Castile and Andalusia. If a comparison is made between the large and medium-sized capitalistic agrarian concerns and the small family-run farms, this heterogeneity and difference in the structure of landowning is still characteristic of Italy. In Greece and Turkey the small farm system has been fully developed as a result of the political choices made after the fall of the dominant Ottoman landownership. Those choices made the Greek agricultural sector the basis of consensus of the oligarchic dominion of the ruling classes. The case of Turkey is different. In spite of the lack of agrarian reforms after the Second World War, the Turkish farmers were stronger and were backed by the state, by technology, by availability of credit and by non-taxation (as in Greece) in order to increase the value of family property and to favour the merging of medium- and small-sized farms, while the depopulation of rural areas and emigration continued.

The persistence of family-run farms and small-holdings can be understood only by considering the writings of Chajanov,[6] the most important social scientist in the field of agrarian history. The study of his theories on family-run farms enables us to appreciate the exceptional role played by this economic form, which many considered confined to an out-dated tradition, in the pursuit of modernity.

The agrarian vicissitudes of Southern Europe have other points in common. One of the most remarkable characteristics of the Southern European countries, when compared to those of Continental Europe, is the importance that agriculture had on their overall economic potential. The agrarian society, with its wealth of values, its close family ties, with its sharing of specific social mores, has not only resisted the spread of market forces but it is the specific form by which the economy has been institutionalized. In this way, a complex mechanism of regulation and administration of economic transactions was formed that was the negation of the market economy according to neo-classical models. The most significant paradox of the negation, together with institutionalization of market forces, can be considered the relation between the spread of monetary regulations and the EEC's agricultural policy. It is the negation of the market in agriculture in the context of a price-fixing policy and fierce protectionism with regard to the rest of the world. No matter the reforms being carried out, or the conflicts breaking out all over the world as a result of the contradictions created by this mechanism (into which only Turkey is anxiously waiting to be admitted), it is a problem that does not alter the controversial substance, between modernity and tradition, of the historical experience we are living through.

When Southern Europe and Continental Europe are compared, one of the characteristics of the former to emerge is the lack of historic continuity in the relation between the primary and the secondary sectors during the development of the economy and society. Here lies the strongest taproot of the falsification of the so-called virtuous circle of the theory of modernization:[7] economic development that produces democracy and the consolidation of contractual relations as theorized by Max Weber.

For Southern European societies, the heart of the problem lies in the fact that the high rate of employment in the agrarian sector was not followed by a high rate of employment in industry (as happened in Continental Europe): it was followed by high employment in the service sector. For a brief period, Italy was an exception to this. In this way, social relationships were not touched by the changeover from systems of power and cultural values based on status to those based on contracts. These systems are typical of societies where the market economy has prevailed. The Weberian capitalistic society is the ideal example. However, this model has had little success in Southern Europe.

It is easy to see what has happened to the market in the agricultural sector. What will happen to the service sector is easily imagined if one thinks of the role that public administration, the distribution system and a far-reaching, but legal-rational to a small degree, state have played, and still do, in these countries. This explains why some of the most brilliant scholars of Southern European history have been able to talk about the 'ruralization of the city'[8] and of 'urbanization without or before industrialization',[9] underlining the social continuity of the anthropological relationships typical of rural societies in a world which has undergone rapid changes. We are talking about changes over a few generations while in Continental Europe the same changes evolved over centuries.

Thus, there has been a very quick transformation in the structures of Southern European countries which has not been followed by a strong cultural change. One of the factors which helps us to understand this process fully is emigration. All the countries which make up Southern Europe have supplied the capitalist Continental countries with labour. However, starting in the 1960s, the flow of emigrants almost stopped and a reverse process started with emigrants returning to their country of origin. At this point, those countries which had supplied labour were subject to immigration from countries outside Europe. This had very important consequences as emigrant remittances played a fundamental part in the balance of payments. These were slowly replaced by the increasing economic weight of tourism.

But emigration, the return home of emigrants and, to a lesser extent, urbanization have been, above all, important factors in the formation of social mobility for large masses of the population. Consumerism has changed life styles and creeds. But this modernization has preserved and given new life to traditional structures. State mechanisms and styles of reciprocity in social and political behaviour have been preserved. That which has happened over the last fifty years can be epitomized by the theory of the so-called 'modernization without development',[10] a model which is more characteristic of Southern Europe than of the rest of the other Europes.

IV Different roads to industrialization

Modernization has undoubtedly happened, though not in the hopefully decisive and revelatory terms that many had foreseen. Industrialization was a wide-spread phenomenon in Southern Europe after the Second World War. Two variables were decisive. The first was the industrial potential of the countries at the moment of their inclusion in the international economy. This created the linkages and the possible synergies with the more advanced centres of capitalist growth. The second was the adoption of an export-oriented policy and economic liberalization, and the abandoning of the policy of import substitution and protectionism. The different historical moments in which these variables appeared and the diverse degrees of integration between them determined the degrees of intersection in the international division of work and the quantity and quality of industrial growth.

The most obvious proof of the truth of this interpretative outline – as long as it is not applied mechanically as so many do – lies both in the Italian experience and the Greek one. In Italy, the early opening up to the international markets of an economy already based on a solid structure of capital goods and of a consistent system of small- and medium-sized light industries laid the foundation for rapid industrial growth. The State played a decisive role in this process, according to the criteria of the mixed economy. In Greece, the difficult and intermittent process of liberalization was not able to provide either a structure capable of competing internationally or economic actions which were not speculative and parasitic.

Thus it can be seen that policies of opening up markets and increasing exports are not miraculous recipes but are a difficult and precarious mix. The test of this is shown by the Portuguese and Spanish experiences. In the case of Spain, the abandoning of authoritarian protectionism and political clientship of a management nature came about thanks to the stimulus of a complex and differentiated social structure and a knowledgeable technocratic strategy. In the case of Portugal, it was above all the return to normality after the revolution which allowed Portuguese industry to find the rationalization and the international specialization due to it, thanks to its past experience of partial integration with foreign markets.

The quality and extent of foreign capital and the timing of the opening up of the economy to foreign markets were decisive factors in the process of industrialization. It can be said that the first of these factors was extremely positive for the growth of the various countries, especially where there was the possibility of synergies and local expertise. The second factor was decisive – even considering the distortions it caused – in determining the shape of the financial and industrial structure of these countries.

The fact that countries like Spain and Portugal, and later Turkey, had to face the full force of competition in the middle of the international crisis caused by the oil price wars, forced them into the difficult situation of intensive capitalistic growth based on labour-saving technologies and on the shrinking of the industrial base. The consequences on employment were very heavy and were never compensated for by the service sector. The administrative and financial sectors of the economy can cause speculative monetary enthusiasms but cannot lay the foundations for growth.

The presence of the state in the economies of the Southern European countries was much heavier than elsewhere. However, the degrees of intervention and the final historic outcomes were different. Where the state allowed the production of capital goods and provided for the essential supply of energy, as in Italy, Spain and

Turkey, its historic function was generally speaking positive. The crisis that now affects these countries, and in particular Italian state-owned industry, was caused by the absence of alternatives to the impulse given by the state as well as by the European crisis in those sectors in which the state traditionally acted. In this sense, the policies of the EEC over the last twenty years have imposed a hard test on the countries of Southern Europe. They do not have the powerful industrial structure made up of large and medium-sized industries typical of Continental Europe. The industrial future of Southern Europe will be largely determined by the part that small and medium-size firms, another characteristic of the socio-economic structures of Southern Europe, will be able to play. The system of small and medium-sized businesses, particularly wide-spread in Italy and Portugal but also economically and socially significant in Spain and Turkey, will have to face growing international competition. The intervention of the state as a regulator and supporter of the economy rather than as a controller, more of a 'director than an owner',[11] will be decisive, but unfortunately this kind of state is lacking in all the Southern European countries. This is an historical problem that, in all its gravity, constitutes the greatest unknown factor for their future.

V The dividing effects of welfare

Though the state has been relegated by industry to the role of guardian or protectionist, it has, over the last twenty years, developed rapidly in the context of social citizenship. For those countries, like Spain and Portugal, that overcame their authoritarian regimes in the middle 1970s, this phenomenon should be seen as a specific historic result of the vicissitudes of Southern Europe. The advent of political democracy coincided with the advent of social democracy. The creation of welfare states is a characteristic of this change.

The result of this process was the growth of societies similar to those of already industrialized countries but connected to a reproductive structure typical of peripheral countries and latecomers to industrialization. These have a prevalence of middle classes, underclasses and mobile workers who cannot be directly defined by a permanent productive role like the classic industrial workers. A marked degree of social heterogeneity prevails in this case.

This lack of synchrony between social structures and productive structures is at the base, together with a lack of a strong state technocracy, of the particular clientship character of the Southern European welfare system.[12] This system tends to pander more to individual needs than to provide universal well-being, thus dividing society into groups instead of unifying it naturally through mechanisms of solidarity. From this point of view, the enormous difficulties of reaching the monetary unification of the European market offer more unknown factors for the countries of Southern Europe than they do for those of Continental Europe and the British Isles. The common market could perhaps produce exogenous shocks for social and state rationalization through the diffusion of meritocratic and contractual systems that those nations are unable to express by themselves.

15

VI Specific forms of modern authoritarianism

The distinctive characteristics of Southern European socio-economic formation become even more evident if one looks at the political and institutional structures. These countries are lands where authoritarianism reigns, that is to say lengthy dictatorships, limited dictatorships and short, intermittent ones. The South of Europe has produced, at different times, all the varieties of modern authoritarianism. This is not the same thing as Fascism or Nazism which are typical of a Continental European reaction. Compared to them, Spanish and Portuguese authoritarianism can be defined as administrative and military dictatorships with varying degrees of institutional violence without those mass movements typical of the totalitarian versions of contemporary dictatorships. The southern authoritarian forces do not stem from the same source as Nazism. They rose from the contrasts between the land-owning classes on one hand and the agrarian and industrial labour force on the other. This happened above all in Spain. Linked to this was the political weakness of the urban middle classes.[13] This characteristic is shared by Italian Fascism which was a transitional dictatorship marking a change from the supremacy of the agrarian classes to that of the industrial classes. This is demonstrated by the part played during the Fascist period by the single party as a political force for the authoritarian mobilization of the masses. This did not happen in Spain and Portugal. This type of force is necessary in societies which are no longer divided but are functionally already different as are those that start to be or were already industrial societies. For that matter, that is what happens under Stalinism and Nazism. In the cases of Italy and Spain, thanks to the choices made by their elites, there was economic growth followed by important institutional changes. The Portuguese and Spanish dictatorships can be defined as limited as there was always space for autonomous political movements. The regime was too weak to control the whole society but, on the other hand, the political opposition was not strong enough to overthrow the dictators.

The military played an important part in all the Southern European countries, except Italy, starting with Spain and Portugal. The Greek dictatorship of the Colonels was the culmination of a process of limitation and exclusion from democracy and from the political citizenship of a large part of the country in which the military played a fundamental role. The role of the Turkish military was different. It intervened recurrently on the political scene in an authoritarian way, but the long-term political process towards democracy did not come to a halt. The military used violence to stop the disintegration of society, but they always handed power, in various forms, back to the civil authorities.

The different types of relations between the military and the social and economic societies in Southern European countries had in common the fact that the military were autonomous from the civil authorities because of a weak degree of institutionalization of the political-democratic system.[14] The intervention of the military substituted this institutionalization. The greater the social and political cleavages based on class and nationalism, the more this substitution was made by continued and violent forms of dictatorship as happened in Spain. The greater the cleavages in the governing classes, and between these and a political system incapable of finding a point of aggregation and stabilization, the greater the substitution of the political institutionalization that occurs intermittently and in a fragmented way, as in Turkey. All the other cases fall between these two poles.

VII The anomic division of political work

The greatest distinguishing feature of the Southern European countries is their limited capacity to institutionalize politics as demonstrated by the interests of a great number of parties. The weakness of the societies of these countries has been *in primis* that of not knowing how to form a strongly institutionalized politically democratic society[15] where norms and democratic procedures of negotiation, compensation and regulation regulate the diverse interests of the various political groups. This is a completely different thing from democratic consolidation[16] meant as a cultural trend towards democracy. Here it is a typical case of social integration. In the case of Southern Europe, the capacity to create systemic democratic integration is under discussion. Or rather, the capacity to create institutional rules and procedures which outlast the wishes of the group or groups of people currently in power. Rules are in fact a system used for the control and regulation of social violence. The theoretical weakness of the formalist and functionalist approach made it difficult to give the correct amount of importance to this problem. This is a classic theme of sociology and political history. Inadequate political institutionalization explains, on one hand, the persistence or the intermittent appearance of dictatorships and, on the other hand, the importance of the processes of patronage and of the 'anomic division of political work'[17] which are typical of Southern Europe.

This last point is decisive and it is worthwhile explaining it more fully. Spain and Portugal managed to create from nothing a democratic political system that (as in Italy on the other hand) did not exist in any other Southern European country prior to the dictatorship, except in a restricted form in Spain. Liberalism and caciquism (*caciquismo*) were the most widespread forms of politics. These states achieved, in a very short time, that which Italy managed to do in two well defined periods of her political history, from 1945 to 1956 and from 1962 to 1989, i.e. to move from a party system based on polarized pluralism[18] to a system based on centrist pluralism.[19] That which counts in this process was not the presence or otherwise of two-party systems or multi-party competitive ones or of coalitions but the fact that the conquest of the centre of society – made up of the higher strata of the working class and the middle classes – gradually became the essential objective in the fight for power. This provoked a generalized leaning towards the centre by a large part of the political forces. This process produced, until the end of the 1980s in all countries, an impressive simplification of party systems. All this happened with the persistence of the clientship system. This is not, however, restricted to Southern Europe. The exchange of favours for votes survives within the institutional practices of democracy. However, when the habit becomes so ingrained and overwhelming as to destroy or significantly limit all forms of relations between electors and elected, it can undermine democracy.

In Southern Europe there is a close relationship between clientship and what can be called the anomic division of political work. Or rather the 'balkanization' of the state, its submission to the desires and needs of particular sectors of the political and economic elites, the omission of the formation of an administrative technocracy or its destruction. The cause of this lies in the spreading of political control over all the resources that can be placed under the authority of political clans. This process can be called the anomic division of political power because the state becomes the state of parties that is none other than the division of the spoils (or the spoils system) and it reflects the incapacity of a political class[20] to produce a governing class which is not under the influence of the pressures of clientship and lobbies, all in a growing decline of the Weberian concept of 'belief in the law'.[21] It is the collusion between clientship, a lack of a sense of state and the ubiquity of clannish parties which creates the weakness of Southern European politics. These societies have all undergone, for different reasons but always with dramatic results, rapid and wide-reaching processes of placing their ruling classes under discussion, leading to acute crises of their political obligations.

Italy is a very significant example of this. Until the 1980s the political system was characterized by the ability of the big parties to attract strong electoral consensus, which compensated for the innumerable short-lived coalition governments.[22] The strength of the consensus was made possible by the cohesive capabilities shown by a political class which had its origins in the fight against the dictatorship, and in the Resistance movement against Fascism. This political class was exogenous to society as it was formed during the long fight against Fascism and it values. When, for reasons of age, that political class handed over to the new politicians who were disciples of the theory of modernization without development, the ability for aggregation of the party system with regard to society weakened. In recent years, there has been a continuous fragmentation of the electorate while political-economic corruption has been highly visible and rife with an ever-growing protest by the citizens with regard to the ruling political classes. It is difficult to say whether or not the Italian way of political fragmentation is the first step in a general tendency. It must, however, be noted that new political formations have recently grown out of this fragmentation.

It seems almost certain that Spain is moving in this direction with the progressive decline of the Spanish Socialist Labour Party's (PSOE, Partido Socialista Obrero Español) control over the centre and the emergence of Italian-like phenomena. One of these, corruption, has already reared its head in Greece, however. One problem which should be analyzed more carefully is to what degree the growth of political fragmentation has been favoured by the weakening of the splits between classes. The series of mainly Italian but also Spanish, Portuguese and Turkish social struggles of the 1960s and 1970s were followed either by systems of industrial relations which dispersed the frequent conflictual tensions or by corporative micro-conflicts of groups or quasi-groups[23] intent on dividing the increasingly scarce resources of systems hit by the economic recession.

At this point, we can go back to the difference proposed at the beginning between low systemic integration and high social integration. It is clear that the latter cannot be a factor of stability and social well-being, as a mediocre functionalist rhetoric would have us believe.

The role played by strong systems of horizontal alliances in unifying interests was lacking. The cleavage which now appears in an acute way, even though different from the past, is that between centre and periphery; it is the conflict between country and state.[24] The manifestations of ethnic identity ranging from terrorism to claims of autonomous institutions were dealt with, in Spain and Italy, by trying to create autonomous regions within the state. This could be a possible solution to the ever more marked emergence of neo-localisms and neo-regionalisms in the whole of Europe. But we need more institutional and cultural courage.

The only possible solution seems to be that of building a state capable of becoming polytheistic about nationality, or rather that takes on the non-identity between state and country as an institutional element. Social inequality, in the crisis that follows rapid growth and the weakness of partisan institutions, strengthens local or nationalistic movements. These situations are also a variation on the theme of modernization without development and when they mix with the lack of identity between state and country they can give rise to an endless chain of conflicts. An example of this can be found in the bankrupting consequences of the dictatorial unification from above carried out in the Balkans and the ex-USSR. The linkages between domestic and foreign politics become more evident and the nationalistic reply becomes violent and threatening. On this subject, the history of the Kurdish nation is exemplary of the interweaving of foreign and domestic politics and the solution can be found only in the institutional difference between state and country.

The lack of democratic political institutionalization can lead both to fragmentation and to the use of force. Behemoth and Leviathan always appear together in historic evolution. Both are apocalyptic monsters of chaos. The first is the symbol of disorder and illegality, the second is the symbol of coercion and maintains only a minute trace of lawfulness and respect for human rights. It seemed that for a brief moment we had left Behemoth and Leviathan behind us. Now they are before us, as Balkan Fascism reaches the shores of the Mediterranean and throws its shadow over the whole of Europe – a vile and cowardly Europe confronted by an exterminating ethnic violence which, with its wave of nationalistic claims, could also involve Greece and Turkey at any moment.

The vicissitudes of Southern Europe, with its particular problems and characteristics, is the story of achieving freedom from Leviathan. The battle against Behemoth has been less victorious thanks to the continued lack of institutionalized politics and the persistent anomic division of political work. It would be a demonstration of foolish and petty optimism to think that there is an easy solution to these problems.

VIII Many Europes

In order to reach a conclusion about these last considerations, the distinctive characteristics of Southern European experience must be underlined again. In the international anthropological debate, the analytical unity of the Mediterranean, from Maghreb to Catalonia, to Pisticci[25] has been subject to discussion. When this does not lead to a negation about the differences between Southern and Continental

Europe, it is useful in bringing out the degree of heterogeneity, also on the level of anthropological history, of the consolidated social and institutional structures of the two shores of the Mediterranean. If we look at these centuries-old structures, we see experiences which are completely different in their historical development of political societies and institutional systems even though there are also some similarities. The consolidation of a parliamentary democracy with the creation of party systems, linked to economic growth, are elements which definitely differentiate Southern Europe from the non-European Mediterranean countries (together with the countries which made up Yugoslavia).

But the variables which differentiate Southern Europe from Continental Europe and the British Isles are the late industrialization coupled with the presence of a state that was as interventionist as it was administratively weak; the low degree of political institutionalization together with the disintegrating consequences of clientship already mentioned. We are dealing with a distinct and specific socio-economic formation as this book will attempt to show.

Szúcs wrote a book entitled 'Three Europes'.[26] It contained the synthesis of an historical journey from the medieval roots of modern freedom to the relations between state and aristocracy up to the French Revolution. The East, the Centre and the West of Europe were the geographical designations for distinct social and political experiences. Today we know that this three-part division is not enough. Southern Europe also has its own distinct personality. The destiny of Europe is that its multiform differences should be accepted fully by its collective conscience and institutional solutions. From the end of the Second World War to today, the changes that have taken place have been more intense and radical than ever before.

Chapter 2

FROM MILITARY BALANCE TO
PROBLEMATIC SOLIDARITY

I The military question and national conflicts

The dynamics of social and political change are closely connected with the placing of the Southern European countries in the international sphere. The foundations of these countries lie in the redefinition of the geo-political spheres of influence decided after the Second World War. The alliance between the Western democratic powers and the USSR broke down and the Mediterranean became a battleground of the cold war.[1] First the conflict between the USSR and Turkey for control of the Dardanelles Straits,[2] and then the Greek civil war[3] were crucial moments in that process. One of the basic elements of this process was also the changeover from British to US hegemony in the Mediterranean.[4] The withdrawal of British troops from Greece, the decisive role played by the USA not only there but also in Turkey and gradually in Italy, Spain and Portugal (where, by tradition, British influence was extremely strong) are the salient moments in the construction of a new hegemonic power. The Truman Doctrine was proclaimed in 1947, and with that the inclusion of Greece, Turkey and Italy in the Marshall Plan became the continuation on an economic level of international power politics.[5] The objective, as the inclusion of these countries in the Atlantic Pact shows, was to prevent the expansion of the Soviet bloc and to guarantee the widening of a capitalist market.

Greece and Turkey in the Balkans and Iran in the Middle East were meant to act as mediators and controllers, and to circumscribe Arab nationalism and the USSR. Inevitably, Israel gradually assumed this role too.[6] One not secondary aspect of the whole process was the fight for the control of oil supplies.[7] In the area between the southeastern part of Southern Europe and the Middle East, the changeover from British to American hegemony was not without difficulties. How to come to terms with the de-colonization of the Arab world which had become aggressively nationalist? This was the basic question. The USA's solution was less tainted by a colonial heritage than Great Britain's. The Suez crisis of 1956 brought to a head the conflict not only between Egypt, ruled by Nasser the leader of the new Arab nationalist movement, and Israel but also between the USA on one hand and a united France and Great Britain on the other.[8] This crisis area bordered on to the Northern Tier, made up of Turkey, Iran and Pakistan.[9] Here the consequences of the conflict between Israel and the Arab nationalists were less acute because Soviet pressure was extremely strong and of a potentially disruptive nature. But the disagreements between Great Britain and the USA, which came to the boil during the changeover in Mediterranean hegemony, did not cease.

The Baghdad Pact of 1955, signed, under British influence, by the countries of the Northern Tier, is a clear effort to avoid the isolation of Egypt and Israel from the Arab world and the Middle East in general. It favoured the status quo and balances built up after the First World War rather than their replacement under the impulse of de-colonization. This complex diplomatic game was played in order to guarantee an effective anti-Soviet front in which Turkey was to play a fundamental role. Together with Greece, it was included in Nato (ex-Atlantic Alliance) as were Italy, Spain and Portugal. All the various countries that gravitated between the USSR, the Balkans and the Middle East saw the outlining of a central role not only for Turkey but also for Greece, as the civil war of 1946–9 had so dramatically shown. In this context, the break-up between Tito and Stalin in 1948 was beneficial for the anti-Soviet front. Yugoslavia could now play the part of linchpin in an area like the Balkans which were exposed to the dangers of conflict with the countries of the Warsaw Pact.[10] On the other hand, the lessening of tension favoured the growth of nationalism and tendencies towards self-government in opposition to the rigid division into blocs, thanks to the international role played by Yugoslavia in the formation of the non-aligned nations group and its desire to annex Macedonia. Evidence of this was the signing of the Treaty of Bled between Yugoslavia, Greece and Turkey in 1954. This showed the need to join together those countries threatened by the possibility of conflicts between the Nato bloc (with Greece and Turkey) and the Warsaw Pact bloc (with Bulgaria, Romania and the USSR).[11]

The rise of nationalistic conflicts, in spite of the membership of Nato, was even more evident in the conflict between Greece and Turkey over Cyprus in 1959.[12] This is the most unpleasant legacy of British supremacy in the Mediterranean. As in the Middle East, and with disastrous results, the British rule of Cyprus was based on the principle of divide and rule in its dealings with Greece and Turkey. This caused an accumulation of growing tension and violent nationalism which gradually excluded any hope of peaceful coexistence between the ethnic groups. Tension on both sides was increased by the needs of both the Greek and the Turkish domestic political situations. The conflict between these two countries was so violent that the integrity of Nato's southern borders was threatened. In 1964 it was only the USA's threat to suspend military aid which frustrated Turkish military action in Cyprus. The Soviets backed the neutral policies of Archbishop Makarios, the charismatic religious and political leader of the Greek community, but their threat of intervention continuously and persistently caused tensions during the peace negotiations. Nato proved incapable of solving the conflict. The main enemy of the Turks and the Greeks, in the growing spiral of nationalism, became not the USSR but the bordering states on the Aegean Sea which had become a bone of contention after the discovery of oil deposits and for military reasons.[13] Even the strategies of Nixon and Kissinger, which were aimed at a global approach to foreign policy, had to take note of the real situation.[14] Choices had to be made and the USA chose to be passive when the Turks invaded Cyprus in 1974. Makarios had fallen from power as a result of the coup ordered by the Greek colonels who could not bear the idea of a democratic and progressive Cyprus. The Turks invaded the island and the USA did not interfere. However, the pressure from the powerful Greek lobby stopped all supplies of arms to Turkey from the USA until 1978. The Turks retaliated by setting limits to the use of their military bases by Nato. The Greeks did the same.

Greece even left Nato temporarily, to return to the fold five years later.[15] A process of centrifugation was inexorably set in motion. Greece made approaches to Bulgaria by proposing the de-nuclearization of the Balkan area. Turkey started to move closer to Syria, Lebanon and Iraq in spite of the conflict between these countries and the USA in the 1980s.

The Cypriot crisis gave rise to two important questions. The first is the basically military nature of the geo-political situation inside Nato. It cannot, in spite of its unquestionable economic basis, overcome conflicts and contrasts which stem from a rebirth of nationalistic feelings helped, within limits, by economic growth. The second question is the growing geo-political weight of Turkey, rather than Greece, in the Middle Eastern and Balkan areas, an influence that is destined to grow even more with the dissolution of the Warsaw Pact.

More than fifty million Turkish speakers live in the Caucasus and in central Asia. Their demographic expansion helped to increase the weight of Turkish regional power. This process became evident half way through the 1970s, and even more so after the advent of so-called nuclear equality and the growth of the Turkish military forces. These leaned more towards the Arab world than towards Israel; proof of the inseparable mix of synergies and vetoes that link the Balkans to the Middle East.

> The Greek or Turkish search for support for their respective positions among the Arab countries produced an Arab demand for reciprocity, that is a cooling down of Greek–Israel and Turkish–Israel relations. This proved sufficient reason for the impossibility of achieving any durable agreements among the three countries. In other words, the Israel – Arab conflict and the Cyprus problem will, unless resolved, prove a permanent impediment not only to triparty relations but to normal bilateral relations as well.[16]

There was a strong tendency in Southern Europe to create middle-sized powers on a regional scale. Confirmation of this can be found in the geo-political and geo-strategical vicissitudes of the two Iberian countries, Spain and Portugal. In 1960, the integration of the Spanish air force into the USA Air Command in Europe made explicit a long-term tendency already emergent immediately after the Second World War. The last traces of British hegemony in Portugal disappeared with the weakening of the European Free Trade Area (EFTA), Great Britain's membership of the EEC and the appearance of an international political power vacuum on the southeastern front of Nato.[17] The consequences were first of all a certain insularity in relations with Spain and then the full integration of Portugal into the Atlantic defence system. However, in spite of the strategic value of the Azores, the role of Portugal was strongly down-graded. With regard to British hegemony in Portugal, the two countries were traditional natural allies of very long standing. Spain was a potential rival, as seen in the frequent disputes over Gibraltar and control over the entrance to the Mediterranean. However, Spain became the central medium-sized power for the USA to count on.[18] Proof of this seems to lie in the fact that the Portuguese revolution of 1974 developed without any interference from the USA. It was only when a communist threat appeared that the United States started to bring pressure to bear.[19] Spain was considered the anchor point of the southwestern Nato front, especially after the French withdrawal from membership in 1966.[20] Faced with Turkish and Greek instability, the stability offered by Franco became a strong

23

point for a global approach to anti-Soviet strategy. Thus the Pact of 1953 between the USA and Spain bore its fruits,[21] allowing Spain to create the basis for its appearance as a medium-sized power. Gradually the post-war isolation was overcome until Spain reached its present dual role: Mediterranean, as shown by its participation in the 1991 war against Saddam Hussein and Iraq; intercontinental, as demonstrated by the increasing ties and links with the countries of Latin America.

Italy was the country which had, prior to Spain and Portugal, a role of medium-sized regional power. At the end of the Second World War, while busily engaged in a confrontation with Yugoslavia for the control of Trieste and Istria, Italy joined Nato. The reasons for this were connected more to domestic affairs than to the Warsaw Pact, especially after the break-off in relations between the USSR and Yugoslavia in 1948 and between the USSR and Albania in 1961.[22] Italy was the country where, from the 1950s until the 1980s, the Communist party was the most active in the whole of Western Europe and where the Vatican exercised a very strong influence on foreign policy.[23] From the viewpoint of undeniable fidelity to the Atlantic alliance in the long term, Italy has been able to develop a largely independent policy with regard to the USSR and the Arab world, particularly on the Palestinian and Israeli questions. The oil crisis and problems of supply were the backdrop against which many of these actions were played out,[24] but they are not the explanation for the originality of a foreign policy that had its origins in the democratic, Roman Catholic, Italian culture. When, in the second half of the 1970s, the communists ideologically accepted the country's role in Nato,[25] though with mixed feelings over the problems of nuclear balance, Italy was freer to play a fundamental part in the opening towards the East and in the attempts to resolve the Israeli-Palestinian conflict.

Finally two basic tendencies in international Southern European politics make their appearance. The first was the realization of the central importance of the military question. As there was no strong political integration between the countries of Southern Europe before the 1970s because of the diverse political regimes, the international military link was the only one possible. In a vacuum of political initiative this central importance becomes a rousing element for disruptive nationalistic movements. Each single country used its need to keep a defensive armed force on its territory as a powerful weapon in any negotiations linked to US hegemony. When peace-making moves started to be made, these were a cause of ulterior fragmentation. On the other hand, the problems inherent to the USA–USSR antagonism world-wide were reflected in the equilibrium of Southern Europe.

In 1959 Italy and Turkey accepted the installation of medium-range missiles on their territory. But when the Cuban crisis occurred in 1962 and the proposal was made to dismantle the Soviet missiles in Cuba if the American ones in Turkey were dismantled too, Nato was put in a very difficult and embarrassing position.[26] Greece and Turkey (and Italy) felt abandoned and the tendencies towards a more defensive national model became stronger and went beyond an exclusive relation with Nato and the USA. When political disagreements were added to military and strategic ones, the distances could not but increase.

The period of Eurocommunism is a case in point. This affected Spain, France and Italy. Henry Kissinger was quite clear and firm in his opposition to enlarging the domestic political alliances in these countries.[27] The second basic trend of Southern European international politics emerges from all this. Given the opposition between centrifugal tendencies and the affirmation of international alliances, the historical connection between foreign and domestic policies emerges. The Cold War did not in fact stop the display of high degrees of political flexibility in the countries concerned. They were extremely quick to take advantage of the potential autonomy that the protection of the Atlantic alliance guaranteed them. Their faithfulness to Nato became a strong instrument in their domestic political struggles. On the other hand, nuclear competition meant the down-grading of 'fortress' countries like Malta, bringing out their role as a bridge between Europe and the Middle East.[28] A clear example of a more general tendency can be found in the fact that the geo-political areas of vital importance for Western interests were used as means towards domestic ends, strongly influenced by domestic politics, to the point where the stability of the Atlantic alliance was put to test.

II New responsibilities and old continuities

After the collapse of the Warsaw Pact, the situation changed and the crisis points multiplied. At the present time they are the Balkans, the Middle East, the Caucasus and the Islamic and ex-Soviet Turkish-speaking republics. Greece, Turkey and Italy, as always, will be the most exposed countries and the most involved in the redefinition of both Nato policies and their own diplomatic ones. The impression is that it is no longer possible for these countries to use the benefits deriving from their position. The external framework of the Atlantic alliance has been broken up.

The war in ex-Yugoslavia and the problems with Iraq illustrate the consequences of this breaking up, showing that a more direct and responsible approach must be taken. This must be based on the relations that each country has with the crisis areas. This will mean new, strong competition between the countries of Southern Europe and the other European countries. First let us consider Yugoslavia. Italy has adopted a foreign policy supporting the residual and illusory hopes of maintaining a confederative arrangement, with essential autonomies used to solve the problems of the internal ethnic minorities. This has, in fact, favoured Serbian aggression. Germany, for example, ever faithful to its tradition of disputes with France, Great Britain and Italy, has from the very beginning sustained the recognition of Croatia and Slovenia. This paved the way for the formation of what should have been national states but which are becoming, unfortunately, ethnic states with the massacre of entire peoples.

Now let us look at the ex-republics in the south of the ex-USSR. Turkey's role is and will be of fundamental importance if it wants to be a stabilizing influence and a cultural and economic reference point in the whole region, thus emphasizing its important role as link between East and West. If it can overcome the heritage of its violent past with regard to important realities like the Armenian and Kurdish nations it will become even more important.

Greece, threatened by Macedonian claims (this is the part of the break-up of Yugoslavia which most affects it), could develop a role of moderation and attraction with regard to the Serbs. It will be ineffective, though, because of the terrible radical violence this war has assumed. If Greece can overcome the many direct nationalist tensions in the area, it could put itself forward as a protagonist in a Balkan policy of overcoming the conflicts.

Italy can do the same, above all in the Middle East, as its presence in recent operations under the UN flag has shown. However, its inability to act in the Yugoslav crisis demonstrates the limits of a foreign policy that is still trying to find the right balance between its Mediterranean and its Atlantic roles. In the Mediterranean area the foreign policies of the medium-sized powers like Italy, Spain and Turkey face the foreign policies of small powers that are unable to play a leading part in the area or to overcome conflicts internal to the area. One example of these is the Greek and Turkish dispute over Cyprus which has reached the unfortunately irreversible state of dividing the island into two ethnically distinct and separate nations. Another example is the marine platform of the Aegean.

Since the change from British to US domination after the Second World War there has not been a leading medium-sized power in the area. This is due mainly to the fact that none of the Southern European countries or, for that matter, European countries *tout-court* were capable of taking a leading role. All this is part of a European incapacity to find a stable solution to the process of continental union which would lead to military and political stability in the Mediterranean. The economic vicissitudes make this evident. This implies the need to continue to base international collaboration on the central point of integration with the USA.

All this is happening at the same time as the endemic crisis in the Middle East between Arab nationalism and the conflict with Israel, Islamic fundamentalism, civil war in the ex-Soviet Caucasus, the Kurdish guerilla warfare (which threatens to disrupt an important oil-producing area), and the ethnic war of the Yugoslav fascists. We are living through a paradoxical historical process. In Southern Europe, nationalisms are going back to being a powerful resource for political-cultural mobilization. These states incorporate various nations that cannot be identified in a deterministic way as social and cultural units. They continuously produce hotbeds of conflict which upset the balance of the Southern European international situation. From this arises the need for external intervention, given that regulation does not come naturally in relations between the countries of Southern Europe. The compulsory presence of the USA emerges because of a lack both of an hegemonic sub-regional project and an effective cooperative project connecting all Continental Europe. Taking into account the profound changes which have come about, this is perhaps the element of greatest continuity to be found in the Mediterranean. There are exchanges of goods, capital and human resources, but no political project has developed out of the economic collaboration. And only politics can be the basis for international order.

It must not be forgotten that, in spite of these contradictions and limits, the entry of Southern Europe into the Atlantic bloc was one of the fundamental elements in hastening the change and allowing the Southern European countries to adopt political and economic philosophies which were typical of Continental Europe. However, this often occurred in the absence of the necessary cultures and experiences. One of the specific features of Southern Europe is this lack of homogeneity between institutions and structures, which the foreign policy exalts and places in great evidence. It is to be hoped that the following pages will demonstrate this thesis.

Part Two

SOCIETY AND ECONOMIC GROWTH

Chapter 3
EMIGRATION AND SOCIAL DIFFERENCES

I The general trend

It is vital to have a complete understanding of the socio-economic effects of emigration on Southern Europe in order to proceed with an analysis of the other aspects of social and economic growth in the area.

The movement of large masses of human beings is the most relevant testimony to the great economic and social changes in Southern Europe. Emigration towards foreign shores is the most evident and distinctive sign of the inclusion of the Southern European countries in the international division of labour and in the process of economic growth that affected the whole of Europe. At the same time, it is also the most visible proof of social and territorial inequality and of the cyclic phases of growth, as shown in the strict connection between migratory flows and the international situation.

The 1970s saw a change in the migratory flows towards western Europe. The serious downward trend in the ability of industrialized markets to absorb the labour force following the oil crisis of 1973–4 was the foundation for the change in the intensity, the content and the direction of population movements.

> The flow of active people is reduced, the proportion of the non-active increases, the migration of people from the countries on the northern shore of the Mediterranean and Turkey towards the traditional markets of Western Europe diminishes while the requests for sanctuary and political refugees (mainly from Eastern Europe) increases. If we think of the 1960s as the period of the immigrant workers, we can say that the 1970s were the period of family re-grouping (kin joining the head of the family abroad) and the 1980s were the moment of the refugees.[1]

This trend is shown clearly in the following tables. Table 3.1 refers to the percentage of foreign population on total population from 1960 to 1986.[2] Tables 3.2 and 3.3 give general population statistics (past, present and future), while Table 3.4 gives birth and death rates.[3] It can be seen that a considerable decrease in the birth rate has occurred only in more recent years against an absolute increase in the total population. Table 3.5 gives statistics on the number of emigrants from 1960 to 1980.[4] These statistics allow us to see the characteristics and size of a general tendency in countries with different-sized populations.

Rather than concentrate on the role played by emigration towards the countries of Central and Northern Europe, about which a great deal has been written,[5] it would be preferable to look at the reasons, characteristics and effects of migration with regard to the countries of Southern Europe. The first thing that needs to be

Table 3.1 Percentage of foreigners on total population in some countries of Western Europe and the north shore of the Mediterranean 1960–86

	1960	1970	1976	1981	1985	1986
Germany	1.2	4.9	6.4	7.5	7.1	7.4
France	4.7	5.3	6.6	6.8	n.a.	n.a.
Great Britain	n.a.	n.a.	2.9	3.9	n.a.	n.a.
Italy	n.a.	0.3	n.a.	0.5	n.a.	n.a.
Greece	n.a.	n.a.	n.a.	1.8	1.4	n.a.
Portugal	n.a.	n.a.	n.a.	1.2	0.4	0.9
Spain	n.a.	n.a.	n.a.	0.6	0.6	n.a.
Austria	1.4	2.8	3.6	3.9	3.6	n.a.
Belgium	4.9	7.2	8.5	8.9	9.1	n.a.
Denmark	0.4	0.8	1.8	2.0	2.1	2.3
Luxembourg	n.a.	n.a.	24.0	26.3	n.a.	n.a.
Netherlands	1.0	2.0	2.6	3.7	3.9	3.9
Norway	0.7	n.a.	1.8	2.0	2.4	n.a.
Sweden	n.a.	5.1	5.1	5.0	4.7	4.6
Switzerland	9.2	16.3	16.4	14.5	14.5	14.7

Sources: Penninx, R., 'International Migration in Western Europe since 1973: Developments, Mechanism and Controls', *International Migration Review*, 4, 1986, pp. 951–72; Sopemi, 'Continuous Reporting System on Migration', *Annual Reports*, OECD, 1988.

emphasized is that Portugal, Spain, Italy and Greece have had a long migratory history, primarily towards the American continent and then to Europe, that goes back to well before the Second World War. This was due to the attraction of the growth of these countries.[6] That growth made the migratory trend legitimate. That is to say, it consolidated the practice and it activated mechanisms which allowed the phenomenon to expand. The culture of emigration was born of misery and unemployment. It caused the exit[7] from the homeland more than stimulating the siren song of collective mobility. The growth of Central and Northern Europe thus generated a series of expectations which became social choices and action in the cyclic process of individual and family life. This was gradually reinforced by the network of friends, relations and family. Thus, community by community, area by area, migratory chains were created which swelled the migratory flows from the country of origin to the new country, according to certain constant factors that withstood all the economic and political cyclical changes of Southern Europe.[8] This process manifested itself everywhere, from Portugal to Turkey.

Table 3.2 Population breakdown by age group in 1985 and previsions for 2000 and 2020 in Mediterranean countries

	1985 population (thousands)					2000 population (thousands)					2020 population (thousands)				
	Total	0–14	15–39	40–64	65+	Total	0–14	15–39	40–64	65+	Total	0–14	15–39	40–64	65+
Portugal	10,157	2,389	3,775	2,775	1,217	10,756	2,007	4,071	3,080	1,598	10,927	1,718	3,319	3,976	1,914
Spain	38,602	8,830	14,451	10,632	4,689	41,027	7,340	15,307	11,802	6,578	41,672	6,490	12,120	15,297	7,765
France	55,170	11,698	21,294	15,033	7,145	58,060	10,633	20,141	18,125	9,162	58,354	8,912	17,506	19,955	11,980
Italy	57,128	11,187	21,175	17,489	7,276	57,981	8,881	20,427	18,467	10,206	54,834	7,251	14,566	20,821	12,196
Malta	344	83	137	90	34	372	70	133	122	46	388	64	120	129	75
Yugoslavia	23,118	5,580	8,899	6,671	1,969	25,203	4,821	9,238	7,790	3,354	25,687	4,051	8,093	8,928	4,616
Albania	2,962	1,022	1,235	550	156	3,819	1,087	1,614	868	250	4,809	1,087	1,792	1,460	469
Greece	9,934	2,115	3,513	2,985	1,321	10,286	1,749	3,597	3,154	1,785	10,133	1,584	2,973	3,493	2,083
Turkey	50,345	18,309	20,699	9,201	2,136	63,817	18,274	28,042	13,706	3,793	76,345	15,554	29,697	24,289	6,806
Cyprus	665	168	270	156	71	761	170	282	222	86	857	165	287	268	138
Syria	10,458	5,031	3,870	1,268	289	18,264	8,526	6,971	2,253	515	35,736	15,100	14,117	5,449	1,071
Lebanon	2,668	1,000	1,061	470	136	3,554	1,135	1,552	643	223	4,597	1,110	1,816	1,341	330
Israel	4,233	1,378	1,645	837	372	5,245	1,426	2,081	1,258	480	6,639	1,568	2,401	1,879	791
Jordan	3,506	1,686	1,270	455	96	6,285	3,009	2,377	726	173	12,429	5,255	4,962	1,858	353
Egypt	47,578	19,264	18,969	7,489	1,855	65,563	22,705	27,326	12,573	2,960	92,181	26,719	37,327	22,128	6,006
Libya	3,786	1,757	1,389	552	88	6,378	2,901	2,360	932	185	12,263	5,190	4,800	1,819	454
Tunisia	7,261	2,876	2,946	1,160	279	10,328	3,674	4,320	1,831	502	14,669	4,206	5,890	3,690	883
Algeria	21,699	9,905	8,181	2,819	794	33,615	13,752	13,922	4,774	1,166	54,140	18,528	22,256	11,054	2,302
Morocco	22,120	9,329	8,722	3,208	861	31,961	11,944	13,318	5,421	1,278	47,664	14,945	19,248	10,953	2,518
North Shore	197,416	42,905	74,479	56,225	23,807	207,505	36,590	74,528	63,408	32,978	206,803	31,157	60,489	74,060	41,097
East Shore	71,875	27,571	28,815	12,388	3,101	97,926	32,540	41,305	18,811	5,270	136,603	38,752	53,279	35,083	9,488
South Shore	102,444	43,131	40,208	15,228	3,877	147,845	54,976	61,246	25,531	6,091	220,918	69,588	89,521	49,645	12,163
Mediterranean	371,735	113,607	143,503	83,841	30,785	453,276	124,106	177,079	107,750	44,341	564,324	139,497	203,289	158,788	62,748

Source: M. L. Bacci, F. Martuzzi Veronesi (eds), *Le risorse umane del Mediterraneo. Popolazione e società al crocevia tra Nord e Sud*, Il Mulino, 1990.

Table 3.3 Surface, population and average rate of increase in Mediterranean countries 1950–2020

	Surface (thousand Km²)	Population (thousands)				Average annual rate of increase (%)			
		1950	1985	2000	2020	1950–5	1985–90	2000–5	2015–20
Portugal	92.1	8,405	10,157	10,756	10,927	0.5	0.5	0.2	0
Spain	504.8	28,009	38,602	41,027	41,672	0.8	0.5	0.2	0
France	547.0	41,829	55,170	58,060	58,354	0.8	0.4	0.1	-0.1
Italy	301.2	47,104	57,128	57,981	54,834	0.6	0.2	-0.1	-0.4
Malta	0.3	312	344	372	388	0.1	0.6	0.4	0
Yugoslavia	255.8	16,346	23,118	25,203	25,687	1.4	0.7	0.3	-0.1
Albania	28.8	1,230	2,962	3,819	4,809	2.5	1.9	1.4	1
Greece	131.9	7,566	9,934	10,286	10,133	1	0.3	0.1	-0.2
Turkey	780.6	20,809	50,345	63,817	76,345	2.8	1.8	1.2	0.7
Cyprus	9.3	494	665	761	857	1.4	1.1	0.7	0.5
Syria	185.2	3,495	10,458	18,264	35,736	2.6	3.8	3.5	3.2
Lebanon	10.4	1,443	2,668	3,554	4,597	2.3	2.1	1.5	1.2
Israel	97.7	1,258	4,233	5,245	6,639	6.8	1.5	1.3	1.1
Jordan	20.8	1,237	3,506	6,285	12,429	3.2	3.8	3.7	2.2
Egypt	1,759.5	20,330	47,578	65,563	92,181	2.5	2.4	1.8	1.6
Libya	446.6	1,029	3,786	6,378	12,263	1.8	3.5	3.4	3.1
Tunisia	1,001.5	3,530	7,261	10,328	14,669	1.8	2.6	1.9	1.7
Algeria	2,381.7	8,753	21,699	33,615	54,140	2.1	3.1	2.5	2.3
Morocco	163.6	8,953	22,120	31,961	47,664	2.5	2.7	2.1	1.9
North Shore	1,264.8	150,801	197,416	207,505	206,803	0.8	0.4	0.1	-0.1
East Shore	1,103.9	28,736	71,875	97,926	136,603	2.9	2.2	1.8	1.6
South Shore	5,752.9	42,595	102,445	147,845	220,918	2.3	2.7	2.1	1.9
Mediterranean	8,121.6	222,132	371,735	453,276	564,324	1.4	1.4	1.2	1.1

Source: M. L. Bacci, F. Martuzzi Veronesi (eds), *Le risorse umane del Mediterraneo. Popolazione e società al crocevia tra Nord e Sud*, Il Mulino, 1990.

Table 3.4 Birth and death rate in Mediterranean countries 1950–2020

	Birth rate (per 1,000 inhabitants)				Death rate (per 1,000 inhabitants)			
	1950–5	1985–90	2000–5	2015–20	1950–5	1985–90	2000–5	2015–20
Portugal	24.1	14.0	12.1	10.5	11.7	9.3	10.1	10.6
Spain	20.3	13.1	11.5	10.7	10.2	8.3	9.6	10.3
France	19.5	13.7	11.3	10.1	12.8	9.8	10.0	10.7
Italy	18.3	10.8	9.7	8.7	9.9	9.2	10.9	12.6
Malta	29.3	14.6	12.8	10.8	10.1	8.4	9.2	10.4
Yugoslavia	28.8	15.1	12.2	10.3	12.4	8.1	9.1	11.2
Albania	38.2	24.6	19.2	16.1	14.2	5.8	5.7	6.3
Greece	19.4	12.6	11.1	10.4	7.2	9.2	10.4	12.2
Turkey	48.2	26.2	18.7	14.2	23.5	8.5	7.2	7.2
Cyprus	27.4	18.1	14.3	13.2	10.5	7.5	7.5	8.4
Syria	46.6	45.8	41.6	36.3	21.4	8.2	6.2	4.6
Lebanon	41.0	28.5	21.6	17.8	18.7	8.0	6.8	6.3
Israel	32.5	21.8	19.4	16.8	6.9	6.7	6.4	6.2
Jordan	46.7	46.0	42.7	25.8	26.0	7.8	5.8	4.3
Egypt	48.6	34.2	25.9	22.4	24.0	10.2	7.8	6.6
Libya	48.0	44.4	42.2	36.4	22.5	9.9	7.8	5.6
Tunisia	46.4	33.8	25.4	22.2	22.6	7.9	6.5	5.7
Algeria	51.0	40.7	32.1	28.0	23.9	9.5	6.7	5.3
Morocco	50.4	36.6	28.7	25.1	25.7	10.1	7.5	6.0
North Shore	20.7	13.0	11.2	10.0	11.0	9.0	10.0	11.2
East Shore	46.5	29.9	24.9	21.9	22.2	8.3	6.9	6.2
South Shore	49.3	36.5	28.6	25.1	24.2	9.9	7.4	6.0
Mediterranean	29.5	23.1	20.0	18.7	15.0	9.1	8.4	8.0

Source: M. L. Bacci, F. Martuzzi Veronesi (eds), *Le risorse umane del Mediterraneo. Popolazione e società al crocevia tra Nord e Sud*, Il Mulino, 1990.

Table 3.5 Emigration 1960–80 (number of emigrants)

	Spain	*Portugal*	*Greece*	*Italy*	*Turkey*
1960	30,500	32,732	47,748	383,908	n.a.
1961	43,000	34,796	58,827	387,123	n.a.
1962	65,336	38,210	84,054	365,611	n.a.
1963	83,728	53,970	100,072	277,611	n.a.
1964	102,146	86,282	105,569	258,482	n.a.
1965	74,539	116,974	117,167	282,643	117,696
1966	56,795	132,834	86,896	296,464	34,410
1967	25,911	106,280	42,730	229,264	8,855
1968	66,699	104,149	50,866	215,713	43,204
1969	100,840	153,536	91,552	182,199	103,975
1970	97,657	173,267	92,681	151,854	129,575
1971	113,702	151,197	61,745	167,721	88,442
1972	104,134	104,976	43,397	141,852	85,229
1973	96,088	120,019	27,525	123,302	135,820
1974	50,695	70,273	24,448	112,020	20,211
1975	20,618	44,918	20,330	92,666	4,419
1976	12,124	33,207	20,374	97,247	10,558
1977	11,300	28,758	18,350	87,655	19,084
1978	11,993	30,253	14,482	85,550	18,852
1979	13,019	20,622	11,050	88,950	23,630
1980	14,065	18,044	n.a.	83,007	28,503

Source: See Ch. 3, n. 4.

II From society to economy

The starting point of the migratory process was the permanent state of backwardness of all the rural areas of Southern Europe compared to the economic conditions of the 'social reference groups'.[9] Industrial progress overseas made this evident to the farm workers and the workers living in a more enclosed world.[10] The deficiencies in the services provided by the state in rural areas contributed to the internationalization of labour.

One of the main causes of emigration was the desire to free oneself and one's children from the lack of those opportunities made necessary by new expectations: schools, health service, the widening of social mobility. This movement, confirmed by the quality of the emigrating labour force, provided a deep and irresistible push towards new levels of civilization. The proof of this lay in the institutional failure of the measures taken to slow down or limit this process.

This was the experience of Spain, Italy, Portugal and Greece which, until 1970, had been suppliers of workers to other countries but, from the start of the 1970s, had gradually become receiving countries. Above all it must be remembered that the majority of emigrants were young people under 30 and young adults (30–49 years old), all active, with a high rate of illiteracy.[11] They found work mainly in the primary and secondary sectors but they were frequently industrial workers. This was particularly true of emigrants from Turkey. Emigrants over 50 or under 14 are included in the family groups in the migratory chains that are so important in these processes. Usually emigration had a definite gender-defined cycle. First the men leave to be followed by the women. The links between socio-economic factors and migratory social action are evident. Over the centuries migration proved to be worthwhile and became legitimized among the lower classes as it offered possible social betterment abroad.

If the consequences of agrarian transformation were enormous, no less enormous were the cultural changes revealed by migration. The prevalence of small family holdings in the homeland does not imply that migration was the consequence of cultural and social stagnation: it was the result of a profound change in the structure of agricultural society. The first cause of migration was, on the one hand, the expulsion of men from the rural areas and, on the other, their escape from them. Machines were the cause of the first and the glitter of the city lights caused the second. If the wretchedness of the countryside did the rest, it was not, however, the vital factor. That was the craving for betterment, the thirst for civilization.

Let us look at an identikit of the typical Turkish emigrant worker. This person was male, about thirty years old, married with children. It was fairly common for him to have two children if he had lived in a city prior to emigrating, or three if he had left directly from a rural area. But the higher his professional qualifications, the higher was his level of schooling and culture; he was better educated than his friends who stayed behind. He had most probably played a solid, productive role in life. When the migratory flow from Turkey towards Germany started in 1962, two thirds of the population were active in agriculture. But for the most part, the emigrant left behind a job in industry where, normally, his earnings were higher than average.[12]

This explains the incredible amount of energy and individual ingenuity, rather than desperation, of the emigrant who went overseas to face a long and difficult adventure. It also explains the difference between these people and those who migrated towards the cities of their own country.

It is extremely important to understand the socio-territorial articulation and differentiation of the migratory process. The factors leading to the decision to emigrate arise out of local conditions. Naturally, this migratory process was also encouraged by some governments to help the dispersion of social tensions.

Italy is an excellent example. Internal migration was favoured by dismantling the old controlling apparatus – inefficient and useless[13] – created by the Fascist regime to stop urbanization and increase its capacity to control the lower classes. Incentives were given to emigrate overseas. Between the end of the Second World War and the beginning of the 1960s, the laws governing the labour market were reformed to allow a more elastic and mobile use of the labour force. At the same time, an attempt was made to mollify the disputes caused by the spread of unemployment in the south.[14] Emigration, both internal and external, became an instrument of social and economic policy not only for its social significance but also for the part played by emigrants' remittances in the balance of payments. This is why there was an enormous increase in the migration of workers towards countries like France, Belgium, Germany and Switzerland and a continual increase in the movement of people from the south of Italy to the north in the 1950s and early 1960s.

One of the more relevant consequences of migration was the effect of emigrant remittances on the general economy. For example, in Portugal:

> Remittances that were insignificant in the early 1960s, reached £1 million in 1972–73. In 1972 workers' remittances comprised 29% and tourism 13% of the country's current exchange resources; combined, they exceeded Portugal's receipts from commodity exports by 2%. By 1974 remittances represented 30% of foreign exchange earnings and 10% of national income.[15]

The period of most intense growth coincided with the period of highest emigration: from 1968 to 1973 the Portuguese GDP reached 7 per cent with industrial production at 9 per cent.[16] In spite of this, growth did not stop the population loss and it accentuated regional differences. Emigration and tourism were fundamental to the economic growth of all Southern European countries after the Second World War as they produced an influx of hard currency, allowing the constraints of the balance of payments and the start of industrialization to be overcome.

After 1972, Spain changed from being a country with a regular and constant deficit to a country that had the highest surplus in the world (as a percentage of its GDP), with foreign exchange reserves of $5 billion. This was a decisive contribution to a pattern of growth in which exports were not able, by themselves, to overturn the historic tendency. Between 1962 and 1972 remittances went from $150 million to $1.4 billion in 1973.[17] Then, in 1974, the first wave of re-entries started[18] and it was greater than the exits. The decrease of remittances resulting from the re-entries began to be worrying even though in 1974 there were still 575,000 Spaniards outside the country: 3.5 per cent of the resident population. When the emigrants remaining abroad were faced with the possibility of inflation and crises eroding the value of the money which they sent home, they preferred to keep their savings in the more stable and secure currencies of the country in which they were resident. Between 1970 and 1981 Spanish inflation reached 16 per cent compared to the much lower inflation rate of other countries with a high number of Spanish emigrants. For example, the average inflation rate from 1970 to 1981 in France was 9.9 per cent, in Germany it was 5 per cent and in Switzerland it was only 4 per cent.[19] From 1981 remittances followed a cyclical movement without, however, ever being a decisive economic factor again.

From the point of view of emigrant remittances, the situation in Greece is particularly interesting. During the 1960s, remittances covered 35 per cent of the balance of payments deficit, making up 30 per cent of all the invisible imports.[20] The incapacity of the industrial and service sectors to create employment became even more evident after the crisis of the 1970s with the return of the emigrants and the decrease of remittances from those remaining abroad. In the last forty years the Greek balance of payments, rent by deep structural weaknesses, managed to overcome its undeniable contradictions. The repayment for war damage, foreign aid, remittances from maritime transport and capital from Greek citizens resident abroad, combined with the emigrant remittances, allowed Greece to have an exceptionally high growth rate. In the period following the 1970s there was a progressive decline in growth due to incapacity in initiating a process of internal development, not based on foreign loans, to finance the growing balance of payments deficit. The continuation of this trend meant that the abandon of the rural areas and the exodus abroad were the dramatic social costs of failure instead of stages towards growth. In any case, official statistics[21] show that remittances had a percentage influence on a constantly deficit balance of payments: from 7.1 per cent in 1964, to 109.1 per cent in 1973, to 152.8 per cent the year after, while in 1980 it reached 43.5 per cent. Overall, from 1964 to 1981 remittances accounted for 49.9 per cent on a deficit of $30,358,000 – a really considerable contribution, even though not decisive, given by a large number of people. In 1985, estimates made by the Ministry of Labour and Social Security showed that there were 2,283,661 overseas residents of which 1,071,313 were workers. The overseas population decreased between 1983 and 1985 by 120,309 people with a decrease in remittances in absolute value from $2,286,500 in 1982 to $1,696,000 in 1986.[22]

Generally speaking, remittances contributed to the profound transformation of the emigrants' country of origin while at the same time accentuating the characteristics of irregular development. This emerges clearly from the case of Portugal where, from 1960 to 1979, 952,926 people emigrated to France, 134,825 to Germany, 5,346 to Holland, 7,735 to Great Britain and 9,719 to Luxembourg for a total of 1,110,553 people. The remittances were not used directly by the emigrants as 'the best utilization still consists in depositing the money in the banks: it is probably drained off from the region, but at least it is channelled towards productive investments which benefit the country as a whole'.[23]

This problem is present elsewhere as well and is important for understanding what emigration means for the homeland. The effects of re-entry are linked to the conditions of exit and emigration has altered social heterogeneity.

III Social heterogeneity

The consequences of emigration have been lacerating everywhere. Let us start by looking at the Portuguese situation. From 1950 to 1974, a twenty-five-year period, 18.3 per cent of the population left the country with a great number leaving the north. This represented 1,514,300 people out of a total population that went from 8,851,299 in 1960 to 8,568,703 in 1970. 'The northeastern regions are subject to population loss due to emigration while those of the central and south are subject to population loss due to migration.'[24] The population became older[25] and there was an increasing predominance of females (greater in the 20 to 40 age group) with a large decrease in the birth rate. The effects of these changes on the labour market are evident. In those small and medium-sized businesses where there had been no wage increases or introduction of better working conditions, the supply of labour was scarce.

The desire to emigrate must be evaluated in all its importance if we are to understand the conditions of the country. Until 1971 the government, under the effect of the colonial war, followed a severe and restrictive policy. Even so, clandestine emigration was the rule: the movement of people to France increased from 23,700 in

1968 to 111,100 in 1970. But emigration played an important part in political stabilization and in lessening the tensions of social conflict.

Spanish industrialization, for example, apart from being helped by the expulsion
of workers from the countryside, was propelled above all by the high-density capital sectors, which offered few job opportunities, in a situation of slow population
growth.[26] The supply of new jobs rose by only 0.9 per cent between 1960 and 1974
and these were mainly in construction and services. The elimination of 1,500,000
(male) jobs in agriculture between 1960 and 1970 was parallel to 889,000 new jobs
in industry and 727,000 in the service sector. The rest of the male labour force was
forced to look for work abroad.

In Spain, as in the other countries, emigration did not reduce social differences: it
created them. There are two distinct cycles with regard to this. First, unequal development caused internal migration concentrating the population in the main cities of
the three important regions of the country, Madrid, Barcelona, Euskady (Basque
provinces). In the meantime, tourism increased the population of the coastal areas
of southern Spain.[27] During the second phase, the same massive reallocation of the
labour force provoked unequal development and, at this point, emigration became
international. Spain and its regions became subject to growing polarization. This is
shown by the different trends of the poles of emigration: Andalusia, Extremadura,
Valencia, Galicia, Murcia.[28]

This differentiating mechanism reached its peak, without any doubt, in Greece.
Greek emigration was very intensive. Between 1946 and 1955, 88,239 people left
the country and from 1956 the yearly figures went from approximately 20,000 to
approximately 40,000. The high point was reached in 1965 with 117,167 (in 1962
the number was 84,054 and in 1974 it was 105,569) after which there was an irregular decreasing pattern until 1973 with 27,529 (a year before it was 43,397 and in
1970 it went up again to 92,681). But in 1968 re-entries became intensive, reaching
18,882 and increasing to 34,214 people in 1975.[29] Between 1951 and 1981, 12.2
per cent of the Greek population emigrated. In a thirty-year period emigration went
from 7,632,801 to 9,740,417 people. It is important to underline the fact that emigration meant a loss for the Greek economy and its society because the people who
left had been economically integrated and active.[30] It must also be pointed out that
often, and particularly in the initial years of mass emigration, the emigrants were
ideologically orientated away from the political right that had, apart from a brief
interval in 1963, governed the country until the Panhellenic Socialist Movement
(PASOK, Panellinio Sosialistico Kinima) came to power. The greater part of the
emigrants came from the north, from the Peloponnese and from the islands. This
resulted not only in a labour shortage in agriculture but also in the most serious depopulation ever seen in Greece. In fact, in those same years, massive urbanization
was added to emigration overseas. From 1951 to 1981 the population of the cities
went from 36.84 to 57.59 per cent with a total population increase from 7,632,801
to 9,740,417. The population of the cities with more than 100,000 inhabitants grew
from 3.89 to 12.13 per cent of the total population. The population of the metropolitan area of Athens went from 18.06 to 31.08 per cent of the total, which in terms of
real population was from 1,378,586 to 3,027,284. Salonica went from 297,164 to
706,180. The rural population decreased over the same thirty-year period from

4,803,583 inhabitants to 4,131,276, equal to a drop from 63.16 to 42.41 per cent of total population.[31] Faced with these statistics, we cannot help but remember Burgel's words:

> Athens has a fundamental vocation for being able to destroy the sources of its own power; consistent with regard to financial capital, this destruction assumes a dramatic aspect with regard to human capital: abandoned villages, small cities impoverished, entire regions deserted. As in the case of the draining off of provincial savings, all this states the problem of the renewal of the sources of growth.[32]

This is the real and profound problem of Greek agriculture. Agrarian problems became national ones and urbanization, with emigration, transformed more than just agriculture. In the years between 1950 and 1970, all the urban growth of Greece was concentrated between Athens and Salonica.

> Everything happened as if the activities of the peripheral regions had become mummified: Thrace like the Aegean islands, Peloponnesus like the Ionic coast. Paradoxically, the continental regions of Greece became prosperous ... it has never been, without doubt, a maritime state on a level of those of the north-east of Europe and the Greek merchant navy has adapted well under Liberian or Panamanian flags, though this has never stopped it from recruiting its crews from the homeland. The regions provide the labour force for the Greek shipowners but in doing so, they lose their population, and live only on the sailors' remittances and on pensions.[33]

It is easy to understand that while emigration reduced the pressures of unemployment, it also meant a change in the income levels of the receivers of the remittances. Naturally the consequences for the emigrants' families were astonishing.

For example, it has been estimated that the average earnings of a Turkish family between 1965 and 1975 underwent an annual increase of 3.1 per cent while that of families containing at least one emigrant increased annually by 24.3 per cent.[34] A survey carried out in 1976 'showed that the Turks in France had an average annual income of 28,000 francs – with an annual transfer to Turkey of 7,300 francs, 26 per cent of the total income; at the time this amount represented an average annual Turkish salary.'[35] A considerable addition to income (although a large proportion of the workers took their families with them) if one takes into consideration the fact that from 1964 to 1980, emigrants numbered 872,463, a number that, though not constant, reached its peak in 1973 with 135,820 exits. The figure then fell to 10,558 in 1976: the year in which the flow towards Germany practically dried up and the flow towards the Middle East started. It must be remembered that the transfer of wealth of migratory origin underwent a transformation after the first half of the 1970s. This was caused by the ebb and flow of Turkish workers to the Arab states. In fact, starting from 1975, after the first energy crisis and with the contemporary introduction of the first measures to limit the entry of foreign workers into Europe, the oil-rich Arab countries started massive projects of infrastructural construction which needed a considerable amount of foreign labour, but it was fairly unstable employment. However, thanks first to the Iran–Iraq war and then to the international war against Iraq when it invaded Kuwait, there was no lack of construction work. Turkey's migratory space changed enormously, distinguishing it from the other Southern European countries which became receivers of foreign workers. In 1984 276,696 Turkish citizens lived in the Arab states (Libya, Saudi Arabia, Iraq, Jordan, Kuwait, Yemen). Of these 195,853 were workers. They were a minority presence among the emigrant workers who numbered some 7,000,000 at the beginning of the 1980s. The majority of these came from other Arab countries or from Asian countries like Pakistan, India, Sri Lanka, Bangladesh, Thailand, South Korea and the Philippines. There are two distinct cycles in Turkish emigration. In Europe industry absorbed the majority of the workers while in the Arab countries a very large proportion were employed in construction with a minority (save in Iraq where they accounted for 27.6 per cent) employed in agriculture.

Perhaps the most important and significant factor which reveals the geo-economic integration between Turkish and Arabian capitalism was in the methods of hiring. As the number of Turkish companies working in the Arab countries was high, taking on labourers was carried out by the Turkish building concerns in collaboration with the civil authorities. The same thing happened in the 1960s and 1970s with the agencies of the European multinationals.[36] The fact is that the less developed regions of Turkey, having participated only weakly in inter-European migration, now provided the majority of emigrants to the Arab countries. For the most part, the emigrants were men specialized in building construction who left for a few months, very different from Germany where 54.1 per cent of the 1,400,000 Turks living there in 1985 had been there for more than ten years. This evolution represents 'the adaptability of Turkish emigration and is an example of its role as bridge between Europe and the Arab world.'[37] But it is also a sign, greatly accentuated after the fall of the USSR and the creation of new republics in Central Asia, of the growing importance of the Middle East and Central Asia to Turkey, which should, in 1997, become a fully integrated member of the EU.

In any case, whatever the Turkish migratory space is, it is certain that we should now ask what the effects of overseas migration were on regional development. There seems to be no doubt that the Turkish experience, like that of Greece and Portugal, shows the fallacy of the theses of balanced development proposed originally by Lutz and Kindleberg and then by Griffin and Rist. These theories assumed, like those on modernization, a virtuous circle between the balance of payments, the increase of internal investment, the decrease of unemployment and, with the return of the emigrants, a new economic development thanks to the skills these had acquired abroad.[38] Obviously, historical experience does not show the total fallacy of some of these theses. It is rather the non-realization of the predicted self-sustained balancing mechanism. It does not prove mechanical dependence, it proves the unequal development of capitalism world-wide, according to Myrdal's thesis on the cumulative causes of inequality.[39] On these themes, research carried out on Latin America, first by Baran and then by Furtado,[40] gave important results concerning models of development that, purified of some ideological detritus, are still of great analytical value. Gradually the hypothesis of asymmetric and unbalanced development has been empirically confirmed by the effects of emigration on the country of origin starting with Turkish experience.[41]

The major factors to influence emigration were low agricultural productivity, the inadequacy of rural incomes, the inequality of land distribution, the grave regional disparity in income distribution, mechanization and property fragmentation.[42] But there is no doubt that the re-entry of emigrants increased territorial and social tensions in spite of increased incomes and a relatively good standard of living. The Turkish case is clearly indicative of this.[43] While a small minority reinvested its money in the acquisition of a house in the native village, the majority tended to settle in the big cities. The cities offered infrastructures and services almost comparable to those found in Europe: the rural native villages did not. The same thing happened to remittances. The tendency was to invest in regions that were already more developed and this increased the imbalance. Certainly[44] many returned emigrants aspired to becoming independent workers, above all in the service sector, even if this choice did not mean getting rich but meant being independent and one's own boss. Thus the long and difficult process that started with the transformation of the countryside finished in the city. This is completely understandable if one bears in mind that the transformation of the countryside was much more than mere mechanization and commercialization: it was a diversification and reorganization of production which involved large masses of human beings. Super-mechanization,[45] with the ensuing excess of human resources, was most certainly one of the causes of emigration and of the changed situation emigrants found on their return home.[46] This leads us to think that the transformation caused by the intense urbanization of the 1950s to 1980s will continue. Statistics for 1950 to 1980 show[47] that the population of typical villages multiplied by 1.5 while that of the cities multiplied by 2.85. Only 8.8 per cent of the urban population lived in cities with less than 100,000 inhabitants while 53.4 per cent lived in 41 cities with more than 100,000 inhabitants. This demographic change had its roots in the agrarian transformation, as we have seen, but it caused incredible changes even in the city.

This became not a place where traditions were destroyed but one where they were regenerated. This was exemplified by the reintroduction of marriage traditions like the dowry. The same thing happened in Greece,[48] and with emigrants who took their traditions with them to the new land.

> An emigrant family in Europe with a marriageable daughter could ask 30,000 or 40,000 French francs (or the equivalent in Belgian francs or German marks) as the engagement price. It was worth it as the future husband could join his bride, daughter of registered immigrants, legally, under the laws of re-grouping of the family and thus recover his investment.[49]

And tradition, in emigrant communities, also meant the re-proposal of religious brotherhoods and popular rituals. It is an extraordinary process which deeply involved Turkish cities, where, as Karpat shows us, the 'ruralization of the city' took place.[50] The 'social effects of mechanization'[51] spread until they became cultural and anthropological effects which radically transformed the society and the politics of the Turkish cities. Was it still an urban world? Certainly it was no longer a classic example of modern, secular city life. Tradition embraced and regenerated everything, intimately transforming the social networks of an environment to make it become patriarchal or matriarchal, clannish, part of a clientship system and neo-patrimonialistic. Therefore, a tight solid bond linked emigration, domestic migration and the process of urbanization: it was the regeneration of tradition.

However, this process which occurred in the context of modern life belonged, without doubt, not only to Turkey but also to those vast regions on the frontiers between Europe, Central Asia and the Middle East of which Turkey itself is the most sensitive weather-vane.[52] In fact, the old horizons, while being represented in newer forms in the towns, were smashed to bits in the villages:

> Because each kin group is concerned primarily with its own welfare and because the only role traditionally able to override this discreetness has been eliminated and not replaced by functional alternatives, we may conclude that in this one respect prosperity now weakened the village as a community.[53]

The increase of incomes and monetary economy made their effects felt, and this reclassified consolidated hierarchies and social practices. The tendencies of the migratory process reflect this cohabitation of old and new, this living together of apparently opposing habits perfectly.[54]

> In the last thirty years, only Italy, among all the European countries, has simultaneously exhibited the following two tendencies: an almost entirely free and unrestricted migratory flow abroad and, at the same time, an internal interregional migration that involved distances no less extensive than the distances required to go abroad. This fact must be kept in mind when examining the role that migration to the European countries has had on the Italian labour market.[55]

For these reasons Italian emigration requires more specific definition than that of the other Southern European countries. Between 1951 and 1960 2,937,000 workers left the country. Between 1961 and 1970 the number was reduced to 2,646,000 but between 1971 and 1980 the number of emigrants fell to 1,082,340. At this point Italy became a permanent host country for immigrants.

On the other hand, migration from the south to the north of Italy was determined by expectations of higher earnings and work in those areas in the north which were undergoing rapid industrial growth. More than 2,000,000 people found work and new conditions of life in the large northern cities of Milan and Turin. This created problems of urbanization, though they were fewer and less serious than those found in general in Southern Europe. One consequence of internal migration was to create a situation of urban concentration and congestion that had never happened before in Italy.[56]

Also, Italian migrants tended to reproduce and strengthen the models of reciprocity and family ties, on a local basis, in the cities where they settled. Summoned by the migratory chain of friends and relations, these models and ties became, from the moment of arrival to the moment of settlement, a strong and resistant cultural heritage. They were then grafted onto the city way of life with its modern consumer habits – the 'affluent society'.[57] The average age of migrants to the north was between 30 and 45. They had been either irregularly or under employed in the fragile and precarious economies of the south.

As Reyneri,[58] a scholar who has studied the problem, so brilliantly demonstrates, the local societies gained socio-political stability and increased incomes from emigration. This produced a generally favourable approach towards emigration by the people concerned. Emigration on one hand and public spending on the other (even more if that of the EEC is added to the national one), became the main instruments for maintaining social control and for increasing political consensus in the areas affected by the exodus.[59] Between 1951 and 1971, 4,000,000 people left the south of Italy: half of them settled in the north. The effect of internal migration on the finances of the Italian economy started to change with the changes in the labour market as a result of the intense and bitter social struggles which broke out in industrial Italy at the end of the 1960s.[60] At that point, bottlenecks in the labour market started to form, caused mainly by the division between jobs which needed highly qualified workers and work which required unqualified workers. The distances from the work place and the absence of social services increased their difficulties. All this happened while, particularly in the south, there were vast numbers of people existing on the margins of the economy who were not qualified for industrial work and were completely separated from the productive process.[61] The over-population of the rural areas continued to be the main problem in the south,[62] especially when internal and external emigration ceased during the late 1970s.[63] The migratory movements ceased because the standard of living in the native village had risen. This was due to an increase in public subsidies to needy families. These subsidies were not given to support economic activities,[64] but to provide money for private consumption. Only from this point of view, the north and the south were united, as the north produced the goods bought in the south. A vast area of parasitic social action discouraged moves towards industrial work as this was less profitable than being a beneficiary of a welfare state perversely hostile to any productive initiative. All this was empirically proved when, during the 1970s, emigration abroad started to decline and the emigrants' remittances could no longer be counted on as income. The state's method of counteracting this was to increase public spending: from fake invalid pensions to reforestation projects which guaranteed a yearly salary to whole families for just a few months' work. This 'agrarian aid' system[65] was the main cause of the distortion of the labour market in the south.

This complex of social and political changes is the cause of the phenomenon of migration which changed the face of Italy in the post-war years. The movements of vast masses of people unified the country culturally in a way that no amount of action from above could possibly have done.[66] The drain of labour from the south to the north[67] was intense and it was joined by emigration to countries like Germany and Switzerland, particularly in the 1960s. Before then emigration was towards Switzerland, France and Belgium.[68] In the period from 1947 to 1959 between 200,000 and 300,000 people emigrated to those countries. The peak year was 1961 with 387,123 emigrants.[69]

Interestingly, the EEC's Free Movement of Labour Provision, inserted in the Treaty of Rome largely at the insistence of Italy, has had little noticeable effect on the pattern of Italian emigration to EEC countries. Indeed, during the 1960s (the period when free movement provision progressively comes into force), the quantity of Italian emigration to EEC countries declined more rapidly (180,000 in 1960, 66,900 in 1969) than it did to the main non EEC destination of Switzerland (128,250 in 1960, 69,650 in 1969).[70]

It is necessary to evaluate the connection existing between the quality of jobs offered by the host country and the strength and tenacity of the kin and friendship networks of the migratory groups rather than the strength of political institutions as mechanisms to incentivate and stabilize migratory movements.

The links with the homeland never break. In fact, they are strengthened, even at a distance, by factors like nationality, inheritances, the processes of civilization within the family group (schooling, purchase of durable goods).[71]

Migration started to decline in 1966, with 229,264 emigrants, as against 83,007 in 1980. Starting in 1972, the tide turned as emigrants returned home giving a positive balance between ins and outs.[72] This process started in 1975 in Spain and Greece and in 1978 in Portugal. All the studies carried out on the subject of return migration[73] show that in all countries the majority of those people who return home while still of working age did not continue with the work they did when abroad. They moved into that gap between agriculture and industry called the service sector which is one of the distinguishing factors of southern economy.[74] When emigrants returned home, they realized their dreams of buying a house, of consuming more than the average and of being self-employed,[75] thus increasing internal demand and the fragmentation of economic activity.

Italy, like all Southern European and OECD countries, is a long way from reaching full employment but in the 1970s and 1980s it became a host country for foreign labour forces.[76] The whole of Southern Europe is characterized by the amplitude of clandestine immigration and by the part that illegal emigrants play in the informal or submersed economy of these countries. For the most part, these emigrants come from Africa and Asia, but Latin Americans go to Spain, and Turks and Cypriots go to Greece. The Indians, Chinese, Filipinos, Moroccans, Pakistanis and Egyptians are among those who request resident permits. Portugal, which has a high proportion of possible emigrants (today about 4,000,000 Portuguese live abroad against a homeland population of 10,000,000),[77] is starting to receive immigrants from the ex-colonies of Angola, Mozambique, Cape Verde and Guinea, all countries sunk in the poverty of new despotism and civil war. This problem must be underlined because it invites discussion of the question which more than any other explains the enormous transformation of the societies of Southern Europe, that of urbanization. The population of Southern European cities is continuously increasing as Tables 3.6 and 3.7 show.[78]

Table 3.6 Urban population and primacy in Greece compared with the rest of Mediterranean Europe 1961–81

City population (in thousands)	1960–1	1970–1	1978–81
Athens	1,852.7	2,540.2	3,027.3
Salonica	380.6	557.4	706.2
Patra	126.0	143.0	154.6
Greece, primacy (%)	20.5	21.9	23.3
Rome	2,363.5	3,033.5	3,228.0
Milan	2,531.8	3,200.6	3,344.0

Naples	1,905.0	2,140.0	2,284.9
Turin	1,351.4	1,775.6	1,854.7
Italy, second city (%)	107.1	105.5	103.6
Lisbon	1,373.9	1,674.5	2,300.0
Oporto	835.7	928.3	1,200.0
Coimbra	106.4	110.2	140.0
Portugal, second city (%)	60.8	55.4	52.2
Madrid	2,393.7	3,564.4	3,188.0
Barcelona	2,451.6	3,401.5	1,755.0
Valencia	769.7	1,056.7	752.0
Spain, second city (%)	102.4	95.4	55.1
Ankara	713.1	1,400.4	2,242.9
Istanbul	1,581.7	2,772.9	4,656.5
Izmir	568.1	904.1	1,276.1
Turkey, second city (%)	221.8	198.0	207.6

Sources: Adapted from various tabulations of OECD, *Urban Statistics in OECD*, OECD, 1983 and NSSG (National Statistical Service of Greece) 1940–84. Published and unpublished data of the General Population and Employment Censuses; Annual Employment Survey; Statistical Yearbooks of Greece; Land Use Surveys.

Notes:
1. All cities over 1 million inhabitants as well as the 3 largest cities of each country are included above.
2. Primacy measured as a percentage of second city population in relation to the capital city (as in Jones, E., *Towns and Cities*, Oxford University Press, 1977, p. 82).
3. City boundaries rather than metropolitan area, 1981/82, adapted from OECD 1982 volume on Spain; no information on metropolitan areas in OECD 1983.

Table 3.7 Employment structure in large Mediterranean cities 1970–1

	Economically active population	Percentage composition, of the economically active population				
	(000s)	1	2	3	4	5
Athens	868.3	0.88	11.23	32.98	15.15	39.76
Salonica	185.8	2.71	10.78	34.31	11.84	40.36
Patra	72.0	4.17		29.17	30.56	36.11
Rome	1,011.8	2.14	9.71	18.47	19.67	50.01
Milan	1,296.3	0.71	5.89	51.22	3.83	38.35
Naples	552.8	7.18	10.78	30.30	8.98	42.76
Turin	692.5	1.67	6.10	56.19	4.04	33.50
Lisbon	693.6	3.39	8.93	25.48	27.17	35.03
Oporto	363.1	5.92	9.10	40.36	18.58	26.04
Coimbra	39.6	11.87	9.00	25.31	28.29	25.54

Table 3.7 *Continued*

	Economically active population (000s)	Percentage composition, of the economically active population				
		1	*2*	*3*	*4*	*5*
Madrid	1,240.1	0.85	11.29	29.64	58.22	
Barcelona	1,286.4	1.54	10.66	48.92	38.88	
Valencia	366.6	7.25	10.58	36.03	46.14	
Ankara	299.5	3.94	6.94	13.03	45.08	31.01
Istanbul	950.0	4.82	7.12	31.23	23.22	33.61
Izmir	188.7	4.65	8.54	27.97	24.14	34.69

Sources: Adapted from various tabulations of OECD, *Urban Statistics in OECD*, OECD, 1983 and NSSG (National Statistical Service of Greece) 1940–84. Published and unpublished data of the General Population and Employment Censuses; Annual Employment Survey; Statistical Yearbooks of Greece; Land Use Surveys. Since errors were found (and corrected) for the case of Greece, this table should be considered provisional for the rest of the countries.

Notes:
1. All cities over 1 million inhabitants as well as the 3 largest cities of each country are included above.
2. Columns 1–5 indicate percentage composition of the economically active population by sector:
   1 primary sector
   2 construction
   3 manufacturing industry
   4 administration, public and social services
   5 rest of activities
3. Only those who declare sector payment are included here.

Very few of the large emigrant cities have been subject to the development of urban areas directly linked to consistent industrialization. In the last twenty years the presence of industry in the cities diminished as the processes of relocation got under way. The majority of the large cities, national capitals or not, are mainly occupied with construction, services and informal sectors. The main part of the extra-European immigrants find some sort of employment in these cities, and in the industrial or service jobs left vacant by the resident populations who are no longer socially or economically interested in them. Thus cultural and religious heterogeneity increases, and the tertiary vocation in Southern European societies is confirmed around the few central areas of industrialization that continuously intensify and restrict their capital investments. It is one of the causes of social disintegration. Historically speaking, as Bairoch[79] tells us, urban dimension and social forms of growth go together. Thus the circle of this type of modernization that leads to social fragmentation, closes with ethnic segregation and the constant threat of new imbalances and social conflict.

Chapter 4

SOUTHERN EUROPEAN AGRICULTURE AND PERIPHERAL PROTECTIONISM

I An overview

The history of Southern Europe's agrarian system is emblematic of the extent and nature of the transformation which took place, after the Second World War, in those countries whose social mechanisms were most homogeneous, especially when compared with the countries of Continental Europe. One common denominator is, without doubt, the persistence of state intervention to maintain control of agrarian activities. Another is the higher proportion of workers in agriculture as opposed to other sectors. Yet another is the very high share of GDP for agriculture.

Though the common denominators are numerous, there are also many factors of differentiation within Mediterranean Europe. Naturally, some of the features that distinguish the European continent from the rest of the world cannot be understood without considering the cyclic economic and institutional ebbs and flows of world economy.

The end of the First World War saw the division of the European continent into four clearly defined agricultural areas (USSR, Eastern Europe, Western Europe and Southern Europe), all suffering a bad economic depression.[1] There is no doubt that protectionist policies for agriculture were started at the beginning of the 1920s to combat this crisis. These policies allowed productivity to increase in the primary sector, thus increasing the proportion of total exports from this sector.[2]

After the 1940s the Southern European states continued to modernize and expand their economies under the hegemony of the USA. This changed in the 1960s and an independent European front emerged thanks to agrarian policies. At the beginning of the 1980s a conflict over agricultural policies started between the USA and Europe. This conflict continues and the agro-alimentary fate of the whole planet will depend on its outcome.

After the Second World War, European agriculture was still under the influence of past protectionism. Unlike the agricultural sector of the USA, the European one was heterogeneous, with strong geographical specializations. Compared to the rapid modernization which spread in Continental Europe after the Second World War, Southern Europe lagged behind mainly because political and institutional ties hindered the modernizing forces. Everywhere except in Greece, there was a change from administrations which favoured the old agrarian classes to new ones more favourable to the farm-working masses and to a sharp increase in small-holdings. The prevalence of small-holdings and of a vital but limited agrarian capitalism, together with territorial imbalances, is distinctive to southern agriculture. Small-holdings mean slower technical and productive progress, making transformation

49

costly for the whole economic system, much more so than for countries of early industrialization.

In the 1950s, the six European countries with the most advanced agriculture, 'with Italy as the only representative of the Mediterranean area and in a tail end position',[3] even though it had been one of the first countries to bring in protectionist policies for agriculture at the end of the First World War, became strongly protectionist with regard to the rest of the world in the same way as had happened in the industrial sector. The objective was to make the modernization of the various national agricultures possible. This was to be done by price control, by subsidizing incomes and by intense mechanization leading to a decrease in employment. This brought 'the ratio of land to labour to tolerable levels in a segmented productive structure that can modify only very slowly'.[4] All this was marked by the spread of technologies which increased the productivity of the land, in the context of increasing agricultural prices and volumes on world markets. This political-economic plan proved very attractive as the farming populations stood to gain great benefit from it. Thus it was adopted by all Southern European agricultures except for Turkey. It was a very dynamic change. It was 'a complex process of transformation that . . . was characterized both by its size and the speed with which it developed in the last decade . . . the decrease of the active agrarian population from a half to a quarter on the total of active population happened in France in three-quarters of a century, in half a century in Germany, in a third of a century in Italy and in only twenty years in Spain.'[5] Of all the countries of Southern Europe, Italy was the first, in the 1940s, to reduce its agrarian population after it had reached its point of maximum expansion. In the USA and in large part of Central Europe this process had started in the second decade of the 1900s, though Great Britain, Belgium, Denmark and Holland had passed that point in the second half of the 1800s. It is a phenomenon that, after the Second World War, gradually appeared in all the other Southern European countries. In the 1950s this process started in Spain and Portugal and in the 1960s it was the turn of Greece. In 1989 Turkey was the only country where employment in agriculture was more than 50 per cent (50.1 per cent) of overall national employment.[6] This phenomenon is essential for understanding the general pattern of southern agriculture after the Second World War.

During the Fascist dictatorship in Italy, capitalism spread to the rural areas[7] in a non-linear fashion. The strengthening of the large capitalistic farming concerns in the north and the big southern estates, combined with the deterioration of the living and working conditions of the day-labourers and leaseholders, obstructed the widening of the domestic market and maintained almost feudal productive relations.[8] Between the two world wars the farming of quality produce gave way to cereal production, inflating the relative over-population of the rural areas together with the premature subordination, compared to Southern Europe, of agriculture to industry. This was clear from the pattern of agricultural prices and the reduction of consumption.[9] In 1951, 12.4 per cent of all workers were employed in agriculture but there were considerable territorial variations: the north had 35 per cent, the centre 43.5 per cent, the south 55.2 per cent and the islands (Sicily, Sardinia and the minor islands) accounted for 47.9 per cent. Industrial employment, with 35.4 per cent of the active population, also showed much the same pattern for 1951: the north with

42.5 per cent, the centre with 30.6 per cent, the south with 26.3 per cent and the islands with 30 per cent. The reason for Italy's premature agrarian reorganization is understandable in the light of the high integration between the primary and secondary sectors which already existed in the 1930s and 1940s. From 1950 to 1989, Italian agriculture went from 23 per cent of the value added of GDP, while the level of agrarian employment fell from 43.8 to 9.3 per cent. The transformation was characterized by a cyclic pattern with modest growth rates from 1945 to 1957 (1.2 per cent annually), slightly stronger ones until the end of the 1960s (from 2.6 to 3 per cent) and a fall during the 1980s to the same rates as the first period. These results were, however, not sufficient to cover an increase in the consumption of more expensive products made accessible by the increases in family income. The consumption of these products meant a steady increase in imports and of the alimentary deficit.

The process of growth started with imbalances due to high productivity in the plains but widespread deterioration of the conditions in the hills and mountains, while southern agriculture had to wait for the 1960s before development started with the cultivation of Mediterranean specialties. There was a major change in cultivation, with a fall in the production of cereals (now half of what it was in the 1950s) and an increase in the production of fruit, vegetables and livestock. In spite of this, Italy, with strong inter-EEC trade relations, imported cereals, oilseed and livestock, while its main exports were wine, fruit and vegetables. Agricultural machines took the place of men, allowing industry to benefit, at the beginning, from low wage labour. In 1951, the employment figure for agricultural workers was 8,600,000 but by the 1980s it had dropped to 2,500,000. In the same period there was an increase of 10,000,000 in total population.[10]

Spanish agriculture underwent a process which has many points in common with the Italian one. The main difference is that it did not start until the beginning of the 1960s. Until then Franchist autarchical policies had discouraged any tendency to change. In the 1950s, the function of Spanish agriculture was to permit the accumulation of capital to finance industrial growth, favouring the big landowners and starving the masses.[11] With the breakdown of the old model of growth in the 1960s, agriculture started to lose labour to industry (and to emigration) and to play an increasing part in industrial markets, with a growing inflow of mainly public capital.

Between 1960 and 1970, about 2,000,000 workers left the agricultural system (the agricultural population decreased from 50 to 29 per cent in the years from 1950 to 1970), while agricultural wages increased (more than 40 per cent) and there was an incredible increase in the rates of mechanization and the consumption of fertilizers.[12] This was the beginning of the greatest period of Spanish agriculture which lasted until half way through the 1970s. All this took place during a general period of industrialization. In 1950 agricultural production was 31 per cent of GDP, by 1970 it had fallen to 13 per cent, while its relative importance in foreign trade decreased from two thirds to one third of the total during the 1960s and 1970s. The subordination of agriculture to industry was clear. In the 1960s, agriculture caused inflationary trends in the system; over the next twenty years agricultural prices fell but the effect of this was partly transformed into increased production, thus helping all the industrial economic system. Employment in agriculture continued to fall, reaching 13 per cent at the end of the 1980s (going from 4,300,000 in 1964 to 1,980,000 in 1987; overall employment was 12,032,000 in 1964 and 14,298,000 in 1987), and was 5 per cent of GDP, with agricultural exports at 10 per cent.

There were, however, distortions in the pattern of the agricultural supply with regard to the growing changes in the demand. From 1965 the agrarian foreign trade balance was negative, with meat and livestock products heading imports. This was not compensated by exports of cereals, fruit and vegetables. This imbalance created an agriculture based above all on the production of those products not exported which produced an exceptionally dynamic effect with regard to international competition. The treaty signed in 1970 between Spain and the EEC favoured this process, though it created considerable problems concerning prices as the Spanish ones were considerably lower than those of the EEC.

Portuguese agriculture did not undergo a similar process. Though the physical features of the Iberian peninsula are common to both Spain and Portugal and these countries share common experiences such as the existence, in the past, of large estates, the historical differences, starting with agriculture, are great. The first significant difference is in the relation between agriculture and industry.[13] The nineteenth century saw agricultural growth without industrialization. The period between the end of the Second World War and the 1974 Revolution saw the start of industrial development and the complete stagnation of agriculture. This lack of synchronism is the reason for the lateness and the distortions in the overall development of the country. Salazar's dictatorship had profound consequences. It was based on the stationary balance of a ruralized capitalism and small businesses. These were 'protected from the uncontrolled abuses of economic power and from the social and political dangers of massive proletarization, the lowest point of a possible convergence of the projects of the different actors involved in production, a backward synthesis of "modernity and tradition".'[14] The colonies played a decisive part in the economy. They were the primary source for the raw materials needed for industrialization, while the overwhelming predominance of cereals gradually took over the interests of the producers. A relation between agriculture and industry was established which curbed all drives to modernize and widen agricultural production. Even when the policy of massive grain support came to an end, according to the autarchy model common to Fascist Italy and Franchist Spain, the state continued to subsidize cereal cultivation.

In the north and centre there was a prevalence of small-holdings with diverse specialized products and livestock. In the south the cultivation of cereal products on a wide scale prevailed where labourers worked small areas under lease or as employees. This structure led to a social and economic down-grading of agriculture which, in turn, led to emigration. In fact, employment went from 43.9 per cent of total employed in 1960 to 19 per cent in 1989, with a decrease in value added as a percentage of GDP of 23.5 per cent in 1960 to 7.4 per cent in 1986.[15] The weakness in growth is easily seen by the stagnation of the gross output over a twenty-year period: with a pattern of less than 1 per cent per year as opposed to a 7 per cent growth in GDP. The absence of investment both in small-holdings and in large estates (low on capital and diversity of cultivation) was marked. And there was constant growth of imports to satisfy the increased demands for alimentary products and raw materials that the colonies could not meet. The situation became dramatic with the return home of hundreds of thousands of Portuguese after the end of the colonial war. It must be stressed that only the output of the small and medium small-holdings prevented the collapse of production. For example, in 1968 holdings with less than 20 hectares (equal to 95.3 per cent of total units and 38.7 per cent of surface) produced 74 per cent of the vegetables; 50 per cent of the annual harvest of wine and fruit was produced by 52 per cent of the small-holdings. It was an extremely backward form of agriculture: in 1978 Spain used 20 per cent more fertilizers per hectare than Portugal, Greece and Italy used double, France used 4.4 times as much, Germany used 5.4 and Holland used 10 times more.[16]

The agrarian revolution affected the Portuguese land division very strongly. However, not many years later the results of price fixing and the use of technology were questioned and rejected. Thus the problems of a system hit not only by almost a century of stagnation but also by institutional instability became progressively worse. All this came on top of a complex of geographical and technical fetters that led towards stagnation, and is shown by the results of policies of price control to support output. Though these policies worked for some products, generally speaking they were very different from those achieved by the European Community. If the technological changes allowed the fall of final prices in other countries, in Portugal, before joining the EEC, the increase of productive efficiency was inadequate with a vicious circle between price increases, higher wages and subsidies. The end of the first decade of European Community integration (1986–96) should be decisive for verifying if the fall of prices of many Portuguese products (excluding potatoes, rice, sunflower and green wine) has led to new levels of competition. After ten years of institutional stability, only the production of livestock shows growth. There is a decrease in the production of vegetables and cereals, with low levels of mechanization. Because of EEC and national policies of subsidizing farm workers' incomes, the surplus population does not need to emigrate.[17]

The transformation of Turkish agriculture is different and more composite. It was not only extremely important for its effect on the active population of the country but also because of its implications for the demographic situation. In 1988 Turkey had 53,960,000 inhabitants. Within the Southern European countries, it was second in size only to Italy which had 57,441,000. Spain had 38,996,000, Portugal 10,305,000 and Greece 10,016,000. But a comparison of the annual rates of growth is decisive. While these have oscillated over the last twenty years between one and zero in all the other countries, Turkey shows, for that period, growth rates from 2.2 to 2.8 per cent. In about twenty years the Turkish population has increased by 18,000,000 people. Alimentary self-sufficiency was the aim of the new democratic Turkey. And, in effect, thanks to decreases in the tax rates and price subsidies, the massive process of mechanization and more effective methods of cultivation caused a great increase in production. Mechanization also increased the amount of arable land considerably. In the first three years of the 1950s production increased by 50 per cent. But unfortunately that process was not yet technically autonomous: the drought of 1954 would have caused famine had it not been for the import of American grain. Following the 1958 drought and after a brief wave of liberalism, Turkey suffered anew from an excess of state intervention.[18]

In any case the process of transformation progressed even if it was geographically diversified. The coastal regions, with their sub-tropical intensive cultivation, are very different to the cereal-producing internal areas with their harsh countryside. A long oblique line divides industrial Turkey from rural Turkey, even though only 20.5 per cent of the population was employed in the industrial sector in 1989, a much lower percentage than that employed in agriculture. During the 1960s it was not possible to stimulate cereal production, which would have eliminated the need to import grain. The same happened for meat and milk production, leading to heavy imports and low production per head growth. Only agricultural cultivations for industrial use increased in spite of widespread mechanization and a considerable reduction in the land put to pasture. The spread of technology and price subsidies began to give widely differing results, and this was to be a constant factor in the Turkish economy. The effects on output, in fact, though modest in the case of grain, oilseed, livestock and dairy products, are better for cotton, tobacco, grapes and figs. In a country which has had a continuous trade deficit due to the import of medium and high technology products for the last thirty years, only the trade in raw materials and food products shows a long-term surplus,[19] with a strategic influence of the primary sector on the whole national economy. In the 1930s, with a considerable increase in the use of fertilizers and machines, the tendency was towards rapid fluctuations and different trends in the sub-sectors. While the production of animal products, vegetables and fruit increased, that of livestock, cultivation for industrial use and forestry weakened, even taking into account the contribution this sector made to exports, and even though international competition became much fiercer.[20]

The general picture of Southern European agriculture up to this point is one of unequal progress, but it is indubitably one of growth and transformation.

The Greek case is completely different. Here we must discuss a consolidation of original characteristics, with a strong tendency towards stagnation. The linkage between industry and agriculture, so diversified elsewhere, is almost non-existent. Even the migration towards Athens and Salonica was aimed at employment in the service sector (or construction and the informal economy) rather than towards industry. The lack of industrial development, the overwhelming part played by bureaucracy and, above all, the almost complete prevalence of small-holdings (much more so than in Turkey and the other countries), are the main causes for the lack of development, even though agriculture was at the centre of the attention of the political powers and it dominated the national economic scene for a long time.

But here we are dealing with the general stagnation of a system. Though between 1948 and 1960 the percentage on GDP changed only from 28.6 to 25 per cent, these figures must be compared with the overwhelming weight of the tertiary sector, with a share of GDP of 55.6 per cent in 1948 and of 48.2 per cent in 1960 while industry went from a 10.7 per cent share of GDP to 17.3 per cent during the same period. Only investments in construction remained high: 33.3 per cent of GDP in 1948 and 21.2 per cent in 1960, with a peak in 1953 of 43.1 per cent.[21] In spite of the fact that the active agricultural population went from 56 per cent of the total in 1951 to 30.6 per cent in 1980, agriculture does not show important indicators of modernization.

> Although the overall agricultural out-put increased and it contributed about 8.6% to the rise in GDP over 1963–79, this was caused more by greater use of machinery, fertilizers and a withdrawal of marginally productive farms than by restructuring the composition of out-put or the rationalization of land ownership.[22]

Cereal production continued to be dominant, and there was state commitment to sustain it, instead of supporting products which would be more useful to the balance of payments. Therefore, there was stagnation in the production of livestock and its by-products, cotton, and cultivations for industrial use. These categories suffered, after integration into the EEC, from the reduction of subsidies. All this produced a strong dependence on exports.

The only sub-sectors with interesting and positive diversification are those of sugar-beet and citrus fruit, but this did not change the general trend. The emptying of the land due to emigration and urbanization caused a labour shortage,[23] starting in 1955 while the need for expert labour for the extension of intensive cultivation and mechanization increased.[24] The situation is different from the general Southern European one, with the most massive and widespread consolidation of the small producer incapable of generating increases in productivity, to the detriment of the businessmen and wage-earners in relative and absolute figures. This did not stop the consolidation of the agro-alimentary industry in segments of the domestic and foreign markets, but it did not allow it to set the general tone of the agrarian situation in the country. In the last ten years the contradictions – in the framework of membership of the EEC agricultural policies – are becoming even more marked. Mechanization and fertilizers are being used massively and the income of Greek farm workers, thanks to the EEC guarantees and to the continual state subsidies, which reached the equivalent of 40 per cent of the contribution of the sector to GDP in 1986,[25] has increased considerably, going from 45 per cent of agricultural income in 1976–80 to 53 per cent in 1981–5. The crisis not only has not come about but a certain improvement in output emerges which is strongly complementary (except for grain) to that of the EEC. The production of vegetables, olive oil, meat and dairy products, and tobacco has increased and these products are exported. Even though this does not equalize the alimentary balance, it does allow survival in a system based on a growing national public deficit and the EEC subsidies, at least while this artificial level of income and production subsidy can be maintained. The Greek situation, with all its characteristics, is the deformed mirror of agrarian policies of protectionist Europe.

II The various roads to change

When compared to the other areas of the European continent, one of the more characteristic and differentiating results of the agrarian growth of Southern Europe was the stabilization of a structure of landownership strongly dominated by smallholdings. The economic and social role of these and the reasons for their predominance are, however, diverse and they must be examined accurately as much for their differences as for their similarities. It is not possible to understand the specifics of Greek experience, for example, unless one bears in mind the history of a country that inherited a landowning structure from the Ottoman empire,[26] and then, in the 1920s, gave a home to refugees from Asia Minor. Therefore, there is a client-ship and political participation which had its roots in the small-holdings and the Greek hierarchy's links to international finance.[27] The priorities of agricultural policies were the strengthening of the small family farm, rather than agrarian capitalism.[28]

This is the perfect example of that extraordinary, perverse and vital thing known as the 'Balkan model'.[29] This is completely different from the two Western models: the 'Prussian' way or the 'French' way, the way of large capitalist concerns or small to medium-sized ones, with or without the full realization of the middle-class revolution in the rural areas. Southern European experiences are a mixture, a variant of the Prussian way (because there was no middle-class revolution) and a variant of the French way (because of the massive spread of small-holdings).

If Italy and Spain managed to avoid the more negative effects of the Southern European model, Greece is the tragic version. The reason for this is that both an aristocratic landowning class and a widespread agrarian middle class were lacking. These two elements were both present in Spain and Italy and also, in a lesser way, in Turkey and Portugal. The Chajanovian family concern,[30] that optimizes the survival of the family rather than its economic efficiency, became, in the case of Greece, a factor which reinforced stagnation. This is shown by the statistical levels of technical and chemical developments in agriculture: much lower than elsewhere, but with slight superiority over Portugal.[31] The prevalence and importance of farms from 1 to 10 hectares in size is incontrovertible: between 1951 and 1971 the figures for productive units of this size went from 68.4 per cent of all units to 73.2 per cent, and the area cultivated went from 65.3 per cent of total area to 73.2 per cent. In those same years, independent family labour went from 91 to 95.1 per cent of the total agricultural labour.

The part played by the small-holdings must be considered not abstractly but in its social and cultural rather than economic context. During the first half of the 1970s, as proof of this and according to the teachings of Ward and Roustow,[32] a comparison was made between the Turkish situation and the Japanese one with regard to the very high productive capacity of the latter in spite of Turkish state aid to the small farmer, and the heavy mechanization of the former.[33] The cause of this was traced to the widespread technical and economical capabilities of the Japanese farmer rather than in structural causes,[34] as also shown by the positive Italian experience of the early 1900s.[35] The Greek and Turkish situations are very similar from a structural point of view. But they are completely different when considering the characteristics of the political elites and the rapidity of change which has been noted over the last ten years. The cause is to be found mainly in the Turkish law of 1984 on the improvement of the territory in the areas of irrigation which gave strong incentives for re-grouping pieces of land and to the growth of general productivity. This law concerned a very large irrigation project on the borders of Syria and Iraq and it caused arguments on the use of the water. For the first time in

Turkish history there was a project that was not aimed at creating small-holdings but whose intent was to form a strong network of medium-sized capitalistic agricultural concerns.

The agrarian law of 1858 was the point which marked the end of state landownership and created the basis for the formation of small landowners: Muslims in the internal regions and non-Muslims along the coasts of Anatolia and the eastern Mediterranean.[36] From that date, the problem of land to the farmers also appeared in Turkey. Kemal Atatürk's revolution in the 1920s tackled the problem but the results were controversial. At the end of the single-party domination after the Second World War ('after 1945 even the small agrarian towns and villages aspired toward fuller participation in politics and economics and were subject to their effects'[37]) a law on land distribution was passed. This was the second land reform after that of Atatürk. In spite of the fact that it was abrogated in 1950 (the same thing happened to the Bülent Ecevit reform of 1973 which concerned a region in the southeast and was declared unconstitutional in 1977) it widened the area of small-holdings by distributing the state-owned pastures rather than the land of medium to large owners. The influence of past habits was great. The bigger the estates, the more effective were the price subsidies that the state continued to give with both hands.[38] But, in spite of this, the small-holding continued to dominate, with regional variations: the smallest around the Black Sea and the largest in eastern Anatolia. This latter area was marked by small-holdings with multi-crop cultivations owned by rural families with very low per capita incomes which were integrated by mainly non-agricultural activities. These families accounted for about a quarter of all rural families. In 1973 only 20 per cent of farming families had an income above the survival level.[39] The 1980 census shows that Turkish owners of land were 68 per cent of the EEC total.[40] This fact, as in the case of Greece, has its roots not only in the policies of modernization promoted from above but also in the laws of land inheritance. The land must be divided between the heirs, so the more people there are to cut the cake the less cake there is for each one.[41] This did not happen, for example, in Catalonia, Galicia and north Portugal. Here the property was not divided up, it had to remain whole as it was the patrimony of the 'house' which had precedence over the rights of the heirs.[42]

The Portuguese experience is different from the point of view of landownership. A basic fact is the cultural, landownership differences between the north and the centre on one hand and the south on the other. Not even the 1974 revolution had radical effects against the large landowners. Change occurred, in fact, with the law of 1975 that expropriated the large estates and gave them to the Production Units, the political trade union organizations of the workers.[43] This happened about five months after the occupation of the land by farmers who had apathetically watched the fall of the regime and the coming to power of the military revolutionaries. The reform concerned only 14 per cent of the arable land and 2 per cent of the active population of continental Portugal (1.5 per cent of the gross agricultural product).[44] It was a 'landowning capitalism'[45] divided between the typical old-style landowners on one hand and the more modern, capitalistically minded ones on the other. The aim of this move was not to give the land to the farmers, as it was with the struggles led by the communists[46] in Alentejo.[47] In fact, it gave birth to a collective structure on Soviet-Stalinist lines, even to the point where the state paid wages,[48] along the lines of the practices of aid spread by the policies of the European Community. However, it at least satisfied the needs of the labourers.[49] The significance was above all political-national and was very different to the reform attempted in Spain in the 1930s,[50] which led to the polarization of the country by the political and social forces. In the north and centre of Portugal the small farmers, backbone of social conservatism, burned the communist centres[51] and the military were deeply split, losing control over the revolutionary process.[52]

After only two years the effects of the reform were diminished and by 1990, 85 per cent of the Production Units' land had been given back to the old owners. Only 6.3 per cent was given to the small farmers and 0.3 per cent to the labourers. 9 per cent was given to people who had not previously worked in agriculture.[53] After 1980, with the centre-right governments, whose programmes included the defence of small-holders and the increase of medium-sized holdings, the predominance of family concerns became still more marked. In 1979 these represented 82 per cent of productive units and in 1981 – with a 10 per cent increase over the last ten years – 71 per cent of the rural population.[54] These family concerns became larger because their production was complementary to that of the EEC even though it was more influenced by the labour market than by goods. This is shown by the experience of part-time work and the connections between agricultural activities and non-agricultural activities.[55] Industrialization based on small businesses is the other aspect of this system of concerns governed by matrimonial strategies and by multi-activities.[56] These businesses, whilst associated with levels of consumption similar to those of the most developed capitalistic societies, are tied to completely different social practices from those governing capitalism, with a fine mix of modernity and tradition.[57] This is one of the crucial aspects of 'modernization without development'.[58]

The Italian land reform was different. It was the answer found by the left of the Christian Democrat party (DC, Democrazia Cristiana) to break both the estate-owning bloc of the south and the many farmers' revolts. It led to a particularly bitter struggle, with many deaths and jail-years, and with the occupation of the uncultivated land of the landowners. In 1950 the reform laws affected both the south and the Lombardy plains in the north and led to the expropriation of 2,805 owners, 64 per cent of those who owned over 1,000 hectares and 10 per cent of those owning between 500 and 1,000 hectares.[59] This was uncultivated land and the farmers were without technical assistance. Only 57 per cent of those people who were then given the land stayed there. The rest migrated to the north, attracted by the more secure industrial wages. But in spite of this, decisive results were achieved. The Italian land (more than agrarian) reform was the only successful one after the Second World War and it proved to be irreversible.

It created a network of small and medium-sized farming concerns that stimulated market forces rather than stifling them as happened elsewhere.[60] The 1959 law on small farming concerns affected some 650,000 families and laid the foundation for the formation of a social bloc in the rural areas. This bloc's productive growth forged the links between agriculture and industry. Italy's weak point was the breakdown of a network of small inefficient agricultural concerns supported by massive and continual succession of state aid, plus regional aid, all added to the aid given by the EEC. The main difference compared to Portugal, Turkey and Greece lay in the fact that in each case the agricultural sector kept up with those countries in the central area of the EEC even though the levels of income and efficiency were inferior.[61] The pillars that held up this policy were numerous. One was the Chajanovian family concern which, in 1970, accounted for 93.6 per cent of all farming concerns and 51.8 per cent of the arable land, producing 67.9 per cent of Gross Saleable Product. Another was the capitalistic farming concerns which accounted for 4.7 per cent of all farming concerns and 21.1 per cent of the arable land, yielding 14.3 per cent of agricultural production. Yet another pillar was the capitalistic firms which accounted for only 1.7 per cent of the farming concerns and 27.1 per cent of the arable land, producing 17.8 per cent of the agricultural production;[62] 60,000 capitalist concerns produced about one-third of the production of 3,300,000 small family concerns.

This was the most distinctive aspect of Italy, with very little difference between regions: a strongly polarized landowning structure which was at the same time, fragmented.[63] It was the result of reforms aimed at strengthening the small-holder as capitalism spread in the rural areas. The effects of this were balanced both by the endogenous persistence of the family structure, and by the intervention of political power, aimed at obtaining and keeping electoral consensus.[64] Therefore, it is not surprising that both part-time[65] agricultural work and other activities, and the large agro-alimentary industry,[66] advanced side by side as incomes were complemented and multi-activities intersected, and with financial aid transfer.

Italy had a stronger and more intense social agrarian transformation than Greece, Turkey and Portugal. It was a largely social process promoted by political participation and the strategies of the governing political parties of the country. The plan to defeat both the old landowners and the social revolution was met with the economic and political mobilization of the farming classes. It overran, thanks to powerful trade union movements, both catholic and social communist,[67] both large estates and the semi-feudal share-farming structures. Thus the small farmer could own the land and agricultural capitalism grew.

The Spanish case is different. It has a great many points of contact with the Italian one but it differs from it in some essential elements. The large landownership question helps us to understand the fascinating history of the modernization of Spanish agriculture. The question of estate owning – a description which could not be used in Portugal before the revolution without accusations of being subversive[68] – is basically that of a system of cultivation where the agricultural activities were controlled by a handful of big owners. Some comparisons can help to clarify the problem. Large estate ownership, which disappeared for good in its semi-feudal form in Italy at the end of the 1940s, remained in its capitalist version as a still important economic and social force in the Iberian peninsula. It appeared territorially as a continuous trans-border area, the result of centuries-old conditions. In any case, the different recent fate of Italian, Portuguese and Spanish estate ownership is evident. Starting in the 1960s, rapid economic growth and emigration led to a great transformation in Spain. Machines replaced men and the dependence of agricultural workers on the landowners diminished. This led to increased productivity.

Portuguese estate ownership was subject to the same changes but these came later on and in the context of weaker economic development and the more traditional outlook of the big landowners.

The vicissitudes of Iberian landownership reflect the fact that Spain and Portugal are deeply different: their entrance into the world of industrial growth took place at different times.[69] The basis for the difference in their fates is to be found in the way they dealt with the problem of emigration and the emptying of the rural areas, phenomena that started to appear at the end of the 1950s. In southern Portugal, this process was less massive and occurred later than in Spain. The difference between the ability of the two systems to import the elements needed for agricultural transformation was a decisive factor. Equally decisive was the increase in the Spanish standard of living. This was shown by a change in eating habits and the growth in the demand for food such as meat, fruit and vegetables. The possibility of developing the production of some industrial agricultural products such as sugar-beet, cotton and tobacco was unique to Spain. The low cost supply of these products from the Portuguese colonies left Portugal no immediate alternative other than the intensive cultivation of cereals. This was extremely profitable for the big landowners but it was disastrous for the physical condition of the land and it did not generate enough employment to satisfy the large masses of labourers. The land could be abandoned without triggering off the mechanism of substituting machines for men which was decisive for Spanish agriculture.

In Spain, on the other hand, without the same type of revolutionary break Portugal had, estate ownership became a productive system similar to the large modern capitalist agricultural concerns. It is essential to stress the fact that Andalusian estate ownership was not of the 'overlord' (*señorial*) type and that wage paying was adopted early on. The political stability of this form of production derived from this.[70] The tremendous defeat of the civil war and the constant political repression of the farm workers both played an important part in the transformation of the political attitudes.[71] But this political and social stability, made up of repression and pragmatic acceptance,[72] is flanked by great entrepreneurial and organizational flexibility. Indubitably, geographical factors also contributed to the speed of the transformation. It was easy to make changes in the fertile plains (*campanas*) while in the mountainous regions (*sierras*) it was much more difficult and complex.

With the exodus from the Spanish rural areas, estate ownership was able, thanks to entrepreneurial action, to assume the connotations of capitalist concerns, while still maintaining the social forms of the large landowning estates. From a certain point of view, it can be said that the modernization of Spanish agriculture allowed large estate ownership to survive under the guise of rural capitalist concerns.[73] In order to do this, it was necessary to abandon the very rigid autarchic structure which Spain, Portugal and Italy had set up in the 1920s. The Grain Campaign was an administrative system which supported the estate owner and traditional classes. It collapsed in Italy with Fascism, and in Portugal with the Revolution. In Spain its gradual disappearance is linked to the agrarian income subsidies which are common to all agrarian European countries whether or not they are members of the EEC.[74]

In Spain the overcoming of the counter-revolution which followed the civil war, with the return of the military hand of the landowners, was slow and difficult. It was the product both of the desire for reform by the elites of Franchism,[75] and of the insoluble contradictions of the regime's economic policies.[76] However, agrarian reform was the impassable limit with which these policies collided. The solution was modernization, orientated in the first place to meet the growth of demand for better quality products.[77] After the 1940s, rife with speculation and black marketeers, the markets gradually became normal. The basic question in this period was the start of mechanization, mainly with the direct commitment of the owners, accompanied by the opening-up of the markets for imports and wage increases for the labourers: very different to the Portuguese situation. This process started with the large Spanish landowners but it also spread to the medium-sized ones. This was in complete contrast to Turkish mechanization where there was a prevalence of small-holders. Because of the objections of those who wanted more cautious, less liberal and more autarchical policies in Spain, the process did not move in a straight line and it often went two steps back for every one step forward. Basically, these people defended the cultivation of traditional products like grain, and this preference marked the logic of the 1950s.[78] The result produced considerable imbalances in the markets, with large surpluses of grain and other traditional products and insufficient production of quality consumer goods. However, the traditional balance was crumbling at the base, with the transformation of the agricultural population, both wage-earners and small-holders, that started in a significant way in the first half of the 1950s.

With regard to the problem of salaried work, this was characterized by the emigration of Spaniards towards the cities and Europe. This caused a rise in wages and it began to become profitable to substitute work with capital.[79] At the same time, and unlike Portugal, the opening up to foreign markets and industrialization guaranteed a supply of products. This swept away the internal resistance to the regime. The changes underway were part of a deeper change: the break with a protectionist past which ran from the beginning of the nineteenth century until 1939 when it culminated in complete isolation. Thus it is easy to understand how every attempt at liberalization, whether it came from below with the escape from the rural areas or whether it came from above with the reforms of a 'limited dictatorship'[80] and upheld by contrasting forces, could not but cause lacerating effects. These were most felt between 1960 and 1970 when almost 2 million labourers left the land. The increase in agricultural wages resulting from this meant that the landowners, who did not act in their normal landowning fashion, substituted the labourers with capital: this practice very quickly became widespread. The transformation of Spanish agriculture is exceptional when looked at in the context of the other Southern European countries which were under dictatorships. Neither Fascist Italy nor Salazar's or Caetano's Portugal had anything like it. Neither did Greece and Turkey, with their rather different, less stable types of dictatorship. It is a very important problem and one which is specifically Spanish. All this occurred in the permanency of the heterogeneity of the landowning structure, with great inequalities in the distribution of property. While in 1961, 91.59 per cent of owners possessed 18.96 per cent of the arable land, only 0.86 per cent of the people owned 53.51 per cent.[81]

However, this inequality did not stop the modernization of Spanish agriculture. In fact, the success of modernization strengthened the anti-Franchist economic stand, as did the movements for profound and irreversible change which came from the people. The changes concerned the large estates and the small-holdings. The answer to the increase in wages on the large estates, which grew by 418.6 per cent from 1957 to 1970,[82] was to invest heavily in mechanization in order to reinforce the capitalist character of the large properties. With the small-holdings, where the development of productive forces had traditionally been held back, the solution was the slow but irreversible concentration of the properties. This led to the loss of the strongly individualistic character of the small concerns, a strong subordination to the market and the beginning of the economic exchanges typical of capitalist production. Added to this were the more limited actions of increasing self-employment and part-time work. The small-holdings that produced use value goods for home consumption were shaken up by the changes and started to fall to pieces – not to disappear, it must be understood. The classic split between large estates where the profits went into the owner's pocket and the small-holdings where nearly all the money earned was ploughed back into the land appeared under other forms.

The agrarian changes in Spain were of domestic origin and they marked the end of the predominantly agricultural nature of the country. Basically it was the labour force requirements of the industry and service sectors, both at home and abroad, that caused the drastic reduction in the rural population which, between 1960 and 1970, lost 1 million workers. This reduction was closely linked to the requirements of industry.[83] This was in the context of a considerable reduction in the land cultivated and in the number of farming concerns (1,300,000 hectares and 560,018 farming units in the period 1962–82), as proof of a rationalization of production, while at the same time the prevalence of small farming concerns remains marked. This is demonstrated by the 1982 figures giving the division of the arable land by the size of farming concerns: 45 per cent of the land was worked by very large farms (more than 300 hectares), while at the other end of the scale, 2.9 per cent of the land was worked by extremely small farms (less than 3 hectares) which accounted for 50 per cent of all farming concerns. Above all, these figures mirror the disappearance of self-sustaining agriculture due to urbanization, the growing and irreversible influence of the market, the growth of intensive cultivation by family concerns and the network of services and subsidies to bolster the agricultural sector.[84] The state, even after the elimination of its corporative trappings, was still very strong, particularly in the field of price subsidies which ended up by increasing the number of marginal, inefficient farming concerns by guaranteeing the farmers a basic level of income. However, this is common to a large part of European agriculture.[85]

Chapter 5

WEAK INDUSTRIALIZATION

I Alternatives and choices

The industrialization of the Southern European countries can be understood by using an interdisciplinary approach. In these countries, the growth of the secondary sector started late, in synchrony[1] with the cyclical movements of the economy and competition with the more powerful industrial and financial complexes of the first-comer countries.

Industrialization was constrained by conditions typical of the extended reproduction mechanism of capitalism. Southern European countries used two weapons to combat the system. The first was to adopt a protectionist strategy based on the restriction of imports, to boost the domestic market. The second was a strategy of entering the European and world markets through exports. The first strategy was directly subsequent to the nationalistic and autarchic closing down of markets world-wide after the Great Depression and the collapse of world trade. It was an ideal system for the totalitarian and authoritarian dictatorships that developed at that time. The democratic regimes – or those that went back to being so after the Second World War like Italy – chose to open up external markets by adopting a strategy based on exports. This opening up did not mean a total acceptance of market forces. These countries maintained state intervention in the economy and protected their industries from world competition through the *Zollverein* of the EEC. In any case, they dismantled most of the barriers put up between the two world wars to regulate administratively the localization of industry and the allocation of the labour force.

The country that followed this line of development was Italy, and this led to the so-called economic miracle of the 1950s and 1960s.

In all the Southern European countries the acceptance of market forces in societies which had always been protected from it became a controversial element of change and novelty. These countries abandoned their protectionist policies in different ways and at different times. In some cases they managed to do so under the same dictatorships which had pursued the closure of the markets as well as violence. This happened with different degrees of intensity in Spain under Franco and in Portugal under Salazar. It happened in other countries like Turkey, with deep political instability only recently overcome with the help of the military and their limited and temporary dictatorships. This was a process which gave rise to socio-economic formations which cannot be defined simply as capitalist. They were of a new type. They had been determined by the character of the mixed economy and by the stratification of classes typical of societies where services had become predominant either after a very brief period of industrialization or by skipping industrialization completely. Market forces were more evident than before, but in a social context dominated by reciprocity and patronage which did not allow the development of a complete contractual system. State and society were the foundation of a mechanism of status that dominated and enveloped the contractual system of the market. In these countries capitalism was induced from outside rather than being the result of autonomous development. In this sense the merits and positive aspects of the strategy of opening up to international markets (export oriented), were accompanied by limitations and obstacles. In this way a weak model of industrialization was born, but it barely penetrated society. So it was left to society, with its centuries-old traditions, to introduce what was elsewhere the essence of post-industrialism: the expansion of the service sector. In Southern Europe this meant skipping over or bypassing the industrial phase of development without it ever having been the predominant sector to influence cultural and social relations as happened in the rest of Europe, admirably described by Weber's conceptual model. This is the other face of incomplete or undeveloped modernization. This induces us to abandon all foolish optimism about the future. These various topics will be developed by discussing first of all the problems arising out of protectionist pasts, then discussing the export-oriented strategy and the different results obtained. A rapid synthesis of the problems raised by unequal development and by the creation of new socio-economic structures will close this chapter.

II Opening of the markets

Nothing is more misleading than statistics on economic growth. If read without an historic eye, they can lead to grave mistakes of evaluation.

In 1981, as proof of this, someone remembered that Greece had been 'a star performer in the world economy before the oil crisis'.[2] Between 1960 and 1973 GDP of this country increased by an average of 7.4 per cent, with an increase of per capita income of 6.8 per cent per year. In 1973 the average income per head reached $1,870, against $2,450 for Italy, $2,150 for Ireland, $1,710 for Spain and $1,410 for Portugal. 'The described developments indicate the favourable effects of the adoption of policy measures aimed at the "opening" of the Greek economy.'[3] However, the reality was and is rather more complex than that deduced from these statements. The final result was a prematurely tertiary and disintegrated society, with territorial and social imbalances. The reason for this was that export-oriented policies do not automatically create the conditions for success. These policies are a social product before being a political or economic one and their total or partial absence can lead to brief upsurges of growth. However, such policies cannot lead to the long-term formation of a sufficiently large industrial base which would allow their continued adoption. In order to reach a critical understanding of the strategies of southern industrialization, we must start from the Greek situation.

In Greece, an examination of the movements of GDP from 1950 to 1988[4] shows some very interesting and salient results. The first is the dramatic and continuous decline of industrial activity without any relevant cycles after the recession and the end of the dictatorship up to the present day. The next is the drying up of sectors crucial to quantitative growth but which, like construction, were disastrous for their speculative and parasitic effects and were potentially damaging to tourism, one of the country's most crucial resources. Last is the collapse of the utilities which became marked in the 1980s. Greece was behind Portugal for per capita income and the economic and social entropy threatened to become dramatic. Would a strategy of protectionism and prolonged substitution of exports have given better results? Perhaps so, in a short-term time-frame. In any case, it is best not to believe in miraculous remedies. It should be clearly understood that countries like Greece need a mix of strategies and a good dose of pragmatism rather than ideological determination.

Let us look for a moment at the background of the non-industrialization of Greece. The period between 1944 and 1952 'can be characterized by a single word: instability.'[5] During this period the Greek dominant classes were under the monetary, military and political protection of the great powers, first under the British, then under the Americans. At the same time, the civil war had been going on for much longer than had been imagined, but it had to be ended.[6] Hyper-inflation and frequent devaluations of the drachma were helpful in the recovery of economic activities like commerce, black market, smuggling and financial speculation.

However, in this context Greece assumed a fundamental strategic position against the advance of Stalinist communism which, thanks to the policies of the Greek Communist Party (KKE, Kommounistiko Komma Elladas),[7] did not seem likely to respect the Yalta agreements (which had given the control of Greece to Great Britain). The KKE was one of the signatories of the agreement for the setting up of the Organization for European Economic Cooperation (OEEC). This was signed in April 1948, right in the middle of the civil war. Shortly after this, a commission was formed to guarantee the application of the Marshall Plan.[8] It was only after the end of the fighting, the defeat of the communists and the start of international recovery after the Korean War, that Greece started the growth process.

The first consequence was the gradual but determined dismantling of the mechanism which, in combining the ideas of free market and planned economy, had unfortunately mixed only the defects, not the merits. This hybrid scheme was supposed to do something about the scarcity of productive resources, the chaos of the public services and the general lack of confidence in long-term investments.[9] The gravity of the situation was such that the drama of a country where there was absolutely no industrial base, or rather, no essential network of infrastructure of capital goods, was evident to all. In 1952, foodstuffs, tobacco and textiles accounted for 50 per cent of total production, while chemicals and clothing accounted for 10 per cent each. The 1951 census shows that 89.6 per cent of all manufacturing industries employed less than 5 workers. This was artisan rather than industrial production, and these small factories accounted for 38.4 per cent of the workers in that sector, with a marked concentration around those centres that would become the poles of successive urbanization. The 50 per cent devaluation of the drachma in 1953 should have laid the foundation for relative price stability and for overcoming the difficulties of the preceding period which had been characterized by the collapse of industrial activity, by the difficulty of exporting and by import restrictions complicated by the existence of a system of multiple exchange rates. The opening up of the economy to foreign trade gradually became more marked and in 1962 Greece was able to undersign the act of association with the EEC.[10] In 1953 came the onset of increasing faith in the national currency, shown by the rapid growth of bank deposits and gold coins.[11] In 1936, 60 per cent of the active population was in agriculture and 13.2 per cent in industry. In the ten years between 1960 and 1970, industry's share of GDP went from 14 per cent to about 19 per cent and fixed capital investments continued to absorb 25 per cent of GDP. The growth of a large chemical industry was a prime factor in changing the industrial sector but the production of mechanical, metallurgical capital goods actually diminished. From 1953 to 1974 the chemical industry went from 7.8 per cent of total industrial output to 12.5 per cent. The other group went from 13.2 to 13 per cent. There was a slight reduction in foodstuffs and tobacco (from 22.3 to 17 per cent). There was a slight increase in textiles (from 14.8 to 15.9 per cent) but there was a reduction in the production of footwear and clothing (from 11.6 to 9.5 per cent).[12] The low degree of interdependence between sectors remained and none had enough strength 'to change its fundamental characteristics or provide the condition for self-sustaining growth'.[13] Businessmen operated under structural conditions which did not encourage the profitability of industrial investments. More could be gained from investments in other sectors. This was a long-lasting tendency in Greek social and economic history.[14] As the events of the nineteenth century show:

> The weak attraction of industrial investments in Greece was not only due to depression and international competition, but also to the possibility of alternative investments promising higher returns. . . . The transactions of the silver lenders offered much higher interest rates than industrial profits. The gains to be had from trade were also more interesting and the income from land, about 4 per cent, must be considered competitive in comparison to that given by industry, bearing in mind the lower risk. For the whole of the 19th century, there was another form of investment competitive to industry: Government bonds.[15]

These were the structural conditions that obstructed industrial growth.

From the time of the Ottoman dominion, Greek society and culture had always legitimized risk and business activity, giving rise to a very varied and complex economic elite, formed by multiple stratifications. Entrepreneurial boost was brought in by the migratory wave of the Greek community from Asia Minor after the Turkish victory in the 1920s. The orientation may have been entrepreneurial but the functional culture was commercial, speculative and agrarian. It could have become industrial only if the structural conditions had been favourable.[16] Added to this was the pervasive state intervention in economic activity brought about by using bureaucrats incapable of any sort of managerial activities, or by protectionist acts.

Figures for investments or fixed capital between 1961 and 1980, measured in millions of Greek drachma and at constant prices, show the differences between those for construction and those for machine goods.[17] The investments in construction had always been higher than those for machines goods. Between 1961 and 1980 the first oscillated between a maximum of 73.7 per cent (1963) and a minimum of 58.3 per cent (1980), while the second went from 17.9 per cent in 1960 to

26 per cent in 1980 with a peak of 35.6 per cent in 1970, all this even though it had been shown that 'to reach the same economic benefits as those from industry, the amount invested in construction should be eight and a half times as much'.[18] The reasons for the predominance of construction must certainly be attributed to the absence of a capital market. But another reason can be found in the extremely low level of housing ten years on from the civil war, in the absence of alternatives for investing capital in a period of rising incomes, in the intense and rapid urbanization, in the persistence of the dowry in marriage contracts and in the fact that the land was fragmented by the laws of heredity and by the historic absence of feudal owners and large landowners.[19]

Urban construction must be placed in the same category as 'renter capital'.[20] It was largely responsible for the under-development of industry and for the growth of a culture which was against productive activity. It was wealth accumulated without production, in a system that was not only economic but also social, connected by the close network of clientship fed by a political class that had developed thanks to the depression of industrial activity. The proliferation of construction by small family concerns must be seen in the context of the creation of political consensus among the less wealthy and the middle classes of the population[21] by guaranteeing them easy credit and building speculation. The example of Greece allows us to understand fully that a strategy of opening up to external markets is not, by itself, a remedy that automatically solves problems which are not only economic but are also social and cultural.

However, Turkey shows us a different kind of reality. Policies of protectionism and export substitution can be tragically dangerous if pursued without any consideration of the conditions of inefficiency and ineffectualness that they produce when applied integrally. However, at the beginning they can be an indispensable stage in laying the foundation for an industry of capital goods. The Turkish case shows both the advantages and disadvantages of protectionism. As protectionism had not been abandoned in the second post-war period when it would have been both possible and necessary, the disadvantages outweighed the advantages. The decision to trade with foreign markets was taken late, and under difficult international conditions. In this sense, Kemal Atatürk's revolution of the 1920s produced very mixed results. A bureaucratic, dictatorial failure? Too long a step, taken too soon? The revolution was also a decisive step towards Turkey's integration into world capitalism, paradoxically through a break with the capitalist, entrepreneurial classes that had formed half way through the 1800s[22] and which made up the more positive elements in the progressive dissolution of the Ottoman Empire. In this sense, Atatürk as a revolutionary was very near to the Leninist model. Therefore, continuity must be looked for within the republican experience, after the revolution of the 1920s. Turkey continued to follow a policy of import substitution in harmony with the nationalistic ideas like interventionism and government control that had taken shape in the 1930s. This policy was finally questioned in the late 1960s when an attempt to continue the financing of imports with foreign loans suffered a final defeat. The turning point came in 1980 when, with a 90 per cent inflation rate and a disastrous balance of payments, the government, under the auspices of the International Monetary Fund (IMF), introduced an orthodox policy for stabilization

67

with an intensely liberalizing programme.[23] This included export subsidies, the gradual removal of trade barriers and exchange restrictions, tax reform and incentives for foreign investors plus radical industrial reconstruction. It was the changeover from an era of protectionism and government control to a market economy.

This was not the first time that such experiments had been tried in Turkey but, until this one, they had always had a very short life. The first one, at the beginning of the Republic in 1924,[24] was a programme of industrial policies but it foundered under the Great Depression and gave rise to massive state intervention. In 1950, after the Democratic Party (DP, Demokratik Parti) came to power, a second liberalist experiment was tried not only because of the party's ideology but also because of the pressures of the Marshall Plan. In any case, after three years of inflation, the collapse of the balance of payments and the over-valuation of Turkish currency, this brief interlude came to a close. A rigorous policy of import substitution was followed for the next decades. It was only in August 1970 that a new phase opened with the devaluation of Turkish currency, with a two-year reduction of the quantity controls on production and prices, the revival of an orientation to market and with incentives to attract foreign investments. The balance of payments was readjusted by emigrants' remittances while the world-wide economic boom of 1971–3 got under way. But the remittances were undermined by the inflation differential and the over-evaluation of Turkish currency which, in a short time, led to the return of old ways. The conflict with Greece over Cyprus was another contributing factor as it increased the country's financial crisis and the decision to return to the 1967 policy of 'convertible currency deposit' led the economy towards a crisis which could have proved irreversible.

It is worth pointing out here that starting in 1960, and at approximately ten-year intervals after that date, the military, with authoritarian methods, imposed renewed democratic rules on the civilians.[25] So in September 1980 a new military government produced an intensive and coherent programme that was completely different from any that had been tried before.[26] It had to complete the programme that had been proposed by the civil government in January of the same year but which the fragile Turkish democracy did not have the force to carry out. This was a very important event because Turkey, not only in Europe but also internationally, is the first, though not the only, developing country to have adopted a system of mixed economy on a large scale.[27] Turkish economic development must be looked at under this light, because it must not be forgotten that the Turkish state-owned companies guaranteed an industrial base.[28] (These state-owned companies were, institutionally, very similar to the Italian state-owned enterprises, where the state does not hold, at least at the beginning, all the company shares.[29]) They carried out a policy of import substitution and imposed monopolies.

However, they were not the sole, undisputed protagonists of economic life in the country, particularly after the second post-war period. During the war these companies accounted for one quarter of the total industrial and artisan production.[30] Even then the private concerns, though smaller, showed good growth levels compared to the difficult managerial performances of the state-owned companies. American aid was a fundamental support for the economy and particularly for the balance of payments.[31] The Marshall Plan had no effect on Turkish culture while in other countries, for historical and cultural reasons, it did. Western interest for such a militarily strategic country was a constant factor. Thanks to a 1955 law, foreign investments were allowed. These were mainly in chemicals, rubber, light engineering and agriculture, while investments in the oil sector were prohibited. Of these investments, 40 per cent were North American, 15 per cent were Swiss, 13 per cent were German and 12 per cent were Dutch.[32]

Turkish industrialization was financed mainly by public banks. However, they were not able to do this for private companies, which were always subject to a weak inflow of capital compared to the easy credit given to state industry. State industry gradually assumed the characteristics of a political-administrative organization linked to the party system by a personalistic network, whereas at the beginning public industry, with the creation of a managerial elite, had taken over the role that the private entrepreneurial elites of the old Ottoman Empire (Greeks, Armenians and Jews)[33] had played. And yet, in spite of a thousand problems, the importance of private industry continued to increase. The 1963 Census gives some very interesting figures.[34] The number of state plants was 238 against 2,774 private ones. The state plants employed 140,400 people, equal to 25 per cent of the total active population. The private plants employed 185,000 people, equal to 17 per cent of the total active population. The production of public plants accounted for 42.6 per cent of value added and private plants accounted for 38.1 per cent. The private sector was dominant in foodstuffs, clothing, wood and skins, while both private and public concerns were equally present in all the other modern sectors. The de facto monopolies had, in fact, been broken and private industry started to develop under the state's wing. At this point, the costs and lack of efficiency of the state-owned enterprises became apparent, while in 1971–2 the private companies underwent a real boom even though the state played a growing part in naval and automotive construction.[35]

However, the balance of payments fully demonstrated the failure of the policy of closure to foreign trade. In spite of rigorous controls and restrictions, for twenty years, until the crisis in the 1960s, the value of exports did not balance the value of imports. From 1952 to 1954 the percentage of exports on imports was 70.4 per cent, from 1962 to 1964 it was 62.9 per cent and from 1970 to 1971 it was 59.7 per cent, in spite of a gradual increase in exports that, however, from 1951 to 1971, evolved with a progression inferior to that of all the other developing countries.[36]

It must also be remembered that exports were always guaranteed first by agriculture (from 1961 to 1972 the value went from $305,600,000 to $694,500,000), then by industry (from $22,600,000 to $155,400,000) and lastly by mining products (from $18,500,000 to $35,000,000). These figures show the importance of the domestic market for products which were not exportable.

From this point of view, protectionist policies had not only badly damaged the sector's quantitative performances but they had also diminished its competitive efficiency with regard to overseas markets. In this sense, the difference with Japan is important. In fact, as late-comers, both countries have protected their growing industries in order to form an industrial base protected by trade barriers rather than by customs duties. But there is an enormous difference between the two industrial policies. Japan had developed a detailed plan to develop a system of production aimed at the export market, while Turkey intensified its protectionist policies to support an inward-looking industrialization. This was made possible by the enormous potential of its domestic market and by the rigid ideology of its elites. A high cost had to be paid for the inefficiency of this policy. An important point to make here is that the more this policy was carried out, the more it revealed the impossibility of controlling the society, which reacted by using all the private economic powers it had at its disposal. International trade exchanges provoked the failure of that system of industrialization. The management of the foreign deficit has made this problem even more evident. Until the 1973–4 crisis Turkey had had no need to ask for foreign loans to cover the balance of payments deficit. This was largely financed by aid received from the Union for Turkey which was made up of the sixteen OECD countries, the European Community Commission and the World Bank. Turkey received the equivalent of $250–300 million from this organization. However, at the end of the 1960s, with the worsening of the terms of trade and the increase in the volume of imports, Turkey had to resort to commercial credit given under market conditions with another increase in the foreign deficit.[37] Therefore, the position of the Turkish economy with regard to international markets is fundamental.[38]

The strategy followed until the 1970s gave rise to serious problems linked to the rapid expansion of a manufacturing industry in a prevalently agricultural economy, which put intolerable pressures on the balance of payments. The 1980s were decisive for the Turkish economy. Enormous human resources were available with a labour force of 18,493,000 divided between agriculture with 9,450,000 employed, industry with 1,910,000, construction with 596,000, transport with 515,000, commerce with 684,000 and services with 2,530,000.[39] But this structure had to work in the context of a market economy. Sacrifices had to be made by the bulk of the population and political consensus was limited. A contradiction arose between the reproductive and the productive system due to the uncontrolled expansion of clientship public spending. For example, the pensionable age in Turkey is 55 years for men and 50 for women and the social services are in a state of complete inefficiency.

At the start of the 1980s, Turgut Özal introduced a new economic plan to privatize state enterprises gradually. This was then continued by his successor, Süleyman Demirel. A parliamentary law of June 1986 was approved which contained a series of measures aimed at reducing new state intervention to a minimum and making public enterprises use the criteria of a market economy. Party membership and political activity were considered illegal for state managers.

Even though the funds given to these enterprises by the public budget had been cut, these were still considerable for the mining industry (90 per cent of all fixed investments), for the energy industry and transport (60–70 per cent) and for tourism (20 per cent). These privatization measures must be inserted in the fundamental change made to Turkish political and economical life by Turgut Özal after 1983. It was a true cultural revolution that legitimized market economy and free enterprise, a revolution which favoured the nascent entrepreneurial class and which gave the entrepreneur and the economic motivations a high degree of respectability. The last ten years have seen an average rate of growth of GDP at 4.3 per cent per year with an almost continuous increase of 6.3 per cent for industrial production. The percentage of GDP for industry went from 25 per cent in 1980 to 32 per cent in 1989, with an increase in industrial exports of 20 per cent per year. This represents 80 per cent of Turkish exports against the 30 per cent of ten years ago. It is interesting to see that the opening up of trade with abroad meant increasing the proportion of heavy industry on total production and a reduction in the importance of light industry. In that sector the production of foodstuffs and textiles showed signs of improvement. 'Everything leads . . . to the belief that the reform of foreign trade in Turkey has produced structural changes in industry.'[40] In spite of the progress made on the industrial front, the Turkish economy had not yet overcome its problems. In the last half of the 1980s the rapid, intense cyclic movements of growth and recession became more frequent and inflation got worse. The trade balance figures for the last thirty years[41] show that Turkey's trade deficit was caused mainly by the import of medium to high technological products from 1980 on and low technology imports in the preceding twenty years. Only trade in food products and raw materials showed a long-term surplus. The programme started in 1980 led to an increase in exports, but that was not enough to stop a deterioration in the balance of payments for high and medium technological products. In any case, even with a continuous surplus in the invisible exports, the trade deficit continued to grow and the current one now exceeds 2 per cent of GDP for 2 billion dollars, combined with the foreign deficit that burdens the Turkish economy. Between 1984 and 1987 this reached $40.2 billion to stabilize at around $45 billion in 1990. This was a result of the liberalization of exchange rates and foreign trade, with an increase of short-term credit from foreign banks and government bonds. There is, however, a lack of synchrony between financial stability and productive recovery so that the increases expected from the liberalization programme did not take place. Bearing in mind the increase in exports, productive capacity and profits, the behaviour of the entrepreneurs is surprising. Most certainly the fall in the value of money, the high interest rates and the inflation rate of about 48 per cent all played their part.[42] One of the chief structural causes of the high rate of inflation was the enormous public sector deficit and the need to produce enough money to service it even though other variables like the fluctuation of exchange rates and prices and the increasing cost of labour also played a considerable part.

But the real social, historical reason for inflation and the foreign and trade deficit lies in the narrowness of the Turkish industrial base compared to the other public and private service sectors. In spite of the continual changes in its characteristics, the Turkish economy is still a long way from that of an industrial society, even though it is no longer the agrarian society of the post-war period.

The case of Turkey demonstrates most clearly that the real problem of export promotion depends on the more developed countries' capacity to absorb manufactured products. Perhaps from this point of view, a period of import substitution combined with a low distortion of incentives is necessary in order to make the opening up to foreign markets feasible. Given that there are limits to market expansion and competition can harm not only businesses and industries but also the countries, it is best to examine the various cases one at a time without resorting to dangerous generalizations.

The Portuguese experience is interesting as it allows a discussion of these themes at a highly articulated level.[43] In fact, it must be noted that between the end of the period of import substitution and the beginning of the export oriented one, when the country joined the European Free Trade Area (EFTA) in 1959, there was an increase of exporting industries. However, the only ones which managed to maintain their position as exporters were clothing, footwear, paper products and textiles while the others (petroleum products, machinery, etc.) failed. The imports of machine goods were high and exceeded the entire quantity of all exports. Thus the nucleus of Portuguese industrial specialization was made up of textiles and pulp products together with important results in naval and non-metallic minerals production. 'This polarization of the specialization in traditional activities . . . is peculiar to Portugal in the context of Southern Europe.'[44] This polarization has the disadvantage of not being very dynamic compared to the changes in world economy and it is, besides, subject to the only advantages of the levels of real wages (doomed to fall after the post-revolutionary years) and the exchange rate devaluation. These two factors together would seem to be the last thing needed for an economy with such a long past of distortion of incentives. From this point of view, the results of privatization and the development of new investments will be fundamental.[45] Privatization proceeds with difficulty and, when it succeeds, it returns those industries, nationalized after the revolution, to the previous owners – the fiefdoms of the financial hierarchy. The first problem to be underlined is that, in spite of the model of stationary balance,[46] Portuguese industrialization in the second post-war period established itself. From 1890 to 1950 the average annual growth of GDP per capita was 1 per cent, while from 1950 to 1970 it grew to 5 per cent, though with a less steady growth rate than this figure would suggest. From 1930 to 1944 it was 2.4 per cent, from 1940 to 1945 it fell to almost 0 per cent, while between 1945 and 1950 it went up again to 2.7 per cent. In the 1950s it stabilized at 3.7 per cent and it reached 6.5 per cent in the 1960s.[47] The cause of these movements was without doubt the pressures of international markets which increased after the country joined EFTA. This is shown by the change in exports where foodstuffs, chemicals and electric machinery join textiles and clothing.[48]

That this could have happened is proof that the original project of industrialization from above, when seen in action, was more lethargic than active, thanks to the support of laws which protected those industries already functioning, and then secondly there was the formation of a patronage network between state bureaucracy and representatives of the industrial and financial worlds. This gave rise to that ideal entrepreneurial type, justly defined as political industrial, born of '*compadrio* and clientship',[49] which had the chief effect of preventing innovation in industry. In this sense, the influence of the tradition and archaism of the authoritarian dictatorship was significant. Unlike what happened in Spain, it allowed the industrial system to exercise a fatal influence on the attempts at entrepreneurial growth which were appearing in the society. The 'traditionalist *pender*'[50] was decisive, particularly in the 1950s. Naturally this contrast caused the slow, tardy formation of an autonomous entrepreneurial class endowed with a solid social and cultural status.[51] Portuguese industry, dominated by the bureaucratic clientship of the dictatorship, was characterized not only by the stability of the large groups but also by the flourishing of innumerable tiny and unprofitable businesses. They flourished under protectionism and import substitution and often they were family owned and run. These businesses grew rapidly and, when faced with the competition of the 1960s, died rapidly. Between 1957 and 1964 10,000 small businesses disappeared as did 100 of the larger ones. Small businesses had an undisputed quantitative predominance even though they did not have an equally strong ability to bring pressure to bear on the government.

In the 1960s, however, integration into the European market, which coincided with the start of the colonial war, forced the regime to change its economic policy in favour of industrialization. The mid-1960s saw growing inflation which was increased by the war effort as well as a massive exodus from the rural areas. In spite of this, growth stabilized: from 1960 to 1970 the active population in agriculture fell from 42.8 to 33 per cent (it was 49 per cent in 1950), while industry went from 29.5 to 35.8 per cent (24 per cent in 1950) and the service sector went from 27.7 to 31.2 per cent.[52] These figures clearly show that the main source of growth was the opening up to foreign markets with membership of EFTA which gave Portugal a privileged treatment for industrial products, rather than import substitution in a very small, poor domestic market. In 1965 the member countries were already the main importers of Portuguese goods: a part which so far had been played only by the colonies. In spite of the success of imports, the trade balance started to show a growing deficit, barely mitigated by the invisible exports of tourism and emigrant remittances.

The shape of industry in the 1960s was different from that of an underdeveloped country because its structure was more articulated and heterogeneous. Its comparative advantages were not in labour-intensive goods where it could not compete with the East and South Asia, nor were they in capital-intensive products as this field was in the hands of the OCDE countries with low cost capital. Its competitive advantages lay, and still lie, in a wide range of goods that fall between these two extremes, chiefly in more skill-intensive sectors.

This is the result of the stratification of Portuguese industry in two distinct historic periods. Until the end of the Second World War, the colonies supplied consumer goods and raw materials while the cities supplied the often stagnant demand of the industrialized countries for products like quality wine, cork, olives and sardines, which all came from the country's natural resources. This resulted in low industrial specialization in a slowly expanding economy. The low cost of labour guaranteed by the dictatorship gave the country new importance in the world economy. In the second half of the 1960s, the high cost of wages in Europe induced new industries in sectors like electro-mechanics, optics and mechanics to move to Portugal. This was the start of export diversification with the development of new industries especially in the agro-industrial field. Portugal's geographical position on the maritime shipping lanes encouraged naval construction and maintenance. This was the time when the large, state supported, strong national industrialized groups developed productions which were essential for the domestic market like mechanics and chemicals. Unlike Spain, however, Portugal did not grow by opening its borders to the world. It was only in the petroleum and the iron and steel industries that there were, before the revolution, significant inter-industrial linkages.

73

Unfortunately these projects suffered from the upheaval of the 1974 revolution. Administrative inefficiency and an adverse world economic situation did the rest, while investments by foreign companies fell for fear of nationalization and the price of imports rose sharply. Traditional industry continued to be important. At the beginning of the 1970s, with devaluation, the fall of real wages and the unfavourable performances of the other industries, the labour-intensive sectors represented about 40 per cent of all exports.[53] At this point, though it had not yet finished the phase of import substitution, Portugal could have been called a semi-industrial country that was already in an export-oriented phase. Direct foreign investments played a considerable part in this.

It would be a mistake to over-evaluate these or to make a negative judgement about them. They gave Portuguese growth an important economic stimulus, particularly in the Lisbon and Oporto areas. Foreign industries accounted for some 32 per cent of the total capital funds of the Portuguese companies in 1970–1 and 18 per cent of the value of gross production in 1975, maintaining control of 65 per cent of the industries.[54] The difference between direct foreign investments in Portugal and Spain was the fact that in Portugal they were used to produce exports as the domestic market was so small. Even though these investments meant a high quota of imports, at least they helped with the balance of payments. Perhaps the most serious problem was that generally speaking high quotas of exports were aimed at internal trade between businesses and that the multinationals developed only a low rate of technological spread in the local businesses. In any case, it is a mistake to think that foreign investments have, by themselves, a negative effect.[55] It is rather a question of economic policies and industrial policy aimed at the development of non-subordinate ties.

Above all, direct foreign investments give rise to the question of the growing regional differences. This is a problem faced by all the Southern European countries. In 1987, investments continued to rise everywhere. The following industries, mentioned in order of size of investments, benefited from them: cement manufacture, mechanics and electro-mechanics, paper, petrol-chemical, clothing and footwear.[56] The major part of these were owned by the British, Swiss, Germans, Spanish, French, American, Japanese and Brazilians. The reasons for these investments were low labour costs and the strategies of direct transformation. These caused an increase in the polarization between Lisbon and Oporto on one hand, and the marginal and agrarian areas on the other. This accentuated urban-industrial concentrations which became more dependent on centres outside of the country as Portugal became more peripheral in the international division of the labour force. But it provided employment and income to the whole system. Historical continuity is stronger than any change[57] so the next few years are going to be very important for Portugal, not only because direct foreign investments are shifting to the property and financial sectors and to the service sector, which they did not do in the past, but also and above all because the government party led by Anibal Cavaco Silva started a massive programme of privatization in 1989. This required modifications to the constitution but it should radically change the shape of Portuguese economic structure.

The question of foreign investments is also one of the problems of Greece. Laws made in 1953 and 1962 favoured a massive invasion of multinational companies.[58]

These controlled those industries vital to the economy and showed a high rate of growth between 1961 and 1964 when they held 37 per cent of the capital assets of Greek businesses. In 1972 they held 29.8 per cent of capital assets but in 1979 this figure fell to 14 per cent. Industries like iron and steel, chemical, electrical and plastics were under complete foreign control until the beginning of the 1970s (cellulose until the middle of the 1960s), while at the end of the 1970s investments moved towards light industries like clothing, wool, etc.[59] At the beginning of the 1970s there were a few hundred light industries: 264 in 1971 and 398 in 1977. They accounted for 46 per cent of net profit and 30 per cent of industrial employment[60] and they were closely connected to the development of the Greek political system.

Between 1961 and 1964, the new Prime Minister, Georgios Papandreou, threatened the oil export rights of Esso-Papas and British Petroleum, to the extent that these two companies plotted against his government. In 1964, Georgios Papandreou was replaced by the military dictatorship because of the conflicts which had arisen in the political field between himself and the financial and monarchical hierarchy. At the beginning of the 1970s, Andreas Papandreou's government nationalized Esso-Papas and started a battle about the aluminium monopoly with Pechiney. This was done in the context of a more general plan of socialization which was interrupted only in 1985 under the weight of domestic and foreign debts.[61] These events must be judged pragmatically, as in the case of Portugal.

Foreign investments in Greece most certainly increased the amount of concentration, thus creating monopolistic situations. But the contribution made to employment was considerable even though it was mainly in industries with a high intensity of capital. However, this trend has changed over the last few years. The major part of these industries aimed at the domestic market, or at intermediate goods for the production of the mother company in the case of branches of multinationals. The volume of imports generated[62] by them is higher than that for exports. Obviously this has repercussions on the balance of payments, and the balance of payments is one of the main problems of the Greek economy. This fact is the key to understanding Greek problems. The crux of the matter lies in the domestic production that can develop alongside the foreign investments.

Portugal is a good example of this. In 1988 GDP stabilized slightly above 17.5 per cent at constant prices, compared to 1984, at the beginning of the new process of economic stabilization. Employment grew by 5.5 per cent from 1985 to 1988. Unemployment fell spectacularly in the final years of the 1980s when it reached points lower than 6 per cent of the active population. The strategies adopted to stimulate public and private investments gave good results. Inflation fell from 28 per cent in 1984 to 10 per cent in 1988. But the danger of inflation is still there and the international factors which were favourable to the Portuguese economy are disappearing. Added to this is a less marked flexibility of wages which had always been a distinctive competitive advantage of Portugal. Therefore, the future of Portuguese society seems difficult.

This seems to be the future of the majority of those Southern European countries (with the exception, as we will see, of Turkey), that abandoned the policy of encouraging the growth of the domestic market in the late 1950s, and turned to encouraging exports. This allowed an almost full use of productive capacity and a reduction of costs by using economies of scale, which contributed to an efficient import substitution. This in turn exposed the country to foreign competition with a resulting positive stimulus to technological change.[63]

Compared to Portugal and Greece, Spain followed this policy in a more effective way. With regard to exports, for example, in the twenty years from 1960 to 1980, Spain's more important exports were footwear, clothing, iron and steel as well as metal goods. These exports, typical of a mature economy, started to suffer in the 1970s from the world recession, but nevertheless changed the proportions of the specialized exports.

> In the 1960s agricultural products accounted for more than half of the total. In the 1970s, a wide variety of manufactured products dominated with about 70%. In the last ten years [1970s] exports ceased to be, for many industrial activities, a mere temporary extra of the domestic market. On the contrary, they grew considerably in the years of rapid domestic development as compared to that which happened in the 1960s.[64]

The trade balance was always in deficit and it increased sharply: in 1959–69 it was $1,104.98 million but in 1974–80 it had grown to $7,019.67 million. It was only in the interim period from 1970 to 1973 that it showed an active balance. In that period the deficit was compensated for by the exceptional growth of the invisible imports of tourism and emigrant remittances.[65] Growth until the middle 1970s was characterized by cyclic fluctuations caused by the close correlation between the rate of production growth and productivity. With the enlarging of the productive base, and a better use of the labour, productivity increased; the opposite happened when production fell. Investment rates and productivity were decisive factors for growth. The cyclical nature of the Spanish economy had always been influenced by the possibility of acquiring imports to satisfy the end user demand. This created problems with the balance of payments and led to a see-saw of stop and go policies.[66]

Policies of this sort were needed in Italy from 1950 to 1970 both to keep inflation down and to contain the overseas trade balance. However, Italy had one very special characteristic compared to the other countries of Southern Europe. At the end of the Second World War, it already had a complex and powerful industrial structure born of the import substitution in the capital goods sectors which took place before and after the First World War and which allowed Italy to be considered as one of the industrial powers, though its position was a fringe one. So Italy was able to open up its economy to world trade not only before any other country in Southern Europe, but also well before the constitution of the EEC in 1957, and it did so successfully. Italian production covered many different sectors and was developed between the two world wars. Though corporative Fascism helped the concentration and oligopolies (as it did in Portugal and Spain), it did not have a substantial impact on growth. This followed the cyclic pattern of world economy. Thus Italy's answer to the period of protectionism following the crash of 1929 was a policy of autarchy and the formation of that vast complex of public businesses and banks called IRI – Industrial Reconstruction Institute (Istituto di Ricostruzione Industriale). (Now, in the 1990s, this whole set-up is being opened up to privatization with an eye to easing the public debt.)

State intervention was decisive in the fields of shipyards, arms, iron and steel, telecommunications, oil drilling and distribution. The only field in which state intervention was monopolistic and totalitarian was that of telecommunications. Private industry was able to develop successfully in the same fields as the state and also it had never abandoned those traditionally exporting sectors with high labour intensity like the mechanical sector which was an essential and vital part of Italian industry. The physiognomy of the national productive structure, and therefore of society, was already clearly outlined between the two world wars. In the first place there was a strong oligopolistic group of public and private businesses in the fields of heavy engineering, iron and steel, electricity (nationalized in 1964), vehicles and minerals. Numerically these were weak compared to other countries in North-Central Europe and to the needs of the Italian economy but were, none the less, very important. In the second place there was an extensive network of small and medium-sized businesses in traditional and mechanical sectors that developed as vigorously in the second post-war period. Finally, there was an intrusive state system, bloated by public employment and a highly politically aware bureaucracy with a vocation of clientship and little dedication to the job of administration.[67]

III Economic dictatorship: political capitalism

That particular aspect of Italy's past introduces one of the central themes in the analysis of contemporary society: the correlation between dictatorship, economic constraints and growth.[68] This is not a deterministic correlation. During dictatorships there have been cases of growth as well as cases of stagnation. The decisive factor was the orientation of the dominant elites with regard to the balance and dynamics of power between the social groups of which they were part. Portugal and Spain, as well as Italy, are excellent examples of this: stagnant dictatorship the first, development dictatorship the second.[69] The analysis of the lobbies and power groups that face each other within the bureaucratic system of the state is of central importance.

Both in Portugal and Spain the corporate institutional structures had a marginal and limited role, and reached stability thanks to the strategic parts played by Salazar and Franco.[70] Both were the final arbitrator, using a carefully calibrated mechanism of compensation of interests, all this within a culture of formalism, of hierarchy, of awareness of the stratifications of status that 'are naturally old world characteristics but they are characteristics of an old world that largely died in 1914 in the rest of Europe but continued to live only in corporativist Portugal'.[71]

The Spanish version of clientship, that is to say the network of contacts that an actor can create and exploit for his own ends, ends up by being the way pressure is brought to bear by the lobbies. The armed forces, the church, the nobility, the industrial middle class and the big landowners formed a power bloc that shaped the structure of the authoritarian dictatorships thanks to the role played by the powerful political police and army. The dictatorial lobbies cannot be compared to the North American lobbies, which are pluralistic and operate through the administrative mechanisms of a parliamentary democracy. The absence of this type of democracy favoured direct relationships between lobbies and bureaucracy and between lobbies and the policies of the dictatorship.

> Portugal has been called an administrative state, a corporative state, a dictatorship or an autarchy, it has also been called a capitalistic state. That is true only in a restricted sense, however, since Portugal wholly lacks some of the prime ingredients of capitalist systems: free competition, individual initiative and entrepreneurship and a laissez-faire market economy. In Portugal it is the state that initiates virtually all economic enterprises, that helps raise capital, that grants charters of monopolies to prospective business establishments, and that continues to regulate the economy at all levels. . . . The Portuguese economy under Salazar and Caetano was dominated by a handful of large *grupes*, *sociedades*, and oligarchies closely tied in with and, again, inseparable from the state.[72]

The financial groups operated through a network of informal and personal contacts, in a sort of oligopoly of influence exercised on the state, rather than through formal channels. This is the essence of the Portuguese experience. The pressure of financial groups combined with Salazar's wishes, as he never wanted to give the corporative agencies a real role and real power. In this sense, corporativism served to kill the parliamentary democracy and it allowed the privileged levels of society to wield their power and influence better. 'For twenty-three years Portugal was a "corporative state without corporation" and . . . when they were finally adopted in 1956, they acquired little real power.'[73]

However, corporativism produced one important result: that of creating, following the example of Italian Fascism, a legal mechanism of 'industrial conditioning'[74] (formed in 1931 and perfected in 1952) that is essentially the real question to be examined. It is the essence of economic regulation, the origins of the restrictions placed on the birth of many enterprises to the advantage of the big oligopolistic private groups that grew with the state and for the state.[75] In Portugal, the authoritarian restrictions of the economy had a special meaning because it was accompanied by a closed economic system formed by the ties between the metropolis and the colonies. As the last colonial empire, Portugal had both capitalism based on slavery[76] and an imperialistic mechanism of disparate trade exchanges. All this was threatened at the beginning of the 1960s with the start of the war of liberation of the colonies, when the two great powers, USA and USSR, faced each other in Africa. However, that which seemed to be a guerilla war to be finished quickly lasted for thirteen years and had important repercussions on the Portuguese economy.

The key for understanding the importance of the colonies lay in the balance of payments of these overseas provinces. They had a constantly positive balance in their foreign trading while that with the motherland was always negative. The explanation for this is to found in the part the colonies played as a protected market, always importing more from the Portuguese mainland than they exported to it.[77] The motherland imported raw materials from the colonies and exported manufactured products, reversing the relations it had with other European countries. Besides this, the colonies were an important source of foreign exchange for Portugal,[78] thanks to the credit balance of the balance of payments that the overseas provinces achieved.

The creation of the Common Portuguese Area in November 1961[79] should have effectively guaranteed this objective by abolishing any barriers to the free movement of goods and by increasing the colonial economy. From this point of view, Angola was the most important nation, while Mozambique sent a large part of its raw materials to Portugal. Special terms for foreign investments were introduced in this period and there was an increase in white colonization aimed at absorbing the excess of workers. From 1951 to 1960 122,000 Portuguese emigrated and this trend continued after the formation of the Common Area. The start of the war caused a change in 'a mixed system of feudalism and capitalism (in a dependent and colonial capitalistic society)'.[80] Maintaining the army and facing the challenge of a somewhat timid economic opening up imposed extraordinary changes. It should be noted that the first divergences within the Salazar regime arose because of the colonial policies.

> According to the first, traditional faction, Portugal should continue to dedicate its efforts to it [colonial policy] by seeking to integrate the colonies into the Portuguese economy; the second faction wants the integration of Portuguese economy into capitalist Europe and does not seem to give much importance to the conservation of the colonies ... [even though the competition with European capitalism] is only possible thanks to the colonies [that allow the cost of labour to be kept low] as Portugal, because of its weak position in the capitalist field, is not in a position to become a neo-colonialist country.[81]

In this way, both factions continued to support the effort of fighting against the liberation movements of Angola, Guinea and Mozambique.[82]

Thanks to the injection of foreign capital all the resources had to be exploited more intensely, breaking with ancient balances and inserting the colonies more widely into a market economy.[83] In Angola a similar policy was aimed at overcoming a system based on over-exploitation, which reduced the productive capacities of the land, of the labour force and of capital, and at changing the methods of cultivation. White colonization and the flow of foreign capital were meant to achieve this aim. This meant that the seat of government in Portugal kept its control over the more advanced sectors of industry and over the financial markets, leaving the colonies the mining and basic manufacturing industries that could profit from the low cost of labour and from monopoly profits.[84]

The 1974 revolution broke the association between the centre and the periphery. With the creation of the independent countries of Angola, Cape Verde, Guinea and Mozambique, the Portuguese economy had to work with new parameters as it could no longer count on the invaluable contribution made by its overseas hinterland to the balance of payments.

Spain and Italy not only no longer had colonies overseas, but in the second postwar period, Italy had already overcome a situation of protectionism typical of economy between the two world wars, while Spain, though still under a dictatorship, managed to do this more quickly than Portugal.[85] In the period between the two world wars 'protectionism, corporativism, state intervention or the existence of oligopolies and monopolies were not features exclusive to the Spanish economy and politics. ... These phenomena appeared in Spain with an intensity and a distinction which was not seen in other countries. . . . After 1950, Spanish economy and politics were [instead] rather unusual in the international framework.'[86] The Franchist system, after all, proved to be different from the Portuguese one in as much as it was more flexible in the face of the stimuli arriving from abroad, from domestic politics and from the international economic conjuncture. The groups in power[87] had a great capacity for adaptation but the international pressure brought to bear on Spain, mainly by the USA,[88] was also considerable. Spain's geographical position was strategically more important than Portugal's and the pressure from the EEC on Spain was greater than that from EFTA on Portugal. Events like the 1953 agreements with the USA, the reentry in the UN and the Treaty with the Vatican,[89] proved to be important, and they softened the policy of corporative interventionism and gave the entrepreneurs hope for possible future growth. This hope did not die even after the riots of the Madrid universities in 1956 and the tightening of controls that followed with the transient triumph of the conservatives. From that moment the clash between the regime's political, bureaucratic elites became crucial for the economy. At this point, there was the danger of the proclamation of a law giving the totalitarian single party control over all aspects of national life. Once this danger was averted, the clash between the parts was solved by the polarization of the power groups. On one hand, there were those in favour of a monarchical, institutionalized and normalizing solution of the regime. On the other, various proposals were made by the Falange and the trade unions incorporating anti-monarchical and socialist ideas.[90] But the real solution to the dead end reached after 1956 was to come from the pressure brought to bear externally from international organizations and the USA. A Plan of Stabilization and Liberalization was produced and it was carried out by a group of technicians, civil servants and intellectuals oriented towards a market economy. The existing system was clear and simple: prices, wages and exchange system had to be reorganized. Public enterprise (the National Institute for Industry, Instituto Nacional de Industria – INI, was founded in 1941)[91] was to be the main instrument for import substitution without consideration for the economic costs. The new plan, instead, involved doing away with ministerial authorization and everything that blocked the invisible hand of the market. This process had been started at the end of the 1950s, with caution and a great many steps backwards by the first technicians. Those were very different from the planners (non-corporative!) of the 1960s who counted members of Opus Dei in their number. This difference has not yet received the attention it merits.[92] Naturally, both the domestic situation before 1959 (that had influenced the adoption of the plan), and the foreign situation did not halt the hostile protests. Finally a sort of paternalistic capitalism was reached in which market forces were widely substituted by political decisions. This lasted until the end of the regime.

> The 'men of the development' [in fact] did something else [from establishing a market economy]. They deformed the market in order to shelve possible political reforms which would have cost them their positions of power. If the economy grew it was not thanks to Lopez Redò [responsible for economic policy in the 1960s] and his cohorts, even though the merit was given to them. It grew less than it could have and not in the most effective way. Neither a market model nor planning were chosen. Certainly the market forces were given more space. A so-called indicative programme was

produced but it met with continuous difficulties. The remainder was recuperated by arbitrary intervention. And behind all this there was a political not economic logic.[93]

However, apart from the far-seeing, libertarian spirit of Gonzalez-Gonzalez, the important fact is that, in spite of the protests, even that small opening of the domestic and international markets allowed Spain to profit from the exceptional growth of the European economy. Spain was able to use the moderate financial capacity of its exports of foodstuffs and raw materials to increase its imports of finished goods for transport and industry and the raw materials and semi-manufactured products needed for industry. This represents the main difference separating Spain from Portugal and Greece.

American aid certainly played an important part, especially after the USA removed its trade bloc with the other countries. The USA wanted to make Spain a prime factor in the defence against the USSR. Greece and Turkey were seen in this capacity too, with the difference that these two countries, with their fragile economies and their unstable democracies, were not able to profit fully from it. A comparison between the two different situations shows that Spain's industrial take-off in the second post-war period was due to its own capacity to take advantage of diverse favourable factors.

In the 1940s Spanish industry and economy were extremely backward. Right after the war, France closed its border with Spain. After this Spain remained isolated until 1957 when France supported Spain's entrance to the European organizations.[94] The UN boycott strengthened the isolationist tendencies of Franco's regime. While the index of industrial production from 1947 to 1950 was multiplied by 1.7 in Italy and by 2 in Greece, in Spain it was multiplied by only 1.1, with a fall in the standard of living equal only to that of the 1930s.[95] The effects of 'economic patriarchy'[96] immobilized the entire mechanism without controlling the inflation. From this point of view, the 1950s were a 'crucial decade'.[97] One era finished and another began. Spain started to lay the foundation for ventures which would enable it to catch up with Italy.

The Italian economy differed from the Spanish one mainly because of its lack of raw materials. This made it very dependent on international markets, thus providing an incentive to the Italian productive system to counteract the large quantity of raw materials imported. Added to this was the higher capitalization of the Italian economy, imposed by the need to adapt the productive capacity of industry to the larger dimensions of the domestic and foreign markets.[98]

Nevertheless, in 1958 the index of Spanish industrial production was almost double that of 1950, with the partial renewal of finished goods, strong imports of raw materials and with a considerable increase in the per capita income.[99] This was a decade in which Spain compared most favourably with the other Southern European countries. The index of industrial production was multiplied by 1.9 from 1950 to 1958 while in Italy it was 1.8 and in Greece 2.1. But above all, the Spanish system benefited from trade, emigrant remittances, tourism and capital investments. This happened in spite of the timorous and incomplete opening to foreign markets encouraged by international pressure. Concerning this matter, the 1953 agreement with the USA was decisive and was followed by a law passed by the US Congress in 1957 on 'Economic Aid for Defense'. The availability of dollars allowed the purchase of imported goods, thus overcoming the inflationary bottle-neck caused by a 'programme of expansion not always consistent with our economic prospects, that has produced monetary and credit expansion'.[100]

The long winter of Franco's regime was drawing to a close, as was reflected also by the relations with the labour force. There were the glimmerings of a system of industrial relations in place of the regime's repressive administrative mechanism. From 1953, the workers started to use strikes as a contractual lever, and 'with the approval of two decrees in 1956 that fixed an average wage increase of 30 per cent . . . the door was opened to allow businesses relative freedom to raise wages and to negotiate informally with the workers.'[101] This was a prelude to the law of April 1958 and the decree of 1962 on collective contracts. For the first time, the labour force's contentions were recognized and the possibility of direct negotiations between workers and employers placed the official trade union officials in difficulty.[102] Wage increases, in the context of multiple exchange rate, administrative control and regulation, and used as a demagogic instrument by the dictatorship,[103] played havoc with inflation. The public sector deficit, added to the enormous balance of payments deficit, threatened to dry up the reserves of gold and foreign currency. It must be remembered that these were the years of the Treaty of Rome in 1957 and the birth of the EEC. In short, the bottle-necks in the system started to make their presence felt and to become so obvious that even the most deep-rooted ideologies were shattered. In any case, the industrial nature of the Spanish economy was clearly being established thanks to the surge of imports, mainly of manufactured products, which increased fourfold over the 1961–5 period.

Imports were now made possible by the fall of restrictions. Devaluation had been meant to aid exports, as those from industry were increasing but those of raw materials were decreasing.[104] Foreign investments increased.[105] In 1958 Spain became a member of the International Monetary Fund and in 1959 it joined the OECD. There was still a considerable amount of protection for industry and agriculture in the form of quantitative restrictions and customs barriers. The trade deficit was regulated by foreign investments, the return of capital from overseas, tourism and emigrant remittances.

The entrepreneurs' propensity to invest is the most important factor for understanding the roots of this endogenous development.[106] Above all, Spain managed to change its economy through a better and more intensive use of capital, thanks to savings and their more efficient exploitation. The low level of exports and the scarcity of foreign currency for imports remained some of the most pressing problems. Nevertheless Spain's economic development, after the fall of Franco's regime, was of an endogenous nature, in spite of the difficult international situation.

IV The Italian model

Italy was defeated in the Second World War when it was allied to Germany and Japan. At the end of the war it had to recreate its political and economic role in Europe and the world. The Bretton Woods agreement laid out the parameters for this but the actuation of the agreement was in the hands of the political and economic elites of the nation. The Italian economy had to confront the geo-political bloc of Europe. The Balkans and Central Europe were destined to form part of the Soviet bloc while the Mediterranean remained under the control of France and Great Britain. The possibilities of trading with South America were few and problematical because the USA and the UK had, in differing measures, interests and an incontestable field of action. From the point of view of the geo-political alignment of the world, the reduction of customs tariffs was almost mandatory in the international division of the world's economic spaces – apart, of course, from the American desire to avoid another depression by the total opening of world markets and the subsequent development of the economy.

Italy's performance until half way through the 1960s is a clear illustration of the effectiveness of an economic policy based on competition even for those countries which industrialized late. The reasons for this were the existence of structural, social and cultural conditions. In fact, anyone who studies the long-term perspective of Italian economic development has to wonder about the rapid and impetuous growth in the second post-war period. In the 1950s and 1960s there was a specific model for success which explains Italian growth: high productivity, low inflation and incentives for exports. This model allowed growth with a speed never seen before, in spite of the continued presence of historic imbalances which were mainly territorial not social. Post-war economic policies marked the birth of an industrial society in Italy. Integration into the world economy was decisive because of the existence of the prerequisites needed in order to profit from it.

At the beginning of the 1950s Italy was in a position to take its place in the world's industrial system, due largely to the capabilities of Italian entrepreneurs. Faced with an almost nonexistent domestic market, they put everything they had into exporting. Credit must also be given to the Italian political class for its steadfast pursuit of the conditions that would allow Italy's integration in foreign markets, like the Italian membership of the EEC in 1957. These policies were followed in spite of the opposition of a powerful group of industrialists radically attached to protectionist policies and import substitution.[107] This does not mean underestimating the importance of the development of the domestic market, which was confirmed by the less dynamic growth of exports in the 1950s.[108] Nevertheless the dynamo of growth was provided by exports.

The Italian economy in the second post-war period offers an extraordinary social laboratory in which to study systems subject to rapid and intense change. The agrarian, mercantile Italy in which industry wedged its structures and on which it erected the mixed economy between the wars leaves the scene and its place is taken by one of the world's most evolved industrial societies. Accelerated growth and the qualitative change of social relations are the intrinsic distinguishing features of the process. Between 1952 and 1963 national income doubled, with a percentage increase lower only to that of Japan and Germany and with a trend among the fastest of all the industrialized countries. One specific characteristic of this rapid movement was the amount of private consumption. This was higher than elsewhere, particularly when compared to Germany and Japan where investments were more important. The increase in incomes which occurred all over Europe after the 1950s is the real silent revolution which had its roots in the changes in the economic structure. The composition of GDP changed. Agriculture decreased from 23.5 per cent in 1959 to 15.7 per cent in 1963, while industry went from 33.7 per cent in 1959 to 43.8 per cent in 1963.[109]

The changes in industry were the main factor in the modernization of the whole economic and social face of Italy. Those sectors subject to massive innovation were now the most dynamic and they took over the leading role from the more traditional ones. Foodstuffs and textiles gave way before the incredible vigour of industries like automotive, precision machine tools, chemical, oil derivatives and cellulose, artificial and synthetic fibres. After the end of the war and the entrance into foreign markets, these industries became a challenge to international competition. They were committed to following standards of efficiency and levels of technology unthinkable before in a closed-market situation. The industries gained knowledge and know-how from their contacts with other systems and they used this to reach excellent growth rates in a world-wide market.[110]

It was only natural that the service sector should change too, though the causes were rather different to those that changed industry. The main area of growth was in the commercial sector, but insurance and banking also grew significantly though more slowly. Furthermore, the service sector, apart from being an important element in the formation of income containing many different elements, could employ workers who could no longer find employment in agriculture or industry. Among the characteristics of the great change was one which greatly affected the labour force. The surplus of workers in agriculture could not be entirely absorbed by industry in spite of the rapid rate of expansion, and therefore a part of that surplus was scattered throughout the economic system. In any case, from 1950 to 1962 the number of active workers went from 16,840,000 to 19,950,000 which is an increase of 18 per cent. The labour force increased by about 2,000,000. This figure included the jobless, who were 1,930,000 in 1950 and 344,000 in 1962, and first-job seekers, who were 2,670,000 in 1962. There was a relative reduction in the unemployment rate from 10.3 to 3 per cent. The figures by sector are most revealing: workers in agriculture went from 6,870,000 in 1950 to 5,810,000 in 1962 representing a decrease of 13.4 per cent. Industry accounted for 5,392,000 in 1950 and 7,810,000 in 1962, an increase of 44.8 per cent. The service sector went from 4,578,000 in 1950 to 6,330,000 in 1962, an increase of 38.3 per cent.[111]

This incredible and massive growth was given the name of 'The Italian Economic Miracle'. The name was well earned as it expresses a moment of exceptionally swift development without inflation. There was an annual rate of growth of GDP at 6.7 per cent (with a peak of 7.5 per cent between 1958 and 1961). Wholesale prices were either lower than or the same as their 1953 levels. Retail prices increased by only 20 per cent on the 1953 levels.[112] There was also a significant concurrent fall in the rate of unemployment. In fact, towards the end of those years, the demand for skilled and unskilled labour was higher than the supply in the new model of development. The absence of skilled workers and the importance of unskilled workers in large plants dedicated to mass production caused wage increases and gave the workers strong contractual power. The period 1960–2 saw the beginning of worker and trade union demands which laid the basis for the labour unrest at the end of the 1960s after the 1963–4 recession.[113]

The increase in exports was responsible for the success of the Italian economic system after the Second World War. This increase was due, basically, to the relationship between price (lower than world prices) and quality (high and competitive) of the goods produced. The quality of Italian products was closely linked to the high personal abilities of the Italian industries' workers and technicians rather than to the managers.[114] The low rate of growth of salaries compared to the exceptional productive capacity allowed the overcoming of competition in the world markets.[115] The correlation between productive capacity, domestic demand and, above all, foreign demand was always supported by the uninterrupted growth of investments. This laid the foundation for a real and extensive development of Italian industry. The most salient change to emerge from an examination of the industrial census figures for 1951 and 1961 is that of the expansion, in the northern and central parts of the country, of small and medium-sized businesses. These did not require advanced technology and the average cost of labour was low.[116] The articulation of the development of a mixed economy could, at this point, be considered complete.

V After the 1970s: decline and problems

For all the Southern European countries that had already joined the EEC, the last twenty years have proved decisive as a testing ground for the growth strategies chosen. Turkey is excluded from the analysis of this chapter as it is not yet an integral part of the European Union. The salient factor of the integration of these countries in the world market is the specialization of products based on local strategies of learning. During the 1980s, the growth of industrial integration in the EEC corresponds to the growth of industrial trade between the countries concerned in this study and the other European nations. This is shown clearly by the increasing dependence on foreign markets for input and intermediate phases of manufacture. This dependence increased in relation to the technological level of the manufacturing process.[117] It is worth considering this latest development, as it allows us to define more clearly the economic and social changes that have taken place over a fairly long period. The 1970s was a period in which all these countries had to perform within the context of a particularly unfavourable world-wide situation.

Italy was the first one to experience difficulties. These were twofold and they started at the end of the 1960s. In 1969 there was a period of labour and union unrest and then in 1973 there was the oil shock which led to the energy crisis. This caused a radical change in the value of the factors of production. The cost of labour, energy and raw materials reached unheard-of and unforeseeable levels. The reallocation of factors did not happen through competition, at least as far as the big firms were concerned. Stagflation developed, that unlikely symbiosis between stagnation and inflation.[118] Businesses relied on debts at negative interest rates which were dispensed by an improvident (and politically dominated) credit system,[119] and relied on the exchange rate of a deflated currency as a competitive advantage. The

85

central bank was the only actor who could regulate credit and apply the incentives needed so that the financial intermediaries could act differently. Unfortunately it was paralyzed by the country's social troubles and by the civil and political scruples of its governors. If deflation and credit restrictions had forced the unemployed to join forces with terrorism, the democratic foundations of the country would have been undermined. Thus investments and the accumulation of capital, which would have been the system's positive solution, did not materialize. In 1979 things seemed to improve but at this point the second energy crisis hit, bringing with it increased energy costs. In 1980 inflation reached 21.7 per cent and the current account deficit reached 2 per cent of the national income. The bankruptcy of the public finances was evident from the state deficit, as more than 10 per cent of the national income was a perquisite of the extensive public sector.[120] As a result of all this, Italy had the highest percentage of unemployment in Europe in 1973. It must be said, however, that this happened in the context of a general crisis and reconstruction which influenced the whole continent and subsequently became more severe. In 1982–3 the rate of unemployment was 9.4 per cent but it was lower than the European average of 9.8 per cent. However, we must never forget the part played by the black, informal, submersed economy. Call it as you will, but apart from defusing social tensions, it was also hidden and unregistered employment and it was a symptom of the low degree of institutionalization of citizens' rights.

The varied and composite face of the Italian industrial society started to take shape. In the period between 1974 and 1980 it had, compared to the stronger European countries,[121] the highest rate of inflation, the highest currency depreciation, the highest and fastest-growing public deficit. In spite of the weakness in the accumulation process before the first energy crisis, there was a respectable average rate of development, overall employment improved, as did the competitiveness abroad. But what was behind that apparent well-being? Italian competition was supported by inflation and exchange rates. Employment had the same characteristics it had at the end of the miracle. Jobs in industry increased by only 2.1 per cent between 1963 and 1970, while during the same period the service sector increased by 4.2 per cent and the public administration increased by 1.4 per cent. From 1970 to 1980 these discrepancies became more accentuated. Employment in industry fell by 1.6 per cent and in the service sector increased by 3.2 per cent (there was a 1.7 per cent increase in the non-selling section).[122]

After 1980 the context in which the actors governing the imperfect markets manoeuvred changed greatly. This time the decisive stimulus came from the central bank, which was no longer influenced by the political situation of a country that had won, for the moment, the battle against terrorism. The central bank initiated a new monetary policy which led to the appreciation of the currency in line with Italy's joining the European Monetary System. The entrepreneurs were no longer able to rely on the devaluation of the lira. They had to reallocate resources with new investments, new energy-saving technologies, raw materials and labour, and they had to increase productivity and stop cost inflation.

From that moment, the double-sided process of instability of accumulation and unequal development[123] started, and it was to become a characteristic of the 1980s and the 1990s. From 1980 to 1985 industrial employment fell by 4.1 per cent (compared to a 5.5 per cent increase in the service sector and a 0.8 per cent in commercial services),[124] due to the increase in the variables aimed at reducing the labour force. Investments were concentrated, and were no longer spread out. For this reason the period of stabilization was very difficult. Inflation started to diminish thanks to agreements between the trade unions, entrepreneurs and state to place wages under control. In 1980 it was at 21.7 per cent but by 1984 it fell to 9.8 per cent even though oil was still expensive and the dollar high. However, unemployment became the big problem. In 1992 it was 11 per cent of the active population. Of the 2,667,000 young adults, 71 per cent were looking for their first job. In the north unemployment was 5.6 per cent, in the centre it was 9.4 per cent and in the south it reached the peak of 19.4 per cent.[125]

In Spain, the 1970s started with economic difficulties. From 1974, the cyclic tendencies of a system which was very dependent on the international situation and the world energy market became more accentuated.[126] In the years of the 'democratic transition to democracy'[127] growth was weak, investments diminished and there was a considerable increase in unemployment. This process was common to most of the OECD countries. However, in Spain it was more marked because of the almost uninterrupted growth of the preceding twenty years. Inflation started to be an endemic problem and the current account deficit grew strongly until the devaluation of the peseta helped to halt it. Over this period 'priority in Spain was given to a serious reform of the institutional and political system, and not much effort was put into correcting the growing imbalances of the economy'.[128] It was only after the parliamentary elections in June 1977, the first since the civil war, that the new government started to elaborate a coherent economic programme. The most urgently needed actions were controlling the balance of payments and blocking the capital drain. Priority was given to the domestic imbalances with the introduction of a restrictive monetary policy. This had immediate and heavy consequences on employment. The so-called Moncloa Pact, signed in October 1977 by the main political parties, had little effect on all this. The pact provided for price control, wage control and a series of economic and institutional reforms aimed at creating a new, post-Franco Spain.

Unemployment grew from 3.8 per cent in 1975 to 9.3 per cent in 1979. Male unemployment went from 3.5 to 8.7 per cent and female unemployment went from 3.6 to 10.7 per cent. The deficit in the trade balance increased. In 1979 it was −$4,960,000 but from 1978 this was counteracted by the services and the flow of capital.[129] This economic pattern continued during the 1980s. The most relevant statistics show that the formation of gross of fixed capital reached −3.4 per cent in 1984 with an average of −1.9 per cent between 1979 and 1984. These rates of decrease were higher than the OECD average and the small and medium-sized European countries.[130] A new cycle of growth started in 1985 and continued until 1989 only to be followed by another recessional phase. After the return of democracy, the labour market had maintained its Franchist heredity of rigidity of dismissals linked to wage flexibility. The measures taken to make the labour market more flexible were vital for economic recovery. Investments were the economic aggregate which had the highest growth above all, because of the stimulus of foreign capital that contributed to their increase from 40 to 50 per cent. Trade union moderation and joining the EEC were also important in this period, while demand grew steadily, as did the accumulation of capital.

Compared to the EEC averages, Spain remained technologically backward. The advantages derived from the lower labour costs diminished. In 1983 wages were 43 per cent lower than the OECD averages while in 1988 they were only 25 per cent lower. The service sector became even more crucial to the Spanish economy accounting for 57 per cent of GDP in 1990 and with 60 per cent of the active population employed. Tourism, one of the most important factors in the balance of payments, started to reveal its limits. The boom of the financial sector was also destined for a period of readjustment that inevitably led to a marked concentration in order to regain efficiency and competitiveness in a recently liberalized system. Direct foreign investments held and continued to grow. According to the Bank of Spain, in 1989 foreign investors held 6.4 per cent of all the shares of the country's portfolio and 29.2 per cent of businesses were in the hands of foreign concerns. In 1980 this figure was 19.2 per cent. This represented one of the highest degrees of foreign penetration in a developed economy. There was a conspicuous presence in the sectors with low labour costs while branches of multinationals dominated industries like electronics, pharmaceuticals, tyres, information technology, detergents, chemicals and plastics. They were also significantly present in foodstuffs, glass and mining as well as investment banks and tourism.[131] On the whole, the Spanish economy seemed beset by the weaknesses that marked the beginning of a new cyclic phase of depression. Spanish ills were those of a completely developed country undergoing the challenges inherent to growth.

The most serious problem seemed to be the incapacity of the system to absorb the labour force. In 1993 23 per cent of the labour force was unemployed, almost double the European average. One can rightly talk about a characteristic of Spanish capitalistic accumulation 'becoming a social formation'[132] and which has its roots in a specific kind of industrial development. The striking factor is that 'the most unfavourable aspects of unemployment are associated with its duration which is usually very high'.[133] Unemployment is unequally distributed between the social groups and enhances the differences of income and status. Therefore, the presence of a black economy is not surprising. It was tucked away in the crevices of development with its roots in kinship and the consequent inefficiencies in the allocation of resources by the markets.[134] It had the same function and the same causes found in Portugal.

The 1974 revolution followed by the policy of stabilization in which the International Monetary Fund played an important part, had a traumatic effect on the Portuguese economy.[135] The most critical period lasted for three years, until 1977. A wage increase of 60 per cent in nominal terms meant that inflation rose to 25 per cent in spite of the introduction of administrative price controls. The worst problem was the deficit of balance of payments which reached 9 per cent of GDP in 1977 equivalent to $1.5 billion. Exports fell, the protected colonial markets no longer existed, emigrants' remittances fell because of political instability and inflation. The policy of stabilization introduced in 1977 when the probability of a revolutionary anti-democratic *coup d'état* seemed unlikely, was based on a restrictive monetary policy and on progressive devaluation. The effects were immediate: the current account balance was put right in the most spectacular way and it reached equilibrium in 1979.

However, it was a transitory recovery. Lost markets had to be recuperated, tourism and emigrants' remittances could not, by themselves, save a compromised situation. In 1980 the balance of payments was already in deficit and the increase in inflation was halted only by administrative price controls (it fell to 10.5 per cent). Low production capacity and a still high rate of inflation remained the most pressing problems of the Portuguese economy. These are the years of rapid and uncontrolled expansion of the public sector to which must be added the financial requirements of the nationalized businesses after the revolution. Subsidies to this sector[136] reached 54 per cent between 1974 and 1980. On the other hand, these, compared to the economy as a whole, accounted for 18.4 per cent of value added, 6.8 per cent of employment and 34.3 per cent of the gross formation of fixed capital. Nationalization had involved key sectors like iron and steel and chemicals as well as credit. Indubitably the increase in the cost of the public administration was caused by the extension of the public social services in a country that had never known either social and political citizenship or a welfare state. The growth of the public deficit was inevitable. In the course of the 1970s, the welfare system was extended to cover almost all the population with a rapid increase in the reallocation of incomes: between 1974 and 1980 the average was 38 per cent. This increase was derived more from the number of beneficiaries than from the fairly low value of the assistance given.[137] Another important reason for the deficit was the growth of employment in the public administration. This had become a very important source of income and it also defused social tensions but it was uncontrollable and from 1975 to 1981 it registered an 8.4 per cent yearly growth rate. The pressures on the labour market were enormous with an almost complete halt to emigration, the insertion of the ex-colonial civil servants and the increases in the health service and education. The inadequacy of the tax system and the increase in cost increased the weight of the public sector on the economy in general. This was the arduous condition of Portuguese economy and industry at the beginning of the 1990s. Textiles, the centre of the country's nervous system, was in great difficulty, and it was jeopardized by foreign competition. The deficit in the balance of trade gained no benefit from the currency devaluations of 1992 and 1993.

The situation in Greece was much worse as industry was not the only basic problem. Industry's contribution to GDP fell from 32.4 per cent in 1980 to 30.2 per cent in 1988. The manufacturing sector went from 21.3 to 19.3 per cent while agriculture reached 13.1 per cent in 1988 with 27 per cent employment of active workers. In contrast to the past, the service sector was static in this period, without significant increases, and it continued to attract as many workers as industry and agriculture put together. Even the mining industry, one of Greece's riches with bauxite, asbestos, magnesium and nickel, was in difficulty due to lack of market expansion and to growing competition from Australia and Guyana. On the other hand, the domestic sources of lignite and the recent discoveries of oil deposits to the north of Thasos were unable to compensate for the high price of energy sources and the inflexibility of energy requirements. However, changes in the structure of industry occurred, with an increase in employment in businesses with more than ten workers. These now account for 90 per cent of workers while in 1960 it was only 75 per cent. The vast number of small businesses continue to be inefficient with a rate of productivity equal to one fifth of that of the larger ones.[138] The policy of social austerity, the abolition of protectionist policies and respect for the EU restrictions adopted by the centre-right Greek government faced enormous problems. Social requirements burden the work of any political coalition. This contradiction between economic growth and social consensus is the greatest point of tension for the future of Southern Europe.

Chapter 6

A SPECIFIC SOCIO-ECONOMIC FORMATION

I The traditional market

The 1990s show, across the whole of Southern Europe, the establishment of tendencies towards decline and stagnation. Domestic reasons were added to a difficult international crisis. Southern societies have reached a composite social form which is marked by strong imbalances and by specific social categories and classes. Every country, as mentioned at the beginning of this book, has territorial and economic imbalances. European integration together with high rates of economic development gave new strength to the process of inequality.

The south of Italy is a good example of this process. During the initial period of growth, all efforts were concentrated on those areas where efficiency and competitiveness already existed. Failure to do this would have meant the non-entry into (or expulsion from) international markets. Therefore integration meant unlimited deepening of territorial inequality, diversities that became more functional the more the north moved towards full employment. The south became an enormous reserve of labour as it was from 1958 to 1962. This was a much more serious problem than unemployment. The south and the north are two real and distinct socio-economic formations. Historically the north belongs to Continental Europe, the south belongs to Southern Europe. The centre wavers between the two. Though economic and social policies were introduced, the result has never done anything but confirm the original diversity in a new shape. The policies aimed at eliminating the differences only resulted in increasing family incomes and stopping emigration without being able to stimulate self-supported growth.[1] Instead, they instituted the social custom of welfare. In the 1960s the situation worsened with the crisis in the heavy industry sector, subject to state subsidies.[2] In the 1990s, the untenable public deficit forced a change in economic policy to avoid the collapse of the whole system.

A widening of imbalances affected Spain as well. Both Spain and Italy, more than the other countries, demonstrate that this phenomenon is a product of growth. The traditional stronghold of Spanish industrialization for the production of capital goods is to be found along the Cantabrian Coast in the north of the country. This area is made up of Euskady (the Basque provinces), Asturias and Cantabria. Though these provinces do not constitute an homogeneous area they are linked by having been protagonists of the historical stages of industrialization.[3] With the fall of investments and employment, the de-industrialization of these provinces, particularly Euskady, seemed irreversible.[4] This could not but worsen the national, social and political problems, degenerating into terrorism in such a crucial area of the Iberian peninsula.

Catalonia is another historically important area that has to be considered separately. This region was the key to the process of import substitution of the whole of Spain and its middle class was decisive in the industrial take-off. Besides this, the area played a major part in the diffusion of foreign technology, first by incorporating it into its own productive processes and then by producing goods for the whole country. Now, even these industrial connections have been hit by a crisis thanks to the progressive advance of the service sector of the economy. But the most interesting changes concern the cyclic patterns that have caused the emergence of a transversal connection between the characteristics of Catalonia and the growth of the highly urbanized area along the Mediterranean coast. This area, starting with Barcelona and the coast and embracing Madrid, Galician Pontevedra, Basque Victoria and Andalusian Malaga, has shown the highest rate of net internal growth between 1955 and 1983 (with values that go from 4.9 to 5.1 per cent). The service sector is the most active but agriculture and industry still show considerable and surprisingly well balanced growth.[5] This is similar to the phenomenon produced in the north-east and centre of Italy with the growth of small and medium-sized businesses.[6]

This is only one of the happier aspects of the specificity of Southern Europe. That the economy had been able to maintain good rates of employment and growth, even in the context of its cyclic patterns, was due to the particular structure of production. This economic development was based on three elements: large-scale state enterprises, a few large oligopolistic private enterprises and small and medium-sized firms, institutionalized by the existence of sub-cultures and local networks.[7] It is a composite production system characterized by a social structure and by values that support the impulses deriving from the various actors and that are shown in a stronger way in Southern Europe than elsewhere. Perhaps there are similarities with Japan where these clusters have lived together,[8] even though they appear in almost all the new and old industrialized countries.[9] The emergence of very small and small industries is a general characteristic of both Europe and Japan in the recent past.[10] But in Southern Europe, the basic characteristic of the industrial system is that of having a high number of small businesses, a low number of medium-sized ones and a very small number of large ones.

With regard to Italy, the latter are more than the Southern European average but in any case they are fewer than those of countries in Northern and Central Europe.[11] The social changes brought about by the small and medium-sized businesses were most notable in the north-east and centre of Italy and in some small areas of the south.[12] These businesses are characterized by strong labour mobility. However, they had a new characteristic which became more marked in the 1980s. This was a tendency for the growth of existing small businesses rather than the creation of new ones. In short, the first signs of social rigidity, the blocking of vertical mobility and the consolidation more than expansion of the newly formed industrial lower and middle classes appear. This growing rigidity shows the difficulties these businesses are facing throughout Southern Europe. On the other hand, has it not been proven recently that there is a maximal level for the personal capabilities that an industrial system can accumulate?[13] If these personal capabilities are not supported by a great deal of capital to achieve huge investments, and if they are not coupled with rationalization from outside, they are not enough to face the challenges of global competitors and to overcome the hurdles presented by new technologies, not even with the by now customary help of the state and of associations and cooperatives.

The problem of the personal entrepreneurial ability continued to be fundamental. One of the greatest differences, however, between Southern and Continental Europe (with the exception of the north and centre of Italy and Catalonia), is the smaller capacity for regeneration by the entrepreneurial groups which are able not only to carry out the normal practices of the reproduction of capitalism, but also to create, preserve and renew a culture suitable to their social function. One of the characteristics of capitalism promoted from above, or of political capitalism, is that of basing itself on the socio-economic mobilization, above all by exponents of the traditional elites of the old regime: merchants, landowners and bureaucratic elites dependent on state support, who perpetuate a culture of the values of ascription rather than achievement, of status rather than contract.

These seem to be the real problems of Southern Europe's future growth. They are more important than those generated by the presence of public enterprises. Only an unwise libertist attitude could maintain that these are, by nature, all inefficient and that the real culprit for this state of affairs is the degeneration of political parties and welfare. Or, even more absurd, that state-owned enterprises are typical of the southern political class. These phenomena are found in all the important European countries as are those of privatization of these companies and the end of their state subsidies.[14] Figure 6.1 gives an effective and concise confirmation of this.

The real problems of Southern Europe lie elsewhere, with the structure of its societies. State and public spending continue to ensure the reproduction of a model of growth based on welfare and the transfer of money within the circles of clientship. Consider the rapid growth of the costs of the public sector due to a constant increase in the financial requirements after the beginning of the 1970s. The public deficit and the public debt have exceeded the limits established in February 1992 by the Maastricht Treaty for the creation of the Economic and Monetary Union. Only Ireland and Belgium, among the non-Southern European countries, exceed these levels of public debt. Italy's deficit is less than that of Greece but more than that of Spain and Portugal. Both the needs of public financing and the public debt started to grow at the beginning of the 1960s. The causes were the size of state administration and the important role played by the interest rates of the public debt. As soon as economic growth started to moderate, the swift increase of the financial burden of the state upset all the indicators of financial stability.[15] There was a vicious circle between deficit, debts and the payment of interest. In this period the inflation rate hit the roof. The vulnerability of inflation expresses disproportions between the factors of capitalistic production and the factors that allow the reproduction of social structures. This causes such a financial burden that the development of the productive system is threatened. This typical aspect of southern capitalism will continue to flourish unless the advent of a new political class frees society from its grasp. If this does not happen southern capitalism will undergo a slow but ineluctable decline.[16] The reasons for this kind of decline can be found in the too rapid transition to a service-sector society which has not laid down solid industrial roots. The employment

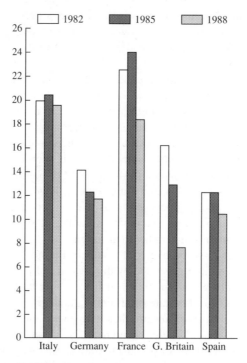

Fig. 6.1 Relative size of public enterprises
Source: see Ch. 6, n. 14.
Note: These measurements represent the average of total value added, total capital formation and total employment of the public enterprises.

structure is the best way to measure this extremely rapid change which developed in Southern Europe over a few decades, whereas in other countries it took more than a century.

In Italy in the 1980s the percentage of industrial workers went back to being 25.8 per cent of the active population. This is only 5,275,000 people, not many more than in 1951 when the percentage was 24.9 per cent representing 4,925,000 people. The stagnation of the industrial sector marked a relevant change in the social order together with two other great social changes. On one hand, the decrease of agricultural workers (from 28.7 to 5.4 per cent) and small-holders (from 12.5 to 4.8 per cent) and on the other, the growth of public and private white-collar workers (from 4.9 to 17.6 per cent). These changes are extremely indicative of the social and political mobility of the country.[17]

A similar tendency is shown in Spain, even though its full extent has not yet been revealed. The percentage of industrial employment on total active employment went from 21.6 per cent in 1955 to 27.8 per cent in 1970, and in 1980 it fell to 26.1 per cent. In 1955 the active population in the services sector was 29.9 per cent, in 1970 it rose to 38.3 per cent to reach 42 per cent in 1980.[18]

In other countries the rapid increase in the service sector caused strong social fragmentation and territorial imbalances. In Portugal there was an enormous move to urbanization with the city of Lisbon as a prime example. The rural population of the country (living in centres of less than 5,000 inhabitants) went from 65.7 per cent in 1960 to 56.9 per cent in 1981, the semi-urban (from 5–10,000 inhabitants) increased from 11.6 per cent in 1960 to 13.3 per cent in 1981 while the urban population went from 22.7 per cent in 1960 to 29.7 per cent in 1981. Eighty per cent of the Portuguese population lives in four districts and in two regions, Lisbon, Oporto, Setubal and Braga, and the economically more dynamic urban areas. Portugal's future will most probably be non-industrial: it will become a service-sector country. In the major urban and semi-urban centres a large part of the population is made up of white-collar workers employed in trade and the services while the rural and minor semi-urban centres have a predominance of skilled and semi-skilled workers. Portugal is a country where the degree of urbanization is fairly low compared to more developed countries. In the area of the north coast and in the centre, industrial development does not follow the classic models of urbanization. The urban and rural characteristics are very similar to those found in the north-east and centre of Italy. It can be described as 'important widespread urbanization' with 'industrialization in the rural centre'.[19] Therefore, it is not surprising to find a growing black, underground or informal economy here. It is due to tax pressure and the part played by family unity. The 1981 estimates show that it accounts for 18 per cent of GDP,[20] which reinforces the semi-rural or semi-urban character of many economic activities. Alongside the entrance of women in the labour force, a new development for Portugal as for all the Southern European countries, there was the re-establishment of family ties, of small merchant production, and of home consumption. All this had an important part in easing social tensions. Society countered the rigidity of norms, more than of salaries, with a high degree of informality that segmented the labour market even more.[21] This is the informal aspect of a growth process that has led Portugal to a semi-industrialized tertiary that seems to be, from many points of view, the future of wide areas in Southern Europe.

So what can be said about the situation in Greece where domestic production is characterized by the predominance of industries producing 'goods' which cannot be traded? Since 1953 the percentage of Greek manufacturing industry on GDP has always been the lowest between Portugal, Greece and Italy (similar to Turkey which overtook Greece after 1980). According to the figures for the last twenty years 10 per cent of GDP came from construction. In the other countries it did not exceed 6 per cent.

The same thing can be said about the service sector that, together with the unexportable activities, produced the majority of income. This reality could not but have grave consequences on social stratification. The years from 1961 to 1975 were crucial to Greek economic growth and change. During this period the active population decreased by 12 per cent, going from 3,638,000 to 3,180,000 people. Of these about a third continued to be employed in agriculture which lost 40 per cent of the active population, going from 1,960,000 to 1,180,000 people. There was an increase of 23.4 per cent in industrial employment which went from 488,600 to 603,000 people. This rate of growth is absurd compared to that of construction which increased by 34.4 per cent, going from 167,000 to 230,000, and transport and

95

communications with 59.2 per cent, going from 153,000 to 245,000 people. In trade, restaurants, hotels, banks, insurance and other services the increase was 23.5 per cent, going from 705,000 to 910,000 people. This is the sector that comes second to agriculture for number of people employed. The fact is that:

> Perhaps the most important characteristic of the structure of employment in Greece is the high share of the self-employed and unpaid family workers in the total active population. This share was, in 1971, nearly 60% in Greece, compared with 10–20% for OECD total, and around 30% for Ireland, Italy, Japan and Spain.[22]

The above description shows that the social and economic structure of Greece is unusual and merits close study as it is indicative of the failure of an export-oriented strategy. The international collocation of the country is certainly important. The structure of the balance of payments was relatively stable for the whole period after the Second World War, unlike that of other developing countries. From 1947 to 1960, it was characterized by a continual deficit in the trade balance and the current accounts balance that could have been much higher, with disastrous results, if foreign aid and invisible exports had not arrived 'to finance the deficit in the balance of payments as the key source of government revenue, and by extension, of state investment'.[23] From 1960 to 1980, the current accounts balance was in constant deficit with emigrants' remittances, foreign exchange from tourism and shipping compensating for a half and a third respectively of that deficit. Industrial exports in this period contributed increasingly to the balance of payments with percentages that went quite incredibly from 3.5 in 1961 to about 50 in 1980. This increase was mainly due to the increase in cotton textiles which earned about 50 per cent of the foreign currency. Machinery and transport industry components accounted for only 4 per cent of industrial exports compared to a marked increase in the imports of products for the not-exportable construction industries as well as crude oil. All this caused a worsening of the balance of payments in the 1970s.[24]

In the light of these events, the relationship between the society and the balance of payments now seems to be clearer. The development of the latter can be seen as a result of the connections between the country's economy and society and, above all, attention can be turned to the substantial increase in the deficit in the 1970s, particularly in 1974 and 1975. An explanation must be found for its increase from the beginning of its growth to the present day. The answer to this question is to be found in the connection between the external factors of the increase and the social structure. This connection takes place at the level of domestic demand, nourished by the increase in the purchasing power transferred to the Greek economy from abroad.[25] Transfers explain 99 per cent of the exchanges of the trade account deficit.[26] This increases because those transfers are in relation to the inelasticity of supply of goods. From this point of view, shipping, as well as tourism and emigrants' remittances, play an important part as it gives Greece, a leading country in this field, an important position in the international division of labour.[27] This activity cannot be considered endogenous to the national economic system. Instead, it is an almost artificial insertion, born from considerable commercial creativity, in an historic patrimony of knowledge of the international financial mechanism. Though shipping does not contribute to removing the historical causes of the

system's low productivity:[28] the loss of allocative efficiency between sectors particularly because of the effect of the self-employed and the non-paid family
employed; the deterioration of the economies of scale; the decline of advances in
knowledge over the last twenty years.

However, the standard of living in Greece has increased enormously and private
consumption is higher in proportion to GDP than in many countries in the EEC.
Between 1980 and 1990 it fluctuated between 64 and 68 per cent of GDP while the
EEC average was 61 per cent in 1987. In spite of its export orientation, the Greek
economy is mainly pulled along by domestic demand with all the implications mentioned previously. For the most part, family income is made up of wages (from 35.2
per cent in 1974 to 38.4 per cent in 1990), but there is also a high percentage of
entrepreneurial and property-owning activities where self-employment is wide-
spread. Self-employment accounts for about 30 per cent, while the government's
transfers grew from 7.4 per cent in 1974 to 15.1 per cent in 1980, causing a relentless increase in the weight of the public sector.[29]

In the meantime, the balance of payments continued to increase its deficit which
was no longer compensated for by the invisible imports. Inflation continued to grow
even though recent government policies seemed to have produced some favourable
results, particularly with regard to wage control which had been upset by the partial
indexing of the cost of living applied by PASOK after 1981. The increase in inflation had stabilized at 6–7 per cent at the beginning of the 1990s. In Greece, as in
other places, the cause of inflation was the growing public expenditure with an
increase in the state deficit and a tax system that was completely inadequate for the
country's needs.

The tax contribution as a share of GDP is the lowest in Europe after Portugal.
The electoral priorities of the country's two large parties had prevented recourse to
a consistent reduction of current expenditure that was among the highest in Europe
with, however, the scant incidence of public services. These accounted for only 7.5
per cent of GDP in the 1970s and 6 per cent in the 1980s. There was also the rapid
growth of foreign debt that went from $6.9 billion in 1980 to $21.8 billion in
1989.[30]

The number of employed went from 3,529,000 in 1981 to 3,593,000 in 1989,
while the unemployed went from 149,000 in 1981 to 303,000 in 1989, from 4.1 to
7.8 per cent of the labour force.[31] The percentage (26) for agricultural workers
hides the under-employment of adults and children in the rural families while, on
the other hand, it is estimated that a third of the labour force was self-employed.
This was a 'parallel' economy[32] rather than an underground one, because it not
only had the characteristics of tax evasion and industrial decentralization, it also
had the continuity of artisan and agricultural traditions. Deprived of its characteristics of home consumption, this parallel economy became both an urban and an
agricultural support to the low incomes, medium-sized consumption and great inefficiencies. Naturally tax evasion played its part in the development of this
alternative economy, but it was more a consequence than a cause and here, as in
Turkey, self-employment was the dream of emigrants returning home. Considering
the unofficial transactions as opposed to the official statistics, in 1984 GDP should
have increased by 29 per cent[33] and GDP per capita should have grown from

$2,980 to $9,800. Confirmation of the pathology of the Greek economic and social structure came from the unofficial parallel economy. Thus the extraordinary stability of a system of interpersonal relations based more on vertical relations (clientship and patronage) and kinship rather than on horizontal ones (associations and collective aggregations), based on status rather than on contract, can be understood. This social process is strictly connected to the Greek method of leapfrogging over industrialization. 'The economy of Greece moved, to a large extent, from agriculture directly to services, neglecting industrialization.'[34]

The Turkish situation is extremely useful for characterizing the socio-economic formation that emerged from the growth of Southern Europe. The figures shown in the 1950 and 1960 census concerning the population's activities are very interesting. In 1950 those who received a wage were 10 per cent of the population, in 1960 they were 18.8 per cent. The self-employed and family workers went from 26.4 to 29.5 per cent. The percentage of non-paid family workers decreased from 62.9 to 47.9 per cent due to the effect of agricultural changes.[35] The levels of education changed enormously: university students increased from 25,000 to 54,000. The population went from 20.9 million to 27.8 million[36] and so the systems of status changed too.[37] But the area of parallel or underground autonomous employment was enormous and reflected the true aspect of social stratification.

This could only reinforce the patrimonialistic heredity of the republican state. The links and ties of patronage were very strong as the social structure broke up on the level of market relations compared to those based on reciprocity and clientship.[38] However, counterbalances to the vertical organization of social links existed. For example, the Turkish trade unions represent a horizontal system of association. This is also a sign of the irreversible changes that industrialization caused in Turkish society. But, as already pointed out, it was a change that cohabited with tradition and the dominance of an agrarian and services society. In 1985, after the stabilization programme, 58.2 per cent of the active population still worked in agriculture, 25.8 per cent were in the service sector and 17 per cent were in industry. This latter figure includes construction.[39]

Modernity really did cohabit with tradition creating new and different socio-economic systems whose mechanisms still have to be fully understood. Scientific and technical education spread and a completely new elite was formed. But the centralized political distribution of resources only recently started to collide with the workings of the market and still defines the systems that govern social stratification.

> The perception of the public and private power as two distinct social milieus characterized by different patterns of stratification is a fact of the relatively concrete, every day level of experience and as such plays an important role in the social construction of that commonly accepted system of meanings which constitutes the stratification system.[40]

However, this observation about Turkey is also valid for the other countries, and needs to be enlarged upon. It must be understood that the conflict and coexistence of the two systems of orientation to action and of value (of the reciprocity and the market), affect all social strata beyond the confines of public and private spheres. In this kind of system, how can self-employment be defined? As an answer from below to the inefficiencies of a dirigist economy, but as a structure that survives because it has political back-up and because it is part of clientship. It is a social and economic formation that grew outside the market in spite of and thanks to its own expansion. It now fills every space and threatens to suffocate the market. Seen under this light, the expansion of the market that started in Southern Europe after the Second World War is not only unequal but also deeply contradictory, full of specificities that need a more analytical explanation.

II Market, society and politics

Economic recovery is a somewhat ambivalent concept. In its objectives, the Marshall Plan was a highly practical mixture of restoring the previous status quo and correcting it to the extent it was unsatisfactory, both within the limits of feasibility. For Southern Italy, Greece and Turkey, the Marshall Plan represented development rather than reconstruction.[41]

The EEC's challenge was that it continued the policies of development and economic integration started with the Marshall Plan. It thought to do this by guaranteeing new markets for the industrialized countries and an opportunity for growth for the developing ones thanks to an association between the two. It was an enlarged reproduction of capitalism and market that, however, did not signify the automatic retreat of the state from the market and society. It was, instead, a case of market regulation and, under certain aspects, continuing state control. The hierarchical hand of the state continued its powerful work in an always imperfect market.

Let us consider agricultural policies. The mechanisms of political negotiations were preferred, on a more general scale, to such things as price and quantity of production. In other fields this type of negotiation had been laboriously eliminated. The forging of the EEC was a political process aimed at solving the more relevant economic problems of the countries involved, thus giving them renewed vigour.[42] This is one of the paradoxes of the relations between state and society in Europe after the 1950s. In this sense the continuity with the 1930s is striking even though the context is different. However, bones of contention existed and they came from that general set-up in which the visible hand of community politics affected the weaker sectors of Europe and the countries that joined after the Treaty of Rome in 1957. The first fifteen years of European integration were characterized by rapid and generally uninterrupted growth in spite of some brief recessions. Towards the end of the 1960s stagflation became a constant danger for European countries, particularly those of Southern Europe. In a recessional period, the penetration of imports into countries that had previously been barricaded inside their own self-contained world could have provoked renewed protectionism or structural difficulties in those countries with a less developed economy. At the same time, contrary to their expectations, these countries could not find markets able to absorb their exports. This resulted in a reclassification of international specializations and the necessary institutional reconstruction in a different mode to the one which characterized the community's policies in the first twenty years of their existence.

The attraction of the EEC customs union lay in the conviction that it would create new trade exchanges between the member countries and thus guarantee their development after joining. All the estimates and predictions, from the more pessimistic to the more optimistic, went in that direction.[43] The elimination of customs tariffs would offer new market opportunities. The competition thus generated would assure gains in productivity and reduction of costs and stimulate investments. In turn this would allow economies of scale and the acceleration of economic development.

From a long-term point of view, the widening and freeing of the markets allowed the European economies a road to growth that had never been seen before. But this does not stop us from putting forward two considerations. This process was deeply influenced by the cyclic phases of the international situation. This process did not encourage industrial growth where original, autonomous conditions did not previously exist, if not in the sense of attracting foreign investment to the individual countries. These two considerations seem to be essential and they are confirmation of the fact that the more developed economies were not always penetrated by the exports of the Southern countries even though the markets broadened. On the other hand, the Southern countries underwent the intense reconstruction of their international specializations according to whether they had high- or medium-tech industries (Italy and Spain), or whether they did not have such industries (Greece and Turkey), or if they had such industries thanks above all to foreign investments. The latter applied to all these countries with the exception of Italy but it applied mainly to Portugal and Spain. The main problem for Southern European countries was determined by the fact that a large part of their industrial concerns had to compete not so much and only with the Northern European countries but, above all, with countries outside Europe that were still fairly underdeveloped. This is particularly true of Portugal,[44] but it affects all the countries including a part of Italian industry.[45]

From this point of view, the dimensions of the small businesses, when not linked to a Shumpeterian specialization of high tech, can be a big disadvantage. And all the Southern countries have a prevalence of small businesses.[46] Therefore, the main danger is that economic integration will block the already existing weak international specializations and the consolidated vertical division of labour between the heart of Europe and its outskirts, exposing them even more to competition from the new industrial countries. Therefore, it is vital for the Mediterranean countries of Europe to intensify the diversification and the vertical integration of their industries in order to base their growth on a solid self-supported foundation.[47] If this happens, the EEC will be something more than just a colossal institutional machine for handing out money to redress imbalances.

This has been particularly true for the Mediterranean area.

In the early years, between 1958 and 1972, over 90 per cent of the £1,400 million loaned by the European Investment Bank went to projects in Italy and the Mediterranean regions of France. Even after the first enlargement in 1973, these two countries continued to get generous allocations of the available fund for regional development with Italy claiming 40 per cent of the £540 million shared out by the European Regional Development Fund in its first three years between 1975 and 1978.

Taking the whole of the period over which they have operated, from 1958 and 1973 respectively, the European Investment Bank and the European Regional Development Fund have together devoted some 45 per cent of their total resource to Mediterranean projects. If the European Social Fund and the European Guidance and Guarantee Fund are also taken into account, then between 1975 and 1981 the '*Mezzogiorno*' [Southern Italy], the south of France and Greece have received altogether £2,622 million in grants and £3,381 million in loans.[48]

All the EEC agencies have had a budget accounting for about 15 per cent of the Community's funds. But in the 1960s more than 90 per cent of the budget went to agriculture and at the beginning of the 1980s it was more than 60 per cent. These funds subsidized live-stock breeding and dairy products in temperate Europe and they subsidized fruit, wine, oil and vegetable production in the Mediterranean areas. Financial transactions are the key to the Common Agricultural Policy (CAP) that had and still has the aim of increasing productivity, guaranteeing farmers an acceptable standard of living and stabilizing the market. The truth is that it is a gigantic process of institutional and political control. The state continues to govern the production of that vast and complex system called agriculture. The CAP prices the products one at a time by an elaborate system – intervening through national agencies who buy up any surpluses, thus guaranteeing the farmers' incomes – while it ensures import controls and subsidies for exports and domestic markets. The costs of this policy continue to grow. $1.8 billion were spent in 1968, $3.5 billion in 1974 and $14 billion in 1979. 'The CAP has, however, been generally inward-looking and it can justly be accused of being protectionist and of adding to instability on the world markets.'[49] This is not the place to discuss the conflicts that this mechanism has produced with institutions like GATT, particularly with the dispute between the only two industrial powers that are exporters of agricultural products, France and the USA.

It seems to be more important to consider two things. The first refers to the inclusion of the Southern European countries in the CAP. Italy, Spain, Portugal and Greece, in spite of the fears and perplexities of many observers, managed to create the premises for their full integration into the big agro-alimentary markets of Northern Europe thanks to a careful policy of mediation between states.

> The expansion of the demand for products typical of these areas, supported by the increase in the level of economic well-being in the industrialized centres, has given partial but appreciable results in terms of income and preservation of employment in agriculture even in densely populated rural areas.[50]

The second consideration is that integration should continue in an inward-looking context, in spite of the changes in the CAP where the trend is to move from policies in support of prices to policies supporting income. In any case it is a hierarchical and administrative intervention, that of a visible hand controlling a gigantic agricultural market.

It cannot be said, however, that the state retreated from the economy and from society and that the market continued to expand regularly after the Second World War. The dynamics of the protection of interests were all-powerful. The wages and working capacity of the European agricultural workers were defended even at the cost of imposing higher prices for the consumer, of destroying vast quantities of surplus production and of creating a protectionist barrier against countries in the Southern hemisphere. This is not an economic problem but a political one, as has been demonstrated by studies on the Community lobbies. The Southern European groups, including the Turkish ones, have rapidly infiltrated into the mechanisms of the pressure groups that are still in an early phase of development.

> In fact, the importance of the European groups in the decision making and running of the European Community was, until recently, relatively marginal with regard to the influence of governments, administrations and national experts, with the exception of agriculture.[51]

All this did not happen by chance. All the protectionist measures and interventions stem from the national political systems. Why have the national political classes vigorously undertaken industrial economic liberalization yet have stopped short when faced with the question of agriculture? Probably because, after the great migratory period, the stability of agrarian employment and the static nature of natural resources called for a continuous and accurate defence of the interests of a very stable and fixed electorate able to bring sanctions to bear on the elected representative.

The Community's agrarian policies contradict, with the use of chemical products in agriculture, the extreme intensification of agrarian technologies, the social waste it produces and the values which are emerging in societies all over the world: respect for ecology and the drive towards tenable growth. There are other contradictions. The combination of pressures exercised by the state and the market with regard to industry on one hand and to agriculture on the other, characterizes the entire South Mediterranean policy of the EEC through the process of association (Malta and Cyprus) and agreements (Tunisia, Morocco, Israel, Yugoslavia, Egypt and Lebanon) that are aimed at the harmonization of the foreign policies of all the EEC members with regard to the other Mediterranean countries. The key to this institutional mechanism is the agreements on reciprocity of quotas and tariffs. This should create a larger free trade area, a customs union, with the formulation of policies aimed at the oil-producing countries and in the periodic revision of the respective concessions. The entrance of Turkey into the EEC after a long wait is the result of a similar process. This country has only recently abandoned its policy of import substitution and its adhesion to the EEC is happening according to criteria that not even the free trading wave of the last decade has been able to modify. This is symbolic and proof of what has been discussed so far.

In conclusion, the market (and this is the great significance of its non-linear relations with the state) is, on the basis of historical circumstances as well as some theories that deny the neo-classical approach,[52] an artificial, not impersonal or spontaneous product. It is the fulfilment of a complicated and difficult process of civilization. It is a long and troubled social construction where politics play an unsuppressible part.

III Induced capitalism

The relations between market, politics and society described in the last section form part of a process general to Europe. Whatever the difficult and uncertain final result will be, at least it can be said that there has been a concrete reduction in the importance of the state as 'political entrepreneur',[53] that is to say, as an interpreter and executor of an institutional economic plan that not only regulates but also controls and forms the markets until it gives life to public enterprises. This process is still under way, naturally, and though there is much talk (and action in some countries) about privatization and stabilization of economic policies aimed at exports, it has not been given up. However, it is not an irreversible process, as the effects of these state practices on the development of the various national middle-classes shows. The extension of the visible hand on society also meant placing, for decades, the accent on the *raison d'être* of the bureaucracy that allocated resources, handed out (and called in) favours and answered to political and clientship obligations, not on individual and autonomous rights based on the individual's conscience and actions. In Southern Europe capitalism was in fact 'induced'[54] more than elsewhere and this had serious social and political consequences. It has been said of Portugal and Spain that 'ascription and kinship rather than achievement continued to exercise an important influence in the assignment of economic roles.'[55] But it is a mistake to think that these distinctive characteristics had been completely surmounted by the advent of economic liberalization. In these capitalist systems, social roles linked to public employment and to non-competitive services continued to be important and this grows with the passing of time. Ascription and kinship continue to be more important than achievement. This is the basis for the growth of political clientship that prospers in systems of status and that refutes impersonal contractual mechanisms as dangerous for its stability.[56] The slow and tardy spreading of the market is the effect of statalism as import substitution on the Mediterranean economies and on Europe. The formidable obstacles faced by the market did not allow the full development of a contractual system based on reciprocal trust between the actors and on impersonal respect of the state's laws. In any case, however, there is no doubt that in the almost fifty years since the end of the Second World War, the interference of the state on economy, both through protectionism and as direct intervention, has diminished in Southern Europe and elsewhere. The market has continued along its road closely linked with every phase of economic growth.

Another process was in act at the same time, particularly in those Southern European countries which were late in forming social citizenship. This process was the result of dictatorships or of the resistance of the more conservative political and social groups. It was the result of autonomous and private structures of social assistance. The state's intervention with regard to social welfare developed and, therefore, public expenditure was expanded, with all the consequences discussed in the previous pages.[57] A comparison of the figures available on social expenditure as a percentage of GDP for the various European countries shows that a large part of the public budget is devoted to social costs. Now even the Southern European countries can be counted among those in which a system of state welfare exists. Statistics for 1985 show that in Italy 27 per cent was spent on welfare, in Greece 20 per cent, in Portugal 17 per cent (1980), in Spain 15 per cent. Among the other European countries France spent 34 per cent, Sweden 32 per cent, West Germany 26 per cent and Great Britain 21 per cent.[58]

This is proof that, as Hirsch said,[59] no market mechanism can survive and expand without social cohesion and it must be solidarity that guarantees the protection of the market, according to the general indications given by Polany.[60] Global competition and the state's fiscal crises have made the realization of the virtuous circle between market and solidarity, between competition and social protection, more difficult. The stage has been reached when it has to be said that capitalism 'cannot coexist *with* neither can it exist *without*, the welfare state'.[61] But there is an accumulation of crisis factors inherent to the state of well-being: all-embracing bureaucracy; inequality of the services provided; discordances between technological changes and social protection; the growing importance of the political and trade union classes as private allocators of public expenditure.

There were also many external crisis factors: demographic change, with the decrease of the active population and the contemporary increase of social coverage; the very strong growth of the costs of longer periods of schooling; the shortening of the active work period and the increased quality of medical services required; the increase of single wage earner families; the increase in temporary and part-time work. 'This has increased the fiscal square on welfare politics and made the search for solutions more urgent.'[62] Here is another characteristic of Southern European countries which distinguishes it from the Continental ones: as soon as they achieved a welfare state they also reached the point in its crisis.

Thus the contradiction between the structure of economic production and that of social reproduction becomes evident. Public expenditure allows the state to insure the mediation between production based on the market and reproduction of society based on services and underground economy, between competition and social protection. The crisis of the welfare system is the crisis of the state's role in social production, at the same time as it gradually retreated from economic production. Because of this, the crisis of the welfare system can have more devastating dimensions in Southern Europe than in more stabilized economies. In fact, the big difference within the European welfare state does not consist either in the resources used nor in the rights of social citizenship that are being formed. It is to be found in the effective percentage of the populations that receive those resources compared to those that supply the social contributions that permit the distribution of benefits. Everywhere in Europe, the welfare system is based on the assumption that the family's wage earner is permanently employed with an acceptable wage which allows that person to pay social contributions. All entitlements are directly linked to the job and the wage or salary paid to the contributor.

But the labour market does not function equally well throughout Europe. For significant parts of the population in the less developed South of the Continent there are only jobs available which pay wages well below the national average, where many of workers' statutory rights do not apply, and which do not carry entitlements to the work-related benefits of the welfare state. Large part of such employment is offered by very small enterprises which can survive only on the basis of cheap labour input . . . the workers concerned are destined to a kind of underclass existence: out of touch with the level of prosperity and the life prospectives of the rest of the population, smoothed for some only by the fact that poverty is embedded in traditional patterns of life and outlooks.[63]

Under these conditions, the welfare system can only accentuate the social divisions between insiders and outsiders, over and above the formal generalizations of Marshallian social citizenship.[64]

In this sense Southern European societies are more dualistic than those of Northern and Central Europe and they must face the prime need to solve the state's fiscal crisis and the lack of legal-bureaucratic rationality in public administration. The overcoming of these problems through social protection from the market can compensate for the divisions and inequalities of the market itself and find a remedy for its failures. The South shows that, alongside competition, the non-competitive nature of solidarity has an unsuppressible value, this over and above all conservative and free-trade ideals and all the social dumping possible within European unification.[65] Market economies are threatened by social disintegration. It is the perverse result of an historical sociological reality. Social disintegration lies in the fact that the increase of social citizenship occurred at the same time as the difficult growth of the market, while in the first-comer countries it occurred after the affirmation of the market. It must also be remembered that there was a continuous movement of political and trade union collective identity as well as that of the state itself before the ideals of the welfare state were accepted in Southern Europe in the 1970s. That was caused by the spreading of the people's identity in the state no matter what political form, dictatorship or democracy, the ruling powers took. The political class placed itself at the head of this collective movement. The characteristics of the social citizenship that was being formed were dictated mainly by its party and trade union origins. The reasons for social citizenship were to be found in the areas of legitimacy and consent, rather than in that of rationality and functionality of the economic system. This could only have happened if the harmonization of the criteria of expenditure with the needs of an industrial society had been guaranteed together with the social citizenship measured by an increase in the standard of living. This could only happen by placing those criteria in relation to a mechanism of state revenue based on taxation and its diffusion over all social levels according to principles of contributory equality. This is exactly what did not happen in Southern Europe.

As proof of this, all that needs to be analyzed is the structure of the welfare systems.[66] The Scandinavian and British systems are based on collective and personal services with uniform benefits that are independent of occupational status. In Southern Europe and those parts of Europe where pro-labour parties have never governed for very long, with the recent exception of Spain, systems of fragmented, institutional arrangements were created. These concentrated on giving monetary aid which largely reproduced the inherent differences in the occupational system from an administrative and distributive point of view, rather than on providing services. These arrangements were then superimposed on a universal form of welfare in the case of health and pensions. But the dissociative effect[67] of such social policies is this form of centralized financial transfers which subsidizes the private claim to

105

goods and services. Such social policies are dissociative because of the effect of division and heterogeneity, rather then homogeneity, induced in the social and cultural systems followed by the corporative struggles. The idea of equality is, however, defeated when it comes to incomes. Here social heterogeneity becomes the crystallization of disparities of group and disparities of class. The latter nourish the former, giving rise to real social divides with profound dissociative effects in the system of values. Here 'the access to benefits is still linked to status and this gives rise to a series of direct and indirect differentiations between social groups and areas.'[68] Certain classes, such as self-employed workers, are excluded from unemployment benefit and health services while other groups, particularly young first job seekers, are completely excluded from the welfare system. The inequalities of class, which impinge on people's ability to get a job, can thus operate with force. This specific system of inequalities reaches its peak in the persistence of poverty, in a European area that has known the development already mentioned. Poverty is the other side of growth and prevents it from becoming development. However, the conclusion that must be drawn from this process of implementation of the welfare state in Southern Europe is, from a social point of view, generally positive.

However, it is positive in the sense that it has produced stability in the levels of inequality in spite of the gravity of the economic crisis and also in times of recovery and strong growth. It has not, however, completely overcome inequality. The welfare system has counter-balanced and moderated the inequalities produced by the market, placing Southern Europe at a half-way point between the British experience and the Continental one. Proof of this lies in the increase in income per capita. From this point of view, Germany, France and Great Britain are part of the group of strong countries in Europe. GDP per capita measured through purchasing power parity for Great Britain went from 125.6 per cent in 1960 to 108.5 per cent in 1986, confirming the relative decline of the economy. France went from 104.8 to 112 per cent, showing the growth and solidity of this economy. Germany went from 121.2 to 121.6 per cent which demonstrates the hegemony and the strength of the system. Italy showed an increase from 83.6 to 94.3 per cent confirming its continuous growth and its position as economic leader in Southern Europe. Spain, Greece and Portugal follow. Between these last three countries, Spain is the one to offer the best performances. In fact it went from 40.2 per cent to a really exceptional 75.6 per cent. Greece went from 38.6 to 58.4 per cent and Portugal went from 35.5 to 52.7 per cent.[69]

But it is this increase in income that leads to the fragmentation of a system based more on the relations of reciprocity and status than on contractual ones without producing upsetting tensions. In fact, the increase of incomes occurred amongst deep heterogeneity and social disintegration. These were also the products of the change in the different cultural approaches of males and females concerning not only the role of the family but also the problem of female employment. In fact, even within the differences of the history of family life in Europe, the emergence of family behaviour in less heterogeneous forms than those of the past with regard to work and the market is an important indication of the political social role that welfare has played in society and the social stratification of Southern Europe. This has had deep and undisputed effects on social mobility. An enormous amount of work still needs to be done on this in order to understand how much social mobility has been affected by economic growth as individual and family incomes increased, if it has been affected by social policies or by a combination of both these factors. The first empirical studies help us to understand this crucial problem. The increase of mobility seems to be linked above all to the changes in the occupational structure together with the positions of fathers and sons. What seems to emerge from the first important studies on this subject[70] is the ties that exist between the limited extent of the social divergences with regard to the position of fathers and sons, the positive part played on the vertical mobility by emigration and education, and the persistent importance of the family in levelling the destiny of class and social behaviour.

All this is further confirmation of the interaction between modernity and tradition that is the most salient feature of the Southern European experience.

Part Three

POLITICS AND PARTIES

Chapter 7

NEO-CACIQUISM

I Modernity and tradition

There are two main differences between the countries of Southern Europe and those of Continental Europe. The first difference is the constant links between modernity and tradition even in political society.[1] The second one is that these countries, with the exception of Italy, went through a period of dictatorship after the Second World War. They were late-comers to democracy and had little ability to institutionalize their political situation. In spite of this, the party system was seen as vital to a democratic way of life. However, while Continental Europe's party systems were 'stable in spite of the changes in society and its stratifications',[2] those of Southern Europe had lower stability. There were also extraordinarily persistent political sub-cultures with an ability to adapt to social changes. For this reason, the democratic parties had their roots in the fight against dictatorship, changing their character through the transition to democracy. In some countries, the modern concept[3] of political party did not exist before the advent of the dictatorships. This very important factor is specific to the political history of Southern Europe.

In the case of Portugal, Salazar's dictatorship was a variation of the European dictatorships of the period between the two world wars. But some of its characteristics distinguished it from Franco's regime and from Mussolini's. It was also very different from the dictatorship in Greece and the sheltered democracy of Turkey.

The first distinctive characteristic of Salazar's regime derived from the fact that the Portuguese dictatorship started with a military coup in 1926. The military had suffered considerable humiliation during the First World War which may have influenced the situation, but the coup was aimed mainly at pacifying a series of revolts in an agrarian society dominated by electoral and political caciquism.[4] These revolts were an attempt, particularly in the metropolitan area of Lisbon, to change the society into a mass society, and to lay the foundation for social and political changes.[5] It was an isolated, clientship-riddled rural world that was changing under the stimuli of emigration and urbanization.[6] When faced with this situation, the dominant, anticlerical republican factions, which were incapable of inspiring political participation in the masses, did nothing but stall the crisis of representation and of legitimization of the liberal state. This started fascist movements which became evident after the First World War, starting with an alliance and a compromise between the pro-modern sectors and the traditional ones.[7] The absence of a mass base for the growing dictatorship of Salazar was caused by the low degree of political awareness in the country. So the Salazar dictatorship can be described as 'fascism without a fascist movement'.

Until 1926, Portuguese political society was a long way from having the characteristics of a liberal democracy based on popular parties. From this point of view, Spain and Italy were very different. The crisis of these then liberal states was caused by the political and social movement governed by popular parties that the oligarchic domination could not contain[8] according to the procedures of a liberal democracy. The class violence of the various and basically different dictatorships stemmed from this.

The situation in Greece was similar to that of Portugal, but there were some important distinctions. After the victory against the Turks a parliament was formed but it was a sort of institutional superstructure on a national reality subordinate to the wishes of the great powers. The monarchy itself was the result of an alliance between Great Britain, France and Russia in 1833 which established the Greek state in counter-position to the Ottoman empire. It had no roots in the native ruling classes. Landowning aristocracy did not exist and the business middle classes had their interests abroad. The farming class was subject to the patronage of elites linked to the oligarchy of the families (*tzakia*) destined to form the monarchic circle. So from the very beginning, parliament had no political participation or institutionalization, and it would remain so until the 1930s. At that point, the dictatorial or semi-dictatorial cycle started as a reaction against the political participation that had, in the meantime, grown. This state of affairs lasted until the collapse of military rule in 1974.[9]

This background is also applicable to Turkish political history. It has a great deal in common with the socio-political systems of Europe. But the fact that it is studied, generally speaking, from a Middle Eastern viewpoint, gives an idea of the historical unfolding of its complex and manifold culture. The history of the Ottoman Empire was as greatly influenced by Islam as its recent past has been. After the Second World War, the secular state created by Kemal Atatürk had to deal with the persistent religious fervour of some sections of the elite and with the peripheral populations, which faced the bureaucratic elite and intellectuals who instead had assimilated a Westernized urban culture.

Turkey has a higher degree of economic development than all its Middle Eastern neighbours. With the exception of Israel, it is the only country in that part of the world to have achieved democracy and political pluralism in spite of its history of continual crises with military intervention.[10] There was a long period of dictatorship between the two world wars, but in 1945 an intermittent dictatorship began. It had a limited time-span, unlike those of Spain, Portugal and even Greece. This fact should make the acceptance of the concept of transforming modernity, emphasized above all else by the social sciences when referring to Turkey, more circumspect. Too often the analysis of the controversial emancipation of society has been overlooked, compared to that of the institutional 'managerealization'[11] of the centralist elites pursued by Kemal Atatürk between the two world wars. The anthropological point of view has contributed greatly to changing this perspective. Turkish political society falsifies all the optimistic interpretative hypotheses by which modernization would have favoured the overthrow of status which was central to social organization. Modernization should have replaced status with contract. It should have brought democracy and political participation.

The regulation and management of associative relations on a microsocial level cannot be accomplished with the regulation and management on a macrosocial level. If there is no systematic connection between these two levels of social order, entropy and anomie take over and the decline of the system is certain. Turkey is an extremely interesting case from this point of view. In the period between the two world wars, the separation between the two levels of regulation was almost absolute given the prevalence of the centristic Weberian reason that wanted to permeate every corner of society. The post-war period was characterized by slow but constant emancipation from centrism with the crises of regulation and control of the whole system. These were caused by the resistance of the authoritarian forces to the changes desired and instigated by the people. Only the synthesis and composition between values, culture and beliefs of the two levels of organization of society can guarantee the regeneration of that society. This should be the function of the political and institutional system which must combine together[12] with society, not be dominated by it. The system must rise above society while at the same time respecting its autonomy and directing it towards universal orientations.

It is extremely difficult to do this. Clientship makes it hard for the political system to be autonomous without actually separating itself from society. The Southern European political systems are not particularly autonomous and Turkey, in spite of years and years of continuous bureaucratic transcendentalism, is no exception. But it does explain its historical weakness.

Southern Europe's more recent history, after the dictatorships, is characterized by the tensions which arose between the creation of the institutions of modern party systems within democratic parliaments and the remains of more traditional methods of political participation. The revival of clientship is a perfect example of these methods. Supporting political parties and other democratic organizations does not mean omitting or undervaluing all the other forms of association which emerge in a democracy. These re-establish their relations with the state by the principles of pluralism and on behalf of interest groups. In Continental Europe 'the party system has been an independent variable and the continuity of the democratic regime was the dependent variable [and] the persistence of democracy was guaranteed . . . in a significant measure by the capability of the party system to keep the conflicts between the subjects of pluralism within the framework of institutionalized democratic competition.'[13] But in Southern Europe this process happened only later, and it was also more difficult and controversial. There is no doubt that the representation of interest groups has always been in the hands of the parties, rather than in the form of direct institutional representation. These were forms of representation which were controlled by the single party or by an administration dominated by the stronger pressure groups in dictatorships, by the parties in competition that filtered the relations with the democratic state. In any case, it was a strongly pervasive political system which was not very autonomous from society, nor did it produce political pluralism. Parliaments assumed a central role but primarily they emphasized the fragmented dimensions of representation and the role of majority parties. Parliaments in all the Southern European countries 'counted on the impetus [of interest groups] to privatize policies and the decisional and administrative options of the legislation and government . . . [they used] their administrative freedom as a power system.'[14] In this way the modern, as opposed to traditional, system of clientship came into being. This system found its distributable resources in the party system and in its control of important sectors of the state rather than in the elites as before. It is always a two-sided relationship that is based on 'the individualistic acquisition of consent'[15] and rests on the weaknesses of the state as an administrative regulator dominated by the universality of the law and by the delivery of the resources. The regulatory body is the party and its rule is particularistic.

II Clientship, weak parties and institutionalization

A careful study of almost fifty years of history since the post-war period – half a century of rapid changes – shows the many complex relations that exist between political society and economic society, between political society and civil society. And political society, with its political and social connotations and its position between the institutionalized political system and civil society, is the key. It is the motive force behind the changes of the last seventy years. Its hub is the new relation between state and economy supported by the political classes.

Modern polyarchies cannot understand each other without acknowledging the role played in them by the political entrepreneur. Or rather by the creation of economic actors by the political class. The peculiarities of Southern Europe, compared to other parts of the continent, are mainly due to the following fact. The creation of political parties comes about, with many contrasts and conflicts, as a result of them being given the possibility to intervene in the construction of market mechanisms. Elsewhere, market forces developed before the democratic parliamentary political classes. The prerequisites of this situation lie in two factors. The first is defined by the original characteristics of induced capitalism. Politics was not the only powerful motive force behind this type of economic development but it was certainly a very important one. The second factor lies in the type of relation between the interests of society and the state during the dictatorships. During that period the state was balkanized by the stronger power groups and subjected to the needs of their clientship and personal networks. In the new democracies, the parties have inherited both the weak balkanized state and the representation of interest groups. This is the legal and rational weakness of the state and the strength of party clientship.

One of the things which radically changed the situation after the post-war period and after the fall of the dictatorships, was the fact that this situation came into being at the same time as the slow but indisputable development of the trade union movement and of the horizontal organizations of the democracy of interests, in a mass society with its parties which are the point of reference for these organizations. This hailed a deep change in the character of political participation compared to the preceding liberal and authoritarian societies. A mixed structure, both vertical and horizontal, of the relations between the socio-economic formations and the political system grew out of this collection of contributory causes. This structure gave the governing political class the most relevant part between those assumed in those years by other sub-systems such as the private entrepreneurial group and the social movement run mainly by the political trade unions class. The mixed structure of political participation exalts the part of continuous, horse-trading clientship between the different parties. The collective movements allow the identification of interests. But the satisfying of these interests is done both in a general way (government laws) and in a particular way (benefits typical of patronage). The difference between this system and that of the political exchange which is typical of modern democracies is that, in Southern Europe, the relations between voter and elected are direct. There is no rational state administration capable of stopping the private use for private ends of public functions or which can act as mediator when the barter vote is normal currency everywhere in civil life and in the administrative machine. The sharing out of resources by government and ministers goes right down the line to the smallest corners of the state and it affects a large part of the economic system. It is an anomic division of political activity without rules and ideals, in a world where ideologies as personal reference points are dead. Because of this, the concept of the anomic division of political activity underlines the absence of norms in social and political action. It is a mistake to think that similar processes were limited to the centre or the right of the political system. The socialist parties, as soon as they became part of the government in democratic societies, either by themselves or in coalitions, headed these processes, widening and strengthening them. From a general point of view, this behaviour is typical of all Southern European politics, and they are very distinctive compared to the other four areas of the European continent: the Central-West, the Central-East, the East and the North.

In Southern Europe the market was late in changing social relations into contractual ones, and there were many difficulties. The Southern European countries are governed more by the division of the spoils by the parties than by legal and bureaucratic rationality. Political and symbolic transitions are segmented and based on clientship rather than universal and based on merit.

Democratic political institutionalization should be based on the creation of parties with a strong base of ideals on one hand while, on the other, they should follow procedural rules that shape the political system within the legality of the state. The institutionalization of politics means stepping over the threshold of modernity by organizing democracy through civil associations and political parties. Or rather, through the acknowledgement of interests and the formation of political solidarity. In the South of Europe there have been two very different ways to reach political institutionalization but this has never been fully realized. The first is the conservative archipelago type of party that does not separate party and associations but governs the relations between them by using both ideological resources and norms for the distribution of resources. It was, and is, not only the expression of clientship but it is also the expression of the attempt at overcoming it. In fact, mass patronage was linked to the creation of a mass sub-cultural party so for a long time it prevented the disintegration of the party at the hands of interest groups and their battles.

Normally the archipelago party is based on solid ideological foundations (the catholicism of the Italian christian democrats, the sacred ideas in the Spanish tradition, etc.), and the economic growth of the system. It permits the distribution of resources to the electorate. After the 1970s, with the economic difficulties and the growth of the public deficit, this road to political inclusion became even more difficult, while the other, sub-cultural, road was slowly argued against by the advancing of the process of disintegration of once consolidated ideologies. This explains many of the difficulties of the conservative parties after the fall of the dictatorships. But it also explains, as we shall see, the difficulties of the socialist groups.

The second way to achieve party institutionalization was that of the communists – a centralized party which, in countries like Italy where it was strong, inherited the geo-political areas of the pre-Fascist socialist reforms and dispensed (and partly still dispenses) ideological resources. Even when it governs locally it is a distributor of material goods. It made good use of its ideological origins and its programmatic severity to establish its difference from the other parties. This became fully compatible with the irreversible defence of the democratic state which the communists followed without duplicity in Spain and Italy. This was not the case in Portugal and Greece, however, at least not until recently. This new communist line clashed with the Stalinist ideology which was held only by a minority. Even so, this clash tore apart the Spanish and Italian revisionist parties and also the small Greek separatist party that was ideologically linked to them. This led to the inability to form a new political class capable of renewing its outlook and its objectives. It led to splits and to the communist contribution to the crisis of the institutions.

The Southern European socialists have never taken the road of modernization and political institutionalization. They quickly adapted to the Mediterranean model of 'multiple caciquism':[16] many leaders fighting amongst themselves together with their faithful followers continuously pulling each other to pieces over the scarcity, of material resources and the overabundance of short-term political resources of narrow strategic vision, an accentuated and quarrelsome splitting up, where the logic of individualistic acquisition prevailed. The victory of charismatic leaders (Felipe Gonzales, Georgios Papandreou, Bettino Craxi) was not an attempt at a modernizing institutionalization (except in the case of Mario Soares in Portugal), as had been proclaimed and believed for a time. Instead, it was a transition from a multi-headed clientship with few resources to a single-headed and authoritarian clientship with wide resources. Caciquism did not become more oligarchic but more democratic. There was one innovation: modern caesarism that was based on a specific method of destroying democracy within the parties and of founding a neo-patrimonialism centred on the boss and his clique. He had arbitrary powers of veto and strongly centralized power of co-optation. This is common to all the Southern European parties. The roots of this are to be found in the fact that, in the 1980s, the electoral growth of all the parties was due to the leaders' ability to attract the new middle classes, only too happy to receive the resources dispensed by the party system of government that controlled the state.

The caesaristic and neo-patrimonialistic phenomena became widely diffused. However, large segments of society began to show signs of disaffection and refusal in the face of clientship practices. This was shown by the increase of non-voters[17] and the formation of new parties covering the entire political spectrum from left to right. The political parties all reacted to this process by increasing the power of the leader within the party and intensifying the personality cult by using mass media. However, party wings and factions persisted as they were essential for the division of the spoils and for forming ever more precarious and unstable coalitions, whereas once they were useful only for ensuring access to the resources supplied by the state of which they were part.[18]

In spite of this lack of institutionalized politics, Southern European societies were the protagonists of an exceptional simplification of the party system. The fall of the dictatorships was followed by the fragmentation of the political forces. This was followed by the rapid affirmation of parties which received the majority of the votes, allowing democratic consolidation. This was the consequence of cultural changes following urbanization. The move away from the rural areas caused changes in behaviour and expectations that led people away from the traditional mores of rural society. This does not mean that certain symbolic elements like dowries, *comparaggio*, etc. were abandoned. In fact, there was a change in political attitudes as these became less controllable by the face-to-face clientship of elite patronage. In fact, new organizations were created by leaders who decided to break with the old political systems, some more vigorously than others. The creation of strong democracies needed stable parliamentary governments. The only way to do this was to form strong parties based on solidarity and long-term interests. However, the past still had a strong influence on the innovative projects. The result was the clientship of the Southern European party.

In Greece, for example, the form this would take was very clear. It would be based on the continuity of clientship by the first political organizations (the Centre and the Radical Union) formed in the post-war period.

> Clientship existed under many forms (distribution of civil service management jobs, concession of subsidies, the giving of emigration permits and import licences ...). But it is clientship practised by the top party management with the individual members of Parliament having to act as collection points in order to obtain the resources needed for their superiors' election.[19]

Twenty-two years later, looking at the post-Junta period, the same things, more or less, can be said. This is because elements of modernity grew out of the old partisan clientship structures, thanks to the enormous heterogeneity of the Greek socio-economic structure. 'It cannot be studied correctly from only one historical point of view: many eras continued to meet within that structure.'[20] This underlines what is mentioned many times in this book: the interrelation and the intersection of tradition and modernity in many of the sectors of public life.

Prior to the Greek dictatorship, the parties were only the extension of personalities, of individuals. This accounts for their number but also for their high mortality rate. The only exception to this was the Union of Democratic Leftists (EDA, Enosi Dimokratikon Aristeron), which contained a strong communist element. It was a modern political organization that had survived its founders. Its reason for being lay in its political programme, not in its personalized network. From this point of view, the situation is full of interesting considerations.

> Greece represents a type of political system that emerged from colonial status of foreign subjugation in the nineteenth century but lagged behind Western Europe and the United States in economic development, in its ability to cope with social change, and the development of strong representative institutions. Many countries in Latin

117

America would be included in this category; several Eastern European states (although their independence came later) would also have qualified before World War II.[21]

The scant social differentiation and the simplicity of associative life contributed to the formation of cliques, whose basic instability could only make political institutionalization more and more difficult. In this context, also noted in studies on southern Italy,[22] socialization processes maximize the persistence of a lack of confidence and therefore the scarcity of horizontal cooperation. Family and local loyalties are dominant because more extensive links are obstructed by the structural character of societies oppressed by uncertainty and shortages. Politics as an individual competition, first to survive and then, with the gradual growth of per capita incomes, for purely personal interests, stems from this. With its two-sided structure in a relationship between unequal components, clientship becomes the exaltation of individual competition.

In Greece, Turkey, southern Italy, Portugal and Spain, internal migration from the rural areas to the cities gave rise to urbanization without industrialization, and this produced the ruralization of the cities. This meant that the old family-orientated models of behaviour were maintained. The permanence of links within the community remained unaltered in the villages and these formed the base for a higher degree of political participation than that found in the cities. The local elites also played a part in this, because of their influence and their patronage system, as demonstrated by the case of Turkey.[23] Thus the persistence of radical two-sided traditional relationships was confirmed in spite of social and political changes. This is true for the changes that indubitably affected local life where the position of the parties gradually became more important. But it was always a variation of the clientship theme within a strongly personalized organization. Or rather, it depended to a great extent on the leaders' ability to lay their hands on resources which they could then distribute easily as subsidies or incentives to the local communities. This allowed them to develop their own groups of faithful followers.[24] Therefore, the party machines rapidly produced political action that was more instrumental than expressive. This occurred in the centrality of vertical relations, not in their exclusivity, as the trade union movement started to emerge.

> Voters are more likely to respond to short-term, concrete, specific material inducements than to long-term, programmatic, sectoral appeals. This type of political participation seems to characterize the more modern rural areas and, at least until very recently, the major cities.[25]

These changes which recycle traditions were well described in that great work called *Gecekondu* (The Shanties).[26] The ruralization of the typical Turkish city, surrounded by settlements and shantytowns and invaded by the values of the population of the villages of the periphery is perfectly depicted. Common agrarian origins were at the base of the persistence of the deferent values which played an important part in selecting the direction of political participation and leadership. However, this recycling lacked the original fabric of community reciprocity. There was a deep sense of insecurity, disintegration and anomie. Faced with this, the use of force emerged to guarantee order and to ensure the support of the family, which was considered fundamental not to existence but to associative life according to the typical principles of 'the amoral familism',[27] while with the move to the city, the old styles of behaviour typical of two-sided relations were preserved. The central position of the family was also maintained, but not as part of a community as it was originally. Urban life was better than a rural one for guaranteeing the survival of the family. Political participation was made of both solidarity and self-interest. It still had to guarantee the conditions for survival. In any case, it was the beginning of 'a more rational and individualized concept of rightness and freedomness, a keener sense of individual achievement and higher aspirations.'[28] Market logic seems to appear here, and also that of political participation derived from making tradition actual again.

Any discussion about the actuality of clientship ties must start from a full understanding of the great changes that came about. An excellent example of this is the case of Turkey after 1983. 'The Turkish state is not the property of its Praetorian guard but (like the armed forces themselves) is a complex entity which already embodies equally complex mechanisms of participation.'[29] The parties' grassroots organizations were the place where such participation took place. However, it was always and above all based on patronage mechanisms. When these mechanisms involved dealings with relatively well-off people in the presence of organizations with strong horizontal links like the trade union movements, they became much more refined than they once were.

An understanding of the reasons for the scarce political institutionalization is therefore essential. Even interest groups were unable to arrive at a form of collective representation without assuming normative forms which could not be based on the ability for self-organization. In turn, the state bureaucracy was penetrated by groups with particular interests. This was the reverse of the typical theory of the penetration of society by the state. The parties faithfully reflected this form of associative life. They were always dominated by families that bequeathed their managerial functions to their offspring. They were associations of groups that defended particular interests. There were some exceptions to this but they were the result of strong shocks inflicted on Southern European politics from outside the area; for example, the Greek refugees from Asia Minor in the 1920s, and the communists who were ever faithful to the Soviet revolutionary ideal. All this had deep repercussions on the parties. They found themselves caught between bureaucratic organizations (therefore durable) and personal organizations (therefore fragile). These were markedly polyarchic and persistent. Legg asserted this principle after studying Greek parties, and his analytical conclusions are valid for the whole of Southern Europe.

> A polyarchic party has a form of collective personal leadership resting on consensus or on some voting procedures; a persistent party's life is measured in decades, whereas a fragile party lasts for years and a durable party for generations. The basic components of Greek political organization as we have seen, have the personal clientelage structures built up by local politicians; these may be described as 'polyarchic and persistent' organizations. However, most of the major parties also contain a 'personal and fragile' component, made up of those attracted by the demagogic qualities of a particular leader and unconnected to the more traditional clientelage structure.

The Greek parliamentary arena also contains a whole variety of other, less important groups. Some parties have been 'personal and durable', no more than families with political labels; others such as the Left are 'bureaucratic and durable'.[30]

How much of this extraordinarily rich and pervasive picture changed, after the end of political fragmentation? As urbanization meant the ruralization of the cities so the creation of organized popular parties brought the cult of clientship in modern politics. This could be the answer. The parties certainly became more bureaucratic and durable, with a clear tendency to stabilization of the political classes as these became older.[31] But this indicator, by itself, does not solve the problem of understanding what type of stabilization it was. Was it personalistic? based on clientship? of a popular party? Without doubt, it continued to be associated with a strong personalization of political life. However, it now appears to be more the product of the need of a Caesar-like power dictated by the widening of participation and by the use of mass media in politics, rather than the re-proposal of the power of the bigwigs in its pure form.

Joaquin Costa's observations made at the beginning of the century should be looked at in the light of the above considerations. The caciquism that he studied is today a specific version of the clientship of the Southern European political society and its party systems. It is neo-caciquism. Party organizations continue to depend on the personal relationship which the person elected has with a society that is intrinsically based on the amoral family. But, at the same time, these organizations are also based on horizontal links with the mass. The persistence of the organization is assured by the relations within the parties and the trade unions, between the leader and the followers. The followers are completely dependent on the leader, who settles their career, maintaining direct relations with society through the clientship organization. A 'bunch' party is formed with centralized power, with a charismatic appeal to the electorate and with the personal welding between the basic caciquistic structure and the party organization. The political invention of Southern Europe is the neo-caciquism of party leaders. The control that the party – any party – has over the state is a decisive part of this invention.

The Spanish regions like Galicia and Leon where, in 1977, the Spanish Socialist Party (PSOE, Partido Socialista Obrero Español) received its lowest electoral results, were once rightly indicated as the basis of a neo-caciquism firmly held by the right and the centre. This neo-caciquism operated through the peripheral structures of the public administration and through the credit and assistance institutions 'and directed consensus towards the right-wing and governing parties'.[32] This is an analysis that completes and coincides with that of modern conservative parties. These are lease-associations where both formal and informal organizations function. The members cannot be defined as militant, they are followers who are united by loyalty to the leader or to interest groups rather than to the party. Therefore, there is a mediation between popular parties and parties of the old elites that is original and persistent in time and space.[33]

When the PSOE was in opposition to Franchism, and when it had not yet spread its electoral roots to the wider social stratifications of the proletariat and wage earners, it was immune to neo-caciquism. This all changed when it became the ruling party. For example, the votes of the Spanish Communist Party (PCE, Partido Comunista de España) that were given to the PSOE in radically leftist areas were only partially based on ideology.

> The success of the very dynamic political initiative of the PSOE in the rural centre started with the agrarian reform law ... but that change is also a sign that a new clientship model linked to the control of the funds for rural unemployment is appearing in the agricultural areas ... and other types of social subsidies and public investments, all controlled by agencies under Socialist control [are also appearing] ... [this is particularly true in the small centres, where] it is easier to create a network of favours and personal contacts through the canalization of public resources.[34]

One of the interesting aspects of neo-caciquism is its links with clientship, typical of world-wide political life acted through the individualized political exchange and with a leadership which tends to centralize material and political resources. Personalization of political life is more marked, particularly where party membership is low[35] and therefore the cardinal role of the local elites and the principal charismatic leader are strong. When clientship is systematically integrated with the caciquistic processes, it becomes part of the regulating structures. The strongly institutionalized popular party does not exist in Southern Europe, apart from the communists.[36] Clans, cliques and factions are useful for party in-fighting and to guarantee the *enchufe* (the handle to open the door of favours). This is the rule of social behaviour.

One of the distinguishing features of the left-wing parties is the fact that they do not have only vertical relations with society. They combine the clientship mechanism with a mechanism based on the control of a considerable section of the electorate by a series of horizontal, collective links (trade unions). But this can give rise to contrasts and crises. For example, in the 1989 elections in Spain, the PSOE lost 800,000 votes because its trade union, the General Workers Union (UGT, Union General de Trabajadores) had, for the first time in its history, refused to indicate the PSOE to its members as the party to vote for. It did that because there was a very difficult social situation and disagreements on economic policy.[37]

Which of these two tendencies will prevail in relations with society, the two-sided type or the collective type? The first is instrumental, the second is expressive. And what is the relation between this situation of transition towards a new relationship between parties and society, and the increase of corruption that is affecting Spain, Greece and, above all, Italy? Corruption for personal gain and corruption for the party's gain, breaking laws regulating the financing of political parties, are everyday news. This applies across the entire spectrum of political parties but the main parties and the top party managements are the most involved.[38] That this should place the legitimacy of the parties under discussion is a new phenomenon. Clientship and corruption have always lain together but this had never been denounced before because this combination was based on the strong anthropological links between the individual and the community. Is there perhaps, in the public opinion's repudiation of political parties, an indication of the longing for democracy and participation that recently roused Southern Europe? Or might it be an indication of a battle between power systems and of the disintegration of the systems of political obligations that could have serious consequences both for the clientship democracy and for democracy *tout court*?

Chapter 8

FROM DICTATORSHIP TO DEMOCRACY

I The stability of southern authoritarian regimes

As has already been pointed out, one of the distinguishing characteristics of Southern European countries is the discontinuity of their democracies.[1] Or, rather, that throughout the twentieth century they were subject to dictatorships for much longer periods than the other European countries. These dictatorships or despotisms of modern times were variations on the theme of authoritarianism. They were certainly not examples of 'limited pluralisms'.[2]

The element of violence, of threats and of class dictatorship against the workers was always present in these regimes in one form or another according to the country and the period concerned. These regimes were based on the destruction of political freedom, civil rights and social citizenship. They lasted for a long time mainly because they were able to generate more or less wide degrees of pragmatic acceptance.[3] This was the only social orientation to action that can be conceived on

Table 8.1 Democratic continuity and discontinuity in European countries in the twentieth century

Continuously democratic countries	Not continuously democratic countries
Belgium	Austria (1933–45)
Denmark	Bulgaria (1923–32; 1935–44; 1947–91)
Finland	Czechoslovakia (1939–45; 1948–90)
Luxembourg	France (1940–5)
Norway	West Germany (1933–45)
Holland	East Germany (1933–45; 1946–90)
Great Britain	Greece (1936–46; 1967–74)
Sweden	Italy (1924–43)
Switzerland	Yugoslavia (1929–45; 1945–90)
	Poland (1926–45; 1947–89)
*Ireland	Portugal (1926–74)
*Iceland	Romania (1938–45; 1946–90)
	Spain (1923–30; 1936–76)
	Hungary (1920–45; 1947–89)

Source: M. Cotta.[4]

Notes:
The dates in brackets of the 'Not continuously democratic countries' refer to the periods of dictatorship; in many cases there is more than one interruption and diverse forms of dictatorship.
* Ireland and Iceland became independent during the course of the twentieth century so their category is slightly different.

a mass scale in a context where the impossibility of political pluralism reigns and therefore it is not possible to make choices supported by liberal processes. Unlike the Nazi and Stalin totalitarian regimes, the dictatorships in these countries were limited, as they did not have complete control over social and political movements. This could have been either because of international pressure or disagreements between the upper classes and the rulers of the dictatorship. These disagreements had different effects on the authoritarian political system according to whether they were backed by electoral consensus or not.[5]

In the case of Portugal, the modern authoritarian dictatorship was limited by the sporadic presence of opposition groups which were tolerated by the single-party regime. They could exist without having any effect on the political balances as they were forced to operate within a set-up that guaranteed restricted electoral result by alterations to the electoral lists, fraud and falsification of the results. The opposition never won any seats. The situation in Spain between 1967 and 1971 was different because there were no alternatives, only autonomous candidates of the single party.

An understanding of why there was an electoral process in Portugal is essential to understand, for example, the peculiarities of the authoritarian Portuguese dictatorship. It was extremely weak and did not have the ability to regenerate itself. Therefore it had to find occasions for reinforcing its control over the personalistic governmental machinery.[6] So from time to time it located and isolated any potential opposition, thus guaranteeing the population's continued pragmatic acceptance.[7]

The absence of a dictatorship party with a management role is decisive because it affected all the characteristics of the relation between authoritarian dictatorship and Southern European societies in the years to come. For example, caciquism and authoritarian clientship,[8] in spite of the scarcity of resources, were of central importance during the Portuguese dictatorship, which was very active in ensuring the political apathy of the masses. It did not need to resort to violence as the Spanish and Italian dictatorships did.[9] In these countries the Italian assassination squads and Franco's troops fought against adversaries determined to defend themselves. From this point of view, and only from this, the Portuguese dictatorship is similar to that of Kemal Atatürk in Turkey which was born from government dictatorship rather than from that of the movement or the party.

> Salazar's regime was neither a movement dictatorship like Nazism, nor a party dictatorship like Fascism. It was a government dictatorship. Control over society was not carried out by the party machine but mainly by the centralized administration. Above all by the police, by censorship and by the corporative structures. Bearing in mind the degree to which the personalization of political direction tended to administer government action, one could just as well talk about an administrative or bureaucratic dictatorship. The party was always subordinate to the state without ever being integrated as a constitutional organ. On the contrary, the party was always kept on the fringes of the state and the government, outside the first and in the hands of the second.[10]

Another distinguishing feature of both Franco's and Salazar's dictatorship was their neutrality during the Second World War. Salazar's policy was truly neutral. It was aimed mainly at preserving the colonial empire but he was also interested in reviving the country's ties with Great Britain, while in Spain, Franco's pro-Germany feelings were evident.[11] Salazar was diffident towards the USA as he felt that, with the 'Atlantic Charter, they were attempting to turn the war into an ideological conflict which, if continued, would have led to the domination of an exhausted Europe by the USA.'[12]

The situation changed in North Africa in 1942 and in U.S.S.R. in 1943. Salazar confirmed his outlook but he had to allow the Allies to use the Azores as an air base. Franco signed an economic agreement with the British after demobilizing his Blue Division which had fought alongside the Germans on the Russian front. The neutrality of Spain and Portugal was the basic condition for the survival of the two authoritarian dictatorships. This neutrality was the basis for the 1953 Pact between Spain and the USA which had such an important influence on the start of Spanish economic growth.

Portuguese economic growth was slower and less stable than Spain's. One of the causes of this was the structure of the Portuguese regime. After the coup in 1926, the Portuguese state was stabilized with the 1933 Constitution which laid out the country's normative character with the publication in the same year of the National Labour Statute (ETN, Estatudo do Trabalho Nacional) which was integrated with the corporative legislation. Nevertheless, this legislation always had a fairly limited role with regard to the administration of the state.[13] In 1930, the National Union (UN, União Nacional) was founded in order to fill the space left by the dissolution of parliament. The new-born party had a clearly anti-liberal and anti-democratic programme. Right from the start, it was meant as an alternative to both totalitarianism and trade unionism. It must be remembered that the UN did not have a popular social base as did the fascist parties. It was the economic elites' instrument for upward social mobilization.[14]

After the two uncertain years from 1945 to 1947, and the challenge to the regime both from the fall of the Nazi and Fascist dictatorships and from international anti-Fascism, a new power compromise between those elites was reached. According to the 'typical line of Salazar's policies [the new equilibria] are not determined by a clear economic and political strategic option but by the overriding desire to last. This was done by concessions and adjustments between the various interest groups which did not, however, solve any of the country's pressing problems, but they at least ensured the survival of the regime.'[15] This was obtained by articulating the strongly repressive power held by the war ministry,[16] together with the compromise between the defenders of industrial modernization and the so-called agrarians. This favoured openings to social groups which did not have political consequences and encouraged those autonomous colonial tendencies that did not question the role of metropolitan capitalism.

This equilibrium was maintained without causing contrasts and tensions within the regime, and it was strengthened in the immediate post-war period by the cold war and by the continuous aid given to Salazar by Great Britain. This last fact is given little consideration today but it was constantly brought to light by anti-Fascists[17] because of its international and economic implications. In 1949 Portugal was admitted to Nato, and in 1955 to the United Nations Organization. All this was essential to the regime for overcoming the domestic disagreements that had developed after the Second World War. Until 1949 the actions of the socialist and communist as well as the military and republican opposition could have caused the fall of the regime. However, these anti-Salazar movements did not produce the results hoped for. They lacked an organization and were too weak to participate in the 1949 elections[18] in which the President of the Republic was unanimously returned to power. The cold war had its effect on the opposition too. This split-up following the broad outlines of the ideological conflict that would affect European political life in future years. Excluding the clandestine part played by the Portuguese communists and the military,[19] the regime had not had to worry about the opposition for years. The golden years of anti-Fascist unity after the international victory over the Nazis and the Fascists were followed by the division of the anti-Salazar group and the international strengthening of the regime. Only the Portuguese Communist Party (PCP, Partido Comunista Portugués) continued its reorganization in spite of fairly important internal conflicts. The last years of the 1950s and the beginning of the 1960s were important as the foundation of a resistance movement dominated by military populism was laid during that period, even though new radicalisms appeared in certain ideological areas. But everyone in opposition was obsessed by the idea of insurrection. With the start of the fight for African independence, this idea grew until it gave rise to the military coup of 1974.

These considerations on the Portuguese regime's post-war crisis help to understand the developments and explain its long life. The crises in stability were, in fact, overcome by intensifying not only the repression but also the state's administrative role and by concentrating on fostering the political apathy of the masses. While Franco's regime offered its subjects a dictatorship with economic and social modernization, Salazar's offered dictatorship and economic stagnation. This stagnation was made possible by the political apathy of the people. Not by chance did the opposition of those years have populist characteristics. Even the rural uprisings in the Alentejo region, after fresh outbreaks in 1961–2, started to die down[20] because of emigration and the appearance of capitalist enterprises. A sort of administrative balance was reached based on repression and political apathy which survived until Salazar's death on 27 July 1971. His place was taken by Marcelo Caetano who had, in 1961, resigned as Rector of Lisbon University. This change gave the opposition hope, but Caetano[21] had all the characteristics of a continuer rather than a reformer both in domestic and colonial affairs. The liberal interlude was brief but it allowed the opposition leaders, Mario Soares and Don Antonio Ferreira Gomes, to return from exile in 1968. In 1969 a catholic liberal was chosen to lead the UN party which was then renamed Popular National Action (ANP, Acção National Popular). A protest movement with trade union characteristics was started in the universities which could have laid the foundation for political opposition.[22] A new electoral law was passed. This begs the question whether the 1969 elections were the start of a change. On that occasion, the Democratic Electoral Committee (CDE, Commissão Democratica Eleitoral), a coalition of progressive catholics, socialists and communists, received 10.5 per cent of the votes while the United Democratic Electoral Committee (CEUD, Commissão Eleitoral de Unidade Democratica), representing catholics and socialists from Lisbon, Oporto and Braga, received 1.6 per cent. The remaining 88 per cent went to the regime.[23]

However, it would be unwise to depict the October 1969 elections as a vote of confidence for Caetano's evolution in continuity. Only about 18 per cent of Portugal's 9.5 million people were eligible to vote, and since there was an abstention rate of around 60 per cent, only about 10 per cent of the population went anywhere near the polling booths.[24]

In any case, the regime started to show signs of wear. A liberally orientated group was forming in the National Assembly, and one of the personalities was Francisco Sã Carneiro. A study group on economic and social development called SEDES (Sociedade para o Estudo do Desenvolvimento Económico e Social) had an increasingly important role as it formed an opposition tolerated by the regime.

But the closing-down of the state apparatus was immediate, with the representative of the most reactionary wing of the regime a candidate for re-election as President of the Republic. Many of the liberals were disillusioned, the colonial war worsened and the dissent among the armed forces became more accentuated. Because of all these factors, the regime was finally challenged. However, it continued to rely on the social control of the corporate structures that had been conceived to demobilize and compartmentalize class interests, whatever they were.[25] The rural clientships did not have any political connotations because the almost complete lack of resources made it impossible to continue the exchange system practised under the dictatorship's policies.[26]

The military were the only elite, the only social force, that had avoided being deprived of political cohesion. This was made possible by their internal tradition of republican ideology (renewed by the colonial wars), and by its own nature as upholder of the state but autonomous from the regime. The military disavowed the idea of leaving society and the administrative structures to sink into a state of irreversible apathy which was, unfortunately, an essential political tool of the authoritarian Portuguese regime.

The situation in Franco's Spain was somewhat more complex because of problems concerning the stability of the dictatorship, the role played by the opposition, and therefore the limitations placed by this on the dictatorship. On one side there was the strength and persistence of modern authoritarianism. On the other was the extraordinary role played by society in questioning the unstable dictatorial balance and then building the irreversible democratic process through the practice of citizenship.[27]

> In other words, a guiding assumption of the story is that the achievement and consolidation of democratic arrangements at governmental level are rooted in the democratic maturation of actors within society; and democracy is thus to be defined as the practice of citizenship, or the achievement of an increasingly autonomous control of the political conditions of social life.[28]

And to make the arguments on this reconstruction of the dictatorial structure more explicit, it must be remembered that:

> In reality the Church, rural caciquism, trade unions, some professional associations, capitalism, the intellectuals: in Spain all these were more important than political life and the state, even during the atrocious crisis of the 1930s and the long period of Franco's authoritarian state. The balance of relative weaknesses meant that society was, even then, stronger.[29]

This means looking at the Franchist dictatorship not according to a deterministic and functionalistic model, but on the basis of considerations of the importance of the social and political actions of the dictatorship's actors; whether they were the dominant elites or whether they were those of the opposition in all their social and political articulation. In this way one can withdraw from the debate on the naturalness of Franchism.[30]

Franchism has one basic distinction compared to the other dictatorships. It grew out of a terrifying civil war fought under the eyes of the whole world only fifty years ago. The character of preventative counter-revolution of the nationalist catholic conservative rising is evident and ruthless.

> In the first place the reaction against the deeds of the Popular Front [must be considered]: wages that sink to the February 1936 levels, land given back to its owners (the farm workers living there for a long time who were not suspect could stay as tenants), compensation to those with property damaged by political events . . . the ruling classes – the army, the rich young, Party members, the higher echelons of the Armed Forces . . . dominated.[31]

Class and military reaction is a very strong element in the original form of Franchism. And it shows the continuity of the chronic long-term inability of the civil institutional system to carry out political institutionalization in an autonomous way, depending as it does on the military and their 'diktats'.[32] This gave rise to the political character of the army and its splitting-up according to the different ideologies. This is shown by the expulsion of those who were against the diktats right from the beginning of the civil war.[33]

This gives Franchism a particular character which sets it apart from Nazism and Italian Fascism, which were essentially civilian dictatorships even though they counted on the support of the army. Furthermore, the army was in a secondary and very autonomous position in the ranks of the forces that formed the background of the dictatorship, compared to the party and its troops,[34] whereas during the full flood of the dictatorship, the Spanish army was given the job of maintaining law and order, using all the repressive methods of the state. It carried out this role right up to the last days of the dictatorship.

Dictatorship, as opposed to democracy, does not separate but unites regime and political system, and it can easily upset the political neutrality of the armed forces by subjecting them to a specific form of dictatorial institutionalization by imposing a political nature on them.[35] In any case, the relation between the military and the dictatorship marks the difference between Franco's regime and those of Mussolini, Hitler and Salazar.

The secondary role of the party is the common denominator between the regimes of Franco and Salazar, which is not shared by Fascism or Nazism. In Italian Fascism the dialogue between the state and the party was continuous in spite of vigorous battles[36] while in Franchism the party is absorbed into the state and neutralized by it.[37] In terms of international politics, this signified the acceptance of the new non-Fascist façade of the regime proposed by Franco in 1945. In domestic politics, this also meant favouring compromise between the power groups. It became essential to solve the problem of the monarchy. The war years constituted a very delicate moment for the formation of the regime and for Franco's power. He was constrained between the military monarchists, the catholic right-wing party of Gil Robles, and the socialist opposition with its contacts with Don Juan di Bourbon.[38] The Law of Succession was passed only in 1947, when the country's isolation was decreasing and the Caudillo's power was strengthened. In a referendum held on 6 June 1947, 82 per cent of the voters confirmed the catholic, social condition of the state, in accordance with its traditions, and declared it a kingdom. Franco was the guardian of monarchical continuity. The culminating moment in his guardianship was when, on 22 July 1969, he nominated Don Juan Carlos de Bourbon y Bourbon as his successor and future king.

The 1947 law of succession had a fundamental significance. It made the institutional balance between the corporative principle on one hand and the dictatorial principle on the other fully explicit. The law on the principles of the National Movement of 1958, after Opus Dei had beaten the Falange in the struggle for power, was the formal recognition of it.

The Falangists became civil servants instead of warriors,[39] but that did not mean the dismantling of the dictatorial structure. More specifically, there was no totalitarian party following its own interests: creating political elites, controlling and educating the masses, maintaining the links between state and society.[40] The control and education of the masses was carried out both by vertical structures of the corporative state and by the Roman Catholic church. The political elites already existed and they formed the groups that dealt with the relations with the rest of society. Under totalitarianism this job had been done by the single party and the relations with society were looked after by the bureaucracy,[41] the military[42] and the entrepreneurial groups. This type of organization gradually became one of the features to distinguish Franchism from the other Mediterranean dictatorships.

> The economic backwardness of Spain in the first thirty years of the 1900s, weighed on the characterization of Franchism as a personal dictatorship with a military foundation based on a repressive fascist system, and it gave the dictatorship an archaic orientation. This dictatorship would have had a repressive logic of containment and elimination of all the progressive social and cultural forces. The paradox lies in the fact that, in spite of this, under Franchism there was space for those basic socioeconomic changes that determined the entry of Spain into 'modern times'.[43]

Thus Franchism can be described as a dictatorship of development (an *Enwicklungsdiktatur*).[44] This feature gives the Franchist experience its particular place in European history and it is the main difference between Spain and both Portugal and Italy. Portugal was not able to emerge from economic stagnation. Italy was hit by the 1929 crash and Fascism represented the institutional shell in which economic policies similar to those of the major industrial countries were formed. Franchism represented the dictatorial way to growth, and in following that road it changed its own political appearance, or rather it modified the relations between authoritarian dictatorship and society.

On this point, one could put forward the theory[45] according to which discontinuity of the power system exists. Due to the Plan of Stabilization and the rise of technocrats and Opus Dei to the nerve centres of economic politics in 1957 and

1959, the regime's orientation underwent a change. The purely repressive measures typical of a landowning oligarchy were abandoned, and a new strategy of industrialization was undertaken. It was a revolution from above,[46] a white revolution that was the twentieth century's version of conservative, modernizing changes. The need of mass participation in the market emerged from this process, and also laid the foundations for it. But it was a compliant civic culture[47] not one which could lead to democratic participation. In this sense, Franco's regime was 'the middle class revolution in act'[48] that until then Spain had not had (excluding Catalonia), and it took the form of despotism. But in order to do this the personalistic military dictatorship had to become more articulated in its elites and more linked with society. The period from 1957, with the Plan of Stabilization, to 1976 with the liberal press law was decisive. On one hand, autarchy ended and on the other, freedom of information was allowed, while the university students' movement and the Workers' Commissions (Comisiones Obreras) transformed the Franchist trade unions into fighting tools and the clandestine socialist trade union movement reappeared. It is interesting to note that the two extreme poles in this transformation process were represented by Fraga Iribarne, Falangist Interior Minister, on one hand, and Opus Dei on the other. This process allowed the actuation of the plan of the monarchic succession at the same time as the expulsion of the Bourbon-Parma family from Spain (this was a hard blow for the ever-present and insinuating Carlismo). Franco indicated Juan Carlos de Bourbon as his successor. In 1969 Juan Carlos proclaimed his unconditional allegiance to the institutions of the regime. The role of the catholic modernizers in this matter was well known and extraordinary. They gave the regime that little bit of conservative innovation that was needed. As already pointed out, this had been impossible in Portugal under Caetano. The last single-party government which lasted from 1969 to 1973, with the overwhelming importance of Opus Dei, closed the cycle whose central point was the preferential agreement with the EEC in 1970 and the new trade union law in 1971.

This was the beginning of a feverish political phase in which all and any options seemed open. However, it was an illusion. It was only with Franco's death on 20 November 1975 that the transitional process could start. The split between the subjectivity of society and the institutional structure of the regime becomes dramatically evident. It was the most exasperated and nihilist type of subjectivity. The military wing of the Basque nationalist movement, Euskady or Freedom (ETA, Euskadi ta Askatasuna) unleashed its campaign of terrorism. It was the demonstration of how radical the conflict inside Spain's nationalistic history was, and the despotic Spanish state was not disposed to solve that politically. Nationalistic radicalism exasperates the basic despotism of the regime. There was something miraculous about Spain's transition to democracy. A very fine but solid point of balance was established between terrorism and the possible inflexibility of the military, between the continuity of monarchical institutions and the development of social and political movements.

II Opposition to dictatorship and the roots of democracy

The history of the opposition to the regimes in Spain and Portugal allows us to understand fully not only the true nature of these countries' dictatorships but also the character of the societies that came afterwards.[49]

There is a sort of breach, organizational and not political, between the two cycles in the anti-Franchist struggle. The first is marked by a kind of 'negative integration'[50] exemplified by the guerilla war. The second is a kind of internal erosion of the dictatorial structures by the opposition's use of all the social and political spaces left open.

The epic of guerilla warfare was caused by two very important historical facts. One part of the ex-combatants of the civil war was faced with either Franchist jail or exile. In 1940 8 per cent of the active population was in jail for political reasons. The political and organizational guidelines of the socialist and communist opposition in exile were to continue the armed struggle. The objective was to return to Spain with the support of the Allied forces. This hope filled the years from 1944 to 1946 as a continuous stream of partisans seeped into Spain. Everyone was convinced that the creation of a more or less stable military presence in the peninsula would have encouraged an Allied intervention, thus provoking the fall of Franco. The guerilla warfare was concentrated in the areas where there was a solid socialist, anarchist or communist sub-culture: Asturias, Leon, Extramadura and Catalonia.[51] The defeat of the partisans was due to political changes and to the failure to sustain the international anti-Fascist alliance until Franco's downfall.

One of the most interesting aspects of Spanish political opposition is the reconstruction of parties. This process started in the concentration camps and jails. For the most part, this reconstruction took forms which were independent from the opposition forces exiled abroad. The organizations were created bearing in mind the preservation of the internal values and the dimension of clandestine life.[52] The history of these dynamics allows the understanding of party institutionalization and the re-formulation of the sub-cultures. The reconstruction of these political forces was carried out against a background of repression, arrests, executions and police infiltrations but also through continual liaison with the exiles. It is a political story made of strategies, of alliances and of contrasts. The basic problem was always the relations with the monarchy and, above all, of the united actions with the communists. The communists were the best organized force inside the country and they had the best organization abroad. The socialists could count on help from the international socialist organizations, particularly the German ones, especially during the latter years of the struggle.[53] From 1956 there were great changes in the relations between the political opposition and the dictatorship, together with the last outbursts of guerilla warfare and the labour unrest. The universities had also joined in the struggle. A part of the future management classes and the lower and middle classes began to move away from the politics of the regime. This is shown by the birth of new democratic forces, of religious and pro-European groups.

The university student movement broke the circle that was tightening around the political opposition and the labour movement. It was an exceptional social and political movement of great intensity and length (from 1956 to 1976), and it is incredible that it took place under a dictatorship.[54] The solidarity between the anti-Franchist political objectives and the moral revolt to establish a new model of interpersonal relationships was profound.

The communist student organization played a decisive role. It is not surprising that, as the party dismantled the movement because of continual disagreements, this coincided with the political and organizational decline of the fight. From this point of view, the movement's crisis was one important aspect of the general crisis of Spanish communism.

The paradox of Spanish communism allows us to understand the relation that existed between the opposition under the dictatorship and the relationship linking the political groups of the transition period with those of the democracy. There is a great difference between political action under a dictatorship and political action in a democracy. The typical organizational structure of Leninist communism was, as a form of collective action, the most suited to clandestine struggle, but it was less suited to the democratic movement in the democracy.

This becomes clear from an examination of social conflict and its relation with political action (the same thing can be said of Portugal). The sign of Spanish political change was the transformation of the actors. The main principals in the fight were no longer the farmers and farm labourers as they were before 1936.[55] Now the leading role was played by the industrial workers and students side by side. Workers' protest movements were few until 1961, though there was the General Strike in Barcelona in 1951 when 300,000 workers paralyzed the city. 'The most important motive was the latent anger among the Catalan working class after eleven years of ... oppression and exploitation.'[56] This was the last great battle in that period of autarchy and economic stagnation.[57] Economic growth eventually gave a new shape to the fight of the working classes. These were made up of young people, often migrants, without the responsibility of family ties and without the historical memory – and the paralysis – of the defeat in the civil war. Everything changed with the new trade union law of 1958 and the decree of 1962 which recognized economic strikes. Conflicts were recognized and turned into norms[58] inside the trade union structure that could thus be used outside the control of the regime. The communists adopted this strategy, but not the socialists, according to an international line of conduct that had its roots in the fight against Italian Fascism.[59] These choices became an occasion for the growth of social citizenship in spite of dictatorship – a citizenship which was not stable and not fully realized, which began as social and not as political, but which none the less allowed democratic expectations to grow. In the 1960s this new capacity of the working classes for social action was fully realized.[60] Conflict arose where there was a history of political radicalism, of anarchic leftism both socialist and communist. This intertwining of political and cultural elements, as well as structural ones, can also be found and verified in the content of the workers' fights. The claims for solidarity were numerous and they were linked to wage and legislative claims.

'Among the contemporary European dictatorships, Spain is an exceptional case of political opposition.'[61] Opposition was born not only from the speed of economic change – a necessary but insufficient reason – but also from the persistence of interpersonal networks that allowed the new generations to access the anti-Franchist sub-culture, in spite of the regime's pressure to eliminate the political identity of the family and of the home and work community. An important role was also played by the heroic organizational capacity of the left-wing parties, mainly the socialists and the communists. This does not undervalue the role played by the new forces born during the student and workers' strife, and the transformation of Spanish Roman Catholicism. The clandestinity of the communists and socialists allowed the workers' and students' movements to become strong, to resist repression and to grow.[62] Naturally, the continuity of anti-Franchism was a basic element even though the political novelty given by the opposition is equally undeniable: the Workers' Commissions; a novelty, and therefore a discontinuity, that must not discount the role played by the socialist tradition and by the UGT, as the years of democracy will show. One can say that the strength of the Spanish opposition, apart from the arguments that developed around the actions of the PCE and the PSOE, lay in the unifying effect of clandestine work and the work done by the masses. The student movement is symbolic of this. Its first actions were within the regime's trade union while, at the same time, a new trade union was being created, until the regime's trade union collapsed to the advantage of the alternative institution.

The question of the workers is more complex. The communists and the left-wing catholics chose to act both through the vertical trade unions and through the founding of the Workers' Commissions. The socialists chose to stay underground with the UGT. The first choice exposed the movement to repression, the second exposed it to isolation. But on the other hand, there is no doubt that the consequences of the first choice laid the basis for the transition to democracy within the Franchist state.

> The extension of society was clearly not a political goal in itself, but rather the result of important political gains which were won by the syndical practices of the commissions and in particular, the infiltration of the Syndicate. The gains included the democratic practice and schooling of the workers' assemblies; the vindication of democratic spaces within the institutional apparatus of the authoritarian state; the creation of an effective if not legal tradition of the authoritarian state.[63]

From when the Commissions were started in 1964 in Madrid by the communists, the dissident falangists, the christian democrats and the socialists, to their spread to Barcelona (in a different form)[64] and in other workers' centres, until the fall of the regime, they went through a long, articulated and contradictory political trajectory. A large part of that was influenced by the communist strategy and by the ups and downs of the Communist party. First the transition and then the birth of democracy had various political and trade unionist consequences. One was the vertical fall of the communists from their central position. Another was the gradual emergence of the socialist trade union, the UGT. In the 1980s this beat the Commissions in the trade union elections. The main cause of this change was the formation, in a democratic context, of a new, spontaneous workers' movement which introduced the negotiating rules belonging to a system of industrial relations in which a trade union movement orientated towards making claims like the UGT could operate. The Workers' Commissions always mixed their trade union function with that of a political movement. This was their strength during the dictatorship as well as their historical merit. In a democracy which was trying to create its institutions, that strength and merit became weakness as there was a growing separation between political and trade union action.

The transition from dictatorship to democracy in Spain surprised the anti-Franchists and the political scientists. They had foreseen an 'Italian' future for the political order. That is to say, a system of parties revolving around two main poles: a christian democratic one and a communist one.[65] This should have been the legacy of the Second Republic. The reality was different and the continuity of the sub-cultural traditions was not enough to make the prophecy come true, in the first place, because that continuity was more socialist than communist and the importance of the PCE was a temporary product of the dictatorship, in the second place because during the dictatorship, the nationalist-catholic bloc had split into two wings, progressive and conservative, thanks to the church's indications after the Second Vatican Council.

In the first years after the transition, there was wide political consensus with a low degree of polarization. The sub-cultural segmentation came before the political party structure, and was still able to characterize the wide rifts of the social struggle but not the institutionalization of the parties. The fall of anarchism is an example of this as the vacuum was filled by the leftist socialists. However, the existence of a catholic sub-culture did not give rise to a catholic party. It spawned a non-confessional right-wing party. The part played by the Democratic Central Union (UCD, Unión de Centro Democrático) of Adolfo Suarez was typical of this. In the most difficult phase of the transition, this party absorbed various political forces (christian democrats, liberals, ex-franchists), and by forming a coalition, avoided the fragmentation of the political system. This, apart from the fact that the economic right withdrew their support, caused the end of a party and of its leader. This mix was possible because the memory of the dictatorship acted as a cushion for antagonisms and as a mechanism to reduce the degree of polarization. This applied to the internal relations of the blocs of 'right and left [where] the moderate options achieved dominating positions.'[66] All this came about in the overcoming of religious cleavages and in the broadening of the catch-all role of the parties, though the class divide still remained[67] and the nationalist fracture deepened in some of its specific variations.

There were two reasons why the prophecy mentioned before did not come true. The first was the changes introduced during the dictatorship. The second was the defeat of the left's hypothesis of a republican, democratic split from the elites of the defeated regime. Inevitably, this would have led to polarization and greater inflexibility in the political mechanism. Instead, the process was completely different.

On Franco's death, Juan Carlos became King of Spain on 27 November 1975. He immediately took a position as the hub of a complex system of forces put into action after the death of the Caudillo. In the first place he guaranteed for the military, where he had grown up and been formed. Secondly he followed a cautious democratic policy. But the pressure that rose in the country and in the international arena favoured the formation of a new government to carry through the transition. It was directed by Adolfo Suarez, ex-secretary of the Franchist movement, favoured by Franco, but determined to change the regime together with the king. There was a sort of self-delegitimization of the system: the governing body (Cortes) passed a law on 17 November 1976 that effectively ended its own power. This law created a democratic assembly elected by universal vote. The referendum of 15 December gave full support to this action. Three basic episodes demonstrate the central importance of the monarchy. The head of the armed forces was substituted by a liberal person faithful to the king. The fiscal privileges for Euskady (Basque regions), eliminated by the regime, were re-instated. Adolfo Suarez declared that he was ready to make the Communist party legal and to start talking to the opposition. These acts would have been impossible without the neutralizing of the armed forces which had always been the guardians of the regime and its foundations. These acts also demonstrate the degree of internal exhaustion of the Franchist system.

Above all, this change from above was possible because the left-wing opposition was deeply divided. It was a social and civil giant but politically it was a dwarf. It was incapable of giving an institutional outlet to decades of fighting. In 1974 the PCE founded a democratic junta (Junta Democrática), together with the small Popular Socialist Party (PPS, Partido Popular Socialista) headed by Tierno Galvan, a intellectually charismatic but politically isolated figure. The PSOE founded the Platform of Democratic Convergences (Plataforma de Convergencia Democrática), which attracted some of the christian democrats. The choices were between opposition to the monarchy by following the PSOE's proposed democratic split and the continuation of a policy of wide alliances embracing all those who wanted democracy, including the PCE with their Italian model. This divergence could never be settled but it was solved by the monarchy. With the legalization of the PCE in 1977 and an amnesty for all the so-called crimes of the civil war, a terrible page in Spain's history was closed.

The opposition:

> understands that a new and fragile democracy cannot, without risk, practice a policy of rancor and sanctions against the actors and partisans of the regime that it is replacing. After the King and Adolfo Suarez, the democrats, until then not very pro-Monarchy, discovered that the adversaries of democracy were ready to fight against them with more fury the more the same democrats did not offer their adversaries other than the prospect of legal and moral exile and that, on the contrary, these last will go along with change on condition that the new regime does not exclude them, giving them the prospect of a natural decline rather than the insult of banishment.[68]

With this game of neutralization, guarantees and legitimization, Spain reached its first free elections on 15 June 1977. Adolfo Suarez's party, the UCD, with its collection of elitists, centrist opposition forces and catholic progessivists, did not reach its aim of absolute majority but took 34 per cent of the votes. The PSOE received 29.2 per cent. These two parties were well ahead of the others. The PCE received 9.24 per cent, the right-wing Popular Alliance (AP, Alianza Popular) led by Manuel Fraga Iribarne received 8.3 per cent. The Popular Socialists had 4.4 per cent, the extreme right had 0.9 per cent and the christian democrats received 1.4 per cent. The nationalist parties in Catalonia and Euskady triumphed, but with moderate candidates who were far from extremist positions. The PCE, in spite of its revised Eurocommunism, was the big loser. Its capacity for mediation and political direction did not carry electoral appeal. The Spanish people refused the polarization of politics and they punished both the Communist party and the remains of Franchism. The changing vote, essentially urban, as the UCD and the AP were more rural, rewarded the PSOE and, in its more moderate version, Adolfo Suarez, even though not to the extent foreseen. The government was formed by the UCD and by minority technicians, and it was based on the desire and need for cooperation as imposed by the Pact of Moncloa. In this period, the overall shape of Spanish politics was defined.

The PSOE followed a different strategy to that of the French socialists who were, at that time, fighting for government with the communists. It was also different from the Italian socialists after the fall of Fascism when they were subordinate to the Italian communists. In the 1979 elections the big division between centrists and socialists was reconfirmed, preventing the UCD from getting the absolute majority. They received 48 per cent of the seats with 36 per cent of the votes. The PSOE bettered its position with 35 per cent of the seats and 31 per cent of the votes. The right lost votes and the communists gained. In order to govern, Adolfo Suarez, not without disagreements, had to count on Fraga Iribarne, but the political and social situation was ever more difficult and gloomy. Electoral abstention grew, reaching 32 per cent at the constitutional referendum. In the first five months of 1979, 80 people fell victim to ETA terrorism and other organizations, and the military threatened to intervene. In November 1978 they had attempted a coup but it was promptly overcome.

The UCD started to disintegrate because of internal conflicts and the crisis of its points of reference in society – Adolfo Suarez resigned and in the summer of 1982 he founded a new party: the Democratic and Social Centre, CDS (Centro Democrático y Social). On 23 February 1981 the government that took over from him saw the occupation of the Cortes by the Commander of the Civil Guard, Tejero. This was the visible and spectacular start to another coup which, however, the government and the crown resolutely quelled. New elections had to be called. The PSOE went to the country with a pragmatic manifesto aimed at attracting a wider electorate than that of the traditional left and they aimed at governing alone without alliances either on the left or on the right. It was a triumph. The elections were held on 1 June 1982 and the PSOE received 48.4 per cent of the votes with 58 per cent of the seats. It was a real change in Spanish political life and it marked the completion of the consolidation of democracy. It produced a radical reform of the political system. The UCD, which received 2.9 per cent of the votes giving it only two seats, was replaced by the CDS; AP inherited a part of the UCD electorate and reached 26.4 per cent of the votes with 30 per cent of the seats, another part went to the PSOE which also gained votes from the PCE which fell to 3.9 per cent. The nationalist Catalan party improved its position, as did the Euskady party which had become more intransigent.[69]

This was the end of an era in Spanish politics. The transition was completed thanks to the convergence of the reformist wing of the regime and the opposition. This meant sacrifices by both political forces and they both placed the interests of a democratic nation before those of their parties. The historical intelligence of two men was of prime importance: Adolfo Suarez and Santiago Carrillo, Secretary of the PCE. Did the transition, like the revolution, destroy its sons as it had done in

Portugal? And in Spain: 'The original impurity of the new Spanish democracy underlines the exceptional merits of it creators. . . . It well demonstrates how two men as different as Suarez and Carrillo can join together in the sacrificial choices they made.'[70]

The role played by the military makes the Portuguese situation completely different. The Portuguese army had very deep liberal, republican cultural roots and these were decisive in laying the foundations for the more or less continuous conspiracies against the dictatorship.[71] Leaders like Captain Henrique Galvao and General Humberto Delgado, who was assassinated by the secret police in February 1965, played an extraordinary part. Delgado made the most effective use of the electoral possibilities available under the regime to those who wanted to fight against its repressive actions.[72] In 1958 he ran as president against the official candidate. Bearing in mind the limited freedom under which the election was held, the result was a triumph. He received 236,528 votes against 758,998 and all his meetings turned into a mass protest against the regime. It is not surprising that after these opposition performances, the direct election of the president was abolished. However, on the other hand, the more conservative elements of the Salazar government were also beaten.[73] The development of such a vast and strong military opposition did not mean that there was a continuous, insinuating opposition between the army and civil powers. The army and the secret police were the power base of the dictatorship. It could be inferred that: 'There was not one Portuguese army or armed force but, in fact, many.'[74] There were three main political divisions: the so-called situationists (*situacionistas*), an authoritarian minority who were in favour of the regime and worked to forward its ideals; the so-called oppositionists (*oposicionistas*), an anti-dictatorship minority who wanted an end to the regime but who were, until 1974, constantly defeated; the so-called 'fence sitters' (*barriguistas*), the majority who fitted into the passive and apathetic climate encouraged by the dictatorship.

During the course of the colonial war which started in 1961 the 'totalitarian model'[75] supported by some sections of the armed forces fell into an irreversible crisis. The recruiting of young, anti-fascist students and the social composition of officers coming from urban areas with a large intake from the lower middle classes[76] changed the processes of political socialization which are fundamental in understanding the orientation of the military institution, an organization that can be influenced by the environment.[77] The movement which was in favour of giving independence to the colonies found many supporters within the military establishment. There were many reasons for discontent. One was a decree passed in 1973 that reduced the period of training for officers with combat experience. The career officers found this humiliating. Added to this were the low pay, not very satisfying duties, growing dissatisfaction over the colonial wars, and the increasing corruption among the higher echelons of the army whose privileges were much reduced compared to those of the economic elites. At the same time, they were fighting a war that seemed never-ending, and in any case they realized that it would not end with victory on the battlefield.

The main problem was that no one was able to find a solution to the colonial wars.[78] The federalists, among others, offered some solutions. They hoped for the more dynamic development of an intercontinental state with its own internal resources. The way to increase these was to remove the military expenditure from the homeland budget and debit it to the overseas provinces. In this way, these provinces would become states in their own right. This position, which was supported mainly by the Creole elites of Angola and Mozambique,[79] also had some well known supporters in Caetano's government and in the armed forces like General Kaulzas de Arriaga and General Antonio de Spinola. The former was Commander-in-Chief of the armed forces in Mozambique and the latter was Commander-in-Chief in Angola.[80] General Spinola's book, 'Portugal and the Future',[81] published in 1974 with Caetano's knowledge, explains the positions most clearly and it represents a kind of last desperate attempt to try to maintain control over the colonies without disgracing the military. The proposal was to create a neo-colonialism able to defend itself in the struggle for African liberation.

What should have been a dispute between the regime's managerial groups turned into a coup which gave rise to a real and true revolution from above. A new fact was the formation of the Armed Forces Movement (MFA, Movimento da Forças Armadas) which was made up mainly of young officers involved in the colonial wars and worried about their professional future. It would be well to remember Walter C. Opello Jr's affirmation that 'Pressure for democracy followed the golpe, it did not cause it.'[82] The coup took place on 25 April 1974 and the regime collapsed. A junta (of National Salvation) was formed with General Spinola at its head. His first proclamation left no doubts: a parliamentary republic would be formed and it would confirm its colonial commitments and the international alliances. But all this changed rapidly for two reasons. The coup gave new life to the opposition forces who were determined to play their part in politics. The PCP was without doubt the most organized. It was much stronger than the others particularly in the south. It had a rich heritage of struggles and sacrifices by its members. It followed a linear strategy of guaranteeing the changeover to socialism by using parliamentary democracy tactically without being influenced by it. This gave rise to stable relations with the more radical wing of the MFA, in rapid growth, and to the tactics of infiltrating the state structures from the mass media to the ministries. The communists were strongly supported by a trade union which they had created. They wanted it to be the only union in order to have better control over it. The socialists had a charismatic leader in Mario Soares but their organization was fragile. It had been created abroad shortly before the collapse of the regime with the support of the German social democrats. Mario Soares and his colleagues were opposed to the strategies of the communists and the MFA radicals. The socialist objective was the return of the military to their barracks and the creation of a parliamentary democracy. The socialists always distanced themselves from the communists both in Spain and Portugal but not in Italy. The other political forces were also organized.

The most important were the Popular Democratic Party (PPD, Partido Popular Democratico) which then changed its name to Social Democratic Party (PSD, Partido Social Democrata), dominated by Francisco Sã Carneiro, whose tragic death came at the height of his political career. This party was similar to the party founded by Diego Freitas do Amaral, the Centre Democratic Social Party (PCDS, Partido de Centro Democratico Social) which was inspired by christian humanism and a conservative tradition, though the ideologies and party line were different. There were many new extreme left-wing political formations, and many which fell between the two main parties. But the most important political fact to emerge in the period immediately following the coup was the MFA's move towards the left after the internal victory of the more radical tendencies. These were encouraged by the presence of the communists in the provisional government formed by General Antonio de Spinola. This represents another great difference between Portugal and Spain (and also Greece) but not with Italy. After Spinola's attempts to isolate the communists, the government fell and the proclamation of a state of emergency did not stop the radicalization. During the second provisional government a special military unit was formed, the COPCON (Comando Operacional do Continente). This became the armed sector of what appeared to be a real revolution promoted by the left-wing sections of the military under the influence of the communists and other extreme left-wing groups.

On 27 July 1975 Antonio de Spinola was forced to recognize the independence of the old colonies which had undergone a de facto liberation, except for Timor which fell into the hands of the Indonesian military forces. Spinola's attempt to get support from the country and to proclaim a state of siege failed and he was forced to resign. His place was taken by General Costa Gomez. In November the MFA openly declared its revolutionary objectives and on 6 December the MFA General Assembly and the Supreme Revolutionary Council were formed. These maintained the principle of the singularity of trade union representation, while the nationalizations went ahead.

The excessive power of the military forced the democratic parties to sign the Platform of Constitutional Agreement on 11 April. This acknowledged the MFA as guardians of the revolution. The agreement was the base for the elections which took place on 25 April 1975, and which gave victory to the Socialist Party (PS, Partido Socialista) led by Mario Soares. The resulting government had to write the constitution. However, the situation in the country worsened with attacks on freedom of speech and conflicts between the moderates and the democrats on one hand and the revolutionaries on the other. The MFA started to split up though attempts were made to find points of contact with the PS and to take the movement back to democratic positions. At the same time the COPCON was central to all the actions in support of the occupation of land. The democratic military (often called moderates by many of the authors who have written about this period in Portuguese history) gained more and more importance within the government and the Revolutionary Council. On 25 November 1975 there were violent altercations between COPCON and the communists and the radical wing of the MFA when they attempted a coup. This failed and many left-wing officers were arrested. This was a decisive moment, and the radical tendencies were beaten. In the meantime, the first constitution was passed. It contained the declaration of intent to promote the transition to socialism. This was approved by all the parties except the CDS.

The elections were held on 25 April 1976. They confirmed the decisive role of the Socialist Party which received 35 per cent of the votes (38 per cent in 1975) with 107 representatives. Mario Soares became head of a minority single-party government after refusing the collaboration of the communists and other parties.

His intention was clearly not to allow the centre-right and the right to participate in the job of getting the country back to democratic normality. This strategy was successful when, on 29 June, the army man Ramalho Eanes was elected as President of the Republic with 62 per cent against the extreme left candidate Otelo de Carvalho who received 16 per cent. This was the beginning of the decline of military populism which was now very different from that of the 1960s. Political and governmental instability, party fragmentation and the disorientation of the people who only saw the worst sides of democracy, were threatening the country's stability and the economy. The importance of the military was still considerable as the President of the Republic was one of them and he was responsible for the Armed Forces and the Revolutionary Council. The president nominated the prime minister after consultations with the council of ministers and he could dissolve parliament. From 1976 to 1980, the military presidents took full advantage of their powers in all of the five governments that followed. These demonstrated the weaknesses of a nascent political class. Therefore it can be said that until 1980 the part played by the military was very strong and it placed a strong mortgage on the new democracy. It was only with the elections held on 2 December 1979 that the Portuguese political situation became favourable to the new democratic political forces. The election was won by a coalition, Democratic Alliance (AD, Aliança Democratica), made up of PSD, CDS and PPM (Partido Popular Monárchico – a small right-wing monarchical party) under the leadership of Sã Carneiro. However, he was not able to offer a stable alternative of government, but he firmly fought the power system of Ramalho Eanes and the Revolutionary Council by demanding a new constitution. The subsequent conflict was not solved even with new elections in 1980 when AD remained stable with 47 per cent, the PS received 28 per cent and the Popular Alliance (APV, Aliança Popular), a group around the communists, had 17 per cent. The strength of the military was still such that AD had to put forward General Soares Carneiro as presidential candidate. However, with only 5 per cent of the votes, he was beaten by Ramalho Eanes who received 40 per cent. Nevertheless the strength of the Parliamentary Assembly was now irreversible and the support of the PS led to the revision of the new constitution which was passed in October 1982. It eliminated the Revolutionary Council and replaced it with the Council of State nominated by parliament. Presidential power was limited. So the step was taken to change the system from a semi-presidential one to a parliamentary one where the military had less scope for action. In 1985 Mario Soares as President of the Republic led the way to full consolidation of the democratic system in Portugal and to its rapid stabilization.

This brought a long era of Portuguese history to a close. It had started in 1926 with the military dictatorship leading to Salazar and Caetano. After the apathy and political demobilization brought about by dictatorship, military populism, together with communism, was for many years the essential element of opposition to the regime. The coup in 1974 and the revolution from above that followed it allowed military populism to reach its climax. It had abandoned republican ideology and embraced that of Marx and other revolutionary ideals from the underdeveloped countries. But paradoxically, its climax was also the last act of its development. Its collapse would not come about in a dictatorship, as had happened with the defeat of its heroic exponents in 1974. It would happen in the full flow of Portuguese democracy which, in that rich, historical heterogenesis of aims, those same military had helped to build.[83]

III Disciplined democracy and intermittent dictatorship

Between the First and Second World Wars, Portugal, Italy and Turkey had long and durable dictatorships with unquestionable institutional continuity. In the period after the Second World War both Greece and Turkey went through a different phase. Rather than strong, long dictatorships both of these countries had short, weak democracies. In Greece democracy lasted until half way through the 1970s while in Turkey it continued until the beginning of the 1980s. In the case of Portugal and Spain there was authoritarianism with limited but not totalitarian dictatorships, while in Greece and Turkey there were fragile and incomplete democracies which could not become stable.

Greece, like Spain, was torn by a civil war that shook the foundations of the nation as a society of people. Pluralism turned into schism which turned into armed violence between opposing factions. The original causes of the Greek civil war, which lasted from 1946 to 1949, are to be found deep in the past and these origins must be traced in order to understand the shape of the country's political development. Greek state-building is a paradox. The ethnic, national irredentism obsessed by the idea of reunification (supported by the Greek Orthodox Church), was the ideological link of the elites separated by dispersion and domestic conflicts rather than united by a higher idea of reconciliation. The 'Great Idea of National Unity' (Megalis Idea) was not enough to avoid the constant subordinate position of Greece with regard to the great powers: to Great Britain until 1945 and to the USA until 1974. At that point there was a period characterized by the reinforcing of national autonomy thanks to political integration into the EEC. This state of subordination is at the base of the great schism in Greek political and cultural life that took place between the pro-German groups and the liberals. The schism was then followed by an even more lacerating division when the world split into two opposing power blocs, giving rise to the fight of the Greek Communist Party (KKE) for power against the reactionaries, centrists, the British and the Americans. The civil war followed, and its wounds were cured and its rivers of blood were dried up only after the fall of the military dictatorship.[84] The fact that the dictatorship collapsed made clear, in the times of the dictatorship of the moderns, a long-term tendency in Greek political life. The nation of the 'Great Idea of National Unity' produced a parliament that became independent of the crown in 1875 and in 1864, eleven years before, it gave everyone the vote. It was the only country, apart from Sweden, to admit universal suffrage before having a working parliamentary government.[85] Unlike Sweden, this country reached the middle 1900s without institutions to organize democratic participation. Thus it is not surprising that unstable political power and oligarchic will, supported by clientship, followed. The violation of constitutional rules is normal in Greek history.

The best proof comes from the constitutions themselves. Not one of them came into force according to the pre-established legal order. They were all products – in one way or another – of power in the broadest sense of the term. They all stemmed from revolutions or coups d'etat. . . . At this point, however, one is compelled, I believe, to note a basic difference between past and present as expressed in the 1967 military coup and this is that the government has over-extended its stay in office beyond any precedent.[86]

In any case, the importance of parties in national life became apparent. Not by chance, before the 1967 coup, Georgios Papandreou was busy changing his party into a mass organization that overcame the particular tunnel vision of Greek political life. The left-wing forces had already done this with EDA. This was one of the reasons for the coup.

The crown and the military had, until then, acted with great judgement, affirming their powers of prohibition, thanks to the lack of a strongly institutionalized political society. Their power was based on the arbitrary possibility of solving political controversies that constitutionally should have been in the hands of parliament and therefore in a mass party democracy. The coup was aimed at the continuation of this power.

The basic moment of change in Greek history came in the 1930s. The 1932 elections were won by the right-wing monarchy and the reactionaries, and the two attempted coups of republican inspiration which followed both failed. This allowed the supporters of the monarchy to purge the teaching fraternity, the state administration and the army and to establish the powers of the crown in 1935. A year later General Ioannis Metaxa took power as dictator. He was ideologically a pro-Fascist but without any of the institutional components of Fascism other than the elimination of all civil rights and of the workers' movement which was weak and split-up internally. Metaxa's dictatorship is similar in its structure to the first years of Franchism but it did not have the cultural legitimization of national catholicism or a victory in a civil war.

The war against invaders gave the dictator his legitimization. He drove the Italians from Greece and Albania before dying in 1941. The Nazi occupation in April 1941 deeply marked the future of Greek political life and it opened a new chapter in Greek history.

The king fled first to Crete, then to Cairo and then to London. He took his exiled government made up of Metaxa's followers and old exponents of Greek politics with him. An armed resistance movement against the Nazis and Fascists was formed within the country by the National Liberation Front (EAM, Ethnikon Apelftherotikon Metopon). It was led by the communist KKE though socialists and democrats participated. The armed section of EAM was the National Popular Liberation Army (ELAS, Ethnikos Laikos Apeleftheratikos Stratos), which started its operations in 1942. In spite of the creation of the National and Democratic Union of Greece (EDES, Ethnikos Dimokratikos Ellinikos Syndesmos) which was strong in Epirus and Crete, the fight for freedom was firmly in communist hands. However, they fought against EDES bitterly. This conflict within the militant opposition was unlike the Italian resistance which, though long and bloody, was always united. This difference was very important as it helped to influence the political order after the war.

During the resistance, contact was made between the parties, the exiled government and the crown. The fighters in the homeland controlled a number of rural areas and formed a clear challenge to the exiled government. Georgios Papandreou had the merit of unblocking a difficult situation with the conference held in Lebanon in May 1944 with the presence of EAM, ELAS, KKE and other left-wing groups. From that point, the guerilla war was commanded by a national unit. But, given Churchill's obsession with a possible communist coup, international events complicated things. However, this did not stop the overcoming of internal opposition and the signing of a new agreement of Caserta in September where ELAS and EDES were placed under British orders. Papandreou returned to Greece on October 18 1944 and became the leader of the first united national government. But other events intervened. In December the communists started an armed insurrection in Athens. This led to repression: the premonitory sign of the civil war that followed.

Papandreou, torn between the reaction of the British and the monarchy on one hand and the Stalinist communist revolution on the other, fought to found a parliamentary regime based on social reforms. Papandreou and the KKE became the determining elements of the future history of Greece. The communist insurrection of December was not to gain power but to eliminate Papandreou who was obstinately hostile to increasing their role in government. The KKE gave an extremist interpretation to the concept of left, of the Stalinist politics of the National Fronts. This error was disastrous. The communists underestimated the force of the British intervention and the inflexibility of political positions created by it. The liberal, republican right wing gave its whole-hearted support to the king who was then able to stand as the last bulwark against communism. Thus a vast area of agreement around revanchism and reactionary positions was created. The Varkiza agreements of February 1945, concomitant to those of Yalta, should have marked the end of the armed fight, with the disarming of the partisans and the fixing of rules for democratic participation: amnesty for political crimes; punishment of collaborators in the police and the army; guarantees of political freedom; preparation of a referendum between monarchy and republic; free elections. But these agreements were not respected. Pressure from the right was too strong and the white terror broke out. It was not stopped by the centrist governments that succeeded each other under the pressures of both the liberals and the populist followers of the monarchy. The elections were programmed for March 1946. The communists refused to take part, citing the violence of the atmosphere, thereby leaving the way free for the right-wing groups. These won with 206 seats out of a total of 354. The National Political Union (EPE, Ethniki Politik Enosis) composed mainly of liberals and centrists, won 68 seats overtaking the liberals and the Panhellenic National Party (PEK, Panellinion Ethnikon Komma) which was the successor to EDES.[87]

The Allied mission declared the elections valid even though only 49 per cent of registered electors actually cast their vote. The first desire of the British was to guarantee the country's stability and to avert more violence, as the country had become a strategic point in the Western line-up. But the right-wing offensive towards the left continued, and at the same time there was renewed large-scale communist military activity. Stalin, who had remained benevolently neutral during the events of December, demanded the withdrawal of British troops from Greece at the onset of the cold war. In October 1946 the formation of the Democratic Army of Greece (Dimokratikos Stratos tis Elladas) was openly proclaimed and the KKE committed itself to a long and painful civil war. What had pushed the Greek communists to this point? What were the links between the domestic and international situations? What consequences would the civil war have on the institutional form of the country and its political system? Various factors caused this largely unforeseeable civil war. Papandreou's weaknesses, the right-wing aggressiveness with the return to Athens of the army people most closely linked with Nazism, and the communist impetus after the victories of the resistance were all contributing factors. The Greek political class, made up of centrists and liberals, was unable to impose the Varkiza Pact agreements or to stop the pressure from the monarchy and the right wing. There was the prospect of an urban revolution against the right's white terror. In spite of the close ties between Moscow and the KKE, the aid given by the Soviets to the communist fighters was minimal. Stalin did not add fuel to the civil war nor did the Greek communists act under his orders, as the interests of the USSR came before anything else and that meant not altering international balances essential for the security of the socialist bloc. The decision to break out the offensive was taken autonomously by the leader of the KKE against the advice of a section of the party. However, discipline reigned and they all followed him. Yugoslavia which had been divided from the Soviets well before 1948 and had argued ferociously with them, supported the Greek choice.[88] The Greek civil war marked the complete failure of the politics of the British occupation. Having been incapable of ensuring democratic freedom in the face of the threats from the right, the British were forced to withdraw. They were replaced by the USA which entered the conflict in support of the monarchy. The fact that Greece remained within the Western sphere of influence was due to American intervention and Soviet disengagement. It was not because of Churchill's frenetic anti-communism. If the communists had won Greece would not have remained within the Western sphere. But the communists were beaten and the idealistic splendour of the resistance against Nazi Fascism was also beaten.

The civil war was completely different to the resistance. It was carried out by a party assailed by disagreements and internecine fights, and it was a desperate and tragic affair; desperate because it was doomed to fail from the beginning; tragic not only because of the deaths and the mourning but also because all through it and for many, many years after, the revolution, that blind and terrible goddess, in the hands of Stalinist, Titoist and Albanian civil servants, devoured her children. The role played by Yugoslavia under Tito must not be forgotten. Macedonia had always been a central point in the Communist party's politics. Its independence and the creation of a Balkan federation, comprising Yugoslavia, Bulgaria and Macedonia, was the dream of the parties in that area.[89]

For many years the KKE had supported the idea of a Balkan federation. This was strongly opposed by the majority of the Greek people who did not want to give up southern Macedonia, particularly after the arrival of refugees from Asia Minor who, in 1922, formed an enclave in what had been until then Slav territory. This problem still exists. Tito had always wanted to join Macedonia to Yugoslavia and this created problems for the KKE even during the resistance. He also created a problem for the Italian Communist Party (PCI, Partito Communista Italiano) in the Friuli-Venezia-Giulia area, in Istria and Trieste which he wanted to annex.[90] He also intended to absorb Aegean Macedonia into his sphere of influence. Stalin was opposed to this as he could not approve of any initiatives which might have led to an enlargement of Tito's realm. Stalin proposed Bulgarian and Yugoslav federations but this was opposed by Tito. The KKE was caught in the middle. Yugoslavia was its military and strategic hinterland but the USSR was its political one. The party had to sacrifice its survival in order to maintain the link with the USSR. It supported the partition of Macedonia, and thus gave the right an exceptional propaganda weapon. When the disintegration of the party and military defeat were near, the declaration against Tito of the KKE, obeying the Cominform decree of 1948, marked the end of the guerilla warfare.[91] Defeat was total. Repression was implacable. When the shooting stopped in 1949, the USA insisted on the safeguarding, at least formally, of democratic rules. But the concentration camps and the prisons were filled with ex-combatants.

On 22 October 1951 Greece joined Nato. This marked a definite ratification of the victory of the Western bloc. That victory had repelled the insurrection and the danger of a change in an area which was crucial for the control of the Mediterranean.

In spite of that, the prisons were not emptied and the executions of the communist leaders were events which became an element in the international politics of the cold war. From the shooting of Beloyannis in 1952 and Kiziridisis and Grekos in 1954, to the assassination of the heads of EDA (resurrected in 1951) by the secret police, Saraphis in 1957 and Lanchatis in 1963, and to the 1964 massacre during an ex-partisan ceremony, the legacies of the civil war continued to stain Greek politics. The last big trial against the communists was in 1960 under the government of Konstantine Karamanlis, and it was only in 1964 that Georgios Papandreou, Prime Minster of the Central Union, finally freed 1,100 political prisoners from the civil war. The right put the resistance against Nazi Fascism on a par with the civil war so the partisans were persecuted as fighters in the civil war. The Greeks had to wait until 22 October 1981 when the socialist government led by Andreas Papandreou, four days after their electoral victory, officially recognized the resistance and its role in the life of the Greek nation.

The refugees in the east, including those from the civil war, could at last return home even though all their possessions had been confiscated and Greece had changed so much as a nation that it was no longer recognizable. After thirty years, Greek democracy was restored, overcoming the wounds of the past and laying foundations which would ensure that such a schism could never happen again. No other country saw such a strong and direct conflict between Stalinist communism and Western capitalism.[92]

The political and institutional reality of the country suffered grave consequences as a result of the conflict between Stalinist communism and Western capitalism. In the 1950s and 1960s a very articulated, state-organized form of 'McCarthyism'[93] invaded the whole of national life. The dependent integration of Greece into the US sphere was the most evident aspect of the institutional changes. On the basis of laws from the Metaxa dictatorship, measures were adopted for purging the state administration of communists, ex-combatants and ex-sympathizers of ELAS, thus creating a powerful anti-subversive security apparatus. Everyone who had anything to do with the state, from the public servants to the agricultural workers in cooperative associations, had to take an oath of loyalty. It was not only a method of exclusion but it also served as a means of distributing state resources on the basis of anti-communist loyalty.[94]

For a very long time after the war, the pressure of the people who wanted to obtain a job in the public administration or to receive public aid (in 1951 one third of the population depended on public subsidies) formed the basis for this imposed loyalty of the masses. This explains the spreading of the mechanism. It affected the whole population, and basically it lasted until 1974. Between 1952 and 1967 21,997 Greeks were deprived of their citizenship. The figure speaks for itself. Thus a form of dualism was created between the 1952 constitution, which formally recognized political and civil rights, and a legislative practice that discriminated against the left. Significant events occurred during the 1961 elections. Gerrymandering and fraud were combined with repressive action by the army's anti-guerrilla teams. The extreme right-wing organization, the Holy Bond of Greek Officers (IDEA, Iéros Desmos Ellinon Axiomatikon), founded in 1944, made its influence felt.[95] In 1962 the anti-communist emergency legislation was formally abolished after pressure brought to bear by the EEC, even though the KKE was still outlawed. The Colonels' dictatorship tore that abolition to pieces. The anti-communist mechanism created a vast organization for controlling society which reinforced state bureaucracy and multiplied the vertical dual face-to-face links. It also prompted the institutionalization of political and ideological clientship. However, efforts to remove the left from the political scene failed.

> In fact, remnants of many repressive controls and discrimination against the left strengthened the opposition leftist forces. This legacy contributed to the 1981 electoral victory of PASOK, which had promised the abolition of all political discrimination.[96]

During the civil war, the foundations for a 'disciplined democracy' emerged,[97] for a 'quasi-parliamentary' regime[98] based on a triad: military, crown and parliament, with the first two having the most important role. The basis of the discipline part of the democracy was the concentration of power realized during the civil war when the legislative function was absorbed by the executive and the armed forces no longer recognized the supremacy of civil power, and became autonomous from it. In the mid-1930s the armed forces had definitely become politically minded. They were the guardians of a disciplined and nationalistic 'statocratic society' which fought against a 'corrupt and cowardly' democracy.[99] The crown did not respect the constitution and was forever interfering in the country's politics. These extra-constitutional activities had a disastrous effect on the disciplined democracy. For example, the king caused the resignation of the right-wing Karamanlis government in 1963 because he did not follow the prime minister's advice on some international questions. He did the same for the centrist governments of Georgios

Papandreou in 1964 and 1965. Papandreou did not want royal interference in the nominations for defence ministers and would not accept indications from the crown. The crisis which followed, with governments in power without the support of parliament, led to the military dictatorship.

It was set up by a group of high-level officers from the army and proclaimed without the king's knowledge on 21 April 1967. This was further proof of the political autonomy of the armed forces. King Constantine at first refused to acknowledge the power of those who had carried out the coup and they used repression against all the politicians, particularly those on the left.[100] In December 1967 a new constitution was drawn up and presented to the people for a referendum. The actual voting and the results were beset by electoral fraud and the terrorizing of dissidents. After a period of benevolent abstention, King Constantine, while his ministers were being arrested, decided to organize a counter-coup with a group of faithful officers for 3 December 1967. This failed miserably. The military regime abolished the monarchy at the end of May 1973 with the pretext of having discovered another plot within the navy, traditionally faithful to the crown. A very difficult period followed. One faction of the regime hoped for parliamentary legitimization. It was that led by General Georgios Papadopoulos, who was elected (he was the only candidate) president in 1974 with 78 per cent of the votes. Another faction of the army, with another coup, installed a government with a civilian at its head but the real power was in the hands of the head of the military police who was famous for his brutality and his tortures.

The reasons for the division of the right lay in the conflicts within the regime over the protest meetings which took place in Athens Polytechnic on 17 November 1973. These shook the military's sense of security very badly. The military government intensified the policy of white terror, of discrimination, of control and surveillance of the communists, which had already resulted in the creation of concentration camps with some 2,000 people deported between 1950 and 1962.

Until the return to a free democracy in 1974, the Greek disciplined democracy was not only selective and limited but it was disciplined by the extra-constitutional powers of the army, resulting from the role it had played in the civil war. From 1945 to 1949 the country was in a state of war. From 1967 to 1974 it lived under a full military dictatorship. In the intervening period of eighteen years, the parties were too weak to constitutionalize fully the state and to control the crown and the military, both deeply anti-democratic. The crown did not have an autonomous supporting base. The military was strong and had autonomous resources of powers apart from the unquestionable and continual support given, for strategic reasons, by the USA. The regime collapsed because of internal decomposition. At that point, its reason for existing, and its ability to defend the nation, were questioned. However, the process of disintegration was slow and gradual due to the lack of a far-reaching and widespread opposition like that which developed in Spain.[101]

This interpretative point of view of the Greek institutional situation cannot be understood fully unless one bears in mind the very important fact that the period of transition between the regime of the civil war and the full flood of military dictatorship first saw the triumph of the right and then saw its fall. The years of triumph started in 1947 when the Greek Union, led by General Papagos, gained power by obtaining 49 per cent of the votes and 247 parliamentary seats on a total of 300 in the elections. After the death of Papagos, Konstantine Karamanlis became party leader. The right was in power almost continuously in that period and was also helped by a complicated electoral system[102] combining a proportional system with a simple majority one. This system gave the National Radical Union (ERE, Ethniki Rizospastiki Enosis), founded in the meantime by Karamanlis, a net advantage. In the 1956 elections this party received 47.4 per cent of the votes with 55 per cent of the seats. It must also be considered that the election results were largely manipulated and falsified. The 1958 elections, which 'were in certain respects a landmark in postwar Greece, the intrigue over the electoral law apparently backfired',[103] gave Karamanlis 41 per cent of the votes with 47 per cent of the seats. But it also marked the unexpected growth of EDA, the democratic leftist party. This was the only united front for all the left-wing forces, including the communists who played an important though clandestine part. EDA gained 24 per cent of the votes with 26 per cent of the seats, and the liberals reached 20.7 per cent with 12 per cent of the seats, having been penalized by the electorate for their ineffective opposition and their alliance with the right. These results showed the deep-rooted tendencies towards democracy and towards communism in spite of repression and clientship. The 1964 elections were won by Georgios Papandreou who presented a programme of reform and liberalization of public life. His party, the Centre Union (EK, Enosis Kentron) won 52.7 per cent of the votes and 57 per cent of the seats. The ERE received 35.2 per cent of the votes and 35.7 per cent of the seats. EDA had 11.8 per cent of the votes and 7.3 per cent of the seats. Thus the centre had the numbers to govern the country but plotting in the Royal Palace made the task impossible. Even the growing rumours about Papandreou's son Andreas, accused of being the leader of a Nasser-style conspiracy in the army, were used. This marked the breaking point in the relations between the king and the army on one hand and Papandreou on the other.

The resignation of the former prime minister was followed by large mass protest meetings which showed that something important had happened within Greece. It was throwing off its apathy and its immobility and it was no longer afraid.[104] The fight against the right worsened as the king nominated a government without parliamentary approval and the elections planned for 28 May did not take place. On 21 April 1967 a coup abolished the parties and democratic freedom, firmly establishing a military dictatorship. International support for the coup was not lacking.

> However, indirectly displaying displeasure with Papandreou and choosing to remain silent during the machinations that followed the November 1963 elections, the United States and Nato gave the Greek military their implicit approval to start a military dictatorship. The United States acted ambivalently, but not negatively to the news of the uprising.[105]

Proof of this ambivalence came in 1970 when the USA removed the arms embargo it had placed against the Junta and renewed its diplomatic relations with it.

A final matter needs to be underlined. The fall of the Greek military regime as a continuous dictatorship was not the result of growing opposition, as has been claimed by others, or of strong international pressure. It was caused by internal disintegration after the loss of honour following the military defeat by Turkey which had invaded and occupied half of the island of Cyprus.

The Republic of Cyprus was born in 1960. For many years it had been under British domination, as the island was an important military post. The new nation under the guidance of Archbishop Makarios followed a policy of non-alignment and therefore ceased to be part of Nato.

The British idea of divide and rule had favoured the growth of the Cypriot Turkish population, though Greece had always considered this island as a part of their nation. It was a part of the *Megalis* Idea, of *Enosis* (Union) which was expressed by all political groups. With the growth of the Turkish community, the *Enosis* principle objectively called for the partition of the island between the two ethnic communities. This had been proposed in the Acheson Plan in 1964 but had been rejected by Papandreou.

> Thus in Greece the political power structure which had benefitted both the domestic elite and the foreign patron had ceased to function satisfactorily at either an internal or external level. The military coup of April 21 1967 can be seen as an attempt to continue this partnership which had formed the basis of postwar political systems.[106]

But the Cyprus question, with the presence of a civil and democratic government in a land that was traditionally Greek, was in itself a challenge for the Colonels. A constant and secret war was waged against Makarios by the military Junta who invoked *Enosis* and the end of the civil government. Armed groups spread terror and put pressure on the democratic authorities.[107] In this context, the tensions between Greece and Turkey increased, particularly after the disputes that arose in 1973 over territorial limits after the discovery of oil deposits in the Aegean Sea.

It should not be forgotten that the Cypriot question acted as a catalyst in the historical conflict between Greece and Turkey. The Greek military were divided between loyalty to Nato, which carried with it the duty to solve any conflicts with other members of the alliance, and the traditional anti-Turkish bias. The Turkish invasion of Cyprus took place on 20 July 1974. The reason given for this was to stop the Greek right from taking over the island after it had attempted a coup against Makarios. The Junta of the Colonels was incapable of organizing any military action on a large scale or of defending areas traditionally governed by the Greeks.

The USA and Nato waited passively. Previously, in 1973, when the Junta had refused to allow the USA to use their bases during the Arab–Israel war, the USA had expressed its uneasiness about the populism of the military. They felt that this orientation could lead to a policy of not respecting alliances. The USA and its Allies did not warn the Junta about the Turkish military preparations. Henry Kissinger used the wide discretionary powers given to him by the Watergate scandal and many of the decisions he took reflected his own personal feelings.[108] Perhaps the security of the southern flank of Nato was best served by a Turkish coup? Would it weaken the military Junta, which by this time had become a danger for the stability of the Mediterranean? This hypothesis seems well founded but it cannot yet be proved.

In any case, the attitude of Greece towards the USA changed radically. A group of military people and politicians (brought into things by the military to organize the transition) decided to offer the government to Konstantine Karamanlis. On 14 August, just one week after his return to power, the old leader took Greece out of Nato. This event ended a long history of subordination and inaugurated a new era in the relations between Greece and the USA. On 24 September he legalized the KKE and paved the way for the pacification of the country. Everything was really changing. The rejoining of Nato in 1980 and the signing of agreements on the US bases in 1983 and 1990 assumed a very different significance to similar acts which had happened before. These agreements had grown from the need to reply to Turkish threats and to counterbalance their presence in Nato as well as from the general international situation.[109] Nevertheless Greece was much less markedly dependent on the USA than before.

Defeat and national humiliation were the most effective incentives to making the armed forces return to their professional role, thereby allowing them to accept the political supremacy of a democratic civilian government. Konstantine Karamanlis returned to Greece after the fall of the military Junta and the committee of civilians and military formed in 1974 decided to entrust him with the task of forming a government capable of guiding the country back to a fully democratic state. The government thus formed had all the characteristics of a pre-dictatorial Greek political system: a high degree of personalization; low, almost non-existent, party institutionalization; an important role played by charisma and traditional power. However, this centre-right government broke with the violently anti-communist right of the past, though it maintained – for a sort of *gratis militarum*[110] – General Phaedon Gezekis as President of the Republic. So there was a gradual transition, aimed above all at preparing the elections of 17 November 1974 without provoking reactions from the military. The anti-communist excluding legislation introduced during the civil war and placing the domination of military power over the political power was abolished. The end of the monarchy, decided by 70 per cent of the people in a referendum, was an important moment in this strategy. The military and the extreme right were disorientated and on the defensive after the defeat over Cyprus. Karamanlis aimed at modernizing the right. This was proved by the foundation of the New Democracy party (ND, Nea Dimokratia), a liberal central-right formation similar to the European conservative parties.

The young technocrats, the new middle-class professionals, the pro-European upper classes: these people formed the base of the ND, which was determined to join the EEC and distance itself from the old right. The idea of creating a modern mass party, not dictated by society, seemed possible while Karamanlis governed the party in 1981. But when the ex-minister for foreign affairs, Georgios Rallis, became prime minister, the party went back to the old habits of clientship and fractionism, showing, in a process of rationalization, the importance of a strong charismatic leader.[111] However, the political system was changing. The most evident sign of this change was the formation of a new political force indubitably set on introducing interesting novelties but still closely descended from the old kinship system. This was the Panhellenic Socialist Movement – PASOK – led by Andreas Papandreou, back from exile in Europe and Canada where he had directed the Movement for Panhellenic Liberation (PAK, Panellinio Kinima) against the

150

dictatorship. The basic watchword '*Allaghi*', meaning change, expressed the genesis of a new political culture very well. Even at the beginning of the 1960s, pressures against the discriminating anti-communist measures and the repressive and vertical inclusive state clientship had been felt and the centre had benefited from it in terms of consensus. PASOK represented the return of this renovating pressure. It was presented as the successor to all the non-communist left-wing and centre-left organizations which had been secretly formed in opposition to the Junta.[112]

The party organization reflected the general need for change, a novelty in Greek history. It had a strong organizational structure, considerable centralization, a wide network of local sections and a powerful ideological message aimed at forming a collective identity which would eliminate the logic of short-term interests. The ideology was that of left-wing extremist populism: biting criticism against monopolistic and oligopolistic capitalism which had reduced Greece to a dependent role; the need for an international policy of peace and non-alignment, and of alliances with both the Warsaw Pact and the Third World countries; development of a welfare system with regular, well planned state intervention; administrative decentralization. The birth and growth of PASOK had immediate effect. The first was the acceleration of the communist crisis. The left-wing groups forming EDA had been the only movement to oppose the anti-communist legislation and they now had to operate in a democratic situation. This proved impossible because the communists were divided by the internal disagreements between the internal and external members, between the pro-USSR members and the 'Italian' ones who wanted autonomy from the Soviets.[113] When Konstantine Karamanlis was nominated President of the Republic in 1980, six years had passed since the fall of the military Junta. Everything pointed to the consolidation of democracy through the strength of the central-right party with a relative, though not dominant, majority with a marked polarized pluralism involving parties with very different ideologies. Even the constitution reflected this polarization at the moment of its elaboration. In 1975 the opposition abandoned the Chamber of Deputies and refused to take further part in the writing of the document.

The presidential regime foreseen by the constitution was meant to give Greece a middle ground stability, the same as that which had been interrupted by the dictatorship. The events that followed put paid to that idea.[114] This will be explained in a later section.

The vicissitudes of Turkish democracy are extremely complex and, as in Greece, have the military at their centre. However, their role was different to that of the Greek military. Perhaps the most important cultural and institutional difference between Turkey and the West and East is the effects of the cleavage between centre and periphery. In its whole post-Ottoman history it is closely connected to a plan of secularization imposed on society from above by a modernizing elite which was culturally hostile to the past and inclined to up-root the wide-spread religious beliefs. In this sense, right from its origins, to use the words of the most penetrating scholar of these problems, Kemal Karpat, 'The modern Turkish political system is the product of the interaction between a continuously changing socio-economic structure and static constitutional models borrowed from outside.'[115]

151

The 'revolution in 1908 of the Young Turks marked the entrance on the scene of an elitist group, new to political decision making.'[116] Unlike the revolutionary elites of the Soviet type who followed a totalitarian plan, the Turks founded the premises for the transformation of the governing elites towards a parliamentary system, thereby ensuring the change from the Kemal dictatorship, which had been formed between the two world wars and was of military origin, to a pluralist democracy.[117] The army had played, for forty years, a decisive role in this nascent democracy. 'The relative weakness of the coercive element in the institutionalization of this regime explains how the relatively peaceful transition from the initial autocratic to the later democratic regime was possible.'[118] In fact, it must not be forgotten that the democratic choice had been conscientiously followed by Kemal Atatürk's elite in the 1930s. It was then realized in 1946 when a new political formation, the Democrat Party (DP, Demokratik Parti) was born. It was an off-shoot of the republic's institutional party, the Republican Peoples' Party (CHP, Cumhuriyet Halk Partisi).

The ideology of the Turkish military dictatorship as laid down by Kemal Atatürk was based on modernizing nationalism with strong references to Western values.[119] These values were nationalism, social reform, constitutionalism and the role of parliament. All this was combined with a certain degree of state intervention. The state did not divorce itself from society but dominated it in order to ensure its growth, according to an original and specific 'transcendentalism'.[120] The military were the backbone of this statalist foundation of politics. Because of this, the army did not opt for a continuous dictatorship as in Greece, nor did it adopt the repressive military type leading to a development dictatorship as in Spain. After their interventions, the military always handed control back to a 'tutelary' democracy[121] in an attempt to give stability to a not very institutionalized pluralistic system. In any case, this type of democracy was so much more advanced than the other Middle Eastern political systems that it could be compared favourably to European ones. And it cannot be said that very strong international pressures were brought to bear on the country. They were certainly no stronger than those aimed at Portugal or Spain.

The Turkish military had always been divided into two factions. On one hand were those who would have remained in power until a state of continuous dictatorship was reached (which would have eliminated the need for a tutelary democracy). On the other hand were those who interpreted the power of intervention as an extension of a political but not constitutional neutrality, following the rulings of Kemal Atatürk.[122] The second group always won: in 1960, 1970 and 1980. However, because of the links between the army and the modernizing elites, this tutelary system could not avoid coming into conflict with the new political class which had been formed after the post-war period. In particular, there was conflict with the Democratic Party (DP). In 1960 this changed its name to the Justice Party (AP, Adalet Partisi) which changed name again in 1980 to become the True Path Party (DYP, Dõgru Yol Partisi).

The conflict between the tutelary system and the DP had profound effects on the state apparatus. For example, the coalition government which took power in 1973 undertook 'a reshuffling of the civil servants'[123] which was unprecedented in the republic's history. Because of this action, it was identified as the government marking the beginning of the end of the legal, administrative rationality of a bureaucracy which, though it was negatively oriented towards parliament (seen as hostile), had not yet been balkanized by the political parties.

The change in the CHP in the period from the mid-1960s to the end of the 1970s, under the leftist leadership of Bülent Ecevit, marked the end of the tight links between the military and the parties which followed the ideals of Kemal Atatürk. Another crossroads was the decision of both Süleyman Demirel (DP) and Bülent Ecevit (CHP) to block the election of the army candidate to the presidency of the republic, thus underlining, in 1973, the primacy of the civil authorities over the military ones.[124] However, a problem was starting to emerge due to the collapse of authority and the fragmentation not only of the parties but also of the state. In this context 'only one element of the earlier bureaucratic centre, the military, kept its autonomy and sovereignty in the policy.'[125] In order to understand the role played by the army, a comparison[126] can be made with the 'Roman' pattern of dictatorship, which was temporary and aimed only at restoring democracy. However, the role of the army gradually underwent a great change from a marked transcendentalism to a moderate political orientation to material benefit.[127] That is to say, its role was seen as having a more direct and precise intervention in the constitutional order wished for by the military, in order to exercise a stricter influence on the political structures. This was different to the events of 1962 when the new constitution was written by civilians. According to Karpat, the long cycle which had started in the 1950s, finished in this way in 1983.

> The present political system in Turkey appears to conform to the Turkish traditions regarding power and authority and to represent the synthesis of various socio-economic forces, and, thus, it enjoys overwhelming popular support. For the first time in its history, Turkey appears to be on the verge of taking upon itself the true essence of democracy. The distribution of power between state (President) and government (Premier) can assure the co-existence of modernism and 'traditionalism' and guarantee the maintenance of order and security.[128]

Until 1983, the visible hand of the military represented the only means for guaranteeing political stability, as the situation of pluralism without institutionalization could not lead to the automatic rebirth of democracy. In the two decades from the beginning of the 1980s to the end of the 1990s, a new era started for Turkish democracy, an era without military guardianship. At that point in time, much depended on the sort of fractures which would materialize, together with the original ones, between the expansion of political participation and the forces of the democratic institutions on one hand, and the precepts of state and nation on the other. An example of this was the conflict with the Kurds. The first of the fractures caused the coup of 1960. The DP was the leader of an alternative social bloc to that which followed the teachings of Kemal Atatürk. It was formed by entrepreneurs, merchants and the rich and middle-class farmers who had been threatened by the agrarian reforms of the CHP in the post-war period when the social changes that would form the basis for the modern Turkish political system first started. A new class of leadership characterized by marked 'achievement orientation' accessed politics.[129] This phenomenon occurred particularly in the cities and in the lower, urbanized social levels.[130] For the first time in the republic's history, with the electoral victory of the DP in 1950, power was given to a party with a very different social base and political orientation to that of Kemal Atatürk. The ideology of the new party acknowledged the idea of market freedom, respect for the Islamic traditions without abandoning the secularism of the state, the necessity of emphasizing the importance of society and its autonomy from the state. This reflected the changes taking place in the country. Three consecutive elections in 1950, 1954 and 1957, gave the DP 408, 503 and 424 seats respectively while the CHP won 69, 31 and 178.[131] Therefore a political and social alternative to the old historical bloc entered politics, taking the place of the professionals, bureaucrats and intellectuals who had governed the political future of Turkey up until the beginning of the 1950s.

Conflict between social groups started to emerge,[132] and entrepreneurial delegations and workers' trade union groups were being formed. It was the beginning of a turbulent phase of political life, with the army standing as the guardian of the institutional revolutionary tradition.

Samuel Huntington[133] maintains that, in a 'Pretorian' society like Turkey, where political participation had already reached the middle classes, the military wanted to exclude from power those social classes which, in a context of civil and political institutional weakness, could have introduced basic changes to the Atatürk institutional order. This could be defined as a coup of prevention as opposed to a coup of attainment. However, in contrast to that theory, the army did not oppose political participation but it made it more rigid. General Cemal Gürsel, leader of the Committee of National Unity (MBK, Milli Birlik Komitesi), though he was responsible for the hanging of the leader of DP and two ministers and had for a time suspended civil rights, practised moderation and compromise (unlike, for example, what happened in the Argentine between Perónists and the military).

In 1965, the Justice Party (AD – ex-DP) led by Süleyman Demirel, its new head, attained power with the alternative social bloc mentioned before. The military, which had previously opposed the bloc, now bowed to popular opinion. In order to evaluate the shape of Turkish domination, it is important to remember that the military were driven by particular corporative needs as well as by the principles of Kemal Atatürk. They wanted their corporative needs to be satisfied in a general process of social mobilization, a process that was caused by, among other things, a clear situation of 'relative hardship'.[134]

> The newly rich politicians, landlords and entrepreneurs placed emphasis on wealth, luxury and material pursuits, all of which contrasted sharply with the ascetic idealism preached in the army. The social standing of the military deteriorated, while the value cherished in the past disintegrated under the assault of the materialism supposedly promoted by the new power groups.[135]

The creation of a secret society with the emblematic name of Society for the Restoration of Respect (IIC, Iade i Itibar Cemiyeti) clearly explains the ideas behind the actions of the military. They wanted to go back to being respected as guardians of republican dignity. They wanted respect for Kemal Atatürk's populist principles based on social justice. They wanted respect for the secularism of the state which was menaced by the ferment of religious activity after the re-opening of the Quranic schools by the DP. The military considered religion to be a natural expression of the Anatolian farmers, but it had to be kept within the limits laid down by Atatürk, and should not in any way have political significance. The military were in favour of a socialist reform of the economy, and they supported economic planning. The constitution, passed immediately after a group of civilians ideologically near to the CHP took power, was the institutional result of the 1960 revolution. The fundamental principles of the constitution were: controls over the executive, full legislative powers, judicial autonomy, a secular state and the rebirth of populism, statalism and reformism, the fight for democracy, a welfare system and an electoral system based on proportional representation. However, this constitution had the effect of paralyzing the fledgling, unstable democracy.[136] The 1960 revolution destroyed the old conception of power and authority, and it became clear that the old elites could not continue to hold power in a statocratic manner. A strong society had to be created but many obstacles had to be overcome. The first of these was the strong competition between the political parties.

In the 1960s, many new political groups appeared. The oldest was the Nation Party (MP, Millet Partisi) which was formed in 1948 by a splinter group from the DP. However, the MP changed its name a number of times. From MP it became the Republican National Party (CMP, Cumhuriyetçi Millet Partisi), then it changed to the Republican Peasant's Party (CKMP, Cumhuriyetçi Koylu Millet Partisi). Its members were from the conservative and traditionalist section of the old MP. In 1965 a new, extreme right-wing leader, Colonel Asparslan Türkes, took over the party which was by that time divided into various factions. He changed the party's name to the Nationalist Action Party (MHP, Milliyetçi Hareket Partisi), and he also changed its characteristics. It had a hierarchical structure and a para-military group of young people. The MHP was nationalist, anti-communist and statalist, and it was an unmistakable sign of the growing polarization of the political system. Its electoral results were weak. In the 1965 elections it received 6.3 per cent of the votes and in 1969 it received 3.2 per cent.

In May 1967 the Reliance Party (GP, Güven Partisi) was founded. This party was the result of a split in the CHP as the new CHP leader was accused of moving towards socialism. This is another symptom of the polarization of the political system, and the growing distance between the ideologies of the various parties.

The appearance of other parties in this decade shows how the problem of class cleavage had been added to that of centre versus periphery. The Workers' Party of Turkey (TIP, Türkiye Isçi Partisi) was founded in 1961 by a group of trade unionists. In 1962 Mehmet Ali Aybar, a very capable person, took over the party leadership. This party was basically Marxist, characterized by the internal divisions typical of extreme left-wing parties of the time and it had limited appeal for the electorate. In the 1965 election it received 2.2 per cent of the votes, and in 1969 it received 3 per cent. It was dissolved in 1973.

The Unity Party of Turkey (TBP, Türkiye Birlik Partisi) was founded in 1966. Its origins were in the Shi'a minority. Politically it was distinctly social democratic, and to left of the CHP. Like the other parties already mentioned, this party too had a small electoral following. In 1969 it received 2.8 per cent of the votes, and in 1973 it received only 1.1 per cent.

155

In 1970 the National Salvation Party (MSP, Milli Selamet Partisi) appeared. This was a religious party which received 11.9 per cent of the votes in the 1973 election, but it was outlawed in 1979. The birth of this party showed that the process of secularization, started so long ago by Kemal Atatürk, had failed. It was also a victory of tradition over modernization. The ideological principles of the MSP were the defence of Islamic morals, culture and values. Its following was made up of merchants, artisans and small Anatolian businessmen.

The general change in society was also felt by the two most important parties, the Justice Party – AP – and the CHP. Süleyman Demirel, the new leader of the AP and a man destined to play an important part in Turkish politics, was unable to avoid the breakaway of the party's right wing. However, the electoral results were good. In 1961 the party received 34.8 per cent of the votes, in 1964 it was 52.9 per cent and in 1969 it was 46.5 per cent.

The CHP also had a new leader in Bülent Ecevit. He moved the party to the left in 1967. This move marked a new phase in Turkish political life. In 1961 the party received 36.7 per cent of the votes, in 1962 this percentage increased to 28.7 per cent and in 1969 to 24.7 per cent.

The spread of Marxism in the universities and the foundation of the Confederation of Revolutionary Workers' Union (DISK, Türkiye Devrimci Isçi Sendikalari Konfederasyonu), which was the result of a break within the pro-government Türk-Is (Türkiye Isçi Sendikalari Konfederasyonu) trade union, were indicative of the general change in the political climate of the country. Before 1960 the trade unions were controlled from above by the government and were detached from political battles. The new constitution legalized contracts, collective negotiations and strikes. This allowed the rapid expansion of the trade unions. In 1967 these were already representing 14 per cent of the non-agricultural labour force and 14 per cent of the industrial labour force.[137] The country's shift towards the left was marked by the breaking-up of the main parties, the CHP's slow, relentless change into a social-populist party and, above all, the organization of the radical right by the military. The birth of terrorism gave rise to the rapid spread of violence.

The time was ripe for another military intervention. On 12 March 1971 the High Command of the armed forces sent a note to the President of the Republic which contained a request to end the anarchy and the civil strife, and to approve certain incisive reforms under parliamentary consideration. It also underlined the duty and right of the army to protect the Turkish republic. A series of technical governments were in power from March 1971 to April 1973. The left and extreme left-wing organizations were subject to repression, and the armed forces were riddled with internecine fights. In the meantime, there were outbursts of guerilla warfare and martial law was declared in 11 out of 64 provinces. Professional associations, left-wing organizations and trade unions were declared illegal. Arrests were made. In 1974 some 4,000 people were awaiting trial. The right was free to act and was condemned by the Council of Europe for its use of repression and torture. Amendments restricting civil and political rights were made to the constitution.[138]

The pressure of international public opinion forced the armed forces back into their barracks. There was a growing awareness that only civilians could solve the political problems of the country, including those concerning state intervention in the economy which had been proposed by the military.

In 1973, civilian government was returned to power with the electoral victory of the CHP with 33.3 per cent of the votes. The DP received 29.8 per cent. The National Salvation Party (MSP), led by Necmettin Erbakan whose electoral campaign was based on direct propaganda and the use of traditional Islamic symbolism to increase the party's influence, won 18 per cent of the votes. In 1974 Erbakan and Bülent Ecevit held the balance of power for the formation of a coalition government which, according to Ecevit, had to follow leftist policies in order to solve the country's problems.

The country had changed a great deal. The problems of political participation in an extremely unbalanced and disconnected society had become a vital question of political stability. In contradiction to the old theories on modernization, the less developed regions were those with the lowest proportion of electoral abstention thanks to the importance of deference systems and clientship networks. In these regions the significant development of the left was accompanied by a wide fragmentation of the right. The party system was thus continually re-aligned and the parties increased their electorate according to well marked territorial divisions.[139]

The CHP's policies differed increasingly from those Atatürkian principles which formed the basis for Turkish national identity. It became a mass socialist party. There were people who opposed this trend but they were unable to act effectively. This last fact should be underlined as it eventually led to the breakaway of the armed forces from the CHP. This had grave consequences on the political system.

As in the 1960s, radicalization and polarization increased. The extreme right grew rapidly. The MHP was strongly nationalist and had an aggressive attitude towards Iraq and Greece for their treatment of the resident Turkish minorities. This party's popularity increased after the military intervention ordered by Bülent Ecevit in July 1974 following the coup in Cyprus. The extreme right started to woo the fundamental Islamic sector of the population in order to increase its electoral strength. This meant supplanting the MSP which was part of Ecevit's coalition. In any case, Ecevit was having problems in remaining in power, and a difficult period of instability followed.

The problem of the lack of political institutionalization was made worse by the CHP's and AP's sectorial and feudal use of the bureaucratic and judiciary administrations. This aggravated the fragmentation and the balkanization of the state.

Süleyman Demirel formed another national front which was made up of MHP, MSP and some other small groups. Because of the importance of the ministries held by the MSP in this period, links were formed between the extreme right and certain sections of the state which then produced disastrous effects on the democratic balance. Terrorism, both from the extreme right and the extreme left, with its political assassinations and street-to-street violence, increased the degeneration and polarization of the political system. The 1977 elections, while confirming the existence of two political poles, did not produce a clear majority. The CHP received 41.4 per cent of the votes giving it 213 seats. The AP received 36.9 per cent of the votes with 189 seats. The two together had 78 per cent and could have formed a coalition government with the aim of restoring law and order and of carrying out a stabilizing economic policy. The main organizations of society, and particularly the entrepreneurial forces, hoped for that solution but the radicalization of the CHP and the AP's fears that such a coalition would strengthen the extreme right meant that all attempts at a compromise were blocked.

Süleyman Demirel formed a right-wing coalition, but the government lasted only six months because of opposition within his own party. Bülent Ecevit returned to power and tried to follow an economic policy of nationalization. At this point the second energy crisis struck and schools and public buildings had to be closed.

After 1974, the USA placed an arms embargo on Turkey. This caused an explosion of anti-imperialist feelings against the USA.

Ecevit resigned after the 1979 senate elections which had shown the weakness of his electoral following. Demirel returned to power. He refused an agreement with the right, and formed a minority government with the support of a small group of independents and some of the military. By December 1979 these military had already threatened to enact a coup if things did not go the way they wanted. The country was on the brink of economic ruin. The minority government decided to actuate a radical policy of privatization and of monetary stabilization.

The Confederation of Revolutionary Workers' Unions (DISK) proclaimed its complete opposition to Süleyman Demirel's fascist regime. Terrorism increased and the martial law proclaimed by the government did not help in enforcing order. The military feared an alliance between the CHP and the MSP, a mix of socialism and Islam which would have meant the end of the Turkish republic and the overthrowing of international alliances.

The 1980 military intervention was quite different to previous ones. This time the military were the ones to establish the details of constitutional principles. They decided the separate roles to be played by the state and by the government. They decided the measures to be taken to return power to the civilians. Another difference from the past was that the military were becoming an entrepreneurial group and so they had an interest in economic privatization and market development. 'The most significant aspect of the take-over was the lack of identification with any specific civilian or bureaucratic group.'[140] The aim of the military was to maintain the status quo as a military unit and to have complete autonomy from the pressures of civilian society. Political society, as an expression of civilian society, had to face the threats imposed to the still weak democracy which, for the first time, was without military guidance.

IV Early transition to democracy and its atypical consolidation

Late transition to democracy and its difficult institutional consolidation are both characteristics of all the countries of Southern Europe. The continuous dictatorships of Spain and Portugal and the intermittent and cyclic dictatorships of Greece and Turkey all reflect the shape of their political societies. However, all these societies have achieved a modern democratic state.

Italy, after twenty years of Fascist dictatorship, moved to democratic consolidation very quickly. The Southern European characteristic of having a political culture based on clientship and kinship are clearly part of Italian culture but the time factor must be taken into consideration in order fully to understand the differences in historical processes which at first appear structurally similar.

Both international and domestic processes influenced Italy's move to democracy.[141] The great powers, the USA, the USSR and the UK, all played a decisive part in influencing Italy once Germany was defeated. Fascism collapsed because of the initiatives taken by that part of the regime close to the king and the industrial middle class. On 8 September 1943 Italy, realizing that the war was lost,[142] asked the Allies for an armistice, and in doing so, changed its international alliances. Unfortunately, this change was accompanied by the disgraceful collapse and disintegration of the military-political ruling class. The king and his government fled from the German troops.[143] The fact that Italy was, at that point, on the side of the Allied forces meant fighting against the Germans, but that did not happen immediately. The Italian army disintegrated. The Allied landing in Sicily meant that the Italian peninsula was divided in half. In the south and southern centre the Allied war against Germany continued with the help of groups of Italian soldiers. In the north and northern centre the partisans were fighting behind the German lines. The partisans were anti-Fascist members of the historical political parties and they were joined by many people who refused to fight the war alongside the Germans and their collaborators. There were not many of these quislings but they were responsible for horrible crimes and terror in the regions where they operated. They were backed up by the Germans and they had no following among the mass of the population. This is the reason why the Italian resistance movement cannot be called a form of civil war, unlike the situations in Spain and Greece. However, this definition is always used by Fascists and Nazis when referring to that period.[144] It is important to remember that the partisans identified with the pre-Fascist political groupings of socialists, catholics (now christian democrats), monarchists and communists. The latter were the most active in the underground movements.

The only real new political formation was the Freedom and Justice group (GL, Giustizia e Libertà)[145] which was a mixture of democratic liberals, social democrats and socialists. The Action Party (PA, Partito d'Azione), which grew out of the GL after the war, had a short life and its members gave their political allegiance to other left-wing parties and the secular centre. Some remained active as politicians while others went into the more prestigious economic professions. The network thus formed constituted an important power centre and it was the only quasi-organization able to counter-balance the clientship system put forward after the war by the strong catholic christian democrats and socialists as the best way to govern.

The development of the armed fight for freedom in northern Italy gave rise to two distinct political societies which have had a great influence on the fate of republican Italy. In the south the fight for freedom did not take place and, as there were no amalgamating forces at work, at the end of the war it became much more difficult to form mass parties. Those that were formed in the north and the centre had a wide membership with ideological orientations. They were the Christian Democratic Party (DC) made up of democratic and liberal catholics, the Socialist Party (PSI, Partito Socialista Italiano) and the Communist Party (PCI). These parties showed great capacity for coordination and collaboration, not only during the fighting but also afterwards when the time came to write the new republican constitution.

The economic and political battles fought by the working classes of the north and centre contributed to the Nazi retreat. An important role was played by the parties and by the politically influenced trade unions that had been founded thanks to political help during the fight for national freedom.[146]

In the south there were protests against living conditions, but only the wave of protest action about land ownership, led by the PCI, had a strong political and social significance.[147]

The political movements which strengthen horizontal links (solidarity) rather than vertical ones (interests) were a characteristic of the north, not the south. This division still remains, even though it is no longer polarized, but the government clientship of the parties has gradually had a disintegrating and demolishing effect on both the centre and the north.

The Italian resistance was very different from the resistance movements in other parts of Europe.[148] It was politically united and of a largely military nature but it did not fight a war of position such as the war fought in Yugoslavia. The Italian resistance was a guerilla warfare. This was due to the part played by the PCI and its leader, Palmiro Togliatti. He was responsible for moving the Italian Communist Party away from its Leninist origins. The unifying elements of the resistance were of far greater influence than the disuniting ones. Togliatti disagreed with the socialists and the Action Party, and he took sides with those people who proposed that the question of the monarchy be raised only at the end of the war. This course of action made the war against the Germans and the Fascist quislings possible. The part of the armed forces which remained faithful to the king joined the partisan forces under the command of General Raffaele Cadorna to form a single fighting force.[149]

As a result of this policy of unity, a communist, Umberto Terracini, was nominated President of the Constituting Assembly and the new constitution was drawn up by all the political forces of the resistance movement. The resistance was the identifying factor in the founding of the Italian Republic and it gave a very wide degree of institutional homogeneity to the political situation. It also acted as a strong link between the political elites responsible for founding the democracy. The majority of these elites had had no recent connection with the cultural values and traditions of Italian political society. Their political awareness had been formed in the Fascist jails, on the battlefields of the Spanish civil war, in the international Stalinist organizations, in the socialist, democratic anti-Fascist networks abroad, and in the cosmopolitan atmosphere of the Vatican Curia. These origins explain the exceptionally progressive part played by the new elites on the Italian political scene. In after years, the decline of these fathers of the republic, for natural or cultural reasons, led to the decline of the political class. The resistance movements in Greece, Spain and Portugal did not have the same effect on the new constitutions of these countries. After the meeting between Churchill and Roosevelt in September 1944 and after the important part played by the Vatican as mediator,[150] the USA emerged as the central point of reference in the Allied occupation of Italy. The

Americans were concerned mainly with reconstructing the country's economy and keeping the expansion of communism within bounds. To this end they wholeheartedly supported the united, organized catholics who founded the Christian Democrat Party – DC.[151]

'Hold back the PCI' became the basic and important watchword. Control over Italy was vital for maintaining the balance of power in the Mediterranean. In 1947 there was already a move towards ending the first republican coalition governments formed by alliances of the left, the centre and the right. Proof of the central role of the USA in Italian politics can be found in the fact that Kennedy's approval was needed when the socialists joined the government at the beginning of the 1960s. It happened again in 1978 when Jimmy Carter expressed his veto with regard to the Eurocomunists.[152]

In 1946, a popular referendum abolished the monarchy, and a new constitution became operative from 1 January 1948. Four months later, on 18 April, the Italians elected the republic's first parliament. The DC, led by Alcide De Gasperi, won a decisive victory over the joint forces of the socialists and the communists with a majority vote of 48 per cent against the 31 per cent of the left.

> Soviet moves were seen as concentrating on the weak limits in the security belt around the Eastern Mediterranean and the Middle East: Italy, Greece, Turkey and Iran . . . on the external front, the election again proved decisive in clarifying Italy's international allegiance to the West, while demonstrating how much post-war Italian politics had become subjected to outside intervention. Indeed Italy emerges at this time as virtually a classic example of . . . 'penetrated system' where the main political forces sought to build and responded to foreign powers.[153]

Italy's membership of the Atlantic Pact in 1949 was the logical consequence of its international collocation. The left wing of the DC was not convinced of the wisdom of this move, and the communists and socialists fought against it. The only other alternative was the Greek one – civil war – to which Palmiro Togliatti was completely opposed. However, in spite of the grave crises which hit the country, such a situation did not arise. The changeover to democracy went through thanks to the unity and cooperation of all the political forces in spite of internal divisions and the cold war. Thus the strong social and idealistic tensions which beset the political society were alleviated.

Basically the sub-cultures of the political system, as in Spain, were reconstructed along the same lines as the pre-Fascist system. However, there was a considerable change in the relative importance of the strengths and mechanics of the parties, and one cannot accept the theory of overall discontinuity with the past.[154] Historically speaking, Italy had a form of social citizenship before it had political citizenship. The trade unions and the Socialist party (founded in 1892) represented the people, particularly in the industrial north and the centre-north rural areas, long before those people were able to elect their representatives in parliament.

The lack of parliamentary representation meant that there was a separation between the legal and the real country which was eliminated politically only after the Second World War. There was also a religious cleavage[155] after 20 September 1870 when armed Italian troops entered the city of Rome which had, until that historic date, been the capital of the Pontifical State. With the conquest of Rome, the temporal power of the Pope came to an end, but the Vatican forbade catholics to participate in politics. For more than fifty years, catholics did not recognize the new Italian state which had been declared in 1861 and so did not take part in its politics.

The lack of catholic integration was the cause of the centralistic structure of the Italian state. Strong regional autonomies could have formed the basis for a restoration of papal power. Particularly in the south, there was a strong element of traditional catholicism and the Bourbons and their supporters made attempts to return to power. This explosive mixture produced a number of revolts which had to be quelled by armed force.

The religious cleavages also vertically divided the agrarian and industrial middle classes, preventing the formation of a British-style conservative party and isolating the rural masses, particularly the smallholders, who were under the church's influence. However, these cleavages did not stop the formation of wide-spread social citizenship thanks to the manifesto of the socialists on one hand and the Papal Encyclical *Rerum Novarum*, which stimulated the catholic social movement, on the other. These doctrines laid the foundations for those catholic and socialist sub-cultures which had such a great influence on the mechanisms of the party system up until the 1980s.[156] Universal suffrage was given to men after the First World War (women were given the vote after the Second World War), and this allowed the emergence of the various parties. Until that time the power of parliament had been limited by the overwhelming power of the executive with its transformist method of operating. Majorities and minorities were formed by secret agreements between the elites which led to swings between maintaining power and caciquism without ever allowing the formation of real political parties.

This was the shape of the liberal organization of power which was incapable of providing a democratic solution to the social and political expectations of large slices of the population. These organizations were swept away first by the political participation of the first elections to be held after the First World War and then by the advent of Fascism. The managing classes adopted a counter-revolutionary solution. They supported the class dictatorship with its Fascist single-party under the leadership of Mussolini. However, the illegal political sub-cultures survived and grew during the Fascist period. The transformation of the sub-cultures into democratic political parties was not modelled on the past. The PCI and GL were the strongest and most compact forces in the underground fight against Fascism. However, GL was not supported by all social levels as it was formed by mainly middle-class intellectuals. The PCI inherited the socialist sub-culture especially in the centre-north thanks to its intelligent political approach to the problems of the agricultural and industrial workers.[157] This process became more marked as Italian socialism spawned breakaway parties. This happened first in 1947 and it happened again in 1964. These splits were always caused by the question of joining governments with the DC or making alliances with the PCI. The PCI continually gained electoral strength until the end of the 1970s.

Another important political change to take place after the Second World War was the disintegration of the bloc formed by the upper agrarian and industrial classes and the middle classes. During the Fascist period this bloc had been bureaucratically united in the National Fascist Party (PNF, Partito Nazionale Fascista).[158] First of all, Fascism instilled these levels of society with its ideology, then it established itself as a regime,[159] with a strict synergy between state and single party. Thanks to its declared anti-communism, it was the only party for the catholics and it inherited the various catholic sub-cultures with their individualist and family-orientated creeds, which were linked to the party by the clientship relations with local leaders rather than by ideological choices. The unification of the middle classes in a political party is a Fascist idea which was adopted by the DC and used to create strong structures which were not only made up of clientship but were also closely linked to the catholic world. Thus the DC facilitated the movement of the middle classes away from reactionary political positions to democratic ones. This prevented the affirmation of a strong right-wing party, i.e. the Italian Social Movement (MSI, Movimento Sociale Italiano), which inherited the mantle of the Fascist party (like Fraga Iribarne's Popular Alliance – AP). There was an inevitable give and take of connections and functions between the role of the DC and the political unity of the catholics. The situation was very different from that in Spain and Portugal.

The Vatican state, heartland of a universal religion, had a strong party (the DC) at its disposal through which it could divulge its principles to the Italian nation surrounding it. World balance was being decided in Italy and Pope Pius XII played an important part in the negotiations by affirming the Vatican state's support of democratic principles and its anti-communism. In fact, the Pope excommunicated all the members of the PCI[160] in spite of the fact that the communists had done everything in their power to stop him. In 1929 an agreement (*Concordato*) was signed between the Italian state and Vatican state which governed their relationship. One of the most important clauses declared that the Roman Catholic religion was the foundation of public schooling and family life. As it was necessary to define a constitutional orientation on this, the DC and the PCI agreed with the extreme right and the Liberal Party (PLI, Partito Liberale Italiano) that the principles expressed in the Vatican agreement had to be incorporated into the new constitution. Togliatti was convinced that this was the only way to help the DC to carry out its basic job of persuading the middle classes both in the rural areas and in the cities to accept a democratic republic, and therefore to accept the role that the PCI would play in it.[161]

In spite of bitter disagreements over religious matters which reached their peak in 1948 and the fact that the church was dealing in propaganda, the PCI did not want a religious war and this was, in fact, avoided.[162] Though religion was repressed under Soviet communism, it is difficult to present the PCI as anti-clerical. Even in this case there is no continuity with regard to the pre-Fascist period when religious controversy was basic to the catholic and socialist identities.

In any case, the reconstruction of the political class was carried out mainly with the drawing up of the constitution. This coincided with the first election for the Constituent Assembly. The political class was renewed with 80 per cent of the votes going to anti-Fascist parties. It marked the end of the liberals of pre-Fascist memory and of the Action Party (PA) which had no sub-cultural base. The socialists received 20.7 per cent of the votes and the communists received 19 per cent. The

DC was confirmed as the majority party with 35.2 per cent of the votes. The Italian Liberal Party (PLI) received 6.8 per cent and the other parties all received fewer votes. In fact, these minor parties were destined to play a secondary role in the entire story of post-war Italian politics.

The Constituent Assembly drew up a constitution which acknowledged the institutional role of political parties and it affirmed the role, even though limited, of direct democracy through abrogative referendums and popular legislative initiatives. It also laid the foundation for overcoming the centralist state by affirming the principle of regional autonomy. On this point no concrete action was taken until the regional elections of 1970. Before, under the constitutional clause affirming the concept of a single, indivisible republic, five regions with a special statute were formed. These were Sicily, Sardinia, Val d'Aosta, Trentino Alto Adige and Friuli-Venezia-Giulia. This move solved, or laid the basis for solving, the question of the linguistic minorities. The agreement between Italy and Austria helped to dissipate the disputes for the protection of the German-speaking minority group in Alto Adige where, for some years, there had been a problem of national independence giving rise to some terrorist attempts. The political alliance between the DC and the South Tyrol People's Party (Sud Tyroler Volkspartei) solved the problem with a statute giving autonomy to the region.[163] There were less serious problems with the Slav minority in the area around Trieste.

No other cleavage had ever had such an important effect on Italian political life. The regions were clearly subordinate to the state, which placed serious limits on their autonomy. The main rationale behind the regions was the creation of decentralized administrative offices and new centres of political power.[164] According to the Italian constitution, parliament has the exclusive right to legislate and control even though the government can pass decrees without going through the parliamentary process. The President of the Republic acts as coordinator of the whole system and as the maintainer of balance between the parts. The electoral system was based on proportional representation in order to effect a complete change from the pre-Fascist period when there were excessive limits to political participation. It was a basically progressive and social constitution aimed at overcoming inequalities in the context of a mixed economy. This was the basis on which the catholic and the left-wing forces reached wide agreement and where the spirit of collaboration born during the resistance reached its institutional peak.

Thus a brief but tormented cycle of Italian political life closed. Contrary to what is generally believed,[165] democratic consolidation was already a fact after 18 April 1948. The revolutionary and rebellious forces that persisted for the whole of the 1950s under the revolutionary push which had inspired a part of the workers' resistance, were always controlled by the PCI leaders who were determined to carry the fight for socialism into the democratic camp. The policies of the PCI were double-edged as they had to use social democratic methods and at the same time maintain the revolutionary ideology invoked by the party's links with the USSR. These links were weakened when the PCI condemned the USSR invasion of Czechoslovakia in 1968.[166] However, the leaders of the PCI used only parliamentary means in their efforts to wean Italy away from the Western alliance. The PCI had already given indications of their democratic thinking in 1948, when Palmiro Togliatti was the victim of an assassination attempt, and they refused to get involved in an armed conflict. The VIII Communist Congress of 1956 offered further proof of their democratic line. Nevertheless, in the same year the PCI approved of the USSR's repression of the Hungarian rebels. This approval caused many of the more prestigious intellectuals to abandon the party.

In any case, the electoral strength of the DC was always the deciding factor in political society. After 1948 the electoral results confirmed both De Gasperi's international policies and Togliatti's policy of avoiding armed actions or strikes which would undermine the sovereignty of parliament. These two faces of Italy were the foundation for the famous Eurocommunism elaborated by Enrico Berlinguer, the new leader of the PCI, in the mid-1970s.

The communist party line of socialism through democracy, was really meant, they were not just empty words. But the PCI was hampered and weakened in its intent by its chronic incapacity to criticize Stalinism. If the party had been able to do so, the effect would have been liberating, and great democratic and transformistic energies would have been released. The PCI carried the extremism and the messianic revolution of the Italian masses onto democratic grounds convinced that this move could be made without breaking the iron bonds binding the party to the USSR. In the end, the PCI paid a very high price for this error of judgement as it hindered rather than helped the party's climb towards being part of the government. Unfortunately, the whole of Italian society paid a price in as much as the people's contribution to social and political change could not be fully utilized. That mistake of forty years ago has had far-reaching effects on Italian political society ever since, even to the present time.

Threats to democracy came from the right of the political spectrum. In 1964 there was an attempted coup directed at weakening the newly formed coalition government of christian democrats and socialists. In the 1970s and 1980s the authoritarian masonic lodge named P2 worked against the established government. Its actions (and membership) were first brought to light by a parliamentary commission especially formed to investigate the matter. This was followed by inquiries by the judicial institutions.[167] But the gravest threats came from extreme left- and right-wing terrorist actions which were directed at crushing the project of opening the government to the PCI in the last part of the 1970s. This was the start of a series of assaults, killings and attempts at disrupting democracy by introducing authoritarian restrictions into the political system. The Mafia joined in too when it lost its christian democrat and socialist governmental supporters. The importance of international implications in this matter cannot be measured with any degree of certainty. It cannot be denied that attempts to let the left in could not but meet obstinate resistance from the USA. After all, the Americans had played an essential part in defeating first Fascism and then communism, and the world was still divided into two opposing blocs.

In Italy democratic consolidation was premature and atypical. There were imbalances between internal forces and international trends. The latter influenced the former, and obscured and limited the purity of the development of democracy. The changeover to democracy, started in 1943, reached the threshold of consolidation in 1948 but did not reach the threshold of stability.

Chapter 9

AFFIRMATION OF THE POLITICAL
MIDDLE GROUND

I Between sub-cultures and the party system

One of the basic characteristics of Southern European political societies in the periods after a dictatorship was the speed with which a non-polarized mass political orientation was affirmed. The most relevant structural causes of this were higher incomes, better schooling and the formation of intermediate social classes. However, the enormous influence of collective historical memory must not be undervalued. The advent and consolidation of dictatorships, whether permanent or transitory, generated such traumas in the population as to prevent the rise of irreversible political splits. The road to democracy was a transition towards a more or less speedy centralized consolidation of the political system. This trend seems to have affected all sub-cultures. It also seems to have favoured the convergence of the elites.

The political systems have accompanied and favoured this centripetal trend with an ever clearer connection between political society and party system. The growth of stable centrist parties in a democracy born after a period of dictatorship is common to all the European countries. The only exceptions to this are Greece and Turkey. In Greece, polarization continues to characterize the party system but it no longer affects the sub-cultures. In Turkey, the central connection between political society and party system came late because of the specific characteristics of the Turkish protected democracy.

The Greek situation is symbolic of the possible imbalances between society and political system. The victory of PASOK in the 1981 elections must be considered as proof of the consolidation of democracy. The party received 48.1 per cent of the votes and 57.4 per cent of the seats. It almost doubled its political influence without any serious risks of a military coup. An entirely new political regime was established. After forty years the right became the opposition party with 35.9 per cent of the votes and 38.3 per cent of the seats. The only other party to receive a significant number of votes was the KKE with 10.9 per cent giving them 4.3 per cent of the seats. The military had remained in their barracks and for the first time in Greek history a left-wing party won the power to govern.

The most relevant institutional modification undertaken by PASOK was constitutional. In 1985 the new constitution gave the power of initiative and intervention to the prime minister (these were previously attributes of the president) who thus became a true 'parliamentary autocrat'.[1] This modification had been sought when the party was in opposition. The PASOK victory was the result of an electoral campaign based on the populist platform of the 'change' (*Allaghi*). The first thing to change was the spoils system. A large number of middle-level managers in the civil service who were linked to New Democracy (ND) were replaced by the PASOK green guards (the party flag was green and white stripes). Governmental power caused considerable changes in the party programme as it had to cope with a fairly difficult economic situation. The austerity measures which PASOK had to adopt caused the party some problems but the 1985 elections confirmed its absolute majority in the lower chamber of parliament. When compared to the previous elections, PASOK lost about 2 per cent and ND gained 5 per cent. However, it became evident that PASOK's initial ardour for change was gradually being dimmed, both concerning foreign policy with the re-entry into Nato and the preferential acceptance of the EEC, and in domestic affairs. The party's relations with society were deteriorating because the structure of the modern mass party was being infiltrated by variations on the clientship and statocratic theme.

Kinship and fiefdom are strong in Greece, and the degree of corruption is high. When Andreas Papandreou was in power in the late 1980s there was an explosion of scandals and corruption. The people protested strongly but the reactions of the government demonstrated their scarce inclination to conceive democratic consolidation in terms of the consensual elaboration of institutional rules. Papandreou changed the electoral system by increasing the quota of proportional representation. This was aimed at preventing a ND victory. In fact, in the June 1989 elections ND won a majority of the seats with 145 against 125 for PASOK but it was not able to govern. The two communist parties and other left-wing forces, finally united after age-old divisions under the name of Left and Progress Coalition (SYNAP, Synaspismos) won 29 seats. At this point, ND and SYNAP formed a coalition government. This event really proves that the schismatic cycle of Greek history was closed with the complete consolidation of democracy. The aim of the new government was to 'purify' (*Khatarsis*) the civil service of socialist political corruption by removing the socialist ministers who were guilty and refusing them parliamentary immunity. The government lasted four months, enough time to actuate the purification programme. On 5 November 1989 the two leaders, Konstantinos Mitsotakis of the ND and Kharibaes Floriakis who was leader of both SYNAP and the KKE, went to the country. However, the results of the election did not allow the formation of a coalition based on a united programme. ND received 46.9 per cent of the votes and 148 seats, PASOK received 40.6 per cent of the votes with 128 seats and SYNAP received 10.9 per cent of the votes with 21 seats. The important thing was that a democracy had been formed and it respected rules and procedures. This democratic victory finally allowed the country to overcome the traumas of the civil war. The country was beset by a very bad moral crisis and the two historically opposed political cultures realized it was the right moment to put aside their differences in the interests of democracy. But the country did not have a stable government until 8 April 1990 when ND won 150 seats with 46.89 per cent of the votes. The PASOK share fell to 123 seats with 38.6 per cent of the votes, and SYNAP took 19 seats with 10.2 per cent of the votes. The small parties were allotted six seats, two of which went to Muslim representatives from Thrace.

The ND leader Konstantinos Mitsotakis had exactly half the seats – 150 out of 300 – and he formed a government by an alliance with a small one-time faction of

ND which had become an autonomous party. Konstantine Karamanlis was elected President of the Republic. The electoral law was changed again. This time it ruled that the party with the most seats would receive a majority prize, and that parties receiving less than 3 per cent of the votes would be excluded from parliamentary representation. The ND confirmed its position in the local elections of 14 and 18 October 1990. However, this was not the beginning of a new cycle in Greek politics. There was strong polarization between the parties. As neither of the two main parties was able to maintain a strong, stable majority, a system of alternation with fierce confrontation was established. However, the ND party leaders split over the question of Macedonia and Yugoslavia, causing divisions within the cabinet and the fall of the government. In October 1993 PASOK won the election by a short lead and yet another Papandreou government held the reins of the country.[2]

The above analysis has shown how Greek political society has become fully democratic without going through extremely radical stages, and with wide agreement over the question of institutional rules and regulations. This process has occurred in spite of protests against corruption, intermittent terrorism and the persistence of the old clientship habits practised by everyone except the communists. The schism is finished and its culture no longer exists. This is the Greek miracle which was not produced by the development of the economy but by the growth of the political sub-cultures.

In the other Southern European countries, the consolidation of democracy came through the affirmation of parties already centrally placed, and by their ability to form wide (and unstable) coalitions if they did not have the absolute majority. However, the historical social cleavages continued everywhere. Italy is a typical example of this.

In Italy the persistence of social cleavages was evident in the thirty years from the end of the 1940s to the beginning of the 1980s. The consolidation of democracy was marked by the strengthening of the role of parties in society. The relations between economic society and the construction of a democratic state were obvious though there were imbalances and contradictions. The connection between the origins of the parties and their workings, which form the shape of political society, was actuated by the sub-cultures whose characteristics become clear when there is democratic political participation. The collocation of these sub-cultures is firstly territorial. It is modelled on economic dualism between north and south and the late affirmation of the market. In the southern areas the market was based more on status than on contract. The amoral family of a desperate society crushed by economic insecurity[3] was transformed by an increase in income but remained culturally isolated within the walls of the family enclave. The differences between north and south are evident.

> In the ... south, politics meant as a process which is relatively free from violence, intimidation and corruption lacks 'credibility', for the good reason that it has never been practised. The development of southern society made some forms of collective action indispensable, but the presence of clientship obliges the group to act through intermediary leaders who, with their particular behaviour, undermine the confidence of the group as a collective entity.[4]

This process prevented the development of modern parties. The communists, with their policy of favouring collective mobilization rather than individual pressure, had trouble becoming popular in the south. The use of the preference vote had always been higher in the south than in the north. This reflected the importance of clientship to the southern electorate. The territorial sub-cultures of the centre and the north-east were not influenced so much by individual gains as by a sense of solidarity and community. These were the areas of the catholic and communist (or social-communist) sub-cultures.[5] The north, not the south, had an associative mentality that gave the parties an extraordinary heartland full of resources and connections. Even in the north, however, the effect of status in relationships was important but, unlike the south, this supported the market and provided it with the confidence and reciprocity it needed to operate. Even the form of clientship is different. It stems more from the characteristics of the party machine than from civil society (while in the south it stems from society). The networks of solidarity are often destroyed by the parties themselves when members of acquisitive groups like the middle classes become part of a spoils system.

There are two other historical forces which wore away these sub-cultures by gradually destroying the system of solidarity. One was secularization and the other was the power of the local administrations. The community structures have been continually corroded by the tendency of local administrations to use the currency of exchange votes. But the solidarity of the sub-cultural base has proved very strong.

The paradox of Italy lies in the fact that there was high government instability[6] together with the persistence of the three main parties, the DC, the Italian Socialist Party (PSI) and the Italian Communist Party (PCI), which played a central and overwhelming role in the political and electoral system until the 1980s. Alongside these three main parties, there were many others which the DC sought to consolidate through coalition governments. But right from the beginning, the PSI showed a marked tendency to move towards the centre. It must be noted that after 1956 and the XX Congress of the Communist party of the USSR, the PSI broke its agreement with the PCI on united action. Then, in the 1970s, the PCI broke its bonds with the Soviet party and started moving towards the centre. The results of the 1953 elections laid the foundation for a centripetal tendency. However, the centre-right coalition government did not reach a stable, secure majority.[7] The DC, the central core of the political system and political society, went back to 40 per cent. The right-wing monarchists and Fascists gained, as did the PCI with 22.6 per cent.

The PCI continued to grow over the following years. In 1958 it went to 22.7 per cent, in 1963 to 25.3 per cent, in 1968 to 26.9 per cent and in 1972 it reached 27.2 per cent. The PSI, after reaching 12 per cent in 1953, went up to 14.2 per cent in 1958 but after that it gradually lost ground until it fell to 9.6 per cent in 1972. The DC reached 42.3 per cent in 1958 but by 1963 it had fallen to 38.2 per cent. In 1968 it went up to 39 per cent and in 1972 it remained more or less stable at 38.7 per cent.

The losses of the DC corresponded to a rise in the votes going to the Liberal party (PLI), the Social Democratic party (PSDI, Partito Socialdemocratico Italiano) and the Fascist party (MSI). This movement was caused by two things. The first was that, at the beginning of the 1960s, the DC started to move towards the left, and the second was that the PSI shifted towards the centre.

In 1962 the PSI joined the government coalition with the DC and this gave rise to the period of centre-left government. This period lasted until 1976. During that time the relations between the parties and society were re-defined, allowing the actuation of a programme of reforms – a substantial novelty for Italian history. However, the strong objections of the industrial and financial right joined to those of the moderate factions of the DC deprived the centre-left of its innovative push.[8]

Programmes of social and political reform were not used as arms in the fight to occupy the middle ground. Clientship was the weapon that counted, and this caused a widespread balkanization of the state by the parties. The years 1968 and 1969 saw protest and unrest, tumultuous and unexpected widening of the rights of social citizenship, violence in factories and society. The political system was faced with great changes, and with an electoral earthquake. From 1972 to 1976 the PCI went from 27.2 to 34.4 per cent. The party took votes away from the other left-wing forces and it gained votes from the 18-year-olds who were voting for the first time. The effects of the general situation benefited the PCI, attacked by both the extreme left and the extreme right, as it was seen as the only alternative to the clientship-ridden political system.

The year 1968 marked the beginning of a very significant period in Italian history. One of the most important aspects was that the parties no longer controlled the collective movements. The trade unions were shaken by the workers' protests. The three trade union organizations, CGIL (Confederazione Generale Italiana del Lavoro), CISL (Confederazione Italiana Sindacati dei Lavoratori) and UIL (Unione Italiana del Lavoro), were fundamental for gathering society's requests and translating them into negotiations in the work place. As the unions were linked to the parties, they also provided political solutions at a legislative level. However, at the beginning they seemed to be supplanted by the waves of protests. But the unions rallied and managed to regain control of the collective movements. They then used their strength to enlarge their organizational structures, turning them into real mechanisms of representation. The unions became more autonomous from the parties, and from the very people they represented.

The students' protest movements followed a different path. They swept away the university unions, which were based on political parties and represented an aspect of the extraordinary growth in the social importance of the middle classes. Unlike what happened in the pre-Fascist and Fascist periods, the middle classes now moved towards the left. The moderate political sub-cultures of the older generation were rejected by the students, who overturned the links between their origins and politics. They founded a completely new culture made up of a mixture of anti-authoritarianism and the various revolutionary left-wing theories of Che Guevara, Stalin and Lenin. The same thing happened on the right, but to a lesser extent, with an outbreak of Fascist, Nazi and racist myths. These myths were very wide-spread in Italy.

This wave of non-party associative movements highlights another basic process. Italy was rapidly becoming an industrial society. The growing autonomy of society was the cause of its alienation from the political system. This autonomy is the result of that social differentiation which stems from industrialization. However, in Italy the weak institutionalization of the political party system did not go hand in hand with industrial growth as it did in the more mature, already industrialized countries. The party system collided with it and thus lost the capacity to control industrial growth and give it procedural rules. The social actors become part of citizenship without having followed that particularistic logic which is a vital part of most of Italian political sub-cultures. But the lack of synchrony between political institutionalization and economic growth creates social divisions and corporativism. Particularism appears in a new shape, in the fight of quasi-groups, that is to say, people with a new professional identity based on interests who group together to obtain advantages thanks to collective mobilization. Class conflict rapidly became corporative conflict.

The working class, which had protested so fiercely and compactly in 1969, was also affected by conflicts. These conflicts were signs of the social unrest of a new political generation, for the most part not imbued with an industrial culture, which overturned the authority of both the management systems and the trade unions, and therefore the parties. For a few years the trade unions tried to control the process of change with demagogy. But by the second half of the 1970s, they had moved from the period of equalitarianism to a deep cultural and social differentiation which was caused by the lack of synchrony mentioned before between political institutionalization and economic growth and the lack of a solid system of negotiating rules.[9] The trade unions were greatly changed by the time they regained control of the collective movements in the second half of the 1980s. The convergence of parties towards the centre of the political spectrum was coupled to the political disintegration of society. At the beginning of the 1990s, the party system started to suffer from the results and the effects were disastrous.

Political and social convergence towards the centre happened in Spain as well, but with a variation on the Italian experience. In Italy the DC was the social hub and the party which represented the centralized groupings of interests and political elites. In Spain, the collapse of the UCD led by Adolfo Suarez immediately following the advent of democracy allowed the PSOE to play the same part as the DC in Italy but without the need to form coalitions, at least until the beginning of the 1990s. The basic question was the considerable cultural de-polarization compared to the past, and the lowering of the degree of haughtiness in force in the party system. The victory of the PSOE and its absolute majority established the indisputable centripetal tendency of Spanish politics. However, the foundations of the system were rather different from those in Italy in the 1950s. The Spanish system moved towards the centre earlier, in coincidence with the single-party PSOE government's predominance. Polarization was based on competition between the parties which helped to moderate radical ideologies rather then emphasize it. The configuration of the system was influenced considerably by the reformist and negotiating orientation assumed by the social relations, isolating the extremist tendencies and assuring the UGT continued consensual growth. This growth gradually allowed the UGT to become more influential than the Workers' Commissions and to have more contractual importance. The orientation of the Spanish workers was decisive. They knew that there was no other way to consolidate democracy.

With the economic crisis, the continued rumblings of some sections of the military (no doubt inspired by the coup in Turkey) and the increase of terrorism, the only realistic strategy had to be based on social pacts at the top and on regulated negotiation of claims at the base.[10] The conflicts between the PSOE and the unions were increased by the centralized negotiations, but those conflicts were part of the reformist stabilization of the system of industrial relations in the birth and general reconstruction of a centripetally dominated political system.

This social process was mirrored by the electoral results and their general political significance. The PSOE lost votes and seats but it continued to be the dominant party and AP could not shift it from power in spite of the various coalitions it had proposed. In 1986 the PSOE had 43.4 per cent of the votes and 184 seats but in 1989 its share of votes dropped to 39.6 per cent and its seats fell to 176. In 1986 AP received 26 per cent of the votes with 105 seats and in 1989 the votes fell to 25.8 per cent but the seats rose to 106.

Parliamentary representation continued to be concentrated. While in 1977 the UCD and the PSOE together received 63.8 per cent of the votes, by 1982 the PSOE and the AP together gleaned 74.3 per cent, with a completely restructured party system. The occupation of the centre by a pro-labour party with an orientation towards monetary policies and pragmatic and conciliatory reformism (except with regard to the church on questions like abortion and education), aimed at becoming a permanent feature of the political system. After the democrats and the liberals left the Popular Coalition (CP, Coalición Popular), Fraga Iribarne, its leader, realized that his project of forming a wide centre-right coalition had failed. In order to succeed, this project needed to count on the regional and national conservative parties' more marked orientation towards the right. However, these were less radical than the national right which was basically centrist. The consolidation of democracy was irreversible and the fact that the PSOE needed to make alliances with the moderate national parties made coalitions transient. But the legitimacy of the system would be enlarged and would become more 'all-embracing',[11] given the importance of the cleavage between centre and periphery in Spain. All this was proved by the stabilization of the political class and its development.[12]

The most important historical contribution to the consolidation of democracy came from the armed forces' acceptance of the change to democracy. The authoritarian tendencies within the armed forces were not lacking but were overcome by internal opposition and decisive actions by the king.[13] The political forces also played a very important part as reforms concerning pay and perks were calmly and gradually introduced which effectively placed the army under civil control. There was no hostility towards the military in the country, which was fortunate as such feelings would have been fatal in the case of renewed terrorism.[14] The PSOE's acceptance of Spanish entry into Nato was decisive in keeping the military happy. After initial opposition to re-entry, the government had realized the importance of Spain to the Western defence system. So, in 1986 the PSOE fought a difficult and crucial referendum on the subject of re-entry into Nato which was necessary for the final consolidation of democracy.[15] The PSOE was alone against everyone else – even against Fraga – but it won with 52 per cent of the votes. This victory was probably more important than the election in 1982.

A stable middle ground in the political system was reached in Portugal too. In spite of the post-revolutionary fragmentation and the deep personal and clientship roots, the rapid formation of the four dominant forces in the country, the PSD, the PS, the PCP and the Democratic Social Centre (CDS, Centro Democratico Social) took place. In Portugal. as opposed to Spain, there were only social cleavages and the positions of the parties faithfully reflected the class structure. The first four elections for the republican parliament were decisive.[16] In fact, they laid the foundation for democratic stability by refusing any revolutionary possibilities and by defining precise limits to the role of the right. The decisive point came in 1985 after a period of great instability. In the elections the PSD with 29.8 per cent of the votes, overtook the PS with 20.8 per cent, and the military were finally subordinated to political society.

Thus Portugal started along the road to a stable political middle ground. This stability had similar characteristics to that of Spain concerning the format of the party system. The absolute majority of the PSD led by Anibal Cavaco Silva both in 1987 and in 1991 was proof of this. The PS was the only party to maintain its electoral position in spite of a leadership crisis. In 1991 it received 29 per cent of the votes. In the same election the PCP fell to 8.8 per cent.

The way in which Mario Soares was re-elected as President of the Republic in January 1991 was a further indication of the centripetal trend of Portuguese political society. Soares was elected with 70 per cent of the votes against the 51.2 per cent he received when he was supported by a left group which included the PCP. Soares did not have any rivals worth worrying about as the PSD decided not to put up any candidates and to support the re-election of Soares. The collaboration between Soares and Anibal Cavaco Silva was emblematic of the consolidation of the democracy. With proportional representation, the party system had, for the moment, found its centripetal consolidation and parliamentary stability. However, attention must be paid to the slogans which appeared in the 1991 elections. They all expressed the typical claims of the right-wing lamentations for the lost colonial past, anti-Europeanism and nationalism. Similar passions and retributions were spreading in all European countries.[17]

The democratic evolution in Portugal was a far more linear process than many thought it was. Taking power away from the military went hand in hand with taking power away from the president and with the democratic institutionalization of the parties and therefore of parliament. In 1976, thanks to an agreement between AD and PS, modifications to the constitution were made affirming the democratic and transforming functions of the parties.

In this way, the Portuguese parliament very quickly became the main seat of party activity. The marked importance of parliamentary activity proved vital for the stability of the political class, especially when compared to the other new Southern European democracies.[18] The strong position of parliament as a true body of representation was made possible by the defeat of military populism and by the army's return to its barracks. It was not in any way the same as in Turkey prior to 1980. In Portugal the military, for the first time in the country's history, accepted the creation of a democratic system based on a party system without any elements of military guardianship. Proof of this came when the constitution was re-written in

1990. This was made possible because the PS and the PSD obtained two thirds of the seats in parliament at the 1987 elections. Nothing remained of the exceptional and tumultuous period in which the first constitution was written in 1976.[19]

The strong institutionalizing power of the parties was reflected in industrial relations. Though the communist predominance had been extremely important during the dictatorship thanks to their ability to infiltrate the regime's trade unions, particularly that of the banks and the iron and steel industry, the new system of industrial relations swept that predominance away.[20]

Trade unionism was based on an ideological and political competitive pluralism, produced by the political party struggle rather than the trade union one,[21] with great similarities to what happened in Turkey, Greece, Spain and Italy. Even though, in Italy, the differences between communists and socialists were less marked as they were both part of the CGIL, a social-communist trade union with communist predominance. The scarce autonomy of the trade unions and the insufficient decentralization of its representatives resulted in a fragile system of industrial relations everywhere in Southern Europe.

The invasion of the system of industrial relations by politics is typical of countries with a party system, based on deep rooted political sub-cultures. Such sub-cultures are well represented in those countries which fought against a dictatorship to win a democratic state. They are also present in countries where the fall of the dictatorship was caused either by internal decadence or by the pressures of international democracy. This was very true of Portugal in spite of the fact that there was no mass democratic tradition prior to Salazar's dictatorship. The role of military populism and of the communists during the dictatorship, and that of the democrats (socialists, christians and conservatives) afterwards were decisive for promoting the institutionalization of the parties and therefore democracy. All social analyses show this line of action to be stable and consolidated.[22] Unfortunately, there is no lack of problems. The most important one, common to the whole of Southern Europe, is the construction of an efficient rational-legal state system with a general orientation.[23]

II Learning democracy

In Turkey the road to centripetal stability was much more difficult and complex. The coup of 1980 dissolved parliament, abolished the right to strike, and proclaimed an iron martial law with the aim of stopping terrorism. The left- and right-wing trade union movements were unable to operate. Süleyman Demirel, Bülent Ecevit and Necmettin Erbakan were placed under house arrest. Asparslan Türkes, leader of the MHP, was arrested. The bureaucracy was purged of its extremist elements. '18,000 civil servants had to answer to administrative or penal sentences.' The army was also purged. Some 80,000 soldiers, both left- and right-wing, were imprisoned. Twenty death sentences were carried out. The death sentence was requested even for Türkes who was accused of having spread right-wing ideology in the army.[24] The general situation of restriction of civil and political freedom and the cases of torture and brutality in the jails, as well as the repression of the trade unions, caused strong international protests.[25] The military dictatorship's efforts were focused in two directions. The first was solving social problems by repression. The other was solving the economic problems. Turgut Özal emerged as the technician who was asked to continue the policy of the last Demirel government and to solve the difficult international economic situation, particularly in dealings with the EEC.

The 1982 constitution was the institutional peak of the temporary military dictatorship. It was completely different to the 1962 constitution in that the powers of the government were most strongly sanctioned. However, the president was not given specific powers and he was closely controlled by the Council of Ministers and parliament.[26]

The TIP, the MHP and the MSP were outlawed because they were linked to socialism, fascism and theocracy; 'There will be no politics in the mosque, the university or the barracks,' said the military leader, General Kenan Evren, in 1982.[27] Associations and political parties were strictly regulated by the new laws. The old parties were abolished, thus thwarting any desires their leaders may have had to continue in politics. In order to eliminate political fragmentation it was decided that only those parties reaching 10 per cent of the votes cast in the elections could be represented in parliament.

In any case, political life was reconstructed with the 1983 elections. Only three political parties ran: the central-right Nationalist Democracy Party (MDP, Milliyetçi Demokrasi Partisi) favoured by the military, the central-left Populist Party (HP, Halkçi Parti), and the Motherland Party (ANAP, Anavatan Partisi) founded by Turgut Özal, a liberal in economy and moderately against the military's political conduct. Özal won the election with 45 per cent of the votes and 53 per cent of the seats. The HP won 30.5 per cent and the MDP won 23.3 per cent. This represented the defeat of the military.

The ANAP was a mixed coalition of old nationalist and Islamic parties, and of left and right moderates. Its strength lay in its autonomy from the military and its ability to draw upon the new religious feeling spreading throughout the country.

The 1985 elections confirmed the validity of the ANAP's policies giving the party 41 per cent of the votes. The other two parties which ran in the 1983 elections proved to be weak and fragile: the HP received 9 per cent of the votes and the MDP had 7 per cent. But three new parties had been born in time for the 1985 elections. There was the True Path Party (DYP) which was the heir of the old Justice Party, and it received 13.5 per cent of the votes. The Party of Social Democracy (SDP, Sosyal Demokrasi Partisi) received 24 per cent and the Democratic Left Party (DSP, Demokratik Sol Parti) led by Rahsan Ecevit, the wife of Bülent Ecevit, reached 23 per cent.

These elections marked the beginning of a period of relative stability. However, in 1987 a referendum was passed with 51 per cent which allowed the leaders outlawed in 1982 to return to political activity. Before the 1987 elections the power of the ANAP had weakened even though the economic situation had improved. However, in the election the party received 36.3 per cent of the votes with 65 per cent of the seats. The SDP received 24.7 per cent and the DYP had 19.1 per cent. None of the other parties won seats. Full democracy returned, as did violence, particularly in the universities. Political assassination continued to be used as a weapon particularly by extremist minorities. It was against this background that Süleyman Demirel's party, the DYP, increased its electoral strength and its social acceptance. It constructed strong ties with the economic circles. Pressure to unify the moderate and democratic right grew. The SDP was in trouble because of internal disagreements, the threat of a left-wing split and personal conflicts. The 1989 local elections had already demonstrated the fall of the ANAP from public favour when it lost Istanbul and all but two of the main cities. In 1989 Turgut Özal was elected President of the Republic. This was the confirmation of civilian power and the definitive start of the change in the dominant party, the DYP, now led by Süleyman Demirel, who could not be halted in his climb to power.[28]

Party fragmentation was greatly reduced and the main parties modified their ideological paradigms. The ANAP was not the reincarnation of any previous party. It was firmly placed in the middle of the political spectrum. It insisted on the power of the local self-government and it marked a considerable renovation in the Turkish political class, supporting decentralization. Its charismatic leadership was very strong. This represented an element of considerable continuity in Turkish politics which, however, began to show signs of discontent and apprehension towards traditional practices. On this point, it has been said that 'An important sign of resentment was the use of the word "dynasty" with reference to decision making by Turgut Özal in consultation with his immediate family, brothers and some close advisers, to the exclusion of the properly elected executive.'[29] Özal showed an authoritarian spirit and a tendency to use kinship tactics in his marked interference in foreign policy.[30] However, this did not stop him from playing a fundamental role in the renovation of the Turkish economy.[31] The collapse of the CHP marked the end of a long political cycle. Bülent Ecevit's leftist strategy was the main cause of the party's failure. The DSP and the HP joined together to form the Populist Social Democratic Party (SHP, Sosyal Demokrat Halkçi Parti) which can, in some ways, be considered, together with the DSP, a successor to the CHP. The fortune of the SHP was determined by the fact that, after 1983: 'In Turkey, as in Western Europe, the main political battle is fought for the possession of the middle ground.'[32] Proof of this statement can be found in the rise of Süleyman Demirel's DYP. This party, based on the charisma of its leader, inherited the consolidated network of the ex-Justice Party. 'The predominantly patroclient type of relationship between the JP [Justice Party] and the party's supporters made such a personal touch possible.'[33] A wide mass rural base was the hub around which all social levels gathered. 'Free democracy' was the basic watchword of the party that continued the anti-centrist and autonomy from the military lines of the DP and the Justice Party. But there was also an underlining of the nationalist line aimed at neutralizing the aggressiveness of the extreme right. The party was decidedly secular but the recapture of religious tradition was seen as one of the cultural contributions needed to reinforce Turkish identity. A free market and the central position of civil power were the basis of the party's actions which tended to converge on the centre with both its programmes and its social background. It would seem, therefore, that the Turkish parties had learnt from their history, as the genetic theory of democracy proposes. 'According to this view, democracy would be consolidated when the actors in question "learn".'[34]

Until 1980 the Turkish political scene was characterized by growing polarization, and by the marked incapacity of the moderate factions of the two main parties to work towards a common political and cultural goal.[35] The explosive combination of fragmentation and polarization made up the essence of the political system as is shown by the extreme volatility of the electorate. Polarization was needed to stabilize the system but the enormous degree of fragmentation made this impossible. The explosive combination mentioned above spread throughout the institutions and, together with their invasion by the political party system was the final cause of the growing ungovernability of the whole system. For a long time the growing instability of parliamentary democracy and endemic violence[36] prevented the rebirth of democracy in the Turkish political system through elections. The authoritarian role of the military with their method of reproducing a democracy stems from that situation. Their 'Roman' dictatorship thus acquires a more general significance.[37] After 1983 many things changed.

The political radicalism of the larger parties decreased and also the religious wing of the party founded by Turgut Özal was moderate in spite of the strong ties which bound it more to the Middle East than to the West. The alliance between the exponents of the moderate religious wing and the liberal democrats seemed to be the road for eliminating the political clout of the extreme left and right. That was the indication given by the Demirel government in 1991. Thus the moderate polarization diminished considerably and it became the, for the moment limited, characteristic of the system. And thanks to the electoral system, fragmentation also diminished. This could lead to important growth for the Turkish political system, above all for supporting parliamentary institutionalization which had been rather deficient until 1983. The stability and consolidation of democracy, through the constitutional institutionalization of the military and the continuity of civil power are, however, essential for preventing Turkey from repeating the experiences of the past.[38] There are reasons for being moderately optimistic. The coalition government formed on 29 October 1991 between the DYP and the SHP confirms this line of thought. Süleyman Demirel became President of the Republic after the death of Turgut Özal. And in 1993 a woman,[39] Tansu Çiller, was nominated as head of the government in place of Demirel. This event can only reinforce the prospects of the continuing consolidation of Turkish democracy. The results of the local elections of March 1994 seem to justify these prospects. Though the Islamic integralists were victorious in very important cities like Ankara and Istanbul, Tansu Çiller's party won nationally. This overall victory consolidates the party's position but the conditions under which it governs have become more problematic.

Part Four

CONCLUSIONS AND NEW PROBLEMS

Chapter 10

SOCIETIES AND MOVEMENTS

I State nationalism

The renewal of conflict between state and country is one of the phenomena to have emerged very strongly in Europe over the last few years. The disintegration of the states created under Stalinism, which started in 1989, was followed attentively by the whole world. The dictatorship was the despotic umbrella of many people who, through cultural conflicts and wars, are now attempting to create their own countries (as happened after the end of the First World War). Conflict has meant the shattering and disintegration of the old states. The lack of identity between ethnic and state confines increases the tension between state and country.

The Centre and East of Europe are not the only areas to be involved in this process, as it is developing both in democracies and where dictatorships have fallen. The question of Northern Ireland and the problem of the Flemings and Walloons in Belgium are but two important examples which allow us to understand that these phenomena are deeply rooted in the construction of the institutional pluralism of Europe. This pluralism created the economic growth which accounted for the European miracle, but it has now become the source of an increasing institutional re-definition with the instability and crisis of the historical geo-political relations.

> The very fact that global political power is more dispersed today provides a more fluid and open cultural space in which ethnic minority movements can operate and grow. Because military and political power have ceased to be so monolithic, other sources of collective power, ethnic, religious, regional, colour based can flourish. New, swifter and denser communications systems can supply ideas, networks, techniques, personnel, tactics, materials and examples for aspiring ethnic movements, together with the hope, even the promise, of support from one of the great powers. In this way, great power rivalry helps to proliferate movements of ethnic autonomy and render existing ethnic conflicts more tractable.[1]

A kind of parabola of European nationalism is drawing to a close. After having fought foreign powers for more than a century, Europe now turns its attention to the construction of its own national state with great vigour,[2] fighting now against the states created by both dictatorships and democracies.

This process is present in Southern Europe, though it is not as strong as in Central and Eastern Europe. In some areas a rapid institutional solution to the conflicts has been found, satisfying the nationalist elites. For example, the situation in Alto-Adige was solved by an autonomistic compromise with the Italian state. This solution, though imperfect, put a stop to the growing desire for separation which was fanned by the actions of a terrorist fringe. However, elsewhere the force of dictatorship was decisive in impeding autonomist evolutions which were the result of long, specific historical journeys. The fact that the nationalist movements oppressed under Franco's dictatorship had a different cultural evolution is significant. It is proof that, faced with the same type of repressive power, the resources available to the people and their leaders for fighting that power were different.

The cleavage between centre and periphery is particularly distinct in Spain. Historically speaking, Catalonia and Euskady are considered peripheral, without in any way diminishing the importance of existing regionalisms or nationalisms or those of recent appearance.[3] One of the historical merits of the Second Spanish Republic was that of adopting a well balanced constitutional solution to this problem by conceding autonomy to Catalonia in 1932 and to Euskady in 1936 when the civil war had already started. In the same year the people of Galicia unanimously voted for autonomy but the Cortes could not approve this concession because of the outbreak of the war.

Franchism, with its centrist, authoritarian, military nationalism, abolished autonomy and heavily penalized the regions which did not accept the regime's diktats. The deepest ideals of the people of these regions, together with their linguistic and cultural identities, were trampled, and assimilating and levelling policies were introduced. The aim of these policies was to instil the masses with the idea of an identity between the Spanish state and the destruction of the roots of national history. This was probably the most ill-omened of Franchist crimes. It affirmed, with violence, the replacement of the polytheistic state of the Second Republic by the Franchist monotheistic state.

However, this destructive form of assimilation from above did not achieve the desired results. Under the dictatorship, the conservation of cultural identity became an instrument for reinforcing the autonomy of society and political and social opposition.[4] In fact, with the advent of democracy the reaffirmation of the Catalan and Euskadian nationalities was very significant. In the 'Territorial Title' (Titulo Territorial) of the democratic constitution a very different choice was made to that made in the 1930s. At that time, the definition of 'regional autonomy' was used. The 1978 text spoke of 'nationalities and regions', affirming the principle of difference between nation and state,[5] with the acknowledgement of both the historical rights of the various nationalities and the 'indivisible unity of the Spanish nation'. Thus the way was opened not only for the autonomy of Catalonia, Euskady and Galicia but also for a slower, more complicated process for other regions, guaranteeing freedom in the case of an eventual choice of autonomy.[6]

In any case, this slow process is, and will continue to be, difficult. Negotiations between the central and peripheral forces have not been easy. The acknowledgement of the traditional rights of self-government by the so-called historical nationalities – Catalonia, Euskady and Galicia – was not enough to reconcile their deeply different political orientations. The autonomist pacts which have gradually been stipulated have not fully eliminated the still fairly strong divisions, both old and new. The Organic Law of the Harmonization of the Autonomy Process (Ley Organica de Armonización del Proceso Autonomico), which has caused, and causes, a great deal of discussion, is proof of this. The right to autonomy was also claimed by areas without any tradition of autonomous characteristics. The 1980 referendum in Andalucia gave the area autonomy together with historical nationality.

The requests for autonomy became requests for self-government which were put forward in order to obtain state intervention against unemployment and de-industrialization. Thus the institutional powers' problems of harmonization and coordination were destined to increase.

The problems were, in any case, the result of the extraordinary growth of the social claims coming from society. The requests for autonomy in the democratic state were one of the strong points of that counter society born during the dictatorship.

Catalonia is an example of this with its party system,[7] and in its cultural strong points. Both the tradition of the industrial middle class and the enlarging of the rights of social citizenship, which was often the base for an unstable and precarious compromise between the middle class and the Franchist state, formed a strong bond capable of resisting the centralist forces in their attempts at assimilation.[8]

This national Catalan identity produced an exceptional experience for Spain. A multi-party, united Catalan government, from communists to centrists, was formed and it united all the parties' initiatives into a single force during the transition to democracy. Thus the Catalan cultural identity, which had always been an example of modernization to the whole of Spanish society, was institutionalized. This culture stood for change rather than opposition. It was reformist and enlightened rather than traditionalist even though the Catalan traditions had always been a very important aspect of this culture.[9] In 1980, in the first elections in the autonomous regions, the Catalans voted according to exquisitely ethnic criteria. They voted for the Convergence and Union party (Convergència i Unió) with its charismatic leader Jordi Pujol. His appeal to the people was based on his birth, his language and his roots – a true Catalan. It is significant that the success of Pujol's party was based on Catalan catholicism and the strong Catalan identity of the economic elites.[10] However, the Convergence party was mainly local because, at national level, it did not have enough general appeal.

The PSOE, though it received fewer votes than the Convergence party in the regional election, increased its electoral return in the national general election and so became the majority party. Above all, the PSOE received votes from immigrants who spoke Spanish not Catalan. The communists also received immigrants' votes but to a lesser degree because of its more nationalist tradition. However, once the PSOE became the governing party it assumed a more centralist character and so lost votes. The Convergence party profited from this situation. The shift in votes also meant gains for AP, thus increasing its presence on the scene in spite of its electoral discontinuity. The collapse of the PC was significant and constituted an historical fracture in Catalan political life.[11]

The political system and culture in Euskady were completely different. First of all, Basque nationalism grew from the protests of a rural society excluded from the industrial process. The historical nationalism of the National Basque Party (PNV, Partido Nacionalista Vasco) wanted industrialization placed under the control of an egalitarian, community-orientated society.[12] The roots of the Basque culture are very strong, as the persistence of its language shows. Secondly, alongside an extraordinary resistance to change, there was a split in the nationalist tradition. In 1961, after about 25 years' gestation, the separatist terrorist movement – ETA – struck for the first time. This paved the way for a strategy of terrorism which, after the split between the Marxist-political wing and the military wing (more anti-colonial and radical), became more vicious, and was pursued rationally and with ruthless lucidity. Many people maintain that the ETA terrorism was a reply, in a perverse cycle of repression and terrorism, to the violence of the Franchist state. Though this point of view is widespread, it is not particularly convincing especially in the Basque case. When considering the explicative variables,[13] other factors like economic conditions and the degree of isolation and inequality must be added to repression. But to maintain that the origins of armed violence lie in the behaviour, the objectives or the structure of the terrorists' social context is not exact. We must explain why only certain people transform the tensions created in society into murderous violence. The anthropological approach,[14] recently given much importance, is an interesting step forward because it throws light on the hybrid nature of the values which legitimize violence. But, valid though this approach seems to be, it is still not enough. As always, the main interest of anthropology is the relation between the values of the community and personal freedom. This relation is filtered and moderated by individual intellectual choices. In this sense, terrorism is a crucial aspect of the problem of the intellectuals and their capacity for organization in contemporary society.

ETA is a perfect example of this and the split with the traditional nationalist party, the PNV, concerned the clerical, conservative, cautious roots of a form of nationalism which was culturally foreign to the idea of a military confrontation with the dictatorship. ETA's mass base was reflected in the importance of Herri Batasuna (HB), the political arm of ETA which had constantly supported the choices of the clandestine movement. Its armed strength was considerable. It had not only struck the dictatorship, but it had also paved the road to democracy with corpses. Thus there was danger of provoking a reaction from the military and compromising any gains made.[15] ETA had widened its previously narrow base beyond the confines of ethnic Basques, to include the immigrants and the unemployed, uniting them in the fight against the oppressing centralist state.

The democratic state, by acknowledging the flag, by restoring fiscal rights,[16] by approving the statute giving autonomy, gave Euskady a level of independence unequalled in its history. However, when the Spanish constitution was approved in Euskady, 55.4 per cent of the electorate abstained from voting. The first autonomous government engaged in a bitter controversy against the central government for its actions which appeared to legitimize violence. But gradually a sort of political, cultural revolution took place in this land exhausted by the economic crisis and by endemic violence. Finally, in 1986 an anti-violence pact was signed between the Basque political parties represented in parliament, with the exception of HB.

The need to put an end to violence and to undertake a civil and political fight against terrorism was causing a profound change on the political nature of nationalism. Furthermore, polarization was becoming more and more evident. Recent successes by the repressive Spanish (and French) forces against ETA were only a moment, although important and fundamental, in the more general fight against a culture of violence which threatened to compromise the cultural patrimony of Euskady.[17] However, the impetus towards self-determination was very strong and constituted the crucial problem in the new period of Basque nationalism.

In the rest of Spain, the political cleavage between centre and periphery did not appear with equal strength. Galicia is an example not only of multiple and multi-form cultural nationalistic orientations but of the crystallization of the party system after a period of transition profoundly dominated by the presence of the centre and the right and a good performance by the PSOE, while the nationalists were fairly weak. The conservative orientation of Galician political culture favoured a tight and organic connection between nationalist autonomy and the preservation of the unity of the Spanish state. This enhances the theory that cultural values cannot be reduced to political contests.[18]

The relationship between national culture, politics and violence is also evident in the conflict between the Turkish state and country and the Kurdish nation. The Kurdish people reacted to the process of secularization, carried out by a moderniz-ing oligarchy dedicated to the ideals laid down by Kemal Atatürk, and to social change, by preserving its tribal organization with its hierarchical, cellular structure. The persistence of tribal loyalty[19] was the Kurdish nation's reply to the state's offensive and it generated the political organization of the Kurdish masses. This organization was based on a tribal structure without, however, reproducing only ascriptive status to legitimize the leadership. It was 'partly an achieved status, gained through competition and political stratagem.'[20]

Political participation broke up the ties of kinship loyalty and encouraged non-ascriptive behaviour. This was not a weakness, it was the strength of a population divided between four states: Turkey, Iran, Iraq and Syria. The solution of the national problem had always been hindered by the inevitable re-definition of a stra-tegic area of vital importance to the balance of power in the Middle East. The conflict between Kurdish nationalism and Turkey started in 1924 when the secular-ization policy of Atatürk destroyed the Caliphate which had guaranteed the union between the two ethnic groups through the Islamic faith, foundation of Turk-Kurd unity.[21] From that moment, all attempts at the colonization and cultural integration of the Kurds in the state of Turkey met with strong resistance. The ideals of Kemal Atatürk meant that war against the Kurds was always seen as an historical mission aimed at affirming the superiority of being Turkish. Mass deportations and military administration were the instruments used to carry out this aim, neutralizing all initiatives aimed at supporting the Kurds' right to self-determination. The question of language was central to bringing the Kurds into the nation as they were forbid-den to use their own mother tongue and made to acknowledge Turkish as the only national language. This prohibition was not removed until 1991. The radical con-frontation with the state polarized Kurdish political society even more and favoured the more intransigent forces. In the 1960s, the Kurdistan Labour Party (PKK, Partiya Karkerên Kurdistan) became stronger. This party was organized along military lines and it proclaimed (continuing the tradition of the Turkish Democrat Party) the creation of an independent state unifying all the Kurds. It created military enclaves as bases both in Turkey and in Iraq. The Gulf War and the international offensive against Saddam Hussein placed the Kurdish question before the eyes of the world when the Iraqi dictator's attempt at exterminating the Kurds became pub-lic knowledge. After the attempted rising of the Kurds in Iraq in March 1991, more than one and a half million Kurds fled to Turkey and Iran. This provoked the intervention of the anti-Saddam allied group and the airspace north of the 36th parallel was closed to Iraqi planes. Terrorist acts, kidnapping of tourists and guerilla warfare were all instruments used by the PKK in its long conflict with the Turkish army. This conflict had wide international repercussions. It seemed difficult, if not impossible, to find a solution. The illusions born in October 1991 soon vanished and the weakened Kurdish forces took the fight into parliament. It was war. The Turkish armed forces attacked the guerilla bases of the PKK in both south-east Turkey and the north of Iraq,[22] and terrorism was carried to the capitals of Europe.

The democratic establishment's acknowledgement of the principle of the non-totalitarian identification between state and nation was the final step in overcoming Kemal Atatürk's legacy. The armed forces also had to acknowledge that principle, as their cooperation was essential. Was this a decisive step for the consolidation of Turkish democracy? The search for an institutional solution was vital. This had been possible in Spain but in Turkey everything was more difficult. The Kurdish problem cannot be compared to the Catalan one, and even though the Basque question led to considerable armed violence, it was not a real war with international implications. The Kurdish question involved global balances linked to the strategic control of access to sources of oil.[23]

Nation and state are still unstable realities in the Middle East, as they now are in Central and Eastern Europe. Once more, Turkish affairs give indications for Europe's future. Dictatorships have deeply conditioned the evolution of national problems. Compared to other dictatorship countries, Turkey has the merit of having actuated its transition to democracy with the persistence of a strong military power whose 'democracy' did not go beyond the democratic principles of Atatürk. Tutorage was the fundamental element of democratic institutionalization which was longer and more difficult than elsewhere. Today, Turkish democracy is faced with one of the most difficult steps to take. An institutional solution must be found to the pluralism of the nations within the same state. This is the only possible prospect for overcoming the historical cleavages between centre and periphery.

II Violence and de-elitization

The use of terrorism in the Kurdish and Basque situations underlines the important role played by armed violence in the political life, past and present, of Southern Europe. Of the Continental European countries, only Germany has experienced anything similar, even though it was of considerably smaller and more limited dimensions. However, in Turkey terrorism was not limited to the nationalist fights. More than anything else, armed violence played an important part in the disrupting of a system in the process of being institutionalized. The increase of the use of force, even of assassination, in political battles can be understood when seen in the light of the process of social and cultural change which, with exceptional speed, was affecting Turkey. The basic elements are to be found in those processes defined as 'radicalization of politics'[24] put forward by the populism which emerged strongly after the 1950s. The ruralization of the city had the upper hand over what should have been the urbanization of the rural areas, and thus the de-elitization of society was encouraged. This meant that the formation of a new managerial class was very difficult. It meant interrupting the regeneration of cultural values both in the villages where the old deferential models of behaviour had disappeared without being replaced by new ones, and in the towns where the political classes were in the grips of identity and authority crises. In a society sunk into anomie and in a world without rules, violence can more easily become social behaviour.

The cultural nativism of the right and anti-Western marxism[25] are cultural paradigms which provide the ideological fuel for young people's violence, and for the disintegration of ancient values.

> In this perspective, student violence in Turkey may be explained as the consequence of a major cultural dislocation which has especially marked the perpetrators of violence. Structural survivals from the body of traditional culture together with the disparate changes have brought about this disjunction. On the one hand family socialization has continued to project strong aggressive tendencies generated within the family to any currently available outgroup. On the other hand other elements of the traditional 'little' tradition have displaced elements of the 'great' tradition without being integrated in a new synthesis. Traditional elite education could not be redesigned to serve the needs of a blueprint which was intended to replace an Ottoman segmented society by a society of organic integration. Collective representation emanating from the centre of traditional society was eroded without being replaced by a successful synthesis of civil religion. These are the elements that need to be studied for the specifically Turkish focus of these student events to emerge.[26]

The process of political participation has provided both the ideological and the organizational fuel. The small extreme left groups, split into a thousand different ideological rivulets, swept away a concept of communism which still clung to pro-Soviet positions and the ideology of the military progessivists. The anti-American and anti-imperialist ideals of Mao and Che Guevara were the ideological principles of a new generation whose actions greatly influenced political polarization but which consumed its youth in terrorism.

On the right, the party led by Asparslan Türkes provided the organizational backbone to mass para-military rallies based on the recovery of pan-Turkish ideology in which irredentism, nationalism and neo-Nazism (indubitably influenced by Italian Fascism and Spanish Franchism) were mixed together to produce ruthless terrorism. The whole world felt the shock wave caused by the attempt to assassinate Pope John Paul II in the middle of St Peter's Square in the Vatican City.[27]

Italy also suffered a long cycle of protests. But the expansion of working-class unrest and the explosive rebellion of new bourgeois student classes, which lasted from 1968 to 1977, did not, in fact, have the positive results noted by many observers.[28] This cycle of protests did not increase political institutionalization and it did not produce new elites capable of heading such institutionalization. This complete lack of political regeneration had unexpected and disastrous effects.

The worst of these effects was left and right-wing terrorism which, from 1974 to 1980, carried out more than 13,000 acts of violence, which killed and wounded some 200 people, reaching one of the highest levels of intensity in the whole world.[29] This happened in a country which had been, for centuries, considered a most refined civilization. The origins of Italian terrorism can unquestionably be found in the meagre degree of social integration among the new classes and groups which, from time to time, were the protagonists of collective mobilization. The persistence of revolutionary myths which champion a regenerative change explains this low degree of integration. All this intersects with the too swift affirmation of the process of citizenship which coincided – also in Italy – with an extensive de-elitization of society, the result of the crisis of consolidated models of authority. The ideological factor was therefore decisive:[30]

> Not the contemporary social situation alone but the social situation historically has created a culture in which radical revolutionary tradition, black and red, are part of the atmosphere in which every Italian lives and breathes. In such an atmosphere the unwanted freedom of capitalism is bound to produce disturbing effects of varying intensity in the minds of those individuals who have been shaped ideologically by political values of the extreme Left and Right, who consequently want to see society reorganized in a revolutionary way.[31]

The choice of terrorism derives from having instilled in the minds of many people a political culture which legitimizes violence.[32] Ideology is one of the most evident incentives of terrorism, in terms of justification of the physical destruction of the adversaries and the emphasis on the heroic role of individuals. These ideological incentives are activated by chains of personal networks which together form the collective identities necessary for the solidarity of the armed conflicts. These chains are gradually strengthened as violence becomes a communicative act[33] that conditions the political system. The most notable case of this occurred in Italy when the leader of the DC, Aldo Moro, was assassinated in 1978. Obviously this does not imply placing the cycle of terrorism on the same level as the cycle of protests. Such a hypothesis would lead to a futile controversy. What it does imply, however, is understanding that together with the paradoxes of economic growth and the scarce institutionalization of Italian politics, there is also that paradox by which the expansion of the process of citizenship in the 1970s when political society was saturated with ideology, came about after so much delay and with such intensity as to give birth to the conviction that violence is the only midwife of history.

III Faith and politics

Southern Europe is the crossroads of the great humanistic and Christian traditions of the continent and the Islamic traditions of the Middle East. One of the characteristics of Europe is the growth of religion as an element of symbolic orientation and of the re-appropriation of identity. The crisis of the consolidated revolutionary ideologies[34] and the wide-spread dimming of faith (defined as life dedicated to relations with the divine) is joined to the growth of a new religious spirit laden with political implications. Religious movements develop[35] together with a decline in the intimacy of transcendental experience. This is a sign of imperfect modernization. Economic growth has not encouraged the growth of cultural conditions capable of giving a significance to everyday life.[36] After the fall of the Spanish and Portuguese dictatorships, religion, as the practice of faith, has no longer been a form of organization and a resource of political society. The Portuguese regime was more secular than Spain's.[37] The Spanish church was more committed to the painful job of renewal[38] than the Portuguese one where the impact of the Second Vatican Council was felt less.[39] A party representing the political unity of catholics has not appeared either in Portugal or in Spain, whereas in Italy, with its earlier democracy and its strong ideological conflicts, such a party existed.[40] In Greece there is no Greek Orthodox party, though the transcendental nature of the orthodox religion makes that fact insignificant. In the orthodox traditions, identity with the nation and loyalty to the constitutional power are principles which are linked to the nation and the state; they are not translated automatically into identity with a party.[41]

The renewal of religious movement and of Islamic faith in Turkey requires a very different comment. This phenomenon is quite distinct from the spread of fundamentalism in the Arab countries. However, the two different situations can interact. The Turkish experience is very specific even though it represents incomplete modernization. The misery of the masses and the rebirth of some currents of Islamic tradition have become an explosive mixture in the hands of active and well organized radical elites. Islam is a religious, cultural and historical force rather than a political one. The enormous development of education and religious practice both in the state schools and the religious ones must be underlined. Since 1976 courses of morality have been compulsory in high schools and courses of religion, though optional, are offered everywhere.[42] Over the last few years, a strategy of affirmation and valorization of Islam, no longer based on the rejection of the Atatürk era but on the synthesis of the two traditions, has met with great success. This represents a specific feature of Turkey when it is compared to the rest of the Islamic world. It is due to the strong Sunni tradition in Turkey, rather than to the Shi'a one, and to the secular orientation of a large part of the political class. The Sunni acknowledge the legitimacy of power and do not admit the constitution of an autonomous, politically minded and radical clergy as the Shi'a do. In Turkey religious leaders are state servants. Only the *Alevi* (*duodecimani Shi'a* – roughly a fifth of the population), are opposed to this relation between the state and the church.[43] After a period of opposition by many clandestine sects to the secular ideas of Atatürk during the transition to democracy, Islam has become, more than anything else, an instrument for mass political mobilization. Islam is being used by the new political opposition to gain power by making a political issue of the religious division between the establishment and the masses. After the 1960s, the religious difference continued to materialize as political diversification between the Islamic left and right. On one hand, the role played by the MSP of Türkes in this context is most important. This extreme right party demanded the advent of an 'Islamic state' at a meeting held in September 1980. The military intervened with a coup.[44] On the other hand, it should be remembered that:

> Some religious men offer free religious education to *gecekondu* [shanty town] children but defend workers' rights and advocate full adoption of technology, modern education and science. Even in the squatters' villages some religious leaders, *hocas* or *imans* as they are called locally, turned into fierce advocates of democracy and urged their village mates to participate in elections, claiming that the Marxist Labor party, active during that period, promoted laudable social programmes.[45]

This plurality of the Islamic political experience is typical of Turkey but it is not exclusive to it.[46] Europeans should study it closely. They must realize that the problems which face Turkey will shortly have to be faced by all the secularized countries of Europe. Islam is already part of European cultural identity. Importing men means importing their religions too.

Chapter 11
SOCIETIES AND PARTIES

I Between innovation and continuity

Attempts at the formation of stable central parties in Southern Europe are character-ized by upheavals and changes in the political system. Such changes are based on the different relations which gradually form between the political society and the political system. The thesis presented here is that political society, meant as the sub-cultural orientations and ideals which grow from civil society itself, is more stable than the political party system which is subject to change and crises.

This explains the contradiction which can emerge in societies where moderate (centre) orientations and equally moderate parties, that govern alone or in more or less fragile coalitions, prevail. However, the moderation of parties does not mean they are static. In electoral competitions such parties take, in often unexpected forms, extreme positions on various themes of national political life.

In Greece, after the fall of the military dictatorship, two dominant parties alter-nated in government. They operated in a political society where consumerism and ideological moderation were unifying elements. However, neither party managed to achieve stability and both continued fighting to win voters offering an often danger-ous mix of populism and nationalism. The Macedonian question is an example of this kind of mix and it reached the point where the principles of the EEC were threatened.

In Turkey, after 1983, the formation of centrally orientated parties produced a more solid stability in the political system than had been foreseen. However, the problems of Islam had to be dealt with, while bearing in mind those particularities which are typical of Turkey.

After the fall of the dictatorships in Spain and Portugal, stable central parties quickly appeared and they held power in complete synchrony with the orientations of political society for about fifteen years.

This affirmation of the middle ground also occurred in Italy but it took place amid fierce conflicts and with the crisis of the stronger parties. The figures shown in Table 11.1 illustrate the situation.

Governments of national solidarity, or rather the formation of coalition govern-ments centred around the DC and the PSI, held power from 1976 to 1979. These coalitions received the external support (non-opposition) of the PCI, which abstained from voting on some issues and supported others. This external support was so important, thanks to the electoral strength of the PCI and the party's pres-tige, that the attempt to build a centrally orientated political system was dominated by the decisive alliance between the DC and the PCI. This move was backed by the efforts of Aldo Moro, leader of the DC, on one hand and by Enrico Berlinguer,

Table 11.1 Italian general elections: percentage of votes received and number of parliamentary seats won

	1976		1979		1983		1987		1992	
	% of votes	seats	% of votes	seats	% of votes	seats	% of votes	seats	% of votes	seats
DC	38.7	263	38.3	262	32.9	225	34.3	324	29.7	206
PCI	34.4	227	30.4	201	29.9	198	26.6	177	–	–
PDS*	–	–	–	–	–	–	–	–	16.1	107
Refounded Communists*	–	–	–	–	–	–	–	–	5.6	35
PSI	9.6	57	9.8	62	11.4	73	14.3	94	13.6	92
Northern League	–	–	–	–	–	–	–	–	8.7	55
Network	–	–	–	–	–	–	–	–	1.9	12
Greens	–	–	–	–	–	–	2.5	13	3	13

Source: Italian newspapers
Notes:
* ex-PCI
The system of proportional representation allows the presence of many parties, not all are mentioned here.

leader of the PCI, on the other. Berlinguer conceived the strategy of the so-called historical compromise (*compromesso storico*) which was basically an agreement between the large popular forces of the christian democrats, the socialists and the communists to collaborate in running the country. This would have overcome the US veto on the presence of communists in the Italian government and would have made the possibility of coups unlikely. This danger had increased after the assassination of the socialist president of Chile, Salvador Allende, and the installation of a military dictatorship in 1973.

Aldo Moro's strategy was nullified by the terrorist actions of the Red Brigades (*Brigate rosse*), which culminated in their assassination of Moro, and by the combined efforts of powerful conservative forces in Italy and abroad. These forces found their ideal interlocutors and political representatives in the right wing of the DC and the PSI of Bettino Craxi. The PSI replaced the PCI as the preferred partner of the DC and this led to the alliance of the DC and the PSI which governed Italy from 1980 to 1992. The peak of this union lasted from 1983 to 1987 with Craxi as prime minister. All available resources were divided between the government forces, allowing very limited space for the opposition. Corruption, involving not just single individuals but also vast organizations in both the political and economic societies, became rife. Successive governments led by Giulio Andreotti continued to follow the same practices, condemning Italian society to degrading immobility and to spurious modernization based on the easy enrichment of a new middle class which despised legality and applauded the arrogance of power without rules.

The political factor which had encouraged this situation was the decline in the strength of the PCI. Its more moderate electorate had hoped for the party's entrance in government and the new generations wanted radical changes. Neither happened so these groups penalized the party by moving their votes elsewhere. The DC also lost votes, particularly in 1983, when, in a direct confrontation with the PSI, its more secular voters moved their support to Craxi's socialists. Thanks to its electoral success, the PSI had the power of veto and clientship holds on the government coalitions. This was the base of the party's victory in 1987.[1] That year marked the decisive 'demobilization'[2] of communist influence. Disagreements and discord started to appear within the government coalition and the traditional electorate of the consolidated parties withdrew their support. The PCI was also affected by the collapse of the USSR's Stalinist system in 1989. The PCI's solution to the problem was to make a complete break with the past and to change the name of the party to the Democratic Party of the Left – PDS (Partito Democratico della Sinistra). This new formation joined the International Socialists. The change of name and direction led to the breakaway of the left wing and the hard-line communists and the formation of a party called Refounded Communists (Rifondazione Comunista).[3]

But the most important occurrence was the rapid break-up of a political system which only a few years before had seemed so firmly based on the partnership between the DC and the PSI.[4] In its place, that which can be defined as a rapid de-institutionalization of the party system occurred.[5] The three main parties lost votes while, on the left, new political formations appeared. One was the Refounded Communists, others were the Network (La Rete) and the Greens (I Verdi).[6] However, the most important novelty was the appearance of the Northern League (Lega Nord),[7] a libertist, popular party markedly hostile towards the state's centralized powers, which explicitly expresses the values of spurious modernization. Its gains came mainly from the electoral bases of the DC in the north of the country, but it also had the ability to erode all the traditional bastions of the electorate. It created a territorially based political and cultural fracture which, not by chance, involved the richer part of the country. This section of society had no desire to give up its recently won well-being when the economic crisis appeared on the scene and the distributive conflicts typical of the state's periods of fiscal crisis started.

This phenomenon explains the collapse of the party system, with the proliferation of new political groups, the volatility of the electorate, the personalization of political life with the rapid rise of heroes and their equally rapid disappearance. The political class attempted to halt this process by changing the electoral system. A referendum held in 1991 resulted in the approval by parliament in 1993 of a first-past-the-post majority system corrected, however, by the proportional attribution of 25 per cent of seats.

Investigations into economic and political corruption[8] carried out by the magistrates were beset by many difficulties and the professional and political independence of the magistrates was threatened. However, the very roots of the political system were affected. The extensive corruption was closely linked to clientship and the oligopolistic control of the markets.[9] Thus the instability of the system was accentuated and this led to the diminishing of the central importance of parliament in the political management of the country.[10] A deep feeling of anomie and insecurity pervaded all parts of society.

This sense of insecurity was accentuated during the local elections of 1993 with the polarization between left and right in some of the most important cities. The municipalities of Rome, Naples and Turin elected mayors from the left. Paradoxically, this insecurity was also accentuated by the advent of a technical government led by the ex-governor of the Bank of Italy, Carlo Azeglio Ciampi. This government leant strongly towards the left and it tackled the enormous problem of the state deficit with a vigour never seen before. But this action raised the unpleasant spectre of the sacrifices required by the electorate in order to overcome the crisis and the inevitable social and political changes resulting from it. A large part of society, orientated towards a moderate right and centre right, could not but regret the destruction of the stability which had been guaranteed by a new political centre. This explains why the party system can change while, at the same time, the inspiring values of political society can be preserved. It meant rebuilding a party system conforming to those values, in the wake caused by the de-legitimization of the old political class by the magistrates' actions and by the hypothesis of a leftist government which was seen by many as a threat to the country. The results of this situation are explained in the following section.

However, emphasis must be put on the fact that the fall of the old Italian party system should be studied very carefully because it reveals more general problems which are valid for all the Southern European political systems.

The Southern European parties, with the exception of the communists, are fragile. This fragility means that they are almost incapable of constructing strong organizations which are free from clientship and the cult of personality. This statement seems a paradox, but such an incapacity produces real weakness if seen in the light of real party participation in politics. The workings of parliament are the *raison d'être* for party politics in a democracy. If the special interests of party action are too pervasive, systems of political solidarity able to institutionalize politics cannot be created. This was the universal message, from a scientific point of view, that Huntington offered to the international scientific community in his classic work[11] which is still of great relevance. Institutionalized societies produce mechanisms of authority to limit the resources that can be used in the battles of political power. Limits which lay down procedures and norms to be respected by those who hold office. The exact opposite occurs where vote-buying is accepted as general practice in a party system seen as a collection of lobbies. If this happens in a pluralist society, the result is not Leviathan but Behemoth, the biblical monster of chaos.

Behemoth takes over when parliament is defeated because of the crises of the political parties. This happened in the USA where the parties reach the democratic executive directly and interests hold unopposed domination on the basis of pure strength.[12]

> The most important ... change ... accomplished by the parties in this century is to have been able to overcome the old dichotomy between society and state, forging a system of government in which social requests are represented directly to the executive. In fact, party government, with its successes and failures, is none other than the institutionalization of the principal and contrasting social requests in a new type of political system which is dependent on parties.[13]

The alternative to this is regression towards a new form of liberalism: the neo-patrimonialism[14] of a society which is unequal from the point of view of political participation.

The collapse of a part of the Italian political system should be studied with great attention because it not only reveals problems of a general, international nature but it also offers many lessons thanks to Italy's position as bridge between the relatively new political systems of Southern European countries and the older political systems of the Northern and Continental European countries.

Signs of the proliferation of the Italian 'sickness' are, alas, already visible elsewhere. In the last Spanish elections in 1993, not only was the parliamentary majority of the PSOE weakened but it was forced to negotiate for the support of the nationalist parties. In the local elections held in Portugal in December 1993, the majority domination of Cavaco Silva's party was undermined by the unexpected advance of the socialists.

Perhaps the most important lesson to be learnt from the Italian experience is the need to reconsider not only the relationship between state and market but also the basic concept of democratic pluralism in newly industrialized societies. The concept of democracy must be reconsidered. It must be seen as a process where the power of decision cannot be limited to the party system and its vote-buying mechanisms.[15]

Once, the problem in Southern Europe was that of the scarce autonomy of the political system with regard to civil society in the absence of the state's role as regulator (clientship). The state was present as a creator of segments of civil society. Society was weak with regard to the capacity for autonomous self-organization in the context of state legality. Thus the vicious circle between clientele, kin and individualistic consent is formed. Today civil society is more mature and its capacity for organization and for making proposals has strengthened. It identifies and organizes its interests and it expresses its growing intolerance of party system guardianship.

There are three basic reasons for this. One is the emergence, in the 1950s and 60s, of a new middle class born of civil, not political, participation. Another is the final affirmation of dependent employment as a subject of groups and associations rather than class, with all the political and trade union consequences. The last reason is society's growing intolerance of the political party system's occupation of large slices of state institutions.

This growing intolerance has its roots in the fact that the innovative cycle of the political class, that lasted until the end of the 1960s, has already reached its end in Italy and its conclusion is in sight in the other Southern European countries. The parties consolidated democracy and laid the foundations for its institutionalization. But while the vicious circle of clientship, kinship and consensus persists, the institutionalization of democracy is impossible. Corruption and political, idealistic anomie are the signs of the slow, ineluctable conclusion of the innovative cycle which, though of spurious form, had been activated. Now this cycle cannot be regenerated. The crisis will arrive and there will be a difficult search for new and more solid democratic institutions. The complete redefinition of the role of the parties and the other systems representing interests is essential.

What happens in Italy indicates the shape of things to come, with different rhythms and forms, in the whole of Europe, not only in the South.

II Back to the future?

The results of the general election held in Italy in March 1994 confirm the thesis put forward in the preceding section. The brief cycle of dismantling seems to be ended. But this does not mean stability or the institutionalization of politics. 'Perhaps it is a still temporary recomposition, a still interlocutory stage on the way to a final arrangement.'[16] One certainty is that those who thought that the reform of the electoral system would lead to the reinforcing of democracy and justice have been disillusioned.[17] Exactly the opposite has happened thanks to the continuation of the scant autonomy of the political system from civil society and to the confusion between economic and political power. This combining of roles has been carried out in full view, with an arrogance never seen before, and no longer masked by the smoke screens of corruption. Now a part of the country's economic power is in the forefront of the parliamentary stage and is directly organizing political society with the consequent personalization of politics, the restoration of clientship and caciquism.

The epicentre of the new political system is a quasi-party organization called Forza Italia (Come on, Italy! – taken from the cry of fans at sporting events, particularly football, when the Italian national team is playing). It was formed from nothing in two months by Silvio Berlusconi who, apart from being the owner of television stations and other forms of mass media and chains of supermarkets and department stores, is also the owner of Fininvest, a very large financial empire which was the axis of the preceding system of socialist power. The use of television (and an exceptional marketing strategy) in the electoral campaign was important to the group's success but it was not the decisive factor.

The decisive factor was the ability with which Berlusconi attracted and unified the followers of the various centre and right parties who had sunk into anomie as a result of the magistrates' investigations and, in some cases, accusations of a goodly part of their elites. This aggregation of forces covers a social swathe of middle classes, upper classes, underclasses and working classes hit by unemployment. Its dominant ideological values are populism and economic liberalism. How will these manage to cohabit? The sympathizers of the Northern League and the pro-Fascist followers of the right-wing populism of the old MSI, were joined by the old followers of the centre-right and the christian democrat and socialist right. The MSI was given a new name, National Alliance (AN, Alleanza Nazionale), by its leader, Gianfranco Fini, a very intelligent and shrewd person who is trying to achieve democratic legitimization for his party.

Thus, in the run-up to the general election, the three unlikely bedfellows, Berlusconi with Forza Italia, Umberto Bossi, the rough and ready leader of the Northern League, and Fini with his ex-MSI, joined hands in an alliance which goes by the name of Polo della Libertà e del Buon Governo (Pole of Freedom and Good Government), known in the international press as the Freedom Alliance. The DC ceased to exist and so its followers dispersed. Some joined the Freedom Alliance and others formed a new party with an old name, the Italian Popular Party (PPI, Partito Popolare Italiano). This was the name of the Italian catholic party before the advent of Fascism. This new party joined with Pact for Italy (Patto per l'Italia), led by Mario Segni, to represent the middle ground, the centre of the political spectrum. The leftist parties, after much discussion and bickering, formed an alliance around the PDS and called themselves the Progressives (Progressisti).

The first general election with the new rules of straight majority was held on 18 March 1994. The Freedom Alliance won 366 seats of the 630 in the lower house giving it a majority. The Progressives won 213 and the Pact and PPI won 46. In the upper house (the senate) the Freedom Alliance won 122 seats of the 315 seats which did not give it the majority. The Progressives won 122 and the others won 31. It is worth noting here that the electorate of the lower house is made up of voters over 18, while voters for the senate must be over 25.

The real substance of this whole process of restructuring of the political forces lies in the political division between the north of the country where the right had such an evident victory and the centre where the Progressives won. In the south, the right won in those areas where clientship and welfare hand-outs continue as a way of life, while the left had success where self-sustained economic development has started to develop. However, the true changes are firstly that the political class has more exponents from the north of the country than before, and, particularly on the right, they are drawn from the middle and upper-middle classes. The new bourgeois of the professions and of the small and medium-sized businesses have entered into politics, in person, for the first time. Secondly, the vast majority of young people voted for the right, particularly in the north and south. This is a sign that the use of mass media had only interpreted and guided a deep anthropological movement which has had an effect on the Italian political sub-cultures.

It will be interesting to see if, in the future, this move to the right becomes a stable factor on the political scene. The crisis in Berlusconi's government at the end of 1994 is significant in this respect. Traditionally the right has never possessed a truly stable voting constituency either in Italy or in Greece, Turkey, Portugal or Spain in spite of the long periods of authoritarianism in the past. When democracy has been organized by parties, the supporters of right-wing parties have always shifted easily from one party to another while keeping within the same ideological parameters. The recent difficulties which beset the traditional central parties and the growing identification of youth with the right seem to be the product of the dependence of political society on the market and its cyclic movements. The market does not have great moral or ethic values. The doubts about the stability of the right stem from this fact, as does the question on the type of relation which exists between anthropology and politics.

Only the left remains as a still strong group of political classes which, in spite of its weaknesses and errors, wants to institutionalize, regulate and improve the institutions of society, reducing the moral and physical violence that stems from civil society itself.

And so the demolition of the centre continues. This is not only because there is a movement towards the right which expresses the anthropological change of the 1980s with its diffused political anomie and social Darwinism, but also because the continuous fragility of the parties does not allow them either to embark on a process of institutionalization or to overcome emotive and clientship aggregation.

Not by chance, the winners are those who best knew how to profit from the changes which are oozing in a sludge-like form over society. And so to the final question. Does the Italian experience indicate the future not only of Southern Europe, but of Europe as a whole? Recent events seem to indicate an affirmative answer.

APPENDIX I STATISTICAL TABLES

Table I.1 Total labour force as percentage of total population (average for period)

	1960–8	*1968–73*	*1974–9*	*1980–9*	*1960–89*
Germany	46.5	44	43.5	47.1	45.3
France	42.4	42.1	42.9	43.4	42.7
G. Britain	46.8	45.5	46.5	48.4	46.8
Average	45.2	43.9	44.3	46.3	44.9
Italy	42.7	39.4	39.3	41.6	40.8
Greece	41	37.1	35.8	38.6	38.1
Portugal	38.3	39.7	45.9	46.9	42.7
Spain	38.8	38.3	37.3	36.9	37.8
Turkey	46.2	41.9	n.a.	35.4	30.9
Average	41.4	39.3	31.7	39.9	38.1

Source: OECD – see Ch. 1, n. 1.

Table I.2 Male/female labour force (aged 15–64) as percentage of male/female population

	1960		*1968*		*1974*		*1980*	
	M	F	M	F	M	F	M	F
Germany	94.4	48.9	91.5	48.4	85.9	49.5	83.5	52.8
France	90.1	46.5	86.3	48.6	83.8	52.4	77.8	55.1
G. Britain	97.5	48.1	94.1	51	91.6	56	88.3	60.2
Portugal	104.1	22.5	103.1	29.9	94	53.4	87.5	58
Spain	97.3	27.1	95	29.2	87	32.8	79.5	34.7
Italy	92	36.4	86.7	33.5	83.7	36.5	80.1	41.5
Greece	88.3	38.6	84.4	32.1	80.3	33	78.3	40
Turkey	101.6	67.6	94.7	60.1	n.a.	n.a.	77.1	44.2

Source: OECD – see Ch. 1, n. 1.

Table I.3 Female labour force (aged 15–64) as percentage of total labour force

	1960	*1968*	*1974*	*1980*
Germany	36.6	36.3	37.5	38.7
France	34.1	35.9	38.2	41.4
G. Britain	33.6	35.5	38	40.5
Portugal	19.5	24.8	38.6	41.2
Spain	22.8	24.2	27.9	30.5
Italy	29.6	28.8	31.3	34.9
Greece	31.8	28.5	30	34.3
Turkey	39.1	38.3		35.7

Source: OECD – see Ch. 1, n. 1.

Table I.4 Employment by sector as percentage of total employment (average for period)

	1960–8			*1968–73*		
	Agr.	Ind.	Ser.	Agr.	Ind.	Ser.
Germany	11.9	47.7	40.4	8.5	47.9	43.6
France	19.3	38.6	42.1	13.3	39.2	47.6
G. Britain	4.2	46.7	49.1	3.2	44	52.8
Italy	27.7	36.4	39.5	20.4	39.1	40.4
Greece	51.9	19.9	28.2	40.3	25.4	34.3
Portugal	39.4	32.2	28.3	29.9	33.4	36.6
Spain	33.4	32.7	33.9	26.7	35.6	37.7
Turkey	72.3	11.7	16	67	14.5	18.5

	1974–9			*1980–9*		
	Agr.	Ind.	Ser.	Agr.	Ind.	Ser.
Germany	6.5	45.1	48.4	4.6	41.3	54.1
France	9.8	37.4	52.5	7.6	32.7	59.7
G. Britain	2.8	39.9	57.4	2.5	32.6	64.9
Italy	16.1	38.5	45.3	11.6	34.7	53.6
Greece	33.6	28.9	37.5	28.5	28.3	43.1
Portugal	32.9	34	33.1	23.3	35.4	41.3
Spain	21.5	37.2	41.2	17.1	33.3	49.6
Turkey	n.a.	n.a.	n.a.	52.6	19.7	27.7

Source: OECD – see Ch. 1, n. 1.

Table I.5 Unemployment as percentage of total labour force (average for period)

	1960–8	1968–73	1974–9	1980–9
Germany	0.8	0.8	3.5	6.8
France	1.5	n.a.	4.5	9
G. Britain	1.5	2.4	4.2	9.5
Italy	4.9	5.7	6.6	9.9
Greece	5.2	3.7	1.9	6.6
Portugal	2.4	2.5	6	7.3
Spain	2.3	2.7	5.3	17.5
Turkey	9.5	11.6	n.a.	10.7

Source: OECD – see Ch. 1, n. 1.

Table I.6 Male/female unemployment as percentage of male/female labour force

	1960		1968		1974		1980	
	M	F	M	F	M	F	M	F
Germany	0.9	0.7	0.8	0.9	2.9	4.4	6	8
France	1	2.4	n.a.	n.a.	3.1	6.9	6.9	12
G. Britain	1.7	1.1	3.2	1	5.2	2.5	11.3	6.9
Portugal	n.a.	n.a.	n.a.	n.a.	4.5	8.3	4.8	11
Spain	2.6	1.3	3.2	1.3	5.1	5.8	15.4	22
Italy	3.9	7.3	4	10	4.2	11.6	6.6	16.2
Greece	4.5	6.9	3.3	4.7	1.5	3.1	4.7	10.1
Turkey	n.a.	n.a.	n.a.	n.a.	n.a.	n.a.	n.a.	n.a.

Source: OECD – see Ch. 1, n. 1.

APPENDIX II NAMES OF POLITICAL PARTIES AND OTHER ORGANIZATIONS

Local name	Country	English name
AD – Aliança Democratica	Portugal	Democratic Alliance
AN – Alleanza Nazionale	Italy	National Alliance
ANAP – Anavatan Partisi	Turkey	Motherland Party
ANP – Acção Nacional Popular	Portugal	Popular National Action
AP – Adalet Partisi	Turkey	Justice Party
AP – Alianza Popular	Spain	Popular Alliance
APV – Aliança Popular	Portugal	Popular Alliance
CDE –Commissão Democratica Eleitoral	Portugal	Democratic Electoral Committee
CDS – Centro Democrático y Social	Spain	Democratic and Social Centre
CEUD – Commissão Eleitoral de Unidade Democratica	Portugal	United Democratic Electoral Committe
CGIL – Confederazione Generale Italiana del Lavoro	Italy	Italian General Confederation of Labour
CHP – Cumhuriyet Halk Partisi	Turkey	Republican People's Party
CISL – Confederazione Italiana Sindacati dei Lavoratori	Italy	Italian Confederation of Workers' Trade Unions
CKMP – Cumhuriyetçi Koylu Millet Partisi	Turkey	Republican Peasants' Party
CMP – Cumhuriyetçi Millet Partisi	Turkey	Republican National Party
Comisiones Obreras	Spain	Workers' Commissions
Convergència i Unió	Spain	Convergence and Union
COPCON – Comando Operacional do Continente	Portugal	COPCON
CP – Coalición Popular	Spain	Popular Coalition
DC – Democrazia Cristiana	Italy	Christian Democrat Party
Dimokratikos Stratos tis Elladas	Greece	Democratic Army of Greece
DISK – Türkiye Devrinci Isçi Sendikalari Konfederasyonu	Turkey	Confederation of Revolutionary Workers' Unions
DP – Demokratik Parti	Turkey	Democrat Party
DSP – Demokratik Sol Parti	Turkey	Democratic Left Party
DYP – Dõgru Yol Patisi	Turkey	True Path Party
EAM – Ethnikon Apelftherotikon Metopon	Greece	National Liberation Front
EDA – Enosi Dimokratikon Aristeron	Greece	Union of Democratic Leftists
EDES – Ethnikos Dimokratikos Ellinikos Syndesmos	Greece	National and Democratic Union of Greece
EK – Enosis Kentron	Greece	Centre Union

Local name	Country	English name
ELAS – Ethnikos Laikos Apeleftheratikos Stratos	Greece	National Popular Liberation Army
EPE – Ethniki Politik Enosis	Greece	National Political Union
ERE – Ethniki Rizospastiki Enosis	Greece	National Radical Union
ETA – Euskadi ta Askatasuna	Spain	Euskady or Freedom; Basque nationalist movement
ETN – Estatudo do Trabalho Nacional	Portugal	National Labour Statute
Forza Italia	Italy	Come on, Italy!
GL – Giustizia e Libertà	Italy	Freedom and Justice
GP – Güven Partisi	Turkey	Reliance Party
HB – Herri Batasuna	Spain	Popular Unity
HP – Halkçi Parti	Turkey	Populist Party
IDEA – Iéros Desmos Ellinon Axiomatikon	Greece	Holy Band of Greek Officers
IIC – Iade i Itibar Cemiyeti	Turkey	Society for the Restoration of Respect
INI – Instituto Nacional de Industria	Spain	National Institute for Industry
IRI – Istituto di Ricostruzione Industriale	Italy	Institute for Industrial Reconstruction
KKE – Kommounistiko Komma Elladas	Greece	Greek Communist Party
La Rete	Italy	Network
Lega Nord	Italy	Northern League
MBK – Milli Birlik Komitesi	Turkey	Committee of National Unity
MDP – Milliyetçi Demokrasi Partisi	Turkey	Nationalist Democracy Party
MFA – Movimento da Forças Armadas	Portugal	Armed Forces Movement
MHP – Milliyetçi Hareket Partisi	Turkey	Nationalist Action Party
MP – Millet Partisi	Turkey	Nation Party
MSI – Movimento Sociale Italiano	Italy	Italian Social Movement
MSP – Milli Selamet Partisi	Turkey	National Salvation Party
ND – Nea Dimokratia	Greece	New Democracy
PA – Partito d'Azione	Italy	Action Party
PAK – Panellinio Kinima	Greece	Movement for Panhellenic Liberation
PASOK – Panellinio Sosialistiko Kinima	Greece	Panhellenic Socialist Movement
Patto per l'Italia	Italy	Pact for Italy
PCDS – Partido Centro Democratico Social	Portugal	Centre Democratic Social Party
PCE – Partido Comunista de España	Spain	Spanish Communist Party
PCI – Partito Comunista Italiano	Italy	Italian Communist Party
PCP – Partido Comunista Portugués	Portugal	Portuguese Communist Party
PDS – Partito Democratico della Sinistra	Italy	Democratic Party of the Left
PEK – Panellinion Ethnikon Komma	Greece	Panhellenic National Party
PKK – Partiya Karkerên Kurdistan	Turkey	Kurdistan Workers' Party
Plataforma de Convergencia Democrática	Spain	Platform of Democratic Convergences
PLI – Partito Liberale Italiano	Italy	Italian Liberal Party

Local name	Country	English name
PNF – Partito Nazionale Fascista	Italy	National Fascist Party
PNV – Partido Nacionalista Vasco	Spain	Basque Nationalist Party
Polo della Libertà e del Buon Governo	Italy	Freedom Alliance
PPD – Partido Popular Democratico	Portugal	Popular Democratic Party
PPI – Partito Popolare Italiano	Italy	Italian Popular Party
PPS – Partido Popular Socialista	Spain	Popular Socialist Party
Progressisti	Italy	Progressives
PS – Partido Socialista	Portugal	Socialist Party
PSD – Partido Social Democrata	Portugal	Social Democratic Party
PSDI – Partito Socialdemocratico Italiano	Italy	Italian Social Democrat Party
PSI – Partito Socialista Italiano	Italy	Italian Socialist Party
PSOE – Partido Socialista Obrero Español	Spain	Spanish Socialist Party
Rifondazione Comunista	Italy	Refounded Communists
SDP – Sosyal Demokrasi Partisi	Turkey	Party of Social Democracy
SEDES – Sociedade para O Estudo do Desenvolvimento Económico e Social	Portugal	Study Group for Social and Economic Development
SHP – Sosyal Demokrat Halkçi Parti	Turkey	Populist Social Democratic Party
STVP – Süd Tyroler Volkspartei	Italy	South Tyrol People's Party
SYNAP – Synaspismos	Greece	Left and Progress Coalition
TBP – Türkiye Birlik Partisi	Turkey	Unity Party of Turkey
TIP – Türkiye Isçi Partisi	Turkey	Workers' Party of Turkey
Türk-Is – Türkiye Isçi Sendikalari Konfederasyonu	Turkey	Confederation of General Workers' Union
UCD – Unión de Centro Democrático	Spain	Democratic Central Union
UGT – Unión General de Trabajadores	Spain	General Workers Union
UIL – Unione Italiana del Lavoro	Italy	Italian Union of Labour
UN – União Nacional	Portugal	National Union
Verdi	Italy	Greens

NOTES

Chapter 1 Many Europes

1. OECD Department of Economics and Statistics, *Main Economic Indicators. Historical Statistics, 1964–1983*, OECD, 1984; OECD Department of Economics and Statistics, *Labour Force Statistics 1969–1989*, OECD 1991; OECD Department of Economics and Statistics, *Main Economic Indicators. Historical Statistics 1969–1988*, OECD 1990; OECD Economical Outlook, *Historical Statistics 1960–1989*, OECD 1991; OECD Statistics Directorate, *National Account Main Aggregate*, vol. 1, *1960–1991*, OECD, 1993.
2. Braudel, F., *L'identité de la France. Les hommes et les choses*, vol. II, Arthaud-Flammarion, 1986, pp. 425–6.
3. Kaelble, H., *Auf dem Weg zu einer europäischen Gesellschaft. Eine Sozialgeschichte Westeuropas, 1880–1980*, C.H. Beck'sche Verlagsbuchhandlung (Oskar Beck), 1987; Fuà, G., *I problemi dello sviluppo tardivo*, Il Mulino, 1975; Wolleb, G., *Sviluppo economico e squilibri territoriali nel sud Europa*, Il Mulino, 1993; Anderson, P., Aymard, M., Bairoch, P., Barberis, W., Ginzburg, C. (eds), *Storia d'Europa I. L'Europa oggi*, Einaudi, 1994.
4. Ziegenhagen, E. A. and Koutsoukis, K. S., *Political Conflict in Southern Europe. Regulation, Regression and Morphogenesis*, Praeger, 1992.
5. Lockwood, D., *Solidarity and Schism. 'The Problem of Disorder' in Durkheimian and Marxist Sociology*, Clarendon Press, 1992.
6. Chajanov, A. V., *The Theories of Peasant Economy*, D. Thorner, B. Kerblay, R. E. F. Smith (eds), Homewood, 1966; Chajanov, A. V., *Oeuvres Choisies*, B. Kerblay (ed.), Mouton, 1967; Chajanov, A. V., *L'organisation de l'économie paysanne*, Librairie du Regard, 1990; Chajanov, A. V., *L'economia del lavoro. Scritti scelti*, F. Sperotto (ed.), Franco Angeli, 1988.
7. Eisenstadt, S. N., *Tradition, Change and Modernity*, John Wiley, 1973.
8. Karpat, K. H., 'Social Effects of Farm Mechanisation in a Turkish Village', *Social Research*, 7, 1960, pp. 83–103.
9. Leontidou, L., *The Mediterranean City in Transition. Social Change and Urban Development*, Cambridge University Press, 1990, p. 29.
10. Schneider, P., Schneider, Y., Hansen, E., 'Modernization and Development. The Role of Regional Elites and Noncorporate Groups in the European Mediterranean', *Comparative Studies in Society and History*, 14, 1972, pp. 320–50.
11. Sapelli, G., *Sul capitalismo italiano. Trasformazione o declino*, Feltrinelli, 1993.
12. Offe, C., *Contradictions of the Welfare State*, Hutchinson, 1984; Sapelli, G., *L'Italia inafferrabile*, Marsilio, 1989.
13. Moore, B., *Social Origin of Dictatorship and Democracy. Lord and Peasant in the Making of the Modern World*, Beacon, 1966; Mouzelis, N. P., *Politics in the Semi-Parliamentarism. Early Parliamentarism and Late Industrialisation in the Balkans and Latin America*, Macmillan, 1986.

14. Huntington, S., *Political Order in Changing Societies*, Yale University Press, 1968.
15. Perez Diaz, V., *El ritorno de la sociedad civil. Respuestas sociales a la transición política, la crisis económica y los cambios culturales de España 1975–1985*, Instituto de Estudios Económicos, 1987.
16. Pridham, G. (ed.), *Securing Democracy: Political Parties and Democratic Consolidation in Southern Europe*, Routledge, 1990; Morlino, L., 'Partiti e consolidamento democratico nel Sud Europa' in M. Calise (ed.), *Come cambiano i partiti*, Il Mulino, 1992, pp. 243–75.
17. Barbano, F., 'Sistema o democrazia dei partiti?', *Quaderni di Sociologia*, 3, 1992, pp. 79–91.
18. Sartori, G., *Parties and Party Systems: A Framework for Analysis*, Cambridge University Press, 1976.
19. Farneti, P., *The Italian Party Systems 1945–1980*, S. Finer and A. Mastropaolo (eds), Francis Pinter, 1985; Farneti, P., *Il sistema dei partiti in Italia, 1946–1978*, Il Mulino, 1983.
20. Farneti, P., *The Italian Party*.
21. Fantozzi, P., *Politica, clientela e regolazione sociale. Il Mezzogiorno nella questione politica italiana*, Rubbettino, 1992.
22. Pridham, G., *Political Parties and Coalitional Behaviour in Italy*, Routledge, 1988.
23. Gallino, L., *Della ingovernabilità. La società italiana tra premoderno e neoindustriale*, Edizioni di Comunità, 1987.
24. Smith, D., *Theories of Nationalism*, Duckworth, 1971.
25. De Pina-Cabral, J., 'The Mediterranean as a Category of Regional Comparison: A Critical View', *Current Anthropology*, 3, 1989, pp. 399–406; Gilmore, D., 'On Mediterranaist Studies', *Current Anthropology*, 4, 1990, pp. 395–6; Herzfeld, M., 'Honour and Shame: Problems in the Comparative Analysis of Moral System', *Man*, 15, 1980, pp. 339–51; Goody, J., 'Culture and its Boundaries: A European View', *Social Anthropology*, 1, 1992, pp. 9–32.
26. Szúcs, J., *Les trois Europes*, Editions L'Harmattan, 1985.

Chapter 2 From military balance to problematic solidarity

1. Gaddis, J. L., *The United States and the Origins of Cold War 1941–1947*, Columbia University Press, 1972; Mayers, D., *George Kennan and the Dilemmas of US Foreign Policy*, Oxford University Press, 1988.
2. Kuniholm, B. R., *The Origin of the Cold War in the Near East. Great Power Conflict and Diplomacy in Iran, Turkey and Greece*, Princeton University Press, 1980; Alvarez, D. J., *Bureaucracy and Cold War Diplomacy. The United States and Turkey 1943–1946*, Institute for Balkan Studies, 1980.
3. Nachmani, A., *International Intervention in the Greek Civil War. The United Nations Special Committee on the Balkans 1947–1952*, Praeger, 1990; Frazier, R., *Anglo-American Relations with Greece. The Coming of the Cold War 1942–1947*, Macmillan, 1991; Jones, H., *'A New Kind of War': America's Global Strategy and the Truman Doctrine in Greece*, Oxford University Press, 1988; Kofas, J., *Intervention and Underdevelopment. Greece during the Cold War*, Pennsylvania State University Press, 1989.
4. Cameron Watt, D., *Succeeding John Bull. America in Britain's Place 1900–1975*, Cambridge University Press, 1984; Valdevit, G., *Gli Stati Uniti e il Mediterraneo. Da Truman a Reagan*, Franco Angeli, 1992.

5. Aga Rossi, E. (ed.), *Il Piano Marshall e l'Europa*, Istituto dell'Enciclopedia Italiana, 1983; Maier, C. S., 'Alliance and Autonomy: European Identity and US Foreign Policy Objectives in the Truman Years' in M. J. Lucey (ed.), *The Truman Presidency*, The Wilson Centre, Cambridge University Press, 1989; Kaplan, L., *The United States and NATO. The Formative Years*, Lexington Press of Kentucky, 1984.

6. Nachmani, A., *Israel, Turkey and Greece. Uneasy Relation in the East Mediterranean*, Frank Cass, 1978.

7. Sapelli, G. (ed.), *Nascita e trasformazione d'impresa. Storia dell'Agip Petroli*, Il Mulino, 1993.

8. Louis, W. R., *The British Empire in the Middle East 1945–1951. Arab Nationalism, the United States and Postwar Imperialism*, Clarendon Press, 1984; Scott Lucas, W., *Divided they Stand: Britain, the US and the Suez Crisis*, Hodder, 1991.

9. Stookey, R. W., *America and the Arab States: an Uneasy Encounter*, Wiley, 1975, Cameron Watt, 1984.

10. Xydis, S., *Greece and the Great Powers 1944–1947. Prelude to the Truman Doctrine*, Institute for Balkan Studies, 1963; Coulóumbis, T. A., *Greek Political Reaction to American and Nato Influences*, Yale University Press, 1966; Harris, G. S., *Troubled Alliance. Turkish-American Problem in the Historical Perspective 1945–1971*, American Enterprise Institute for Public Policy Research, Hoover Institution on War, Revolution and Peace, Stanford University 1972; Barchard, D., *Turkey and the West*, Royal Institute of International Affairs, Routledge, 1985.

11. Bacheli, T., *Greek-Turkish Relations since 1955*, Westview Press, 1990.

12. Ténékides, G., 'Internationalisation et désinternationalisation du problème chypriote. La position des puissances occidentales', *Hellenic Review of International Relations*, 3–4, 1983–4, pp. 51–72; Evriviades, M. L., 'Greek Policy and Cyprus: An Interpretation', *Journal of the Hellenic Diaspora*, 3–4, 1987, pp. 25–48; Drevet, J. F., *Chypre, île extrême. Chronique d'une Europe oubliée*, Syros-Alternatives, 1991.

13. Couloumbis, T. A., 'Assessing the Potential of US Influence in Greece and Turkey: A Theoretical Perspective', *Hellenic Review of International Relations*, 3–4, 1983–4, pp. 27–50; Alford, J., *Greece and Turkey: Adversity in Alliance*, Gower, 1984; Vaner, S. (ed.), *La différence gréco-turc*, Editions L'Harmattan, 1988.

14. Hoff-Wilson, J., '"Nixingerism", NATO, and the Detente', *Diplomatic History*, 4, 1989, pp. 501–6; Isaacson, W., *Kissinger: A Biography*, Faber and Faber, 1992; Stavrou, N. A., *Allied Politics and Military Interventions: the Political Role of the Greek Military*, Paparissi, 1976.

15. Yannas, P. M., 'The Papandreou Government's Decision on the Status of US Bases in Greece: A Structural Analysis', *Hellenic Review of International Relations*, 3–4, 1983, pp. 299–315.

16. Nachmani, A., *Israel, Turkey and Greece*, p. 52.

17. Ferreira de Sousa, J., 'As relações externas na dinamica politica e economica nacional nos anos 80', *Análise Social*, 3–4, 1985, pp. 473–97; Rosas, F., *O salazarismo e aliança luso-britanica (Estudio sobre a politica externa do Estado Novo nos anos 30 e 40)*, Editorial Fragmentos, 1988.

18. Menaul, S., 'The Geo-strategic Importance of the Iberian Peninsula', *Conflict Studies*, 133, 1981.

19. Antunes, J. F., *Os americanos e Portugal*, vol. 1, *Os anos de Richard Nixon (1969–1974)*, Dom Quixote, 1986.

20. Harrison, M. M., *The Reluctant Ally. France and Atlantic Security*, Johns Hopkins University Press, 1981.

21. Hadian, R., 'United States Foreign Policy Toward Spain 1953–1975', *Iberian Studies*, Spring 1978, pp. 3–13.
22. Santoro, C. M., *La politica estera di una media potenza*, Il Mulino, 1991; Santoro, C. M., *L'Italia e il Mediterraneo*, Franco Angeli, 1988.
23. Di Nolfo, E., *Vaticano e Stati Uniti 1939–1952. Dalle carte di Myron C. Taylor*, Franco Angeli, 1979; Riccardi, A., *Il Vaticano e Mosca*, Laterza, 1992.
24. Sapelli, G. (ed.), *Nascita e trasformazione*, 1993.
25. Dassù, M., 'Europe and Detente: the Case of Italy', *Working Paper for the Royal Institute of International Affairs*, 1991.
26. Bernstein, B. J., 'The Cuban Missile Crisis: Trading the Jupiters in Turkey?', *Political Science Quarterly*, 1, 1980, pp. 97–104.
27. Isaacson, W., *Kissinger: A Biography*, Faber and Faber, 1992.
28. Frendo, H., *Party Politics in a Fortress Colony: the Maltese Experience*, Midsea Publication, 1979; O'Neill, R. (ed.), *Prospects for Security in the Mediterranean*, Macmillan, 1988.

Chapter 3 Emigration and social differences

1. Rettaroli, R., 'Migrazioni e politiche migratorie' in M. Livi Bacci and F. Martuzzi Veronesi (eds), *Le risorse umane del Mediterraneo. Popolazione e società al crocevia tra Nord e Sud*, Il Mulino, 1990, p. 281.
2. Rettaroli, R., 'Migrazioni e politiche migratorie', p. 283.
3. 'Appendice Statistica' in M. Livi Bacci and F. Martuzzi Veronesi (eds), *Le risorse umane*, p. 398.
4. King, K., 'Population mobility: emigration, return migration and internal migration' in A. Allan Williams (ed.), *Southern Europe Transformed. Political and Economic Change in Greece, Italy, Portugal and Spain*, Harper & Row, 1984, p. 148; for Turkey: Kutlay Ebiri, 'Impact of Labor Migration on Turkish Economy' in R. Rogers (ed.) *Guests come to Stay. The Effects of European Labor Migration on Sending and Receiving Countries*, Westview Press, 1985, p. 216.
5. Giner, S., 'Immigracio de força de treball dels països mediterranis a Europa: alguns efects socio-economics', *Papers*, 4, 1975, pp. 31–55.
6. Simon, G., *Migration in Southern Europe: an Overview*, OECD, 1986.
7. Hirschmann, A. O., *Exit, Voice and Loyalty: Responses to Decline in the Firms, Organisations and States*, Harvard University Press, 1970; Piselli, F., 'Mercato del lavoro ed emigrazione: il processo d'individuazione di una comunità tradizionale', *Inchiesta*, luglio–agosto, 1979, pp. 44–57.
8. Brettel, C. and Pereira, V. M., 'Immigration and the Portuguese Family: A Comparison between Receiving Societies' in T. Bruneau, V. M. P. Roso, A. McLead (eds), *Portugal in Development. Emigration, Industrialisation, the European Community*, University of Ottawa Press, 1984, pp. 83–111.
9. Runciman, W., *Relative Deprivation and Social Justice. A Study of Attitudes to Social Inequality in Twentieth Century England*, Routledge & Kegan Paul, 1966.
10. Brettel, C., *Men who Migrate, Women who Wait. Population and History: a Portuguese Parish*, Princeton University Press, 1986, p. 12; De Sousa Bettencourt, J., 'El fenomeno de la emigración portuguesa', *Revista Internacional de Sociología*, 68, 1959, pp. 589–620 and 69, 1960, pp. 67–99; Marinho Antunes, M. L., 'Vinte anos de emigração portuguesa: algums datos e comentarios', *Análise Social*, 30–1, 1970, pp. 299–385; Betriz Rocha Trinidade, M. (ed.), *Estudos sobre a Emigração*

Portuguesa, Cadernas de la Revista de Historia Economica e Social, 1–2, Sa da Costa, 1981.

11. Anido, N. and Freire, R., *L'émigration portugaise. Présent et avenir*, PUF, 1978.
12. Ebiri, K., 'Impact of Labor Migration on the Turkish Economy' in R. Rogers (ed.), *Guests come to Stay*, p. 206.
13. Treves, A., *Le migrazioni interne durante il fascismo*, Einaudi, 1978.
14. Paci, M., 'Il mercato del lavoro' in AAVV, *Storia d'Italia*, vol. 1, *Il mondo contemporaneo*, La Nuova Italia, 1978, pp. 640 ff.
15. Gregory, D. D. and Cazorla Perez, J., 'Intra-European Migration and Regional Development: Spain and Portugal' in R. Rogers (ed.), *Guests come to Stay*, p. 237.
16. Baklanoff, E. N., *The Economic Transformation of Spain and Portugal*, Praeger, 1978, p. 130.
17. Alonso, J. A., 'El sector exterior' in J. L. Garcia Delgado (ed.), *España Economía*, Espasa-Calpe, 1988, pp. 330–1.
18. Piore, M. J., *Birds of Passage: Migrant Labor and Industrial Societies*, Cambridge University Press, 1979.
19. Bank, W., *World Development Report 1983*, Oxford University Press, 1983.
20. Freris, A. F., *The Greek Economy in the Twentieth Century*, Croom Helm, 1986, p. 166.
21. Ebiri, K., 'Impact of Labor Migration', p. 224.
22. Bourgey, A., *Flux et reflux des travailleurs turcs dans les pays arabes* in J. Thobie and S. Kancal (eds), *Turquie, Moyen-Orient, Communauté Européenne*, Editions L'Harmattan, 1989, p. 101.
23. Clausse, G., 'Portuguese Emigration to the EEC and Utilization of Emigrants' Remittances' in T. C. Bruneau, V. M. P., Da Roso, A. McLead (eds), *Portugal in Development*, p. 160; Stahl, H. M., 'Portuguese Migration and Regional Development' in Fundação Calouste Gulbenkian and The German Marshall Fund of the United States, *2ª Conferencia Internacional sobre Economia Portuguesa*, Fundação Calouste Gulbenkian, 1980, pp. 369–99.
24. Anido, N. and Freire, R., *L'émigration portugaise*, p. 86.
25. Nazareth, J. M., *O Envelhecimento da população portuguesa*, Editorial Presença, 1979.
26. Gregory, D. D. and Cazorla Perez, J., 'Intra-European Migration'.
27. Berrocal, L., *Marché du travail et mouvements migratoires*, Editions de l'Université de Bruxelles, 1983.
28. Gregory, D. D., *La odisea andaluza. Una emigración hacia Europa*, Technos, 1978; Cayltano Rosado, M., *Emigración: telón de la pobreza*, Servicio de Estudios de la Emigración Extrema 1979; De Miguel, A., *La pirámide social española*, Editorial Ariel, Fundación Juan March, 1977; Garcia Ramon, M. D., 'Agricultural Change in an Industrialisation Area: the Case of Tarragona Area' in R. Hudson and J. Lewis (eds), *Uneven Development in Southern Europe. Studies of Accumulation, Class, Migration and the State*, Methuen, 1985, pp. 140–54; Leizu, M., *Capitalismo europeo y emigración*, Avance, 1975.
29. Freris, A. F., *The Greek Economy*, p. 164.
30. Leontidou, L., *The Mediterranean City in Transition. Social Change and Urban Development*, Cambridge University Press, 1990, p. 99.
31. *Ibid.*, pp. 56 and 104.
32. Burgel, G., *Croissance urbane et développement capitaliste. Le 'miracle' athénien*, Editions du CNRS, 1981, p. 247.
33. Kayser, B., Pechouse, P. Y., Sivignon, M., *Exode rural et attraction urbaine en Grèce*, Centre National de Recherches Sociales, 1971, p. 222.
34. Ebiri, K., 'Impact of Labor Migration', p. 206.

35. Gokalp, A., 'Les Turcs' in A. Gokalp (ed.) *L'argent des immigrés: revenues, épargne et transfert*, PUF, 1981, p. 352.
36. Giner, S., 'Immigracio de força'.
37. Bourgey, A., *Flux et reflux des travailleurs*, p. 109.
38. Lutz, V., 'Some structural aspects of the southern problem: the complementarity of emigration and industrialisation', *Banca Nazionale del Lavoro Quarterly Review*, 14, 1961, pp. 367–402; Kindleberger, C. P., *Economic Development*, McGraw-Hill, 1965; Griffin, K., 'On the emigration of the peasantry', *World Development*, 4, 1976, pp. 353–6; Rist, R. C., *Guest Workers in Germany*, Praeger, 1978.
39. Myrdal, G., *Rich Land, Poor Land*, Harper & Row, 1957, and id. *Economic Theory and Underdeveloped Regions*, Methuen, 1963.
40. Baran, P., *The Political Economy of Growth*, Monthly Review Press 1957; Furtado, C., *Development and Underdevelopment*, California University Press, 1971.
41. Unat, A (ed.), *Turkish Workers in Europe, 1960–75*, E. J. Brill, 1975; Mandel, R., 'Shifting Center and Emergent Identities: Turkey and Germany in the Lives of Turkish Gastarbeiter' in D. F. Eickelman, J. Piscator (eds), *Muslim Travellers: Pilgrimage, Migration and the Religious Imagination*, Routledge, 1990, pp. 153–71; Nikolinatos, M., 'Wanderungsbewegungen, Investitionen und Handelsbeziehungen zwischen Regionen verschiedenen Entwicklungsgrades unter Spätkapitalistischen Bedingungen. Der Fall Mittelmeer', in C. Leggerwie, N Nikolinakos (eds), *Europäische Peripherie. Die Dritte Welt*, 1975; Ramazanoglu, H. (ed.) *Turkey in the World Capitalist System. A Study of Industrialisation, Power and Class*, Gower, 1985.
42. Danielson, M. N., Keles, R. 'Urbanisation and Income Distribution in Turkey' in E. Özbudun and A. Ulusan (eds), *The Political Economy of Income Distribution in Turkey*, Holmes & Meier, 1980, pp. 269–311.
43. Keles, R., 'The effects of external migration on regional development in Turkey' in R. Hudson and J. Lewis (eds), *Uneven Development*, pp. 54–74.
44. Töpfer, H., 'The economic impact of returned emigrants in Trabzon, Turkey' in R. Hudson and J. Lewis (eds), *Uneven Development*, pp. 77–100.
45. Penniux, R., von Reuselac, H., von Velzen, L., 'Social and Economic Effects of External Migration in Turkey' in N. Unat (ed.), *Turkish Workers*, p. 303.
46. Ramazanoglu, C., 'Labour, migration in the development of Turkish capitalism' in H. Ramazanoglu, *Turkey in the World*, p. 175.
47. Gokalp, A., 'Espace rural, village, ruralité: à la recherche du paysan anatolien' in A. Gokalp (ed.), *La Turquie en transition, Disparités, Identités, Pouvoirs*, Maison Neuve Larose, 1986, p. 75.
48. Lambiri-Dimaki, J., 'Dowry in Modern Greece: a Traditional Institution at the Crossroads between Persistence and Decline (in the 1960s)' in J. Lambiri-Dimaki, *Social Stratification in Greece 1962–1988. Eleven Essays*, N. Saokoulas, 1983, pp. 157–80.
49. Gokalp, A., 'Espace rural, village, ruralité: à la recherche du paysan anatolien', p. 75.
50. Karpat, K. H., *The Gecekondu: Rural Migration and Urbanisation*, Cambridge University Press, 1976.
51. Karpat, K. H., 'Social Effects of Farm Mechanisation in a Turkish Village', *Social Research*, 7, 1960, pp. 83–103.
52. Magnarella, P. J. (with Ahmet-Ozkan), *The Peasant Venture. Tradition, Migration and Change among Georgiani Peasants in Turkey*, Schenknian, 1972.
53. *Ibid.*, p. 160.
54. Paine, S., *Exporting Workers: the Turkish Case*, Cambridge University Press, 1974, p. 175.

55. Ascoli, U., 'Migration of Workers and the Labour Market: Is Italy becoming a Country of Immigration?' in R. Rogers (ed.), *Guests come to Stay*, p. 190.

56. Fofi, G., *L'immigrazione a Torino*, Feltrinelli, 1964.

57. Bielli, C., 'Aspects of the social integration of immigrants in Milan', *Genus*, 29, 1973, pp. 183–92.

58. Reyneri, E., *L'emigrazione meridionale nelle zone di esodo*, Università di Catania, 1976.

59. Pugliese, E., 'Farm workers in Italy: agricultural working class, landless peasants or clients of welfare state?' in R. Hudson and J. Lewis (eds), *Uneven Development*, pp. 123–39.

60. Pizzorno, A., Crough, C. (eds), *Conflitti in Europa: lotta di classe, sindacati e stato dopo il '68*, Etas Libri, 1977.

61. Donolo, C., 'Sviluppo ineguale e disgregazione sociale in Meridione', *Quaderni Piacentini*, 47, 1972, pp. 101–28.

62. Ascoli, U., 'Migration of Workers', p. 192.

63. Reyneri, E., *La catena migratoria*, Il Mulino, 1974.

64. Trigilia, C., *Sviluppo senza economia. Effetti perversi delle politiche nel Mezzogiorno*, Il Mulino, 1979.

65. Becchi Collidà, A., *Politiche del lavoro e garanzie del reddito in Italia*, Il Mulino, 1979.

66. Golini, A., and Gesano, G., 'Regional migration in the process of Italian economic development from 1981 to present' in J. Balán (ed.), *Why People Move: Comparative Perspectives on the Dynamics of Internal Migration*, Unesco Press, 1981, pp. 128–61.

67. Migliorini, E., 'Spostamenti di popolazione nell'Italia nell'ultimo quarto di secolo' in A. Pecora and R. Pracchi (eds), *Contributi italiani al 23° Congresso Internazionale di Geografia*, CNR, 1976, pp. 135–201.

68. Golini, A. and Gesano, G., 'Regional migration'.

69. King, I., 'Population mobility: emigration, return migration and internal migration' in A. Allan Williams (ed.), *Southern Europe Transformed*, p. 146.

70. *Ibid*, p. 149.

71. Meloni, B., *Famiglie di pastori. Continuità e mutamento in una località della Sardegna Centrale. 1950–1970*, Rosenberg e Sellier, 1984.

72. Bruni, M., 'Migrazioni mediterranee e mercato del lavoro italiano' in B. Amoroso (ed.), *Primo rapporto sul Mediterraneo*, CNEL, 1991, pp. 1–36.

73. Ascoli, U., 'Migration of Workers'.

74. King, R., Martiner, F., Strachan, A., Trono, A., 'Return Migration and Rural Economic Change: a South Italian Case Study' in R. Hudson and J. Lewis (eds), *Uneven Development*, p. 120.

75. Cazorla, J., Gregory, D. D., Neto, J. P., 'El retorno de los emigrantes al sur de Iberia', *Papers*, 11, 1979, pp. 65–79; Raque Amaro, R., '"Ei-los quevoltam". Problemas e desafios do regresso dos emigrantes', *Revista Critica de Ciencias Socials*, 15/16/17, 1985, pp. 351–73.

76. Rettaroli, R., 'Migrazioni e politiche migratorie', p. 285.

77. Simon, J., 'Migration in Southern Europe: an Overview' in OCDE, *The Future of Migration*, OCDE, 1987.

78. Leontidou, L., *The Mediterranean City*, pp. 107 and 108.

79. Bairoch, P., *Taille des Villes, conditions de vie et développement économique*, Editions de l'EMHSS, 1977.

Chapter 4   Southern European agriculture and peripheral protectionism

1. Fabiani, G., 'Un ciclo comune nell'evoluzione dei sistemi agricoli contemporanei' in P. P. D'Attorre and A. De Bernardi *Studi sull'agricoltura italiana*, Annali della Fondazione Feltrinelli, XXIX, Feltrinelli, 1994, pp. 545–88.
2. *Ibid.*
3. *Ibid.*, p. 560.
4. *Ibid.*, p. 576.
5. Garcia Delgado, J. L. and Muñoz Cidad, C., 'La agricoltura: cambios estructurales en los últimos decenios' in J. L. Garcia Delgado (ed.), *España Economía*, Espasa-Calpe, 1988, pp. 123–4.
6. OECD, *Main Economic Indicators. Historical Statistics 1964–1983*, OECD, 1984.
7. Preti, D., 'La politica agraria del fascismo: note introduttive', *Studi storici*, 4, 1931; Corner, P., 'Considerazioni sull'agricoltura capitalistica durante il fascismo', *Quaderni storici*, 29–30, 1955, pp. 519–29.
8. Giorgetti, P., *Contadini e proprietari nell'Italia moderna. Rapporti di produzione e contratti agrari dal secolo XVI a oggi*, Einaudi, 1974.
9. Coehn, S., 'Rapporti agricoltura-industria e sviluppo agricolo' in P. Ciocca and G. Toniolo (eds), *L'economia italiana nel periodo fascista*, Il Mulino, 1976, pp. 379–408.
10. Fabiani, G., *L'agricoltura italiana tra sviluppo e crisi (1945–1985)*, Il Mulino, 1986.
11. Naredo, J. M., 'La agricultura española en el desarrollo económico' in R. Garrabou, C. Barciela López, J. J. Jiménez Blanco (eds), *Historia agraria de la España Contemporanea*, vol. 3, *El fin de la agricultura tradicional (1900–1960)*, Editorial Crítica, 1986, pp. 455–98.
12. Delgado, J. L. and Muñoz Cidad, C., 'La agricoltura: cambios estructurales'; Garrido Egido, L., 'Eficencia y competitividad de la agricultura. La evolución de la agricultura española en el periodo 1961–1980', *Revista de estudios agro-sociales*, 123, 1983, pp. 69–94.
13. Halpern Pereira, M., *Assimetrias de crescimiento e dependencia externa (Comparãçao entre dois periodos de historia contemporanea portuguesa 1847–1914 e 1940–1970)*, Seara Nova, 1974, pp. 11 ff. Now in Spanish translation in M. Halpern Pereira, *Política y economía. Portugal en los siglos XIX–XX*, Ariel, 1984, pp. 59–86.
14. Marques, A., *Política economíca e desenvolvimento em Portugal (1926–1959)*, Livros Horizonte, 1988, p. 97; Barreto, A., 'O estadío fascista do desenvolvimento do capital-ismo em Portugal', *Polemica*, 1, 1970, pp. 91 and 123.
15. OECD Economic Outlook, *Historical Statistics 1960–1989*, OECD, 1991.
16. Van Rijckelem, W. and Barreiros, L., *Employment and Basic Needs in Portugal*, International Labour Office, 1978, p. 132.
17. Pearson, S. R. (ed.), *Portuguese Agriculture in Transition*, Cornell University Press, 1987; Cabral Cordovil, F., 'A socioeconomia da agricultura portuguesa nos anos 80: factos e ideias', *Análise Social*, 121, 1993, pp. 187–234.
18. Karpat, K. H., 'Social Groups and the Political System after 1960' in K. H. Karpat (ed.), *Social Change and Politics in Turkey. A Structural-Historical Analysis*, E. J. Brill, 1973, pp. 227–81.
19. Stewig, R., 'Bursa, Nordwestanatolien-Strukturwandel einer orientalischen Stadt unter dem Einfluss der Industrialisierung', *Schriften der Geographische Institut der Universität Kiel*, 1970; Maury, R. G., 'Géo-démographie de la Turquie: une transition difficile', *Méditerranée*, 4, 1983 pp. 51–61; Bazin, M., 'Les disparités régionales en Turquie' in A. Gokalp (ed.), *La Turquie en Transition. Disparité, identité, pouvoirs*,

Maison–Neuve Larose, 1988, pp. 17–48; Ramachandran, N., *Agricultural and Industrial Development Policies in Turkey. A Review*, OECD, 1974. pp. 18 ff.

20. Hershlag, Z. Y., *The Contemporary Turkish Economy*, Routledge, 1988, p. 55; Tekelioglu, Y., 'Les structures agricoles, facteurs de blocage de l'agriculture turque dans le contexte de l'intégration de la Turquie à la CEE' in J. Thobie and S. Kancal (eds), *Turquie, Moyen-Orient, Communauté Européenne*, Editions L'Harmattan, 1989, pp. 72–100.

21. Dertilis, G. B. (ed.), *Banquiers, usuriers et paysans. Réseau de crédit et stratégies du capital en Grèce (1780–1930)*, Fondation des Treilles, La Découverte, 1988; Freris, A. F., *The Greek Economy in the Twentieth Century*, Croom Helm, 1986.

22. Freris, A. F., *The Greek Economy*, p. 185.

23. Papelasis, A. A., *Labour Shortages in Greek Agriculture 1963–1973*, Center for Economic Research, 1963.

24. *Ibid.*, pp. 17–18.

25. McDonald, R., *Greece in the 1990s. Taking its Place in Europe*, Economist Intelligence Unit, 1991, p. 23.

26. Mouzelis, N. P., *Modern Greece. Facets of Underdevelopment*, Macmillan, 1978, p. 80.

27. Mouzelis, N. P., *Politics in the Semi-Periphery. Early Parliamentarism and Late Industrialisation in the Balkans and Latin America*, Macmillan, 1986.

28. Vergopoulos, K., *Le capitalisme difforme et la nouvelle question agraire. L'exemple de la Grèce moderne*, François Maspero, 1977, p. 167; Burgeel, G., 'Recherches agraires en Grèce' in J. Dresch (ed.), *Mémoires et documents. Recherches sur la Grèce rurale*, Editions du CNRS, 1972, pp. 8–59.

29. Mouzelis, N. P., *Modern Greece*, p. 83.

30. Chajanov, A., *The Theory of Peasant Economy*, D. Thorner, B. Kerblay, R. E. F. Smith (eds), Homewood, 1966.

31. Mcdonald, R., *Greece in the 1990s*.

32. Ward, R. E. and Roustow, D. A. (eds), *Political Modernisation in Japan and Turkey*, Princeton University Press, 1966.

33. Ramachandran, N., *Agricultural and Industrial,* p. 30.

34. Ward, R. E. and Roustow, D. A. (eds), *Political Modernisation*.

35. Orlando, G., 'Progressi e difficoltà dell'agricoltura' in G. Fuà (ed.), *Lo sviluppo economico in Italia*, Franco Angeli, 1969, pp. 17–95.

36. Karpat, K. H. 'Structural Change, Historical Stages of Modernisation and the Role of Social Groups in Turkish Politics' in K. H. Karpat (ed.), *Social Change*, p. 43.

37. *Ibid.*, p. 67.

38. Tekelioglu, Y., 'Les structures agricoles', pp. 92–5; Hershlag, Z. Y., *Turkey. The Challenge of Growth*, E. J. Brill, 1968, p. 158; Eren, N., *Turkey Today and Tomorrow*, Praeger, 1963, p. 111; Akan, R., 'Problems of Land Reform in Turkey', *Middle East Journal*, Summer 1966, p. 330.

39. Ulusan, A., 'Public Policy Toward Agriculture and Its Redistributive Implications' in E. Özbudun and A. Ulusan (eds), *The Political Economy of Income Distribution in Turkey*, Holmes & Meier, 1980, p. 143.

40. Tekelioglu, Y., 'Les structures agricoles', p. 84.

41. Pianet, C. (ed.)., *Familles et biens en Grèce et à Cypre*, Editions L'Harmattan, 1985.

42. Barrera González, A., *Casa, herencia y familia en la Cataluña rural (Lógica de la razón doméstica)*, Alianza Editorial, 1992.

43. De Barros, A. (F. Ribeiro Mendes and G. Mendes, eds), *A reforma Agraria em Portugal. Das ocupações de terra à formação das novas unidades de produção*, Fundação Calouste Gulbenkian, 1979.

213

44. *Ibid.*, p. 46.
45. *Ibid.*, p. 48.
46. Sereni, E., *La questione agraria nella rinascita nazionale italiana*, Einaudi, 1945.
47. Da Costa, R., *Elementos para a Historia do Movimento Operario em Portugal. 1820–1875*, Assirio e Alvian 1979; Ventura, A., *Subsidios para a Historia do Movimento Sindical Rural no Alto Alentejo. 1910–1914*, Seara Nova, 1976.
48. Barreto, A., 'O Estado e a Reforma Agraria: 1974–1976', *Análise Social*, 77–78–79, 1986, pp. 513–77; Pacheco Pereira, J., *Conflitos Sociais nos campos de Sul em Portugal*, Europa–America (no date); Pacheco Pereira, J., 'Atitudes do trabalhador rural alentejano face á posse de terras aõ latifundo' in A. de Barras (coord.), *A Agricultura Latifundiária na Peninsula Iberica*, Fundação Calouste Gulbenkian, 1980; Pacheco Pereira, J., 'As lutas sociais dos trabalhadores alentejanos: do banditismo a greve', *Análise Social*, 61–2, 1980, pp. 135–56.
49. Cutileiro, J., *Ricos e Pobres no Alentejo*, Sa da Costa, 1977.
50. Malefakis, E., 'Two Iberian Land Reforms compared: Spain, 1931–36 and Portugal, 1974–78' in A. de Barras (coord.), *A Agricultura Latifundiária*, pp. 455–86.
51. Viergas, J. M. and Reis, M., 'Campesinato e Regime Democratico. Uma cultura politica em trasformação', *Sociologia, Problemas e praticas*, 5, 1988, pp. 79–108.
52. Hespanha, P., 'A distribuição de terras a pequenos agricultores. Uma politica para "desproletarizar" a reforma agraria', *Revista Critica de Ciencias Sociais*, 18–19–20, Feb. 1986, pp. 379–403.
53. Cazes, G., Domingo, J., Gouthier, A., *L'Espagne et le Portugal. Le défi éuropéen*, Bréal Montreuil, 1989, p. 329.
54. Oliveira Baptista, F., 'Trabalhadores agricolos e agricultores familiares. Dez anos de factos, debates e projectos', *Revista Critica de Ciencias Sociais*, 18–19–20, Feb. 1986, p. 435.
55. Barbot Campose Matos, M. C., 'As Estratégias das pequenas explorações familiares', *Cadernas de Ciencias Sociais*, 7, Nov. 1988, p. 35; des Mercedes, M. and Covas, C. M., 'Agricultura familiar em Portugal. Que extenção para o seu desenvolvimento?', *Economia e Sociologia*, 49, 1990, pp. 153–68; Reis, J., 'Notas de leitura sobre a intensificação da produção agricola', *Revista Critica de Ciencias Sociais*, 12, 1983, pp. 242–81; Reis, J., 'A pequena agricultura e o desenvolvimento economico. Modos de inserção do sector agricolo na economia portuguesa' *Comunicação a 2a Conferencia Nacional dos Economistas*, Lisboa, 1984; Reis, J., 'Modos de industrialisação, força de trabalho e pequena agricultura. Para uma análise de articulação entre a acumulação e a reprodução', *Revista Critica de Ciencias Sociais*, 15–16–17, pp. 225–60.
56. Laurenco, N., *Familia rural e industria. Mudança social na região de Leiria*, Editorial Fragmentos, 1991.
57. De Sousa Santos, B., 'Estado e sociedade na semi-periferia do sistema mundial: o caso português', *Comunicação ão Coloquio: Mudanças Sociais no Portugal de Hoje*, 1985; de Sousa Santos, B., *O Estado e a sociedade em Portugal (1974–1988)*, Edições Afrontamento, 1990.
58. Schneider, P., Schneider, Y., Hansen, E., 'Modernization and Development', 1972. The Role of Regional Elites and Noncorporate Groups in the European Mediterranean', *Comparative Studies in Society and History*, 14, 1972, pp. 320–5.
59. Barberis, G., *La riforma agraria in Italia. Risultati e prospettive*, Feltrinelli, 1960; I.N.S.O.R., *La riforma fondiaria trenta anni dopo*, Franco Angeli, 1979; Marciani, G. E., *L'esperienza di riforma agraria in Italia*, Giuffré, 1966.
60. Fabiani, G., *L'agricoltura italiana tra sviluppo e crisi (1945–1985)* Il Mulino, 1986 p. 141.

61. *Ibid.*
62. Bertolini, P. and Meloni, B. (eds), *Aziende contadine. Sviluppo economico e stratificazione sociale*, Rosenberg & Sellier, 1978, p. 14.
63. Sapelli, G., *L'Italia inafferrabile*, Marsilio, 1990, pp. 17–18.
64. *Ibid.*
65. De Filippis, F., 'Il part-time nel dibattito sulla stratificazione aziendale', *La Questione Agraria*, 18, 1985; Saraceno, E., 'Il part-time nell'agricoltura dei paesi occidentali: linee evolutive e strumenti d'intervento', *La Questione Agraria*, 18, 1985.
66. Balestrieri-Terrasi, M., 'I fattori di localizzazione dell'industria alimentare in Italia', *Rivista di Economia Agraria*, 1, 1985.
67. Tarrow, S., *Partito Comunista e contadini nel Mezzogiorno* Einaudi, 1972; Villani, P. and Marrone, N., *Riforma agraria e questione meridionale*, De Donato, 1981; AAVV, *Campagne e movimento contadino nel Mezzogiorno d'Italia dal dopoguerra ad oggi*, De Donato, 1980.
68. Pereira, M., 'Algunas reflexões sobre a transformação economica de estructura latifundiária' in A. de Barras (coord.), *A Agricultura*, p. 379.
69. Drain, M., 'Le latifundium en Espagne et en Portugal. Réflexion en vue d'une étude comparée' in A. de Barras (coord.), *A Agricultura*, p. 447; García, T. (Gomez, J.), *La evolución de la cuestión agraria bajo el franquismo*, Edición revisada por A. Lanegro and J. M. Lumpsi, Ministerio de Agriculturas, Pesca y Alimentación, 1993.
70. Martinez Alier, J., *La estabilidad del latifundio. Analisis de la interdipendencia entre relaciones de producción y conciencia social en la agricultura latifundista de la campaña de Cordoba*, Paris, 1968.
71. Giner, S. and Moreno, L., 'La sociedad española en la encrucijada' in S Giner (ed.), *España. Sociedad y Política*, Espasa-Calpe, 1990, pp. 19–74; Perez Yruela, M., 'La sociedad rural' in S. Giner (ed.), *España*, pp. 199–242.
72. Sapelli, G., 'La classe operaia durante il fascismo: problemi e indicazioni di ricerca' in G. Sapelli (ed.), *La classe operaia durante il fascismo*, Annali della Fondazione Feltrinelli, XX, Feltrinelli, 1981, pp. IX–XCVII.
73. Roux, B., 'L'évolution de l'agriculture latifundiaire dans le système capitaliste: les transformations de la grande exploitation en Andalousie' in A. de Barros (coord.), *A Agricultura*, p. 268.
74. Aymard, M., 'Pour une continuité de l'histoire rurale' in P. Villani (ed.), *Trasformazioni delle società rurali nei paesi dell'Europa occidentale e mediterranea (secolo XIX–XX). Bilancio degli studi e prospettive di ricerche*, Guida, 1986, p. 26; Linz, J. J. 'La Frontera Sur de Europa: tendencias evolutivas', *Revista española de investigaciones sociólogicas*, 9, 1989, pp. 7–62; Antunes de Castro, A., Torres, A., Silveira, J., Valadas de Lime, A., 'La campagne du blé et le protectionisme céréalier au Portugal: 1929–1960', *Estudos de Economia*, vol. III, 4, Jul.–Sept. 1989, pp. 524–30; Martins Casaca, J. P., 'Sete falsas hipoteses sobre a "Campanha do trigo"', *Estudos de Economia*, vol. III, 2 Jan.–Mar., 1987, pp. 139–59; De Freitas, E., Ferreira de Almeido, J., Villaverde Cabral, H., *Modalidades de penetração do capitalismo na agricultura. Estructuras agrarias em Portugal continental 1950–1970*, Editorial Presença, 1976; Carrière, J. P., *Les transformations agraires en Portugal. Crise, réformes et financement de l'agriculture*, Ed Economica, 1989.
75. Gonzalez, M. J., *La economía política del franquismo 1940–1970*, Tecnos, 1979, pp. 90–2.
76. Barciela Lopez, C., 'Los costes del franquismo en el sector agrario: la ruptura del proceso de transformaciones' in R. Garrabou, C. Barciela Lopez, J. J. Jimenez Blanco (eds), *Historia agraria de la España Contemporánea 3. El fin de la agricultura tradicional (1900–1961)*, Editorial Crítica, 1986, pp. 293–358.

77. Naredo, J. M., 'La agricultura española en el desarrollo económico' in R. Garrabou, C. Barciela Lopez, J. J. Jimenez Blanco (eds), *Historia agraria*, pp. 455–98.
78. Leal, J., Leguina, J., Naredo, J., Tarrafeta, J. M. and L., *La agricultura en el desarrollo capitalista español*, Siglo XXI, 1975.
79. Perez Diaz, V. M., *Pueblos y Clases Sociales en el campo español*, Siglo XXI, 1972; Mira Castera, J. F., 'Estratificación, generaciones y cambio social en una comunidad rural', *Revista española de la opinión pública*, 19, 1970, pp. 39–56; Perez Diaz, V., *Estructura social del campo y exodo rural*, Tecnos, 1966; Sigran, M., *Del campo al suburbio. Un estudio sobre la inmigración interior en España*, Consejo Superior de Investigación Científica, 1959.
80. Sapelli, G., 'La classe operaia'; Martinez Alier, J., 'Notas sobre el franquismo', *Papers*, 8, 1978, pp. 17–51.
81. Anlió, J., *Estructura y problemas del campo español*, Cuadernos para el Diálogo, 1966.
82. Garcia Delgado, J. L. and Roldán López, S., 'Las Rentas Agrarias en el contexto de la crisis de la agricultura tradicional española' in AAVV, *La crisis de la agricultura tradicional en España (La nueva impresa agraria)*, Centro de Estudios Sociales de Valle de los Caídos, 1974, p. 93.
83. Pérez Yruela, M. and Sevilla Guzmán, E., 'La dimensión política en la reforma agraria: reflexiones entorno al caso andaluz', *Papers*, 16, 1981, p. 89; Sanchez López, A. J., 'La eventualidad, rasgo basico del trabajo en una economía subordinada: el caso del campo andaluz', *Sociología del trabajo*, 3–4, 1988, pp. 97–128.
84. Garcia Delgado, J. L. and Muñoz Cidad, C., 'La agricultura: cambios estructurales', pp. 119–52.
85. *Ibid.* pp. 123–4.

Chapter 5 Weak industrialization

1. Sapelli, G., *Economia: tecnologia e direzione d'impresa in Italia*, Einaudi, 1994.
2. Balassa, B., *The Newly Industrializing Countries in the World Economy*, Pergamon, 1981, p. 281.
3. *Ibid.*
4. McDonald, R., *Greece in the 1990s. Taking its Place in Europe*, Economist Intelligence Unit, 1991, p. 21.
5. Candilis, W. O., *The Economy of Greece, 1944–66. Efforts for Stability and Development*, Praeger, 1968, p. 67.
6. Wittner, L. S., *American Intervention in Greece 1943–1949*, Praeger, 1982.
7. Vlavianos, H., *Greece. 1941–1949. From Resistance to Civil War*, Macmillan, St Anthony's College, 1992.
8. Freris, A. F., *The Greek Economy in the Twentieth Century*, Croom Helm, 1986.
9. Candilis, W. O., *The Economy of Greece*, p. 68.
10. *Ibid.*, p. 91.
11. *Ibid.*
12. Sweet-Escott, B., *Greece. A Political and Economic Survey. 1939–1953*, Royal Institute of International Affairs, 1954, pp. 161–3.
13. Freris, A. F., *The Greek Economy*, p. 158.
14. Alexander, A. P., *Greek Industrialist and Economic and Social Analysis*, Center of Planning and Economic Research, 1964.
15. Dertilis, G., 'Hiérarchies sociales. Capitaux et retard économique en Grèce (XVIIIème–XIXème siècle)' in *Actes du Colloque Internationale d'Histoire:*

Economies méditerranéennes, équilibres et intercommunications XVIIIème–XIXème siècle, Centre de Recherches Néohelléniques Fondation National de la Recherche Scientifique, 1985, p. 328.

16. Alexander, A., *Greek Industrialist*, pp. 75 ff.
17. Contsoumoris, G., *The Morphology of Greek Industry. A Study in Industrial Development*, Center of Planning and Economic Research, 1963, pp. 254 ff.
18. Negreponti-Delivani, M., *Analysi tis Ellenikis Oikonomias*, Papazisis, 1981, p. 39.
19. Mouzelis, N. P., *Modern Greece. Facets of Underdevelopment*, Macmillan, 1978.
20. Petros, J., 'Greek Rentier Capital: Dynamic Growth and Industrial Underdevelopment' and Slouras, A., 'Rentier Capital, Industrial Development, and the Growth of the Greek Economy in the Postwar Period: A Response to Jame Petros', *Journal of the Hellenic Diaspora*, 2, 1984, pp. 47–58 and 1, 1985, pp. 5–15,
21. Petros, J., 'Greek Rentier', pp. 51–2.
22. Kasaba, R., *The Ottoman Empire and the World Economy. The Nineteenth Century*, State University of New York Press, 1988.
23. Balassa, B., *The Newly Industrializing*, p. 301.
24. Hershlag, Z. Y., *Turkey: an Economy in Transition*, E. J. Brill, 1958 (first edition of Z. Y. Hershlag, *Turkey. The Challenge of Growth*) and Nas, T. F. and Odekon, M. (eds) *Liberalization and the Turkish Economy*, Greenwood Press, 1988.
25. Karpat, K. H., 'Social Groups and the Political System after 1960', in K. H. Karpat (ed.), *Social Change and Politics in Turkey. A Structural-Historical Analysis*, E. J. Brill, 1973, pp. 227–81.
26. Nas, T. F. and Odekon, M., 'Introduction' in T. F. Nas and M. Odekon (eds), *Liberalisation and the Turkish Economy*, Greenwood Press, 1988, pp. 3–4.
27. Poroy, I. I., 'Planning with a Large Public Sector. Turkey (1963–1967)', *International Journal of Middle East Studies*, July 1972, pp. 343–64.
28. Walstedt, B., *State Manufacturing Enterprise in a Mixed Economy. The Turkish Case*, World Bank, The Johns Hopkins University Press, 1980.
29. Sapelli, G. and Carnevali, F., *Uno sviluppo tra politica e strategia. ENI (1953–1985)*, Franco Angeli, 1992.
30. Walstedt, B., *State Manufacturing*, p. 79.
31. Hershlag, Z. Y. *Turkey. The Challenge*, p. 152.
32. *Ibid.*, p. 153.
33. Rass, L. R. jr and Rass, N. P., *Managers of Modernisation: Organisation and Elites in Turkey*, Harvard University Press, 1971.
34. Ramachandran, N., *Agricultural and Industrial Development Policies in Turkey. A Review*, OECD, 1974, pp. 42–3.
35. *Ibid.*, p. 47.
36. *Ibid.*, p. 62.
37. OECD, *Etudes économiques*, OECD, Nov. 1978, pp. 40–1.
38. Ebiri, K., 'Turkish apertura' in H. Ramazenoglu (ed.), *Turkey in the World Capitalist System. A Study of Industrialisation, Power and Class*, Gower, 1985, pp. 114–15.
39. Hershlag, Z. Y., *Turkey: an Economy*, p. 31.
40. OECD, *Etudes économiques de l'OCDE: Turquie 1990–1991*, OECD, 1991, p. 89.
41. *Ibid.*, pp. 38–41.
42. Arincali, T. and Rodrik, D. (eds), *The Political Economy of Turkey: Debt, Adjustment and Sustainability*, Macmillan, 1990.
43. Machado, D. P., *The Structure of Portuguese Society. The Failure of Fascism*, Praeger, 1991.
44. Marques, A., 'Promoção de exportações e desenvolvimento. De algums limite de

ensinamentos da experiencia portuguesa', *Revista Critica de Ciencias Sociais*, 15–16–17, 1985, p. 312.

45. OECD Economic Surveys, *Portugal 1990–1991*, OECD 1991.
46. Marques, A., *Política económica e desenvolvimentos em Portugal (1926–1959)*, Livros Horizonte, 1988.
47. Valerio, N., 'Aspectos das finanças publicas portuguesas, 1919–1983' in AAVV, *O Estado Novo. Das origins ão fin da autarcia (1926–1959,)* vol. I, Editorial Fragmentos, 1987.
48. Alvares, P. and Roma Fenandes, C., *Portugal e o Mercado Commum – da EFTA ãos acordos de 1972*, Editorial Portico, 1972.
49. Loureiro, J. A., *Economia e sociedade. A industria no pós guerra. Anos '50–'60*, Cosmos, 1991, p. 195.
50. *Ibid.*, p. 274; see the different opinion of Brandao, J. M., *A Industrialização portuguesa no pós-guerra (1948–1965): o condicionamento industrial*, Dom Quixote, 1989.
51. Cardoso, J. L. (and others), *Empresarios e gestores da industria em Portugal*, Dom Quixote, 1990.
52. Castro, A., *Desenvolvimento Economico ou Estagnação?*, Dom Quixote, 1976, p. 88.
53. Esser, K. (ed.), *Portugal. Industrie und Industriepolitik vor dem Beitritt zur Europäischen Gemeinschaft*, German Development Institute, 1977.
54. Deubner, C., 'The Paradox of Portugal's Industrialisation: Emigrant Labour, Immigrant Capital and Foreign Markets' in T. C. Bruneau, V. M. P. da Rosa, A. MacLead, (eds), *Portugal in Development. Emigration, Industrialisation, the European Community*, University of Ottawa Press, 1984, p. 164.
55. Solgado de Matos, L., *Investimentos extrangeiros em Portugal*, Seara Nova, 1973.
56. Carrière, J. P. and Reis, V., 'Investissements étrangers et disparités régionales: le cas du Portugal', *Estudos de Economia*, 1, 1989, p. 55.
57. OECD, *Les problèmes et les politiques de développement régional au Portugal*, OECD 1978; Peixto, J., 'O crescimento da população urbana e a industrialização em Portugal', *Revista Critica de Ciencias Sociais*, 22, 1987, p. 112.
58. Vasilios, G. F., *Greece and the Transnational Corporations*, Transnational Corporation Research Project, University of Sidney, 1988, pp. 40–3.
59. Freris, A. F., *The Greek Economy*, p. 173.
60. Vasilios, G. F., *Greece and the Transnational*, p. 47.
61. *Ibid.*, pp. 53–4, 99–101.
62. Freris, A. F., *The Greek Economy*, p. 180.
63. Balassa, B., *The Newly Industrializing*, pp. 13–15.
64. Reig, E., 'El sector exterior' in J. A. Martinez Serrano (ed.), *Economía española: 1960–1980. Crecimiento y cambio estructural*, Hermann Blume, 1982, p. 197.
65. Reig, E., 'El sector exterior'.
66. Martinez Serrano, J. A., 'Los rasgos basicos del crecimiento económico español' in J. A. Martinez Serrano (ed.), *Economía española*, pp. 23–58.
67. Sapelli, G., *Sul capitalismo italiano. Trasformazione o declino*, Feltrinelli, 1993.
68. Sapelli, G., 'La classe operaia durante il fascismo: problemi e indicazioni di ricerca' in G. Sapelli (ed.), *La classe operaia durante il fascismo*, Annali della Fondazione Feltrinelli, XX, Feltrinelli, 1981.
69. Wiarda, H. J., *Corporatism and Development. The Portuguese Experience*, University of Massachusetts, 1977; von Beyme, K., *Von Faschismus zur Entwicklungsdiktatur. Mach Elite und Opposition in Spanien*, R. Piper, 1971.
70. Schmitter, P. C., 'Corporative Interest Representation and Public Policy-making in Portugal', paper presented at the Annual Meeting of the American Political Association, 5–7 September 1972.

71. Wiarda, H. J., *Corporatism and Development*, p. 288.

72. *Ibid.*, p. 302.

73. *Ibid.*, p. 329.

74. Brandao de Brito, J. M. 'Corporativismo e industrialização: elementos para o estudo do condicionamento industrial', *Ler Historia*, 6, 1984, p. 53; Ribeiro, J. F., Gomes Fernandes, L., Manuel Carreira Rames, M., 'Grande industria, banca e grupo financeiros. 1953–73', *Análise Social*, 5, 1987, pp. 945–1018.

75. Belmira Martins, M., *As multinacionais em Portugal*, Editorial Stampa, 1976.

76. Anderson, P., *Le Portugal et la fin de l'ultra-colonialisme*, François Maspero, 1963.

77. De Sousa Ferreira, E., *Africa-Austral – O passado e o futuro. Análise de Economia e Politica sobre as ex-Colonias Portuguesas*, *Africa do Sul e Namibia*, Seara Nova, 1977; De Sousa Ferreira, E., *O Fim Duma Era: o Colonialismo Português em Africa*, Sa de Costa, 1977.

78. Pereira Leite, J., 'La reproduction du réseau impérial portugais: quelques précisations sur la formation du circuit d'or Mozambique/Portugal 1959/1973', *Estudos de Economia*, 3, 1990, pp. 365–401.

79. Massart, J. J. and Suetens, N., *L'espace commun portugais*, Université Libre de Bruxelles, 1969.

80. Pereira, M. H., *Das revoluções liberais aõ estado novo*, Presenca, 1993, p. 42 and Pereira, M. H., *Assimetrias de crescimiento e dependencia externa*, Seara Nova, 1974, pp. 57–8, now in Pereira, M. H., *Politica y economia. Portugal en los siglos XIX–XX*, Ariel, 1994, pp. 85–6.

81. De Sousa Ferreira, E., *Africa-Austral – O passado*, pp. 78–9.

82. De Andrade, M., and Allivier, M., *La guerre en Angola*, Maspero, 1971.

83. Duffy, J., *Portuguese Africa*, Harvard University Press, 1968.

84. Torres, A., 'Balança de pagamentos e integração de Angola nos finais do periodo colonial', *Estudos de Economia*, 3, 1983, pp. 313–29; de Sousa Ferreira, E., 'A Logica da consolidação da economia de mercado em Angola. 1930–1974', *Análise Social*, 1, 1985, pp. 83–110.

85. Carreras, A., 'La industria: atraso y modernización' in J. Nadal, A. Carreras, C. Sudriá (eds), *La economía española en el siglo XX. Una perspectiva histórica*, Ariel, 1987, p. 303.

86. Comín, F., 'La economía española en el período de entreguerras (1919–1935)', in J. Nadal, A. Carreras, C. Sudriá (eds), *La economía española*, p. 138.

87. Maya, C., *El poder económico en España 1939–1970*, Tecnos, 1975.

88. Anderson, C. W., *The Political Economy of Modern Spain: Policy-making in an Authoritarian Regime*, Praeger, 1970.

89. Tusell, J, *Franco y los católicos. La política interior española entre 1945 y 1957*, Alianza Universidad, 1984; Hermet, G., *Les catholiques dans l'Espagne franquiste vol. I et vol. II*, Presse de la Fondation Nationale des Sciences Politiques, 1980.

90. Gonzalez-Gonzalez, M. J., *La economía política del franquismo (1940–1970). Dirigismo, mercado y planificación*, Tecnos, 1979, p. 24.

91. Schwartz, P. and Gonzalez, M. J., *Una historia del Instituto Nacional de Industria (1941–1976)*, Tecnos, 1978; Aceña, P. M. and Comín, F., *INI, 50 años de industrialización en España*, Espasa-Calpe, 1991.

92. Martinez Alier, J. and Roca Jusmet, J., 'Economía política del corporativismo en el estado español: del franquismo al postfranquismo', *Revista española de investigación sociológica*, 41, 1988, pp. 25–61.

93. Gonzalez-Gonzalez, M. J., *La economía política*, p. 321; see also Merigo, E., 'Spain' in A. Boltho (ed.), *The European Economy. Growth and Crisis*, Oxford University Press, 1982, p. 578.

94. Gonzalez-Gonzalez, M. J., *La economía política*, p. 161; Whitaker, A. P., *Spain and Defense of the West*, Praeger, 1961.

95. Prados de la Escosura, L., 'El crecimiento económico moderno en España, 1930–1973: una comparación internacional', *Papeles de economía española*, 20, 1984, pp. 151–4.

96. Morodo, R., *"Acción Española": origenes ideológicas del franquismo*, Tucar, 1980, pp. 30–1.

97. Garcia Delgado, J. L., 'La industrialización y el desarrollo económico de España durante el franquismo' in J. Nadal, A. Carreras, C. Sudriá (eds), *La economía española*, p. 170.

98. Cao-Pinna, V., 'Principales características estructurales de dos economías mediterraneas: España e Italia', *Revista de Economía política*, 1, 1958, pp. 23–112.

99. Prados de la Escosura, L., 'El crecimiento económico'.

100. Baldrich, A., 'Balance y efectos económicos de la ayuda norteamericana', *Moneda y Crédito*, 61, 1957, p. 43; Vinas, A., *Los pactos secretos de Franco con Estados Unidos. Bases, ayuda económica, recortes de soberanía*, Ariel, 1981.

101. Maravall, J. M., *El desarrollo económico y la clase obrera (Un estudio sociológico de los conflictos obreros en España)*, Ariel, 1970, p. 90.

102. Maravall, J. M., *Trabajo y conflicto social*, Edicusa, 1968.

103. Sapelli, G., *Fascismo, grande industria e sindacato*, Feltrinelli, 1975.

104. Fuentes Irurozqui, M., 'La balanza comercial de España', *Revista de Economía Política*, 42, 1966, pp. 43–77.

105. De Torres Sino, P., 'Inversiones extranjeras en España', *Revista de Economía Política*, 45, 1967, pp. 19–34.

106. Linz, J. and de Miguel, A., 'Actitud empresarial', *Moneda y Crédito*, 91, 1964, p. 47.

107. Ciocca, P. L., Filosa, R., Rey, G. M., 'Integration and Development of the Italian Economy 1951–1971', *Banca Nazionale del Lavoro Quarterly Review*, Sept. 1975; Rey, G. M., 'Italy' in A. Boltho (ed.), *The European Economy*, pp. 502–27.

108. Graziani, A., *L'economia italiana dal 1945 ad oggi*, Il Mulino, 1979.

109. D'Antonio, M., *Sviluppo e crisi del capitalismo italiano 1951–1972*, De Donato, 1973.

110. Graziani, A., 'Aspetti strutturali dell'economia italiana nell'ultimo decennio' in A. Graziani (ed.), *Crisi e ristrutturazione dell'economia italiana*, Einaudi, 1975, pp. 5–73.

111. D'Antonio, M., *Sviluppo e crisi*.

112. Ackley, G., 'Lo sviluppo economico italiano del dopoguerra e gli insegnamenti che è possibile trarne per la politica economica degli Stati Uniti' in A. Graziani (ed.), *Crisi e ristrutturazione*, pp. 156–65.

113. Graziani, A., 'Aspetti strutturali'; D'Antonio, M., *Sviluppo e crisi*.

114. Fuà, G., 'Notes on Italian Economic Growth 1861–1964', *Quaderni della Scuola Enrico Mattei*, 1965; Fuà, G., *Lo sviluppo economico in Italia. Storia dell'economia italiana negli ultimi cento anni. I. Lavoro e reddito*, Franco Angeli, 1983.

115. Campanella, F., 'Scelte sindacali e teorie economiche' in G. Lunghini (ed.), *Scelte politiche e teorie economiche in Italia 1945–1978*, Einaudi, 1981, pp. 171–202; De Cecco, M., 'Lo sviluppo dell'economia italiana e la sua collocazione internazionale', *Rivista Internazionale di Scienze Economiche e Commerciali*, 1971, pp. 91–145.

116. Graziani, A., 'Introduzione' in A. Graziani, *L'economia italiana*, Il Mulino, 1972, pp. 13–98.

117. Bruno, S., 'Microflexibility and Macrorigidity; Some Notes on Expectations and the Dynamics of Aggregate Supply', *Labor*, Autumn 1987, pp. 127–57.

118. Ciocca, P., 'Inflazione, ristagno, disoccupazione negli anni Settanta e oltre' in P. Ciocca, *L'instabilità dell'economia. Prospettive di analisi storica*, Einaudi, 1987, pp. 85–135.

119. Filippi, E. and Zanetti, G., *Finanza e sviluppo della grande industria in Italia*, Franco Angeli, 1965; Zanetti, G., *Le motivazioni all'investimento nella grande impresa*, Il Mulino, 1977; Cesarini, E., *Struttura finanziaria, sistema creditizio e allocazione delle risorse*, Il Mulino, 1989; Filippi, E., 'Imprese e inflazione: considerazioni sulla politica industriale dell'ultimo decennio', *L'Impresa*, Jul.–Sept. 1983, pp. 347–70; Macchiati, A., *Il finanziamento delle imprese industriali in Italia*, Il Mulino, 1985.

120. Boltho, A., 'L'economia italiana a confronto' in Ente Luigi Einaudi (ed.), *Oltre la crisi. Le possibilità di sviluppo dell'economia italiana e il contributo del sistema finanziario*, Ente Luigi Einaudi, 1981, pp. 106–7.

121. *Ibid.*

122. Graziani, A., *L'economia italiana.*

123. Vercelli, A., 'La "lunga crisi": interpretazioni e prospettive' in Ente Luigi Einaudi (ed.), *Oltre la crisi*, pp. 31–98.

124. ISTAT, *Sommario di statistiche storiche 1926–1985*, ISTAT, 1986.

125. Vicarelli, F., 'La disoccupazione: il problema più grave' in *CISL 1981–85*, 1985, now in F. Vicarelli (ed.), *La questione economica nella società italiana. Analisi e proposte*, Il Mulino, 1987, p. 404; May, J., 'Recent trends in unemployment and the labor force, 10 countries', *Monthly Labor Review*, Aug. 1985, pp. 9–22.

126. Sudriá, C., 'Un factor determinante: la energía' in J. Nadal, A. Carreras, C. Sudriá (eds), *La economía española*, pp. 313–64.

127. Tuñón de Lara (dir.), *Historia de España. Tomo X Transición y democracia (1973–1985)*, Editorial Labor, 1991.

128. OECD Etudes économiques *Espagne*, OECD, 1978, p. 5.

129. OECD Etudes économiques *Espagne*, OECD, 1980; Trullen i Thomas, J., *Fundamentos Económicos de la Transición Política Española. La política económica de los acuerdos de la Moncloa*, Ministerio de Trabajo y Seguridad Social, 1993.

130. Maraval, F., *Economía y política industrial en España*, Ediciones Piramides, 1987, pp. 36–7.

131. Alonso, J. A., 'El sector exterior' in J. L. Garcia Delgado, *España Economía*, Espasa-Calpe, 1988, pp. 273–366.

132. Pérez Infante, J. I., 'Acumulación capitalista y excedente de la fuerza del trabajo: análisis de la experiencia española', *Sociología del Trabajo*, 3–4, 1980, pp. 65–96.

133. Andrés, J., Garcia, J., Jiménez, S., 'La incidencia y la duración del desempleo masculino en España', *Moneda y Credito*, 189, 1989, p. 106.

134. Sauchis, E., Picó, J., 'La economía sumergida. El estudio de la cuestión en España', *Sociología del Trabajo*, 9, 1983, pp. 64–93.

135. Krugam, P., Braga de Macedo, J., 'The Economic Consequences of the April 25th Revolution. Portugal and the IMF: The Political Economy of Stabilisation' in J. Braga de Macedo and S. Serfaty (eds), *Portugal since the Revolution: Economic and Political Perspectives*, Praeger, 1981, pp. 53–100, 101–52 respectively.

136. OECD Etudes économiques, *Portugal*, OECD, 1981, p. 30.

137. De Sousa Santos, B., (P. Hespanha coll.), 'O Estado, a Sociedade e as Politicas Sociais: o Caso das Politicas de Saude' in B. de Sousa Santos, *O Estado e a Sociedade*, Afrontamento, 1990, pp. 193–258.

138. McDonald, R., *Greece in the 1990s*, p. 35.

Chapter 6 A specific socio-economic formation

1. Trigilia, C., *Sviluppo senza autonomia*, Il Mulino, 1992.

2. Gianola, A., 'Problemi e prospettive di sviluppo nel Mezzogiorno d'Italia' in Ente Luigi

Einaudi (ed.), *Oltre la crisi. Le possibilità di sviluppo dell'economia italiana e il contributo del sistema finanziario*, Ente Luigi Einaudi, 1981, p. 213.

3. Nadal, J., *El proceso de la Revolución Industrial en España 1814–1913*, Avril, 1975.
4. Vázquez García, J. A., 'Regiones de tradición industrial en declive: la Cornisa Cantabrica' in J. Garcia Delgado (ed.), *España Economía*, Espasa-Calpe, 1988, pp. 765–94.
5. Pedreño, A., 'Un eje de expansión económica: Cataluña-Mediterráneo' in J. L. Garcia Delgado (ed.), *España Economía*, pp. 797–829.
6. Sapelli, G., *L'Italia inafferrabile*, Marsilio, 1989.
7. Sapelli, G., *Sul capitalismo italiano*, Feltrinelli, 1992.
8. Whithly, P., *Business Systems in East Asia. Firms, Markets and Societies*, Sage, 1982.
9. Burns, P. and Dewhurst, J. (eds), *Small Business in Europe*, Macmillan, 1986.
10. *Ibid.*
11. Sapelli, G., *L'Italia inafferrabile*.
12. *Ibid.*
13. Gershuny, J., *Social Innovation and the Division of Labour*, Oxford University Press, 1983.
14. Myro, R., 'Las empresas públicas' in J. L. Garcia Delgado (ed.), *España Economía*, pp. 471–98 and tables pp. 480–1.
15. OFCE, 'Maastricht: les enjeux de la monnaie unique', *Lettre de l'OFCE*, 96, 1992.
16. Sapelli, G., *Sul capitalismo italiano*.
17. Sapelli, G., *L'Italia inafferrabile*.
18. Maraval, J. M., *Trabajo y conflicto social*, Edicusa, 1968.
19. Reis, J., 'Modos de industrialização, força de trabalho e pequena agricultura. Para una análise da articulação entre a acumulação e a reprodução', *Revista Critica de Ciencias Sociais*, 15/16/17, 1985, pp. 225–60.
20. Dos Anjos, N., Godinho Mira, A. I., 'Economia subterrânea: sua quantificação no periodo 1965–1981', *Economia e Sociologia*, 43, 1987, pp. 57–90.
21. Murteira, A., Branquinho, I., 'A mão-de-obra-industrial e o desenvolvimento português', *Análise Social*, 27–28, 1969, p. 581; João Rodrigues, M., *O sistema de emprego em Portugal. Crise e mutações*, Dom Quixote, 1988, pp. 274–5.
22. Maroulis, D., 'Economic Development and the Structure of the Balance of Payments. The Case of Greece', *Center of Planning and Economic Research Studies*, 18, 1986, p. 38.
23. Freris, A. F., *The Greek Economy in the Twentieth Century*, Croom Helm, 1986, p. 144; see also Prodromidis, K. P. and Anastassakou, J. N., *The Determinants of Greece's Common Trade 1961–1978*, Center of Planning and Economic Research, 1984.
24. Tsoris, N., *The Financing of Greek Manufacture*, Center of Planning and Economic Research, 1984.
25. Maroulis, D., 'Economic Development', pp. 55–6, 57.
26. *Ibid.*, p. 59.
27. Freris, A. F., *The Greek Economy*, pp. 187–8; Maroulis, D., 'Economic Development', pp. 60–1; Petros, J., 'Greek Rentier Capital: Dynamic Growth and Industrial Underdevelopment', *Journal of the Hellenic Diaspora*, 2, 1984, pp. 55–6.
28. Tsaliki, P. V., *The Greek Economy. Sources of Growth in the Postwar Era*, Praeger, 1991, pp. 138–9 and 177.
29. Tsoukalos, K., *Social Development and the State: the Evolution of the Public Sector in Greece*, Themelio, 1981.
30. McDonald, R., *Greece in the 1990s. Taking its Place in Europe*, Economist Intelligence Unit, 1991, p. 90.

31. *Ibid.*, p. 75.
32. Germidis, D. A. and Negreponti-Delivanis, M., *Industrialisation, Employment and Income Distribution in Greece. A Case Study*, Development Centre of the Organisation for Economic Co-operation and Development, 1975.
33. McDonald, R., *Greece in the 1990s*, pp. 75–6.
34. Gianaris, N. V., *Greece and Turkey. Economic and Geopolitical Perspectives*, Praeger, 1988, p. 63.
35. Hale, W., *The Political and Economic Development of Modern Turkey*, Croom Helm, 1981, p. 100.
36. *Ibid,.* p. 101.
37. Karpat, K. H., 'Structural Change, Historical Stages of Modernisation and the Role of Social Groups in Turkish Politics' in K. H. Karpat (ed.), *Social Change and Politics in Turkey. A Structural-Historical Analysis*, E. J. Brill, 1973, pp. 11–92.
38. Mardin, S., 'Turkey: the Transformation of an Economic Code' in E. Özbudun and A. Ulusan (eds), *The Political Economy of Income Distribution in Turkey*, Holmes and Meyer, 1980, p. 43.
39. Hershlag, Z. Y., *The Contemporary Turkish Economy*, Routledge, 1988, p. 30; Aricauli, T. and Rodrik, D., *The· Political Economy of Turkey. Debit, Adjustment and Sustainability*, Macmillan, 1990.
40. Arar, I., 'Social Mobility in Turkey' in E. Özbudun and A. Ulusan (eds), *The Political Economy of Income Distribution in Turkey*, Holmes and Meyer, 1980, p. 484.
41. Lindbeck, A., 'Economic Dependence and Interdependence in the Industrialized World' in OECD, *From Marshall Plan to Global Interdependence. New Challenges for the Industrialized Nations*, OECD, 1979, p. 107.
42. Tsoukalis, L., *The European Community and its Mediterranean Enlargement*, Allen and Unwin, 1981; Milward, A. S., *The European Rescue of the Nation-State*, Routledge, 1993.
43. Balassa, B., 'Trade Creation and Trade Diversion in the European Common Market: An Appraisal of Evidence' in B. Balassa (ed.), *European Economic Integration*, E. J. Brill, 1975, pp. 22–46; Resnick, S. A. and Trumau, E. M., 'An Empirical Examination of Bilateral Trade in Western Europe' in B. Balassa (ed.), *European Economic Integration*, pp. 93–126.
44. Romao, A., *Portugal face à CEE*, Horizonte, 1983.
45. Payno, J. A., 'The Second Enlargement from the Perspective of the New Members' in J. L. Sampedro and J. A. Payno (eds), *The Enlargement of the European Community*, Macmillan, 1983, pp. 1–40.
46. Hudson, R. and Lewis, J. R., 'Capital accumulation: the industrialisation of South Europe' in A. Williams (ed.), *Southern Europe Transformed. Political and Economic Change in Greece, Italy, Portugal and Spain*, Harper and Row, 1984, pp. 198–9.
47. *Ibid.*
48. Blacksell, M., 'The European Community and the Mediterranean Region: Two Steps Forward, One Step Back' in A. Williams (ed.), *Southern Europe*, pp. 269–70.
49. Davenport, M., 'The Economic Impact of the EEC' in A. Boltho (ed.), *The European Economy: Growth and Crisis*, Oxford University Press, 1992, p. 241.
50. Canali, M., *et al.*, 'Il sistema agroalimentare nel Mediterraneo: problemi e prospettive' in B. Amoroso (ed.), *Primo rapporto sul Mediterraneo. Nuove prospettive di cooperazione economica, tecnologica ed istituzionale* Centro Studi sull'Europa del sud e il Mediterraneo, Università di Roskilde, CNEL, 1991, p. 9.
51. Sidjauski, D. and Ayberk, U., 'Le nouveau visage des groupes d'intérêt communautaires' in D. Sidjauski and U. Ayberk, *L'Europe du Sud dans la*

Communauté Européenne. Analyse comparative des groupes d'intérêt et de leur insertion dans le réseau communautaire, PUF, 1990, p. 81.

52. Sapelli, G., *L'impresa come soggetto storico*, Il Saggiatore, 1991.
53. Sapelli, G., 'Lo stato italiano come "imprenditore politico"', *Storia Contemporanea*, 2, 1990, pp. 243–96.
54. Keyder, C., *State and Class in Turkey. A Study in Capitalist Development*, Verso, 1987, p. 201.
55. Baklanoff, E. N., *The Economic Transformation of Spain and Portugal*, Praeger, 1978, p. 168.
56. Sapelli, G., *Sul capitalismo.*
57. Scase, R., *The State in Western Europe*, Croom Helm, 1980; Friedmann, W., *Public and Private Enterprise in Mixed Economies*, Stevens & Sons, 1974; Comín, F., 'Las administraciones públicas' in J. L. Garcia Delgado (ed.), *España Economía*, pp. 438 and 454–6; Pedone, A., 'Public Expenditure' in A. Boltho (ed.), *The European Economy*, pp. 390–408.
58. OECD, *Social Expenditure Trends and Demographic Developments*, OECD, 1988.
59. Hirsch, F., *Social Limits to Growth*, Twentieth Century Fund, 1976.
60. Polany, K., *The Great Transformation*, Holt & Winston, 1944.
61. Offe, C., *Contradictions of the Welfare State*, Hutchinson, 1984, p. 153.
62. Jessop, B., 'Changes in the International Economy, their Impact on European Social Structure and their Implications for the Welfare State' in *Conference on 'Globalization and Systems of Welfare'*, Fondazione Giovanni Agnelli, 1990, p. 18.
63. Pfaller, A., 'The European Welfare States Facing Common Endogenous and Exogenous Challenges: Towards Convergence?' in *Conference on 'Globalization'*, pp. 4–5.
64. *Ibid.*
65. Pfaller, A., *Can the Welfare State Compete? A Comparative Study of Five Advanced Capitalist Countries*, Macmillan, 1990.
66. Ferrera, M., *Il welfare state in Italia. Sviluppo e crisi in prospettiva comparata*, Il Mulino, 1984.
67. Gallino, L., 'Effetti dissociativi dei processi associativi in una società altamente differenziata' in L. Gallino, *Della ingovernabilità. La società italiana tra premoderno e neoindustriale*, Edizioni di Comunità, 1987, pp. 51–70.
68. Ferrera, M., *Il welfare state*, p. 136.
69. Wolleb, G., 'Introduzione: distribuzione dei redditi e regolazione sociale' in G. Wolleb (ed.), *La distribuzione dei redditi familiari in Europa*, Il Mulino, 1991, p. 25; Ahijado, M. and Sastre, L., 'La distribuzione in Spagna: un modello in transizione' in G. Wolleb (ed.), *La distribuzione dei redditi*, p. 139.
70. Landry, B., Matsuda, N., Platt Jendrek, M., 'Clase social y movilidad social en España e Italia', *Papers*, 11, 1979, p. 144; De Lillo, A., 'La mobilità sociale assoluta', *Polis*, 1, 1988, pp. 19–51; Schizerotto, A. (ed.), *Classi sociali e società contemporanea*, Franco Angeli, 1988; Teekenes, R., 'Inequality and Poverty. Portugal Compared with Greece, Ireland and Spain', *Estudos de Economia*, 2, 1990, pp. 111–42.

Chapter 7 Neo-caciquism

1. Farneti, P., *The Italian Party Systems 1945–1980*, S. Finer and A. Mastropaolo (eds), Francis Pinter, 1985.
2. Cotta, M., 'Continuità e discontinuità nei sistemi politici europei' in M., Calise (ed.), *Come cambiano i partiti*, Il Mulino, 1992, p. 211.

3. Martinez Alier, J., 'Notas sobre el franquismo', *Papers*, 8, 1978, pp. 17–51.

4. Tavares de Almeida, P. *Eleições e caciquismo no Portugal Oitocentista (1868–1890)*, Difel, 1991; Opello, W. jr, *Portugal's Political Development. A Comparative Approach*, Westview Press, 1985.

5. Costa Pinto, A., 'Lo "stato nuovo" di Salazar e il fascismo europeo. Problemi e prospettive', *Storia Contemporanea*, 3, 1992, pp. 469–528.

6. Villaverde Cabral, M., *Portugal na Alvorada do Século XX*, A. Regra do Jogo, 1979.

7. Machado Pais, J., 'A crise de regime liberal republicano: algumas hypótheses explicativas' in AAVV, *O Estado Novo. Das Origens ao Fim da Autarcia 1926–1959*, vol. I, Fragmentos, 1987, p. 134.

8. De Lucena, M., *A evolução do sistema corporativo português*, vol. I, *O Salazarismo*, Perspectivas & Realidades, 1976.

9. Mouzelis, N., *Modern Greece: Facets of Underdevelopment*, Holmes & Meyer, 1978; Mouzelis, N., *Politics in the Semi-Periphery: Early Parliaments and Late Industrialisation in the Balkans and Latin America*, Macmillan, 1986; Clogg, R., *A Short History of Modern Greece*, Cambridge University Press, 1986; Kourvetakis, Y. A. and Dobratz, B. A., *A Profile of Modern Greece. In Search of Identity*, Clarendon Press, 1987; Carrey, J. P. C. and Carrey, A. G., *The Web of Modern Greek Politics*, Columbia University Press, 1978.

10. Vaner, S., 'Système partisan, clivages politiques et classes sociales en Turquie (1960–1980): questions de méthode et esquisse d'analyse', *Hellenic Review of International Relations*, 3–4, 1983–4, pp. 449–69; Hermet, G., 'L'exotisme superflu: réfléxion sur les systèmes politiques de l'Europe du Sud', *Politique Etrangère*, 1, 1979, p. 129.

11. Ward, R. A. and Rustow, D. A., 'Conclusion' in R. A. Ward and D. A. Rustow (eds), *Political Modernization in Japan and Turkey*, Princeton University Press, 1964, p. 446.

12. Karpat, K. H., 'The Evolution of Turkish Political System and the Changing Meaning of Modernity, Secularism and Islam (1876–1945)', *International Journal of Turkish Studies*, 1985, p. 377.

13. Cotta, M., 'Continuità e discontinuità', p. 223, U. Liebert and M. Cotta (eds), *Parliament and Democratic Consolidation in Southern Europe*, Francis Pinter, 1990.

14. Morisi, M., *Le leggi del consenso. Partiti e interessi nei primi parlamenti della Repubblica*, Rubbettino, 1992, p. 109.

15. Pizzorno, A., 'I ceti medi nel meccanismo del consenso' in A. Pizzorno, *I soggetti del pluralismo*, Il Mulino, 1980, p. 82.

16. Costa, J., *Oligarquia y caciquismo*, Ateneo, 1902; Palomares Ibáñez, J. M., *Nuevas políticas para un nuevo caciquismo. La dictadura de Primo de Rivera en Valladolid*, Universidad de Valladolid, 1993.

17. Mannheimer, R. and Zajczyk, F., 'L'astensionismo elettorale', *Quaderni di Sociologia*, XX, 1982, pp. 399–436.

18. Caciagli, M., *Elezioni e partiti politici nella Spagna post-franchista*, Liviana, 1986; Caciagli, M., 'Spain. Parties and the Party System in the Transition' in G. Pridham (ed.), *The New Mediterranean Democracies. Regime Transition in Spain, Greece and Portugal*, Frank Cass, 1984, pp. 84–103.

19. Meynaud, J. with P. Merlopoulos and G. Notoros, *Les forces politiques en Grèce*, Etudes de Sciences Politiques, 1965, p. 171.

20. *Ibid.*

21. Legg, K. R., *Politics in Modern Greece*, Stanford University Press, 1969, p. 40.

22. Graziano, L. (ed.), *Clientelismo e mutamento politico*, Franco Angeli, 1974.

23. Tachau, F., *Turkey. The Politics of Authority. Democracy and Development*, Praeger, 1984, pp. 140–3.
24. Mouzelis, M 'Continuities and discontinuities in Greek politics. From Elefterios Venizélos to Andreas Papandreou' in K. Featherstone and D. K. Katsoudas (eds), *Political Change in Greece before and after the Colonels*, Croom Helm, 1987, pp. 271–88.
25. Özbudun, E., *Social Change and Political Participation in Turkey*, Princeton University Press, 1976, p. 222.
26. Karpat, K. H., *The Gecekondu: Rural Migration and Urbanisation*, Cambridge University Press, 1976; Karpat, K., 'The Transforming Impact of the Turkish Shanty Town in Urban and Rural Areas', Paper for Burg Wartenstein Symposium 73, Wenner-Green Foundation for Anthropological Research, 1977.
27. Banfield, E. C., *The Moral Basis of a Backward Society*, Free Press, 1958.
28. Karpat, K. H., *The Gecekondu*, p. 232.
29. Finkel, A. and Sirman, N., 'Introduction' in A. Finkel and N. Sirman (eds), *Turkish State, Turkish Society*, Routledge, 1990, p. 2.
30. Legg, K. R., *Politics in Modern Greece*, p. 140.
31. Alivizatos, N., 'The Difficulties of "Razionalization" in a Polarized Political System: the Greek Chamber of Deputies' in U. Liebert and M. Cotta (eds), *Parliament and Democratic*, pp. 121–41; Lyrintzis, C., 'Political Parties in Post-Junta Greece: A Case of "Bureaucratic Clientelism"?' in G. Pridham (ed.), *The New Mediterranean*, pp. 99–118; Korvetaris, Y. A. and Dobratz, B. A., *A Profile of Modern Greece. In Search of Modernity*, Clarendon Press, 1987, pp. 64–7.
32. Caciagli, M., *Elezioni e partiti*, p. 180.
33. *Ibid.*, p. 212.
34. Parras Nadales, A. J., 'Il voto comunista in Andalusia', *Quaderni dell'Osservatorio Elettorale*, Jul.–Dec. 1990, pp. 91–92.
35. Morlino, L., 'Partiti e consolidamento democratico nel Sud Europa' in M. Calise (ed.), *Come cambiano i partiti*, p. 260.
36. Gillespie, R., *The Spanish Socialist Party. A History of Fractionalism*, Clarendon Press, 1989, pp. 376–413.
37. Sapelli, G., 'Spagna. Il successo del PSOE e la conquista del Centro', *Il Moderno*, 9, 1989, p. 7.
38. Sapelli, G., *Cleptocrazia. Il meccanismo unico della corruzione tra economia e politica*, Feltrinelli, 1994.

Chapter 8 From dictatorship to democracy

1. Cotta, M., 'Continuità e discontinuità nei sistemi politici europei', in M. Calise (ed.), *Come cambiano i partiti*, Il Mulino, 1992; Kircheimer, O., 'The Transformation of the Western European Party-system' in G. La Palombara and M. Weiner (eds), *Political Parties and Political Development*, Princeton University Press, 1966, pp. 177–200; Rokkan, S., *Citizen, Election, Parties*, Oslo Universitetsförlaget, 1970; Rokkan, S., *A Geoeconomic and Geopolitical Model of Sources of Variation Across the Territories of Western Europe*, Fondation Nationale des Sciences Politiques, 1977.
2. Linz, J., 'An Authoritarian Regime: Spain' in E. Allardt and Y. Littunen (eds), *Cleavages, Ideologies and Party Systems*, Westermak Society Helsinki, 1964; Sapelli, G., 'La classe operaia' in *La classe operaia durante il fascismo*, Annali della Fondazione Feltrinelli, XX, Feltrinelli, 1986, pp. IX–XCVIII; Sevilla Gutzmán, E.,

Perez Yruela, M., Ginet, J., 'Despotismo moderno y dominación de clase: para una sociología del régimen franquista', *Papers*, 8, 1978, pp. 103–41.

3. Mann, M., 'The Social Cohesion of Liberal Democracy', *American Sociological Review*, 3, 1970, pp. 423–39.

4. Cotta, M., 'Continuità e discontinuità', p. 217.

5. Hermet, G., Roose, R., Rouquié, A., *Election without Choice*, Macmillan 1978.

6. Schmitter, P. C., 'The Impact and Meaning of "Non Competitive, Non Free and Insignificant" Elections in Authoritarian Portugal 1933–1974' in G. Hermet, R. Roose, A. Rouquié (eds), *Election without Choice*, p. 167.

7. Rouquié, A. 'Clientelist Control and Authoritarian Contexts' in G. Hermet, R. Roose, A. Rouquié (eds), *Election without Choice*, pp. 19–95.

8. Firstenberg, J. and Haupt, R., 'Peasant and Politics in Salazar's Portugal: the Corporate State and Village "Non-politics"' in L. S. Graham and N. M. Makler (eds), *Contemporary Portugal. The Revolution and its Antecedents*, University of Texas Press, 1979.

9. Villaverde Cabral, M., 'O fascismo Português numa Perspectiva Comparada', *O Fascismo em Portugal*, Acta do Coloquio realizado na Faculdade de Letras de Lisboa en Março 1980, A Regra do Jogo, 1982, p. 23; Costa Pinto, A., 'Lo "stato nuovo" di Salazar e il fascismo europeo. Problemi e prospettive', Storia Contemporanea, 3, 1992, pp. 522–3.

10. Braga da Cruz, M., *O partido e o estado no Salazarismo*, Editorial Presença, 1988, p. 255.

11. Telo, A., *Portugal na Segunda Guerra*, Perspectivas & Realidades (no date but 1987) and *Portugal na Segunda Guerra (1941–1945) vol. I Documento historico*, Vega (no date).

12. Telo, A., 'Relações Portugal EUA 1940–1941' in AAVV, *O Estado Novo Das Origenes ao Fim da Autarcia 1926–1959*, vol. I, Fragmentos, 1987, p. 391.

13. De Lucena, M., *A evolução do sistema corporativo português. vol. I O salazarismo*, Perspectivas & Realidades, 1976; De Lucena, M. and Wiarda, H. J., *Corporatism and Development. The Portuguese Experience*, University of Massachusetts Press, 1977.

14. Braga da Cruz, M., *O partido e o estado*, p. 173; Caldeira, A. M., 'O partido de Salazar: antecedentes, organização e funções da Unidade Nacional (1926–34)', *Análise Social*, 94, 1986, pp. 962–77.

15. Rosas, F., *Portugal entre a paz e a guerra 1939–1945*, Imprensa Universitaria-Editorial Estampa, 1990, p. 56.

16. Gallagher, T., 'Fernando dos Santos Costa: guardião militar do Estado Novo 1944–58' in AAVV, *O Estado Novo*, vol. I, pp. 199–220.

17. Fryer, P. and McGowan Pinteiro, P., *Oldest Ally*, Dobson Books 1962; Fryer, P. and McGowan Pinteiro, P., *Le Portugal de Salazar*, Ruedo Ibérico, 1963.

18. Raby, D. L., *Fascism and Resistance in Portugal. Communist, Liberal and Military Dissidents in the Opposition to Salazar, 1941–1974*, Manchester University Press, 1988, p. 30.

19. Raby, D. L., *Fascism and Resistance*; da Costa, R., *Elementos para a História do Movimento Operário em Portugal. 1820–1975*, vol. II, *1930–1975*, Assirio e Alvinu, 1979.

20. Pacheco Pereira, J., *Conflitos Sociais nos Campos do Sul de Portugal*, Publicações Europa-América (no date), p. 127.

21. Graham, L. S., *Portgual. The Decline and Collapse of an Authoritarian Order*, Sage, 1975, pp. 13 and 60–1; Gallagher, T., *Portugal. A Twentieth-Century Interpretation*, Manchester University Press, 1983, p. 161.

22. Namorado, R., 'Para uma Universidade Nova. Cronica de Crise de 1969 em Coimbra', *Revista Critica de Ciencias Sociais*, 27–29, 1989, pp. 91–2.

23. Raby, D. L., *Fascism and Resistance*, pp. 238–9.

24. Gallagher, T., 'Fernando dos Santos', p. 168.

25. Makler, H. M., 'The Portuguese Industrial Elite and Its Corporative Relations: a Study of Compartmentalization in an Authoritarian Regime' in L. S. Graham and H. M. Makler (eds), *Contemporary Portugal. The Revolution and Its Antecedents*, University of Texas Press, 1979, pp. 123–66.

26. Firstenberg, J. and Haupt, R., 'Peasant and Politics'.

27. Foweraker, J., *Making Democracy in Spain. Grass-roots Struggle in the South 1955–1975*, Cambridge University Press, 1989; Pérez Diaz, V., *El retorno de la sociedad civil. Respuestas sociales a la transición política, la crisis económica y los cambios culturales de España 1975–1985*, Instituto de Estudios Económicos, 1987.

28. Foweraker, J., *Making Democracy*, p. 247.

29. Pérez Diaz, V., *El retorno de la sociedad*, p. 11.

30. Vilar, S., *La naturaleza del franquismo*, Península, 1977.

31. Vilar, P., *Historia de España*, Critica, 1978, pp. 157–8.

32. Balbé, M., *Orden público y militarismo en la España constitucional (1812–1983)*, Alianza Editorial, 1983.

33. *Ibid.*, p. 398; Preston, P., 'Decay, Division and the Defence of Dictatorship: the Military and Politics. 1937–1982' in F. Lennon and P. Preston (eds), *Elites and Power in Twentieth Century Spain*, Clarendon Press, pp. 203–28.

34. Almed Gomez, J. A., *Las Forzas Armadas en el Estado Franquista*, Ediciones el Arquero, 1988.

35. Huntington, S. P., *The Soldier and the State: the Theory and Politics of Civil-Military Relations*, Harvard University Press, 1975.

36. Sapelli, G., *Fascismo, grande industria, sindacati. Il caso di Torino*, Feltrinelli, 1975.

37. Tussel, J., *La dictadura de Franco*, Alianza Editorial, 1988, p. 334.

38. Morlino, L., *Dalla democrazia all'autoritarismo*, Il Mulino, pp. 330–1.

39. Balfour, S., 'From Warriors to Functionaries: the Falangist Syndical Elite, 1939–1976' in F. Lennon and P. Preston (eds), *Elites and Power*, pp. 229–48.

40. Neuman, F., *Permanent Revolution: Totalitarianism in the Age of International Civil War*, Praeger, 1965; Payne, S. G., *Falange – a History of Spanish Fascism*, Stanford University Press, 1961; Ellwood, S. M., *Spanish Fascism in the Franco Era*, Macmillan Press, 1987, p. 95.

41. Beltran, M., *La Elite burocrática española*, Fundación Juan March–Editorial Ariel, 1987.

42. Busque Bragulat, J., 'Las cuatros ultimos generaciones militares', *Revista española de la opinión pública*, 7, 1967, pp. 179–95.

43. Elorza, A., 'Le radici ideologiche del franchismo'in L. Casali (ed.), *Per una definizione della dittatura franchista*, Franco Angeli, 1990, p. 71.

44. Von Beyme, K., *Von Faschismus zur Entwicklungsdiktatur. Machtelite und Opposition in Spanien*, R. Piper Verlag, 1971.

45. Hermet, G., *Les catholiques dans l'Espagne franquiste. Les acteurs du jeu politique*, Presse de la Fondation Nationale des Sciences Politiques, 1980, pp. 325–6.

46. Barrington Moore jr, *Social Origins of Dictatorship and Democracy. Lord and Peasant in the Making of the Modern World*, Beacon Press, 1966.

47. Almond, G. A. and Verba, S., *The Civic Culture*, Princeton University Press, 1963.

48. Solé-Tura, J., *Catalanismo y revolución burguesa*, Edicusa 1970, p. 17; Pérez Gorzón, S., 'La revolución burguesa en España: los inicios de un debate científico' in M. Tuñon

de Lara (ed.), *Historia Española Contemporánea y Coloquio del Centro de Investigaciones Hispanicas de la Universitad de Pau. Balance y Resumen*, Siglo XXI, 1980, pp. 91–138.

49. Tussel, J., *La dictadura de Franco*, pp. 297–8.

50. Roth, G., *The Social Democrats in Imperial Germany: A Study in Working Class Isolation and National Integration*, Free Press, 1963.

51. Fernandez Varga, V., *La resistencia interior en la España de Franco*, Istmo, 1981; Sanches, A., *El maquis en España*, San Martin, 1976; Kaiser, C., *La guerrilla antifranquista*, Ediciones 99, 1976; Prades Pons, E., *Las guerrillas españolas 1939–1960*, Planeta, 1977; Romeu Alfaro, F., 'Panoramica sociopolitica de los primeros movimientos guerrilleros en la España de 39 a 46' in J. L. Garcia Delgado (ed.), *El primer franquismo: España durante la segunda Guerra Mundial*, Siglo XXI, 1989, pp. 349–78.

52. Sapelli, G., 'Partecipazione politica e coscienza di classe nel movimento operaio torinese durante il fascismo' in A. Agosti and G. M. Bravo (eds), *Storia del movimento operaio, del socialismo e delle lotte di classe in Piemonte*, De Donato, 1980, pp. 401–52.

53. Alba, V., *El Partido Comunista en España*, Planeta, 1979; Hermet, G., *Les Communistes en Espagne: histoire d'un mouvement politique clandestin*, Armand Colin, 1971; Simon, D., *The People of the Plain: Class and Community in Lower Andalucia*, Columbia University Press, 1980; Semprun, J., *Communists in Spain in the Franco Era*, Harvester, 1980; Tobella, J. E., *El PCE en la clandestinidad (1939–1956)*, Siglo XXI, 1982; Tussell, J., *La oposición democrática al franquismo*, Planeta, 1977; Vilar, S., *La oposición a la Dictadura: protagonista de la España democrática*, Ayma, 1971; Foweraker, J., *Making Democracy*; Hevie, H., *La oposición política al franquismo (1939–1950)*, Planeta, 1983; Gillespie, R., *The Spanish Socialist*.

54. Fuerer, L. S., *Los movimientos estudiantiles. Las revoluciones nacionales y sociales en Europa y el tercero Mundo*, Paidos 1969; Galván, T., *La rebelión juvenil y el problema en la Universidad*, Seminarios y Ediciones, 1973; Camarero Gonzalez, A., 'Características generales, objetivas y adversario del movimiento estudiantil madrileño bajo el franquismo', *Revista internacional de sociología*, 40, 1981, pp. 115–65 and 43, 1982, pp. 349–95; Mesu, R., *Jaraneros y alboradadores. Documentos sobre los sucesos estudiantiles de febrero 1956 en la Universidad Complutense de Madrid*, Editorial de la Universidad Complutense, 1982.

55. Comín, A. C., 'Los conflictos colectivos en Andalucía', *Anales de Sociología*, 4–5, 1968–9, pp. 200–37.

56. Balfour, S., *Dictatorship, Workers and the City. Labour in Greatest Barcelona since 1939*, Clarendon Press, 1989 p. 23.

57. *Ibid.*, p. 28.

58. Inglesia, J., 'De Ussel y Ordis. La resolución judicial de los conflictos laborales: un análisis sociológica', *Revista española de la opinión pública*, 36, 1974, pp. 79–102; Terzanos, J. F., 'Los conflictos laborales en España', *Revista de la opinión pública*, 38, 1974, pp. 93–110; del Pozo, C. B., *La clase obrera asturiana durante el franquismo*, Siglo XXI, 1993.

59. Sapelli, G., *Fascismo, grande industria*.

60. Maraval, J. M., *El desarrollo económico y la clase obrera (Un estudio sociológico de los conflictos obreros en España)*, Ariel, 1970.

61. Maraval, J. M., *Dictadura y disentimiento político. Obreros y estudiantes bajo el franquismo*, Alfaguara, 1978, p. 256.

62. Germani, G., 'Political Socialisation of Youth in Fascist Regimes: Italy and Spain' in S. P. Huntington and C. M. Moore (eds), *Authoritarian Politics in Modern Society*, Basic Books, 1970, pp. 133–61; Maraval, J. M., *Dictadura y disentimiento*, pp. 256–7; Foweraker, J., *Making Democracy*, p. 97.
63. Foweraker, J., *Making Democracy*, p. 212.
64. Balfour, S., *Dictatorship, Workers*, pp. 69–72.
65. Lipset, S. M. and Rokkan, S., *Party System and Voter Alignments: Cross-National Perspectives*, Free Press, 1967; Linz, J., *El sistema de partidos en España*, Bitacora, 1976.
66. Santamaria, J., 'Transición controlada y dificultades de consolidación: el caso español' in J. Santamaria (ed.), *Transición a la democracia en el Sur de Europa y America Latina*, CIS, 1981, p. 121.
67. Coelho, M. B., 'Clivagens do sistema político espanhol da transição (1975–85)', *Análise social*, 2–3, 1988, pp. 6–13; Rijphart, A. 'Typologies of Democratic Systems', *Comparative Political Studies*, 1, 1968, pp. 23–51.
68. Hermet, G., *L'Espagne au XX siècle*, PUF, 1986, p. 275.
69. Hermet, G., *L'Espagne au XX siècle*; Carr, R., *Modern Spain. 1875–1980*, Oxford University Press, 1980; Flaquer, L., Giner, S., Moreno, L., 'La sociedad española en la encrucijada' in S. Giner (ed.), *España. Sociedad y Política*, Espasa-Calpe, 1990, pp. 19–73; Moreno, L., 'Las fuerzas políticas españolas' in S. Giner (ed.), *España*, pp. 285–314; Tuñon de Lara, M. (ed.), *Historia de España X. Transición y democracia (1973–1985)*, Labor, 1991; Preston, P., *Franco. A Biography*, HarperCollins, 1993.
70. Hermet, G., *L'Espagne au XX siècle*, p. 289.
71. Raby, D. L., *Fascism and Resistance*, pp. 151–76; Wheeler, D. L., 'The Military and the Portuguese Dictatorship, 1926–1976: "The Honor of the Army"' in L. S. Graham and D. L. Wheeler (eds), *In Search of Modern Portugal, the Revolution and Its Consequences*, University of Wisconsin Press, 1983, pp. 210–11.
72. Raby, D. L., *Fascism and Resistance*, p. 177.
73. *Ibid.*
74. Wheeler, D. L., 'The Military', p. 206.
75. Carilho, M., *Forças Armadas e Mudança Política em Portugal no sec. XX. Para uma explicação sociologica do papel dos militares*, Estudios Gerais, 1985, pp. 430–5.
76. *Ibid.*, p. 453.
77. Moskas, C., *The American Enlisted Man. The Rank and File in Today's Military*, Russel Sage Foundation, 1970.
78. Bruce, N., *The Last Empire*, David and Charles, 1975.
79. Guerra, H., *Angola. Estructura Económica e Classes Sociais. Os ultimos anos de colonialismo português em Angola*, Edições 70, 1975.
80. Graham, L. S., *Portugal*, pp. 41–7.
81. De Spinola, A., *Portugal e o Futuro*, Arcadia, 1974.
82. Opello jr, W. C., 'Portugal: a case study of international determinants of regime transition' in G. Pridham (ed.), *Encouraging Democracy: the International Context of Regime Transition in Southern Europe*, Leicester University Press, 1991, p. 85.
83. Kayman, M., *Revolution and Counter-Revolution in Portugal*, Merlin Press, 1987; Munster, A., *Révolution et contre-révolution en Portugal*, Edition Galiée, 1977; Fernandes, E., *Sá Carneiro e a Social Democracia*, Estante Editora, 1991; G. O'Donnell, P. C. Schimitter, L. Whitehead (eds), *Transitions from Authoritarian Rules: Southern Europe*, Johns Hopkins University Press, 1986; Bruneau, T. C., 'Continuity and Change in Portuguese Politics: Ten Years after the Revolution of the 25 April 1974' and Lewis, J. R. and Williams, A. M., 'Social Cleavages and Electoral

Performances: Social Basis of Portuguese Political Parties 1976–1983' in G. Pridham (ed.), *The New Mediterranean*, pp. 73–83 and. 119–37; Gladdish, K., 'Portugal: an open verdict' in G. Pridham (ed.), *Securing Democracy: Political Parties and Democratic Consolidation in Southern Europe*, Routledge, 1990, pp. 104–25; Opello jr, W. C., 'Portugal: a Case Study'; Bruneau, T. C., *Politics and Nationhood in Post-Revolutionary Portugal*, Praeger, 1984; Braga de Macedo, J. and Serfaty, S. (eds), *Portugal since the Revolution*; Piselli, F., *Medio Occidente. Una periferia d'Europa tra politica e trasformazione*, Marsilio, 1991.

84. Pentzopoulos, D., *The Balkan Exchange of Minorities and its Impact upon Greece*, Montou, 1942; Chiclet, C., *Les Communistes grecs dans la guerre. Histoire du Parti Communiste de Grèce de 1941 à 1949*, Editions L'Harmattan, 1987; Esche, M., *Die Kommunistische Partei Griechenland 1941–1949*, Oldenburg Verlag, 1982; Loulis, J. C., *The Greek Communists 1940–1944*, Croom Helm, 1982; Vlavianos, H., *Greece, 1941–49. From Resistance to Civil War: the Strategy of the Greek Communist Party*, St Anthony, Macmillan, 1992; Smith, O. L., 'The Problems of the Second Plenum of the Central Committee of the KKE, 1946', *Journal of Hellenic Diaspora*, 2, 1985, pp. 43–62; Houdros, J. L., *Occupation and Resistance: the Greek Agony 1941–1944*, Pella, 1983; Minehau, P., 'Dependency, Realignment and Reaction: Movement Toward Civil War in Greece during the 1940s', *Journal of the Hellenic Diaspora*, 3, 1983, pp. 17–35; Wittner, L., *American Intervention in Greece*, Columbia University Press, 1983; Clogg, R. (ed.), *British Policy Towards Wartime Resistance in Yugoslavia and Greece*, Macmillan, 1975.

85. Markesinis, N., *The Theory and Dissolution of Parliament*, Cambridge University Press, 1972, p. 233.

86. *Ibid.*, pp. 230–1.

87. Clogg, R., *Parties and Elections in Greece. The Search for Legitimacy*, Duke University Press, 1987, pp. 18–19.

88. Vlavianos, H., *Greece, 1941–49*, pp. 69–73.

89. AAVV, *The Cominform. Minutes of the Three Conferences 1947, 1948, 1949*, Annali della Fondazione Feltrinelli, XXX, Feltrinelli, 1994.

90. *Ibid.*

91. Vlavianos, H., *Greece, 1941–49*.

92. Tsoucalas, C., 'The Ideological Impact of Civil War' and Alivizatos, N., 'The Emergency Regime and Civil Liberties' in J. Jatrides (ed.), *Greece in the 1940s: a Nation in Crisis*, University Press of New England, 1981, pp. 328–30 and 226–7.

93. Samatas, M., 'Greek McCarthyism: a Comparative Assessment of Greek Post-Civil Repressive Anticommunism and the USA Truman–McCarthy Era', *Journal of the Hellenic Diaspora*, 3–4, 1986, pp. 5–75.

94. Alivizatos, N. A., *Les institutions politiques de la Grèce à travers les crises. 1922–1974*, Pichon, 1979; Mouzelis, N., 'Capitalism and Dictatorship in Postwar Greece', *New Left Review*, 96, 1976, pp. 57–80.

95. Astavrov, N., *Allied Politics and Military Interventions: the Political Role of the Greek Military*, Paparissis Publishers, 1976.

96. Samatas, M., 'Greek McCarthyism', p. 55.

97. Alivizatos, N. A., *Les institutions politiques*, p. 95.

98. Mouzelis, N., 'Capitalism and Dictatorship'.

99. Alivizatos, N. A., *Les institutions politiques*, p. 140.

100. Athènes-Presse Libre, *Le livre noir de la dictature en Grèce*, Seuil, 1969; Amnesty International, *Torture en Grèce. Premier procès de tortionnaires 1975*, Amnesty

International Publications, 1977; Anonymous, *Verité sur la Grèce*, La Cité-L'Age d'Homme Editeur, 1970.

101. Alivizatos, N. A., *Les institutions politiques*, p. 550.
102. Markesinis, N., *The Theory and Dissolution*.
103. *Ibid.*, p. 213.
104. Clogg, R., *Parties and Elections*, pp. 30–53.
105. Danopoulos, C. P., *Warriors and Politicians in Modern Greece*, Documentary Publications, 1985, p. 55.
106. Verney, S. and Couloumbis, T., 'State-international systems interactions and the Greek transition to democracy in the mid-1970s' in G. Pridham (ed.), *Encouraging Democracy*, p. 105.
107. Markides, K. C., *The Rise and Fall of the Cyprus Republic*, Yale University Press, 1977.
108. Isaacson, W., *Kissinger: A Biography*, Faber and Faber, 1992.
109. Diamondeuros, P. N., 'Transition to, and Consolidation of Democratic Politics in Greece, 1974–1983: a Tentative Assessment' in G. Pridham (ed.), *The New Mediterranean Democracies. Regime Transition in Spain, Greece and Portugal*, Frank Cass, 1984, p. 59; Verney, S. and Couloumbis, T., 'State-international systems', pp. 116–18.
110. Diamandeuros, P. N., 'Transition to, and Consolidation', p. 56.
111. Clogg, R., *Parties and Elections*, p. 153.
112. Spourdalakis, M., *The Rise of the Greek Socialist Party*, Routledge, 1988.
113. Kepetanyannis, V., 'The Communists' in K. Featherstone and D. K. Katsoudas (eds), *Political Change*, pp. 145–73.
114. Lyrintzis, C., '*Pasok in Power: the Loss of the "Third Road to Socialism"*' in T. Gallagher and A. M. Williams (eds), *Southern European Socialism. Parties, Election and the Challenge of Government*, Manchester University Press, 1989, pp. 34–59; Clogg, R., *Parties and Elections*, pp. 133 ff.
115. Karpat, K. H., 'The Evolution of Turkish Political System and the Changing Meaning of Modernity, Secularism and Islam (1876–1945)', *International Journal of Turkish Studies*, Oct. 1985, p. 377.
116. Quataert, D., *Social Disintegration and Popular Resistance in the Ottoman Empire, 1881–1908. Reactions to European Economic Penetration*, New York University Press, 1983, pp. 154–5.
117. Trimberger, E. K., 'A Theory of Elite Revolutions', *Studies in Comparative International Development*, 7, 1992, pp. 191–207.
118. Eisenstadt, S. N., 'The Kemalist Revolution in Comparative Perspective' in S. N. Eisenstadt, *European Civilisation in Comparative Perspective. A Study in the Relations Between Culture and Social Structure*, Norwegian University Press, 1987, p. 151.
119. Karpat, K. H., 'Introduction' in K. H. Karpat (ed.), *Political and Social Thought in the Contemporary Middle East*, Praeger, 1982, p. XXVIII.
120. Heper, M., *The State Tradition in Turkey*, Eothen Press, 1985.
121. Weiker, W. F., *Political Tutelage and Democracy in Turkey*, E. J. Brill, 1973.
122. Hamad, F., *The Turkish Experiment in Democracy, 1950–1975*, Royal Institute of International Affairs, Hurst & Company 1977.
123. Heper, M., *The State Tradition*, p. 91.
124. *Ibid.*, p. 117.
125. *Ibid.*, p. 125.
126. Sunar, I. and Sayari, S., 'Turkish Democracy: Changing and Persistent Problems and

Prospects', Paper for the European Consortium for Political Research Workshop on '"Late Democratisation in Southern Europe', Aarhus, Denmark, April 1982, pp. 2–3, cited in M. Heper, *The State Tradition*, p. 129.

127. Heper, M., *The State Tradition*, p. 153.
128. Karpat, K. H., 'Military Interventions: Army-Civilian Relation in Turkey before and after 1980' in M. Heper and A. Evin, *State Democracy and the Military. Turkey in the 1980s*, Walter de Gruyter 1988, p. 148.
129. Karpat, K. H., 'Structural Change, Historical Stages of Modernisation and the Role of Social Groups in Turkish Politics', in K. H. Karpat (ed.), *Social Change and Politics in Turkey. A Structural-Historical Analysis*, Brill, 1973, p. 57.
130. *Ibid.*
131. Hamad, F., *The Turkish Experiment*, p. 37.
132. Karpat, K. H., 'Social Groups and the Political System after 1960' in K. H. Karpat (ed.), *Social Change and Politics*, p. 231; Bianchi, R., *Interest Groups and Political Development in Turkey*, Princeton University Press, 1984.
133. Huntington, S. P., *Political Order in Changing Societies*, Yale University Press, 1968.
134. Runciman, S., *Relative Deprivation and Social Justice. A Study of Attitudes to Social Inequality in Twentieth Century England*, Routledge & Kegan Paul, 1966.
135. Karpat, K. H., 'The Military and Politics in Turkey, 1960–64: a Socio-Cultural Analysis of Revolution', *American Historical Review*, 6, 1970, p. 163.
136. Ward, R. E. and Rustow, D. A. (eds), *Political Modernisation in Japan and Turkey*, Princeton University Press, 1964, p. 461.
137. Bianchi, R., *Interest Groups*, pp. 26 and 219; Hamad, F., *The Turkish Experiment*, p. 58; Shabon, A. M. and Zeytinoglu, I. U., *The Political, Economic and Labor Climate in Turkey*, Warton School, University of Pennsylvania, 1985.
138. Dodd, C. H., *The Crisis of Turkish Democracy*, Eothen Press, 1990; Hamad, F., *The Turkish Experiment*; Pevsner, L. W., *Turkey's Political Crisis. Backgrounds, Perspectives, Prospects*, Washington Papers 110, Praeger, 1984, p. 26.
139. Özbudun, E., *Social Change and Political Participation in Turkey*, Princeton University Press, 1976, pp. 214–21.
140. Karpat, K. H., *State, Democracy*, p. 151.
141. Leonardi, R., 'The International Context of Democratic Transition in Italy: a Case of Penetration' in G. Pridham (ed.), *Encouraging Democracy: The International Contest of Regime Transition in Southern Europe*, Leicester University Press, 1991, pp. 62–83; Di Nolfo, E., 'Sistema internazionale e sistema politico italiano: interazione e compatibilità' in L. Graziano and S. Tarrow (eds), *La crisi italiana*, vol. I, *Formazione del regime repubblicano e società civile*, Einaudi, 1979, pp. 79–112; Di Nolfo, E., *Vaticano e Stati Uniti, 1939–1952. Dalle Carte di M C Taylor*, Franco Angeli, 1978.
142. Aga Rossi, E., *Una nazione allo sbando. L'armistizio italiano del settembre 1943*, Il Mulino, 1993.
143. *Ibid.*
144. Pavone, C., *Una guerra civile. Saggio storico sulla moralità della Resistenza*, Bollati Boringhieri, 1991.
145. Valiani, L., Bianchi, G., Ragionieri, E., *Azionisti, Cattolici, Comunisti nella Resistenza*, Franco Angeli, 1971; Spriano, P., *Storia del Partito Comunista Italiano*, vols. IV and V, Einaudi, 1973, 1975; De Luna, G., *Il Partito d'Azione*, Feltrinelli, 1987, Cotta, M., *Classe politica e parlamento in Italia*, Il Mulino, 1979, pp. 66–83; Meynaud, J., *Rapporto sulla classe dirigente italiana*, Giuffré, 1968.
146. Vaccarino, G., *La Resistenza europea*, Feltrinelli, 1981.
147. Tarrow, S., *Peasant Communism in Southern Italy*, Yale University Press, 1967.
148. Sassoon, D., *The Strategy of the Italian Communist Party*, Francis Pinter, 1981.

149. Ellwood, D. W., *Italy 1943–1945*, Leicester University Press, 1985; Ellwood, D. W., *L'alleato nemico. La politica dell'occupazione anglo-americana in Italia*, Feltrinelli, 1977; Rossi, E. A., *L'Italia nella sconfitta*, Nuovo Istituto Editoriale Italiano, 1985; Harper, J. C., *L'America e la ricostruzione dell'Italia (1945–49)*, Il Mulino, 1987.

150. Leonardi, L. and Werkman, D. A., *The Politics of Dominance: Italian Christian Democracy*, Macmillan, 1989; Baget Bozzo, G., *Il partito cristiano al potere*, Vallecchi, 1974; Di Nolfo, E., *Vaticano*.

151. Leonardi, R., 'The International Context of Democratic Transition in Italy: a Case of Penetration' in G. Pridham (ed.), *Encouraging Democracy: The International Contest of Regime Transition in Southern Europe*, Leicester University Press, 1991, pp. 62–83.

152. Leonardi, R., 'The International Context', pp. 62–83.

153. *Ibid.*, pp. 76 and 80.

154. On this thesis I am at variance with a friend of mine who has deeply influenced my thought: Farneti, P., 'Partito, stato e mercato: appunti per un'analisi comparata' in L. Graziano and S. Tarrow (eds), *La crisi italiana*. The problem is that Farneti made no distinction between sub-cultural continuity and discontinuity of parties.

155. Farneti, P., *Sistema politico e società civile. Saggi di teoria e ricerca politica*, Giappichelli, 1971.

156. Sapelli, G., *Comunità e mercato. Cattolici, socialisti e 'governo economico municipale' all'inizio del XX secolo in Italia*, Il Mulino, 1989.

157. Caciagli, M., 'Quante Italie? Persistenza e trasformazione delle culture politiche sub-nazionali', *Polis*, 3, pp. 429–57.

158. Sapelli, G., *Sul capitalismo italiano. Trasformazione o declino*, Feltrinelli, 1993.

159. Tasca, A., *Nascita e avvento del fascismo*, La Nuova Italia, 1963; Sapelli, G., *La classe operaia*.

160. Riccardi, M., *Il Partito Romano*, Morcelliana, 1979; Casula, C. F., *Domenico Tardini (1888–1961). L'azione della Santa Sede nel periodo delle due guerre*, Studium, 1988; Giovagnoli, A., *Le premesse della ricostruzione. Tradizione e modernità nella classe dirigente cattolica del dopoguerra*, Nuovo Istituto Editoriale Italiano, 1981; Acerbi, A., *Chiesa, cultura e società. Momenti e figure dal Vaticano I a Paolo VI*, Vita e Pensiero, 1988.

161. Sassoon, D., *Contemporary Italy. Politics, Economy and Society since 1945*, Longman, 1986.

162. Prandi, A., *La Chiesa e la politica*, Il Mulino, 1968.

163. Bibes, G., *Le système politique italien*, PUF, 1974.

164. Rotelli, E., *L'avvento della regione in Italia*, Giuffré, 1967.

165. Morlino, L., 'Consolidación democrática. Definición, Modelos, Hipótesis', *Revista española de investigaciones sociológicas*, 35, 1986, pp. 7–61; Morlino, L., 'Partiti e consolidamento democratico nel Sud Europa' in M. Calise (ed.), *Come cambiano i partiti*, Il Mulino, 1992, p. 251.

166. Blackmer, L. M. D. and Tarrow, J., *Il comunismo in Italia e in Francia*, ETAS, 1976; Belligni, S. (ed.), *La giraffa e il liocorno. Il PCI dagli anni '60 al nuovo decennio*, Franco Angeli, 1982.

167. De Felice, F., 'Doppia lealtà e doppio stato', *Studi Storici*, 3, 1989, pp. 493–563.

Chapter 9 Affirmation of the political middle ground

1. Katsoudos, D. K., 'The Constitutional Framework' in K. Featherstone and D. K. Katsoudos (eds), *Political Change in Greece before and after the Colonels*, Croom Helm, 1987, p. 28.

2. McDonald, R., *Greece in the 1990s. Taking its Place in Europe*, Economist Intelligence Unit, 1991; Catsiapis, J., 'Grèce: reconquête du pouvoir par la droite libérale' in A. Grosser (ed.), *Les pays d'Europe occidentale*, La Documentation Française, 1991, pp. 203–16; Featherstone, K., 'Political Parties and Democratic Consolidation in Greece' in G. Pridham (ed.), *Securing Democracy. Political Parties and Democratic Consolidation in Southern Europe*, Routledge, 1990, pp. 179–201.

3. Banfeeld, E., *The Moral Bases of a Backward Society*, Free Press, 1958.

4. Graziano, L., 'Clientela e politica nel Mezzogiorno' in P. Farneti (ed.), *Il sistema politico italiano*, Il Mulino, 1979, p. 236; Graziano, L. (ed.), *Clientelismo e mutamento politico*, Franco Angeli, 1974.

5. La Palombara, J., *Clientela e parentela*, Edizioni di Comunità, 1969; Istituto Cattaneo, *L'organizzazione partitica del PCI e della DC*, Il Mulino, 1968; Bibes, G., *Le système politique italian*, PUF, 1974, pp. 63–6; Putnam, R., Leonardi, R., Nanetti, R., *Making Democracy Work. Civic Tradition in Modern Italy*, Princeton University Press, 1993.

6. Pridham, G., *Political Parties and Coalitional Behaviour in Italy*, Routledge, 1988; D'Amato, L., *Il voto di preferenza in Italia (1946–1963)*, Giuffré, 1964; D'Amato, L., *Correnti di partito e partito di correnti*, Giuffré, 1964; Cazzola, F., 'Partiti, correnti e voto di preferenza', *Rivista italiana di scienza politica*, 2, 1972, pp. 569–88; Ancisi, A., *La cattura del voto. Sociologia del voto di preferenza*, Franco Angeli, 1976.

7. Farneti, P., 'I partiti politici e il sistema di potere', in V. Castronovo (ed.), *L'Italia contemporanea 1945–1975*, Einaudi, 1976, p. 69.

8. Sapelli, G., 'L'Edison di Giorgio Valerio' in V. Castronovo (ed.), *Storia dell'ENEL*, vol. III, Laterza (forthcoming).

9. Pizzorno, A., *I soggetti del pluralismo. Classi, partiti e sindacati*, Il Mulino, 1980; Bordogna, L. and Provasi, G. C., 'La conflittualità' in G. P. Cella and T. Treu (eds), *Relazioni industriali. Manuale per l'analisi dell'esperienza italiana*, Il Mulino, 1982; Cella, G. P., 'Tipologia e determinanti della conflittualità' in G. P. Cella and M. Regini (eds), *Il conflitto industriale in Italia. Stato della ricerca e ipotesi sulle tendenze*, Il Mulino, 1985, pp. 79–100; Accornero, A., 'La trasformazione nella cultura conflittuale del sindacato' and Cella, G. P., 'Gli obiettivi del conflitto sindacale per gli anni '80' in AAVV, 'Il conflitto sindacale negli anni '80. Ipotesi e linee interpretative', *Quaderni della Fondazione Feltrinelli*, 24, 1983, pp. 15–16 and 59–64; Ceri, P., 'L'autonomia operaia tra organizzazione del lavoro e sistema politico', *Quaderni di Sociologia*, 1, 1977, pp. 47–84; Tarrow, S., *Democracy and Disorder. Protest and Politics in Italy 1965–1975*, Clarendon Press, 1989.

10. Diaz, V. P., *Clase obrera, partidos y sindicatos*, Fundación del INI, 1979, p. 32; Maraval, J. M., *La política de la transición*, Taurus, 1981, pp. 43–7; Gunther, R., Sani, G., Shabad, G., *El sistema de partidos políticos en España. Génesis y evolución*, CIS, 1986; Luiz, J. and Montero, J. R. (eds), *Crisis y cambio: electores y partidos en la España de los años ochenta*, CEC, 1986; Sani, G., 'Partiti e atteggiamenti di massa in Spagna e in Italia', *Rivista italiana di scienza politica*, 11, 1981, pp. 235–79; Sani, G., Gunther, S., Shabad, S., 'Estrategia de los partidos y escisión de masas en las elecciones parlamentarias españolas del 1979', *Revista de Derecho Político*, 11, 1981, pp. 141–86; Montero, J. R., 'Los fracasos políticos y electorales de la derecha española: Alianza Popular, 1976–1986', *Revista española de investigación sociológica*, 39, 1987, pp. 27–43.

11. Morlino, L., 'Partiti e consolidamento democratico nel Sud Europa', in M. Calise (ed.), *Come cambiano i partiti*, Il Mulino, 1992, p. 252.

12. *Ibid.*, p. 253; del Campo, S., Tezanos, J. F., Santin, W., 'La élite política española y la transición a la democracia', *Sistema*, 48, 1982, p. 60; Marau, M. L., 'Un intento de

análisis de la "clase parlamentaria" española: elemento de renovación y de permanencia (1977–1986)', *Revista española de investigación sociológica*, 45, 1989, pp. 61–84.

13. Moreno, L., 'Las fuerzas políticas' in S. Giner (ed.), *España. Sociedad y Política*, Espasa-Calpe, 1990, pp. 297–8; Heywood, P., *Spanish next Five Years. A Political Risk Analysis*, Economist Intelligence Unit, Apr. 1991, p. 43; Caciagli, M., *Elezioni e partiti politici nella Spagna post-franchista*, Liviana, 1986; Caciagli, M., 'Spain, Parties and the Party System in the Transition' in G. Pridham (ed.), *The New Mediterranean Democracies. Regime Transition in Spain, Greece and Portugal*, Frank Cass, 1984, pp. 84–98; Gillespie, R., 'Regime Consolidation in Spain. Party, State and Society' in G. Pridham (ed.), *Securing Democracy: Political Parties and Democratic Consolidation in Southern Europe*, Routledge, 1990, pp. 84–103; Aguilar, S, 'El asociacionismo empresarial en la transición post-franquista', *Papers*, 24, 1985, pp. 53–83.

14. Busquet, J., *El militar de Carrera en España*, Ariel, 1983; Busquet, J., 'Las Fuerzas Armadas en la transición española', *Sistema*, 93, 1989, pp. 13–28; Fernandez Segado, F., 'Fuerzas Armadas-Sociedad: del mutuo aislamiento a la progresiva integración', *Revista española*, 34, 1986, pp. 75–6; Rodrigo, F., 'El papel de las Fuerzas Armadas españolas durante la transición política: algunas hipótesis basicas', *Revista internacional de sociología*, 2, 1985, pp. 349–69; Martinez Paricio, J. I., 'Ejercito y militares: 1898–1988' in S. Giner (ed.), *España*, pp. 397–448.

15. Story, J. and Pollack, B., 'Spain's Transition: Domestic and External Linkages' in G. Pridham (ed.), *Encouraging Democracy: the International Context of Regime Transition in Southern Europe*, Leicester University Press, 1991, pp. 125–58.

16. Opello jr, W. C., 'Portugal: a case study of international determinants of régime transition', in G. Pridham (ed.), *Encouraging Democracy*, pp. 84–102; Aguiar, J., *O Pós-Salazarismo. As fases políticas no período 1974–1984*, Dom Quixote, 1985, p. 197; Aguiar, J., *A Illusão do Poder. Análise do sistema partidario português. 1976–1984*, Dom Quixote, 1983; Opello jr, W. C., *Portugal's Political Development. A Comparative Approach*, Westview Press, 1985, pp. 43–4; Grew, R., 'The Crises and Their Sequences' in R. Grew (ed.), *Crises of Political Development in Europe and the United States*, Princeton University Press, 1978, pp. 3–37; Lewis, J. R. and Willeanis, A. M., 'Social Cleavage and Electorate Performance: the Social Basis of Portuguese Political Parties, 1976–1983' in G. Pridham (ed.), *The New Mediterranean*; Stock, M. J., 'O centrismo político em Portugal: evolução do sistema de partidos, genese do "Bloco Central" e análise do dois parceiros de coligação', *Análise Social*, 1, 1985, p. 65.

17. Gonzales Hernandez, J. C., 'El proceso electoral portugués. Análisis cuantitativa del comportamento político (1975–1976)', *Revista española de la opinión pública*, 48, 1977, pp. 205–62; Stock, M. J., 'Sistema de partidos e governabilidade', *Economia e sociologia*, 37, 1984, pp. 43–84; Morlino, L. 'Portogallo', *Quaderni dell'Osservatorio Elettorale*, Jan. 1986, pp. 113–15; Leonard, Y., 'Portugal: une année de transition' in A. Grosser (ed.), *Les Pays d'Europe*, pp. 191–202.

18. Braga da Cruz, M., 'Sobre o Parlamento português: partidorização parlamentar e parlamentarização partidoria', *Análise Social*, 1, 1988, p. 103; Morlino, L., 'Portogallo', pp. 252–3; Lobo Antunes, M., 'A Assembleia da República e a consolidação de democracia em Portugal', *Análise Social*, 1, 1988, pp. 77–95.

19. Gaspar, C., 'O processo constitucional e estabilidade do regime', *Análise Social*, 12, 1990, pp. 9–29.

20. Barreto, J., 'Os primordios de Intersindical sob Marcelo Caetano', *Análise Social*, 12, 1990, pp. 57–117.

21. Staleroff, A. D., 'Sindicalismo e Relações Industriais em Portugal', *Sociologia*, 4, 1988,

pp. 147–63; Castanheira, J. P., 'Os sindicatos e a vida política', *Análise Social*, 3–4–5, 1985, pp. 801–18.

22. Leite Viegas, J. M. and Reis, M., 'Campesinato e regime democratico. Uma cultura politica em trasformação', *Sociologia*, 5, 1988, pp. 79–105; Stock, M. J., 'A imagen dos partidos e a consolidação democrática em Portugal – resultados dem inquérito' *Análise Social*, 1, 1988, pp. 151–61.

23. Graham, L. S., 'Administração Pública central e local: continuidade e mudança', *Análise Social*, 3–4–5, 1985, pp. 903–24; de Lucena, M., 'Neocorporativismo? Conceito, interesses e aplicação ao caso português', *Análise Social*, 3–4–5, 1985, pp. 819–85; Opello jr, W. C., 'O Parlamento português: análise organizacional de actividade legislativa', *Análise Social*, 1, 1988, pp. 127–50.

24. Ali Brand, M., *The Generals' Coup in Turkey. An Inside Story of 12 September 1980*, Brassey's Defence Publishers, 1987, p. 67; Hamad, F., 'Military intervention and the crisis in Turkey' in H. Ramazanoglu (ed.), *Turkey in the World Capitalist System. A Study of Industrialisation, Power and Class*, Gower, 1985, pp. 191–221; Dodd, C. H., *The Crisis of Turkish Democracy*, Eothen Press, 1990, pp. 51–5; Hale, W., 'Military Rule and Political Change in Turkey 1980–1984' in A. Gokalp (ed.), *La Turquie en transition*, Maison–Neuve Larose, 1986, pp. 155–76.

25. Confédération Mondiale du Travail, *Rapport syndical sur la Turquie avant et après le coup d'état de 1980*, CMT 1981.

26. Dodd, C. H., *The Crisis of Turkish Democracy*, p. 90.

27. Pevsner, L. W., *Turkey's Political Crisis. Backgrounds, Perspectives, Prospects*, Washington Papers 110, Praeger, 1984, p. 114.

28. Ergüder, U., 'The Motherland Party 1983–1989' in M. Heper and J. M. Landau (eds), *Political Parties and Democracy in Turkey*, Tauris, 1991.

29. *Ibid.*, p. 161.

30. Favre, J. M., 'L'élaboration de la politique étrangère en Turquie sous la présidence de M Turgut Özal', *C.E.M.O.I.I.*, 12, 1991, pp. 213–26.

31 Özal, T., *La Turquie en Europe*, Plon, 1988.

32. Mango, A., 'The Social Democrat Populist Party, 1983–1990' in M. Heper and J. M. Landau (eds), *Political Parties*, p. 186.

33. Acar, F., 'The True Path Party, 1983–1989' in M. Heper and J. M. Landau (eds), *Political Parties*, p. 189.

34. Heper, M., 'Introduction' in M. Heper and J. M. Landau (eds), *Political Parties*, p. 6.

35. Özbudun, E., 'The Turkish Party System. Institutionalisation, Polarisation and Fragmentation', *Middle Eastern Studies*, 2, 1981, pp. 23 ff.

36. Soyaray, S., 'The Turkish Party System in Transition', *Governmental Opposition*, 1, 1989, pp. 23–41; Tachau, F., 'Political Leadership in Turkey: Continuity and Change' in M. Heper and A. Evin (eds), *State Democracy and the Military*. Turkey in the 1980s, Walter de Gruyter, 1988, p. 111; Roos, L. L. and Roos, N. P. *Manager of Modernisation. Organisations and Elites in Turkey (1950–1969)*, Harvard University Press, 1971; Özbudun, E., *Social Change and Political Participation in Turkey*, Princeton University Press, 1976; Özbudun, E. and Tachau, F., 'Social Change and Electoral Behaviour in Turkey: Toward a Critical Realignment?', *International Journal of Middle East Studies*, 6, 1975, pp. 460–80; Tachau, F., *Turkey. The Politics of Authority, Democracy and Development*, Praeger, 19, p. 133.

37. Birand, M. A., *Shirts of Steel. An Anatomy of the Turkish Officer Corps*, Tauris, 1991.

38. Dodd, C. H., *The Crisis of Turkish Democracy*, Eothen Press, 1993, 2nd ed.

39. Arat, Y., *The Patriarchal Paradox. Women Politicians in Turkey*, Rutherford, 1989; Koray, M., 'Frauen und Politik. Die aktuelle Entwicklung der Lage der Frauen in der Türkei', *Zeitschrift für Turkeistudien*, 1, 1993, pp. 5–34.

Chapter 10 Societies and movements

1. Smith, A. D., 'The Supersession of Nationalism?', *International Journal of Comparative Sociology*, 1–2, 1990, p. 12.
2. *Ibid.*, pp. 18–19.
3. *Revista Internacional de Sociología*, 44, 1982, is entirely consecrated to the study of nationalism in Galicia, Andalusia, Canary Isles, the Basque Country, and the examination of the Castilian situation too.
4. Solé-Tura, J., *Introducción al régimen político español*, Ariel, 1971.
5. Solé-Tura, J., 'La questión de l'Estat i el concepte de nacionalitat', *Taula de Cauvi*, 1, 1970; Tayne, S. G., 'Nationalism, Regionalism and Micronationalism in Spain', *Journal of Contemporary History*, 26, 1991, pp. 479–91.
6. Fusi Aizpúrua, J. P., 'La organización teritorial del Estado' in J. P. Fusi Aizpúrua (ed.), *España-Autonomias*, Espasa-Calpe, 1989, pp. 11–41; Giner, S. and Moreno, L., 'Centro y perifería: la dimensión étnica de la sociedad española' in S. Giner (ed.) *España. Sociedad y Política*, Espasa-Calpe, 1990, p. 186.
7. Molinero, C. and Ysas, P., *La oposición antifaxista a Catalunya (1939–1950)*, La Malagrana, 1981.
8. de Riquer, B. and Culla, J. B., *Historia de Catalunya*, vol. III, *El franquismo e la transició democratica*, Edicions 62, 1989; Anguiler, S., 'Burgueses sin Burguesia? La trayectoria corporativa de la burguesia empresorial catalana', *Revista española de investigación sociológica*, 31, 1985, pp. 183–211.
9. Borja, J., 'Descentralitzaciò, una qüestiò de métode' and Basaguren, A. L., 'El pluralisme lingüistic dins l'estat autonomic', *Autonomies. Revista catalana de dret public*, June 1985, pp. 21–41 and July 1988, pp. 43–74.
10. Lorés, J., *La transiciò a Catalunya (1977–1984). El pujolisme i els altres*, Empuries, 1985.
11. Linz, J. and Montero, J. R. (eds), *Crisis y cambio: electores y partidos en la España de los años ochenta*, CEC, 1986; Gunther, R., Sani, G., Shabad, G., *El sistema de partidos políticos en España. Génesis y evolución*, CIS, 1986; Colomé, G., 'L'elettorato socialista in Catalogna: composizione e comportamento', *Quaderni dell'Osservatore Elettorale*, Jan.–July 1989, pp. 71–94.
12. Corcuere, J., 'Perspectiva del nacionalismo vasco. Integración y asimilación', *Revista Internacional de Sociología*, 45, 1983, pp. 51–75; Elorza, A. 'El tema rural en la evolución del nacionalismo vasco' in J. L. Garcia Delgado (ed.), *La cuestión agraria en la España contemporánea*, Edicusa, 1976, pp. 121–60; Elorza, A., *Ideologías del nacionalismo vasco*, Haramburu Editor, 1978; Heiberg, M., *The Making of the Basque Nation*, Cambridge University Press, 1989, p. 100; Ben-Amin, S., 'Basque Nationalism Between Archaism and Modernity', *Journal of Contemporary History*, 26, 1991, pp. 443–52.
13. Reinarex, F., 'Sociogénesis y evolución del terrorismo en España' in S. Giner (ed.), *España*, pp. 353–96.
14. Zulaika, J., *Basque Violence. Metaphor and Sacrament*, University of Nevada Press, 1988.
15. Piniel, J. L., *El terrorismo en la transición española (1972–1982)*, Fundamentos, 1986; AAVV, *Terrorismo y sociedad democrática*, Akal, 1982.
16. Tomas y Valente, F., 'Los "derechos históricos" de Euskadij', *Sistema*, 31, 1979, pp. 3–28.
17. Zirakzadeh, C. E., 'Economic Changes and Surges in Micro-Nationalist Voting in Scotland and the Basque Region of Spain', *Comparative Studies in Society and History*,

31, 1989, pp. 318–39; Heiberg, M., *The Making of the Basque*; Urrutia, V., 'Trasformaciones demográficas y urbanización en el País vasco', *Papers*, 22–23, 1984, pp. 27–61; Della Porta, D. and Mattina, L., 'Ciclos políticos y movilización étnica: el caso vasco' and Roiz Celix, M., 'Los limites de modernización en la estructura social de Cataluña y Euskadi', *Revista española de investigación sociológica*, 35, 1986, pp. 123–48 and 25, 1983, pp. 199–313; Gurruchaga, A., 'La persistencia del nacionalismo periferico', *Revista Internacional de Sociología*, 4, 1985, pp. 531–67.

18. Maiz, R., 'Aproximación a la trayectória politico-ideológica del nacionalismo gallego', *Revista Internacional de Sociológia*, 44, 1982, pp. 513–48; Villares, R., 'Galicia' in J. P. Fusi Aizpurua (ed.), *España-Autonomias*, pp. 465–516.

19. Van Bruinessen, M., *Agha, Shaikh and State*, University Press of Rijswik, 1978; Tapper, R. (ed.), *The Conflict of Tribe and State in Iran*, Croom Helm, 1983; Kudat, A., 'Patron-Client Relations: the State of the Art and Research in Eastern Turkey' in E. D. Akorli and G. Ben-Dor (eds), *Political Participation in Turkey*, Bogàziçi University Publication, 1975.

20. Yalcin-Heckmunn, L., 'Kurdish Tribal Organisation and Local Political Processes' in A. Finkel and N. Sirmon (eds), *Turkish State, Turkish Society*, Routledge, 1990, p. 300.

21. Bazarsbou, H., 'Le Kémalisme et le problème kurde' in H. Hakim (ed.), *Les Kurdes par delà l'exode*, Editions L'Harmattan, 1992, pp. 63–89.

22. Ghassemlou Kendal, A. R., 'Le Kurdistan de Turquie' in G. Chaliand (ed.), *Les Kurdes et le Kurdistan. La question nationale kurde au Proche-Orient*, Maspero, 1978, pp. 71–153; Gunther, M. M., *The Kurds in Turkey: a Political Dilemma*, Westview Press, 1990.

23. Verrier, M., 'La guerre s'étend au Kurdistan', *Le Monde Diplomatique*, Jan. 1993, p. 3.

24. Mardin, S., 'Youth and Violence in Turkey', *Archives Européennes de Sociologie*, XIX, 1978, pp. 229–54.

25. *Ibid.*, p. 246.

26. *Ibid.*, p. 235.

27. Samin, A., 'The Left', Agaogullari, M. A., 'The Ultranationalist Right', Toprak, B., 'The Religious Right' in I. C. Schick and E. A. Tonak (eds), *Turkey in Transition. New Perspectives*, Oxford University Press, 1992, pp. 147–76, 177–217, 218–35; Rouse, J. P., *La religion des Turcs et des Mongols*, Payot, 1984; Landau, J. M., *Panturkism in Turkey. A Study in Irredentism*, Hurst, 1981; Gökalp, I. and Georgeon, F., 'Kemalisme et monde mussulman', *Cahiers du GETC*, 3, 1987; 'La Communauté Européenne et la Turquie. Avant la question de l'adhésion. Approche culturelle d'une relation politique', *C.E.M.O.T.I.I.*, 10, 1990; Szyliowicz, J. S., *A Political Analysis of Student Activism: the Turkish Case*, Sage, 1972.

28. Tarrow, S., *Democracy and Disorder. Protest and Politics in Italy 1965–1975*, Clarendon Press, 1989.

29. Drake, R., *The Revolutionary Mystic and Terrorism in Contemporary Italy*, Indiana University Press, 1989.

30. Ventura, A., 'Il problema del terrorismo italiano', *Rivista Storica Italiana*, 92, 1980, pp. 125–51; Ventura, A., 'Il problema delle origini del terrorismo di sinistra' in D. Della Porta (ed.), *Terrorismi in Italia*, Il Mulino, 1984, pp. 75–152.

31. Drake, R., *The Revolutionary Mystic*, p. 159.

32. Della Porta, D., *Il terrorismo di sinistra*, Il Mulino, 1990, pp. 295–6.

33. Mass, D., 'Analysing Italian Political Violence as a Sequence of Communicative Acts: the Red Brigades 1970–1982', *Social Analysis*, 15, 1983, pp. 84–111; Kaare, M., 'Partecipazione, valori e violenza politica' in R. Catanzaro (ed.), *La politica della violenza*, Il Mulino, 1990, p. 34.

34. Wilson, B., *Contemporary Transformation of Religion*, Oxford University Press, 1976.
35. Beckford, J. (ed.), *New Religious Movements and Rapid Social Change*, Sage, 1986.
36. Deconchy, J. P., *Orthodoxie religieuse et sciences humaines*, Mouton, 1980.
37. Cerqueira, S., 'L'Eglise Catholique et la dictature corporatiste portugaise', *Revue française de sciences politiques*, 3, 1973, pp. 473–512; Georgel, J., *Le salazarisme. Histoire et bilan 1926–1979*, Cujas, 1981.
38. Perez Diaz, V., 'Iglesia y religión en la España contemporánea' in V. Perez Diaz, *El retorno de la sociedad civil. Respuestas sociales a la transición política, la crisis económica y los cambios culturales de España 1975–1985*, Instituto de Estudios Económicos, 1987, p. 421; Hermet, G., *Les catholiques dans l'Espagne franquiste. Les acteurs du jeu politique*, Presse de la Fondation Nationale des Sciences Politiques, 1980, pp. 202 ff and 240–6; Lannou, F., *Privilegio, persecución y profecía. La Iglesia Católica en España, 1875–1975*, Alianza Editorial, p. 287.
39. Gomez Perez, R., *El Franquismo y la Iglesia*, Ediciones Rialp, 1986; Ruiz Rico, J. J., *El papel político de la Iglesia Católica en la España de Franco*, Tecnos, 1977.
40. Parisi, A. (ed.), *Democristiani*, Il Mulino, 1979.
41. Vryonis, S. (ed.), *The 'Past' in Medieval and Modern Greek Culture*, Undena Publications, 1978.
42. Bilici, F., 'L'Etat turc à la recherche de la cohésion nationale par l'éducation religieuse', *C.E.M.O.T.I.I.*, 6, 1988, pp. 161–76.
43. Vaner, S., 'En guise d'introduction' in 'Modernisation autoritaire et réponse de sociétés en Turquie et en Iran', *C.E.M.O.T.I.I.*, 5, 1988, p. 14; Toprak, B., *Islam and Political Development in Turkey*, E. J. Brill, 1981.
44. Geyikdagi, M. Y., *Political Parties in Turkey. The Role of Islam*, Praeger, 1984, p. 156.
45. Karpat, K. H., *The Gecekondu: Rural Migration and Urbanisation*, Cambridge University Press, 1976, p. 127.
46. Arkoun, M., *Essai sur la pensée islamique*, Maison–Neuve Larose, 1984; Carré, O., *Mystique et politique*, Cerf, 1984.

Chapter 11 Societies and parties

1. Corbetta, P., Parisi, A. M. L., Schadee, H. M. A., *Elezioni in Italia. Strutture e tipologia delle consultazioni politiche*, Il Mulino, 1988; Caciagli, M. and Spreafico, A. (eds), *Venti anni di elezioni 1968–1988*, Liviana, 1991; Bibes, G., 'La démocratie chrétienne italienne d'un congrès à l'autre', *Etudes*, 3, 1980, pp. 23–38; Bibes, G. and Besson, J., 'La démocratie chrétienne italienne ou les infortunes de la vertu', *Revue française de sciences politiques*, 2, 1984, pp. 259–94; Pridham, G., 'The Italian Christian Democrats after Moro. Crisis or Compromise?', *West European Politics*, 2, 1979, pp. 69–88; Hine, D., 'The Italian Socialist Party under Craxi: Surviving but no Reviving', *West European Politics*, 2, 1979, pp. 133–48.
2. Corbetta, P., Parisi, A. M. L., Schadee, H. M. A., *Elezioni in Italia*, p. 400.
3. Blackmer, D. L. M., Tarrow, S., *Communism in Italy and France*, Princeton University Press, 1975; Belligni, S. (ed.), *La giraffa e il liocorno. Il PCI dagli anni '60 al nuovo decennio*, Franco Angeli, 1982; Sassoon, D., *The Strategy of the Italian Communist Party*, St Martin's Press, 1981; Urban, J. B., *Moscow and the Italian Communist Party*, Townsend, 1986.
4. Martinelli, A. and Pasquino, G., *La politica nell'Italia che cambia*, Feltrinelli, 1978; Mannheimer, R. and Sani, G., *Il mercato elettorale*, Il Mulino, 1987; Caciagli, M. and

Corbetta, P., *Elezioni regionali e sistema politico nazionale*, Il Mulino, 1987; Parisi, A. and Pasquino, G., *Continuità e mutamento elettorale in Italia*, Il Mulino, 1977.

5. Sani, G., '1992: la destrutturazione del mercato elettorale', *Rivista italiana di scienza politica*, 3, 1992, pp. 539–66.

6. *Ibid.*, p. 540.

7. Mannheimer, R. (ed.), *La Lega Lombarda*, Feltrinelli, 1991; Diamanti, I., *La Lega. Geografia, storia e sociologia di un nuovo soggetto politico*, Donzelli, 1993.

8. Sapelli, G., *Cleptocrazia. Il meccanismo unico della corruzione tra economia e politica*, Feltrinelli, 1994.

9. Mouzelis, N., 'Continuities and discontinuities in Greek politics. From Elefterios Venizélos to Andreas Papandreou' in K. Featherstone and D. K. Katsoudas (eds), *Political Change in Greece before and after the Colonels*, Croom Helm, 1987, p. 275; Tussel, J., *Oligarquía y caciquismo en Andalucía*, Ariel, 1976; Ayata, A. G., 'Class and Clientelism in the Republican People's Party' in A. Finkel and A. Simon, *Turkish State* pp. 159–84.

10. Morisi, M., *Le leggi del consenso. Partiti e interessi nei primi parlamenti della Repubblica*, Rubbettino, 1992; Hine, D., *Governing Italy. The Politics of Bargained Pluralism*, Clarendon Press, 1993; Mastropaolo, A., 'Parlamenti e parlamentari negli anni ottanta', *Rivista italiana di scienza politica*, XX, 9, pp. 29–70.

11. Huntington, S. P., *Political Order in Changing Societies*, Yale University Press, 1968.

12. Lowi, T. J., *The End of Liberalism. The Second Republic of the United States*, Norton, 1969; Lowi, T. J., 'Governo di partito e regime presidenziale' in M. Calise (ed.), *Come cambiano i partiti*, Il Mulino, 1992, pp. 299–324.

13. Calise, M., 'Introduzione: cambiare governando' in M. Calise (ed.), *Come cambiano i partiti*, p. 41.

14. Eisenstadt, S. N., *Traditional Patrimonialism and Modern Neo-Patrimonialism*, Sage, 1973.

15. Sapelli, G., 'L'impresa e la democrazia', *Quaderni della Fondazione Adriano Olivetti*, 1992.

16. Mannheiner, R. and Sani, G., '1994: dalla decomposizione alla ristrutturazione?' in R. Mannheiner and G. Sani (eds), *La rivoluzione elettorale. L'Italia tra la prima e la seconda repubblica*, Anabasi, 1994, p. 215.

17. Warner, S., Gambetta, D., *La retorica della riforma. Fine del sistema proporzionale in Italia*, Einaudi, 1994.

INDEX

Political groups are listed under the entries for individual countries.